Victor Serge

Collected Writings on Literature
and
Revolution

Victor Serge

Collected Writings on Literature
and
Revolution

Translated and Edited by Al Richardson

Francis
Boutle
Publishers

First published by Francis Boutle Publishers
272 Alexandra Park Road
London N22 7BG
Tel/Fax: (020) 8889 7744
Email: serge@francisboutle.demon.co.uk
www.francisboutle.demon.co.uk

ISBN 1 903427 16 9
Printed in Great Britain

Al Richardson

Teacher, Historian, Socialist and Revolutionary

1941–2003

Acknowledgments

Al Richardson, the editor and translator of this volume, sadly died before its publication. The publishers would like to thank those people who helped the book into print: in particular, Jim Ring for extricating the text from Al's computer and Ian Birchall, who painstakingly checked the translation and added his own translation of three essays. Thanks are also due to the David King Collection for permission to reproduce the photo of Serge; the Victor Serge Foundation for permission to make the translations; the editors of *International Socialism* for permission to reproduce the article Twice Met (Parijanine); and the *International Instituut voor Sociale Geschiedenis*, Amsterdam, for providing copies of other original articles. Apart from those named at the end of Al's introduction, there are undoubtedly others he would have wanted to thank, and my apologies go to those I am unable to name in person. My thanks, though, to Carl Williams, Ted Crawford and Clarence Chrysostom. It was Al's wish to dedicate this book to Harry Ratner for his contribution to the magazine *Revolutionary History*. It is with great sorrow that we add a dedication to Al Richarson himself, whose enthusiasm and scholarship will be greatly missed.

Clive Boutle

This collection was made to place on record our appreciation of the contribution of Harry Ratner, thinker, trade union activist and Socialist.

Contents

Part Four: Historians of the Revolution

Part Five: The Writers under the Terror

Victor Serge (centre) in Spain during the Civil War

Introduction

This book is intended to bring together the bulk of Victor Serge's literary writings during the revolutionary and post-revolutionary periods in Russia, and its aim is to show how the history of the time is reflected in its literature, rather than for the purposes of literary criticism as such. At the same time it may provide a useful antidote to those whose ideas of the relationship between Marxism and literature are coloured by Mao's 'Great Proletarian Cultural Revolution', which was great only in the sense of its enormities, cultural only in the sense of being a negation of it, and proletarian in no sense at all. On the other hand, those in England who think that Marxist appraisal of culture is about pretty wallpaper might also learn a thing or two.

The present translator is ill-equipped to comment upon the niceties of Marxist aesthetics, which in any case has been the subject of a number of impressive works in English,[1] apart from the fact that an introduction should not presume to tell the reader what he is to find in the book, which amounts to a sustained exercise in Marxist literary criticism over the period under review. However, much of it will be completely unintelligible unless some sort of summary is provided of Marxist views about literature that would have coloured Serge's thinking. Since we are necessarily restricted to what was then in print, we can only offer our apologies to those who expect to find discussions about literature taken from *The German Ideology* or the *Grundrisse*, and find space accorded to Lafargue, Plekhanov, Trotsky or Lenin instead.

S.S. Prawer has shown the amazing extent of Marx's command of the literature of his time, and it is not surprising that he should have formed some very firm opinions about the relations between the intelligentsia, intellectual life and production, and the revolution of the working class. Let us begin where

Serge must have done, with the remarks in *The Communist Manifesto*, that 'the bourgeoisie has stripped the halo from all occupations hitherto considered respectable and regarded with pious awe. It has converted the physician, the lawyer, the priest, the poet, the man of learning into its paid wage-labourers', whilst making 'the intellectual products of individual nations ... common property'.[2] Literature therefore becomes universalised, but along with it comes a differentiation within the intelligentsia who produce it, and 'a part of the bourgeoisie goes over to the proletariat, and in particular a part of the bourgeois ideologists who have worked their way up to a theoretical comprehension of the course of historical development as a whole'.[3] Education, being 'also dominated by society', must be 'wrested from the influence of the ruling class' and 'combined with material production', for 'what does the history of ideas show but that intellectual production is remoulded along with material production? The ruling ideas of an age have always been but the ideas of the ruling class. People speak of ideas that revolutionize a whole society; they thereby merely express the fact that within the old society the elements of a new one have been formed, that the dissolution of the old ideas keeps pace with the dissolution of the old conditions of life.'[4]

Marx had been thinking along these lines for some time. Ideas, he points out in *The Holy Family*, even at their most creative, themselves do not make history: '*Ideas* can never lead beyond the old world order but only beyond the ideas of the old world order. *Ideas cannot carry out anything at all.* In order to carry out ideas men are needed who can exert practical force.'[5] In any case, 'reflection on the forms of human life' usually 'takes a course directly opposite to their real development. Reflection begins *post festum*, and therefore with the results of the process of development ready to hand.'[6] Writers work within a given historical context, and influence how it changes only when they relate to it. So Marx feels justified in criticising Bauer for 'separating "*the pen*" from the subject who writes, and the subject who writes, as "*abstract writer*" from the living *historical* man who wrote'.[7]

Moreover, creative works can themselves partake of the nature of commodities, and derive part of their value from the labour time expended on them: 'even as far as *intellectual* production is concerned, must I not, if I proceed reasonably in other respects, consider the time necessary for the production of an intellectual work when I determine its scope, its character and its plans? Otherwise I risk at least that the object that is in my idea will never become an object in reality, and can therefore acquire only the value of an *imaginary* object, i.e. an imaginary value.'[8] So if this value is not realised by the market, the writer becomes an 'unproductive labourer'. 'Milton', Marx points out, 'who wrote *Paradise Lost* for five pounds, was an *unproductive labourer*. On the other hand, the writer who turns out stuff for his publisher in factory style, is a *productive labourer*. Milton produced *Paradise Lost* for the same reason that a silk worm produces silk. It was an activity of his nature. Later he sold the product for £5. But the literary proletarian of Leipzig, who fabricates books ... under the direction of his publisher, is a *productive labourer*; for his product is from the outset subsumed under capital, and comes into being only for the purpose of increasing that capital.'[9]

At the same time Marx argued that 'in spiritual production another kind of labour appears as productive'. 'The material division of labour is the pre-condition for the division of intellectual labour', and the relationship between the two can only be grasped 'not as a general category but in *definite historical form*'. What Marx calls 'the free spiritual production' of 'the ideological component parts of the ruling class' can only be understood from 'the specific historical structure of their production relations', which are not appropriate to all forms of artistic creation: 'for instance, capitalist production is hostile to certain branches of spiritual production, for example, art and poetry'.[10] Social realism, on the other hand, can flourish in this context, and Marx was particularly impressed with Balzac's 'profound grasp of reality',[11] while criticising Lassalle's *Franz von Sickingen* for 'the transformation of individuals into mere mouthpieces for the spirit of the time'.[12]

Marx was under no illusions that more than a section of the intelligentsia could go over whole-heartedly to the side of the working class. Writing about the ideologists of the democracy, he noted that 'what makes them representatives of the petty bourgeoisie is the fact that in their minds they do not get beyond the limits which the latter do not get beyond in life, that they are consequently driven, theoretically, to the same problems and solutions to which material interest and social position drive the latter practically. This is, in general, the relationship between the *political* and *literary* representatives of a class and the class they represent.' And since the democratic ideologist represents 'a *transition class*', he 'imagines himself elevated above class antagonism generally'.[13]

Karl Kautsky went on to develop the Marxist understanding of culture. Creativity takes place within a given climate of opinion, and 'the historical effect of a thinker does not depend on him alone', for 'a certain mentality of a society is required if certain ideas are to be adopted by it'.[14] He also showed that change in ideas and material change never exactly correspond. For example, during the sixteenth century, a time of economic, social and political upheaval, 'the new ideas, prompted by the new interests, had not discarded the vestments of modes of thinking derived from feudalism, and the latter persisted long after the main props of its material foundation had been knocked away', so that feudalism, 'by force of tradition ... governed the forms of intellectual life'.[15] In addition he points out that when thinkers draw their inspiration from the distant past, the old culture is never revived in its original form. Speaking of the rebirth of classical learning during the Renaissance, he argues that 'if ideas really created material conditions, and not the reverse, a resurrection of antique society ought to have proceeded from the revival of antique ideas', but what really happened was that 'they only adopted these ideas to the degree that they corresponded with actual conditions'.[16]

Kautsky was also concerned with 'the antagonism between the intellectuals and the proletariat'. Whilst accepting that the intellectual 'has to sell the product of his labour, and frequently his labour power', and 'is often enough exploited and humiliated by the capitalists', neither his conditions of work, nor his status and living standards are proletarian, and, 'armed with the general education of our time, conceives himself as very superior to the proletarians'.[17] That being said, 'intellectuals are not a class, they have no special class interests; they are divided into diverse vocations with very different professional interests', and 'are not able to conduct a class struggle on their own'. But they can 'make the cause of another class their own, take part in its struggles, and stimulate it intellectually to a high degree'.[18]

This was a problem that also preoccupied Marx's son-in-law, Paul Lafargue. He identified 'a swarming and famishing throng of intellectuals whose lot grows worse in proportion to their numbers'; 'if only they had understood their own interests, they would long since have turned against the capitalist class the education which it has generously distributed in order better to exploit them', since 'poverty is harder for the intellectual than the workingman; it bruises him morally and physically'. However, in order to sell the results of their labours, the intellectuals have to operate within market conditions: 'spurred on by the mercantile process, they are never better satisfied with themselves or with society than when they succeed in selling their intellectual merchandise at a good price; they even come to the point of making its selling price the measure of its value'. This market, the public, is, of course, the capitalist class itself: 'the intellectuals of art and literature, like the jesters of old feudal courts, are the entertainers of the class which pays them. To satisfy the tastes of the capitalists and beguile their leisure – this is their whole artistic aim.'[19]

Moreover, it is their education itself that prevents them from going over wholeheartedly to the working class: 'they think their education confers upon them a social privilege, that it will permit them to get through the world by themselves, each making his own way in life by crowding his neighbour or standing on the shoulders of everyone else. They imagine that their poverty is transitory, and that they only need a stroke of good luck to transform them into capitalists.'[20]

Plekhanov, who gave more attention to questions of literature and the intellectuals than any other Marxist, firmly rooted them in their historical context. Since 'it has often been observed that great talents appear everywhere, wherever the social conditions favourable to their development exist', this must mean that 'every man of talent who *actually appears*, i.e., every man of talent who becomes a *social force*, is the product of *social relations*'.[21] He quotes Taine with approval that 'the arts appear and disappear together with certain conditions of minds and manners with which they are connected', noting how classical Greek tragedy only flourished after the defeat of Persia and Athens' rise to dominance in the civilised world.[22] Hence 'in the sphere of social ideas a genius outdistances his contemporaries in the sense that he *grasps earlier than they do the meaning of new social relations which are coming into existence*',[23] and 'when artists become blind to the major social trends of their time, the inherent value of the ideas they express is seriously impaired'.[24]

However, Plekhanov was concerned to point out that there was no straight correlation between ideology and social relations along the simple lines of cause and effect. The romantic movement of 1830, for example, was 'essentially bourgeois', but it was far from popular with the bourgeoisie as a whole, who 'failed to understand a considerable part of the aspirations and sentiments which then animated its own spokesmen in literature and art'.[25] In fact, in literature, 'the standard of revolt was raised only later and, moreover, by people who warmly sympathised with the old regime overthrown by the revolution'.[26] The French bourgeoisie was yet to establish its complete political and economic domination, so that 'here, as everywhere, the origin and character of such a discrepancy can only be explained, in the last analysis, by the economic situation of the social class in which it manifests itself'.[27]

The universal character of literature noted by Marx in *The Communist Manifesto* could only come about as a result of the development of common social and economic conditions by means of the capitalist world market. And 'the influence of the literature of one country on the literature of another', Plekhanov pointed out, 'is directly proportional to the similarity of the social relations of these countries. It does not exist at all when that similarity is reduced to zero.'[28]

Nor was the value of Plekhanov's insights limited to his own time. When Serge was grappling with *proletcult* he must have remembered Plekhanov's remarks that 'at a certain stage of the economic development of a country, certain well-meaning stupidities "necessarily" arise in the heads of its intellectuals'.[29] He must also have agreed that political authority 'is most often conservative and even reactionary', that state control of the arts means harnessing 'all ideologies to the service of the cause which it serves itself', and might even 'place human reason under military discipline',[30] as Stalin certainly did.

Lenin's acquaintance with world literature was less extensive than those of Marx or Plekhanov, but he was well grounded in the Russian classics. His writings are peppered with references to Chekhov, Chernyshevsky, Gogol, Krylov, Pushkin, Saltykov-Shchedrin, Tolstoy, Turgenev and Uspensky, and Serge comments upon his relations with Gorky over a number of years.[31]

Lenin regarded Tolstoy in particular as reflecting 'the universal significance of the Russian Revolution', 'in raising so many great problems' and in 'rising to such heights of artistic power that his works rank among the greatest in world literature'. Here again, he pointed out how closely Tolstoy's achievement was connected with the development of the country: 'The epoch of preparation for the revolution in one of the countries under the heel of the serf-owners became, thanks to its brilliant illumination by Tolstoy, a step forward in the artistic development of humanity as a whole.' And whilst all Tolstoy's work was in the context of 'the specific historical features of the entire first Russian revolution', he had 'succeeded in conveying with remarkable force the moods of the large masses that are oppressed by the present system, in depicting their condition and expressing their spontaneous feelings of protest and anger', with 'such emotional power, such passion, convincingness, freshness, sincerity and fearlessness in striving to "go to the roots".'[32] At the same time he did not deny that Tolstoy reflected 'an ideology of an Oriental, Asiatic order', that his socialism was of the pre-Marxist Utopian sort, and was convinced that the 1905 Revolution 'marked the historical end of Tolstoyism'.[33]

He also admired 'how profoundly and splendidly Chernyshevsky understood the realities of his time' in grasping 'the fundamentally bourgeois character' of Tsar Alexander II's land reforms. However, he also regarded them as marking the parting of the ways between the Marxists and the democratic intelligentsia, and that 'the period of Russia's social development, when democracy and socialism were merged in one inseparable and indissoluble whole ... has gone never to return'. For it was the slow tempo of Russia's development that had allowed the intelligentsia to dominate politics for so long, 'when the class antagonisms of bourgeois society were still quite undeveloped and were held down by serfdom, when the latter was evoking the unanimous protest and struggle of the entire intelligentsia, thus creating the illusion that there was something peculiarly democratic about our intelligentsia, and that there was no profound gulf between the ideas of the liberals and the socialists'.[34]

The ideological contribution of the intellectuals was bound to be limited once the workers' revolution became a possibility. They were, after all, 'the mouthpiece of the class that is begotten by capitalism's destruction of the old forms of life', and after the revolution of 1917 'the majority of the intellectuals gravitated towards the bourgeoisie'.[35] However, Lenin reported to Gorky that 'everything is being done to draw the intelligentsia (the non-whiteguard intelligentsia) into the struggle', which he regarded as crucial:

> We know Socialism can only be built from elements of large-scale capitalist culture, and the intellectuals are one of these elements. We had to be ruthless with them, but it was not Communism that compelled us to do so, it was events, which repelled from us all 'democrats' and everyone enamoured of bourgeois democracy. Now we have the chance to utilise the intellectuals for Socialism, intellectuals who are not Socialist, who will never be Communist, but whom objective events and relations are now inducing to adopt a neutral attitude towards us.[36]

Acutely aware of the massive backwardness of the Russian countryside, he regarded the 'vivacious and talented writings of the old eighteenth-century atheists' as 'a thousand times more suitable for arousing people from their religious torpor than the dull and dry paraphrases of Marxism' which 'frequently distort Marxism', and that 'proletarian culture must be the logical development of the store of knowledge mankind has accumulated under the yoke of capitalist, landowner and bureaucratic society'.[37] He took a very firm stand against 'all attempts to invent one's own particular brand of culture' as 'theoretically unsound and practically harmful', blaming 'bourgeois intellectuals, who very often regarded the new type of workers' and peasants' institutions as the most convenient field for testing their individual theories in philosophy and culture, and in which, very often, the most absurd ideas were hailed as something new, and the supernatural and incongruous were offered as purely proletarian art and proletarian culture'.[38] 'We hear people dilating at too great length and too flippantly on "proletarian culture",' he concluded; 'for a start we should be satisfied with real bourgeois culture'.[39]

To be frank, Lenin found the new art 'alien and incomprehensible'. But he did like the work of Demyan Biedny, even if he thought it crude, and tried to get him to collaborate with *Pravda*.[40] To begin with he was embarrassed by Mayakovsky, and even irritated by him: 'he shouts, invents some sort of distorted words, and doesn't get anywhere in my opinion – and besides is incomprehensible. It is all disconnected, difficult to read.'[41] For he was a determined opponent of Futurism, and was extremely angry with Lunacharsky's decision to print 5,000 copies of Mayakovsky's *150,000,000*[42] even if Lenin did later warm to his poem criticising the Bolshevik obsession with meetings.[43]

As a supporter of the Left Opposition, Serge was well acquainted with

Trotsky's writings on the intellectuals and literature, some of which had already appeared in the volumes of his *Collected Works* that had come out before Stalin began to take direct administrative measures against him.[44] Trotsky was deeply interested in the relationship between culture and society:

> Culture binds people together and imposes constraints; it is conservative, and the richer it is, the more conservative it is. In Europe, every new idea cutting its way through the solid body of the old culture was met by the deadening resistance of the old outworn ideology, and by a keen rebuff from entrenched interests. In struggling against this resistance, the new idea gained in strength, captured the minds of ever wider social circles, and finally triumphed as the banner of new classes and strata struggling to establish their own place in the sun. In subordinating the rebellious idea to their own requirements, the new classes bound and restricted it socially, depriving it of its absolute meaning.[45]

The problem of ideology was all the more acute in Russia since the intelligentsia had always been the transmission belt for ideas coming from the West into a country whose traditional culture was so much more backward. For an entire epoch the intelligentsia substituted for classes that were yet to come into existence: 'the intelligentsia has been substituting itself for political parties, classes, and the people. The intelligentsia has experienced entire cultural epochs – on behalf of the people. The intelligentsia has chosen the paths of development on behalf of the people.'[46] But this heroic struggle could only go on for a limited time, and had its disadvantages: 'even when an idea developed in line with general historical development, it was so far ahead of that development in time, under the influence of the West, that the bearer of that idea, the intelligentsia, became connected to the country's political life not through the class that it wanted to serve, but merely through the "idea" of that class'.[47] The revolutions of 1905 and 1917, when modern classes entered directly into political conflict with each other, were to spell the end of the autonomous and progressive role of the intelligentsia as a whole.

Indeed, Trotsky believed that the contribution of the intelligentsia to the socialist movement had been for some time declining on a global scale. Their 'biggest influx' into the movement – including Marx and Engels – took place 'when it was still in its childhood', and 'the easier it has become for each and everyone to understand its mission in history, the more decidedly have the intelligentsia recoiled from it', an 'alienation which increases with the very growth of the socialist movement'. This is partly due to the progress of the capitalist division of labour, dividing the intelligentsia itself into a higher and a lower stratum, the one dependent on the bourgeoisie and the other on the proletariat, and because 'the "spiritual" nature of the work that the intelligentsia do inevitably forms a spiritual tie between them and the possessing classes'.[48]

For all his appreciation of Tolstoy's *War and Peace*, Trotsky was less appreciative of his work than Lenin was, holding him to be 'alien and deeply hostile to the aesthetic of the big-city culture' and 'rejecting the division of labour and, along with it, culture and the state'. Tolstoy thus represented 'the aristocratic and conservative wing' of Russian Populism.[49]

Extensive quotations from *Literature and Revolution* make clear Serge's debt to Trotsky's overall analysis, from which he takes his critique of 'proletarian literature' and concepts of 'internal emigration' and 'fellow travellers'.[50] And with the growth of Stalinism Serge may well have meditated on Trotsky's remarks that 'perhaps the worst thing in a reactionary epoch is the stupidity that spreads in the social consciousness', which 'becomes insolence and, showing its rotten teeth, derides any attempt at serious generalisation'.[51]

Rosa Luxemburg's introduction to her translation of Korolenko's semi-autobiographical *History of My Contemporary Life* clearly influenced Serge's thinking.[52] Whilst praising Russian literature for 'never denying its social responsibility', she agreed with Trotsky that 'Tolstoy's mystic doctrines reflect reactionary tendencies, if not more'.[53] Had she lived, she would obviously not have been a supporter of *proletcult*, for she did not like novels that sacrificed artistic merit to social criticism.[54] Serge shared her view that 'patterns such as "revolutionary" or "progressive" in themselves mean very little in art', and that 'with the true artist the social formula that he recommends is a matter of secondary importance; the source of his art, its animating spirit, is decisive'.[55]

This does not of course mean that she accorded a timeless quality to literature, totally abstracted from its place in history and class society. Speaking of Uspensky, she pointed out that he symbolised the rise, florescence and decline of Narodnism during the crisis that followed the Crimean War up to when the course of time destroyed their illusions in the Russian peasantry, and that in fact what he was doing was describing the *social* being of his characters in that particular situation.[56]

But Rosa Luxemburg appreciated Tolstoy's contribution more than Trotsky did, as 'a deadly enemy of the existing order, a fearless warrior for equality, for solidarity among men, and for the rights of the dispossessed'. And whilst she agreed that he had 'no understanding of the modern workers' movement', she held that 'it would be a bad sign for the intellectual maturity of the enlightened working class if it did not understand that, in spite of this, Tolstoy's art is suffused with the purest, most genuine spirit of Socialism'. For his art properly belonged to 'a revolutionary and enlightened audience freed and cleansed of the shackles of German philistinism, a proletarian public in a position to rise above all prejudice and belief in authority, and which has the courage to reject all craven compromise'. So she concluded that 'there can be no better educational material for the proletarian youth than the works of Tolstoy'.[57]

The foremost literary critic in the ranks of the Bolsheviks was Anatoly Lunacharsky, himself the author of over thirty-six books, essays and plays. He agrees with previous Marxist assumptions that 'a work of literature always reflects, whether consciously or unconsciously, the psychology of the class which the writer represents', but adds that it often 'reflects a mixture of the elements in which the influence of various classes on the writer is revealed'. Considering that 'the Marxist critic takes first of all as the object of his analysis the *content* of the work, the *social essence* it embodies', the distinction between literary critic and literary historian 'loses nearly all its validity' for a Marxist.[58] He, too, accounted for the literary flowering of nineteenth century Russia by the gap between its ideals and the development of the rest of the country: 'Our literature is devoted to ideas, because when such an abyss yawns between the understanding of its bearer – the intelligentsia – and the life about it, it is impossible for literature to avoid thought.'[59]

However, in spite of this common ground, it is likely that Lunacharsky only influenced Serge to a limited extent. He believed Lenin was justified in his disputes with Lunacharsky, Gorky and Bogdanov before the First World War, and Serge strongly disagreed with Bogdanov and Lunacharsky's promotion of the *proletcult* afterwards. Lunacharsky had far more avant-garde tastes in literature than Lenin, believing that 'a writer is valuable when he cultivates virgin soil, when he intuitively breaks into a sphere which logic and statistics would find hard to penetrate'.[60] He cherished the hope that 'the great flood of social revolution and the entrance on the scene of the proletariat will prove capable of refreshing art down to its very base and up from its foundations'.[61] And being in favour of *proletcult*, he was sharply critical of the fellow travellers, describing Blok himself as 'the last poet of the landed gentry' and 'the prophet dreamer and latter day romantic of the nobility', accepting the view that the poet's own attitude to the Revolution was 'left-wing Narodnik dreams of utopia and mystic, apocalyptic ravings'.[62] Nor would Serge have liked Lunacharsky's support for Stalin's censorship, or his claim that identifying a writer as having 'unconscious or even "semi conscious", counter-revolutionary ideas' under the Stalin regime did not amount to informing. He must have been disgusted at Lunacharsky's debasing himself before the Lenin cult,[63] and even more by his attempt to blame Mayakovsky's death on Trotsky.[64]

The recent appearance of an excellent collection of Voronsky's articles on literary criticism also allows us to speculate on the extent of Serge's debt to him. As supporters of the Left Opposition, they shared so much common ground that it is often difficult to distinguish between them. Both argued vigorously against *proletcult*, against the possibility of creating 'proletarian literature', against a negative attitude to the classics, and in defence of the 'fellow travellers', whilst admitting the affinity of these writers with the life of the Russian peasant rather than the Marxist world view.[65] Of course Voronsky never denies that the work of the artist 'is always conditioned by the spirit of the epoch, and the psychology of the class or group to which he belongs', consciously or unconsciously fulfilling the task of this class 'by a psychology which in the final analysis depends on the state of productive forces of a given society'.[66] He also accepts, probably with more than a glance in the direction of Mayakovsky, that 'there are epochs, periods, when applied art, applied sciences, agitational material, feuilletons and propaganda naturally take on overwhelming significance'.[67]

But this does not at all in his view justify casting aside the achievements of previous literature:

> Bourgeois literature lived and developed along with its class. There was a time when the bourgeoisie fought against feudalism, when it was revo-

lutionary. At that time both science and art were revolutionary; after victories came a period of maturity, balance, full-bloodedness, good health and flourishing development. During this epoch the bourgeoisie produced incomparable examples of creative thought and feeling both in science and in literature.[68]

He also shares Marx's enthusiasm for bourgeois literary realism. 'Genuine art consists of thinking with the *aid of images*. Such thinking can be just as objective as scientific, discursive thinking with the aid of concepts. Such true art takes its material from *reality*.' This makes it 'fundamentally realistic and always true', because 'it must correspond to one degree or another to reality'.[69]

This bare catalogue obviously cannot take in all the influences upon Serge's thought, since he was himself a creative writer, and we have not dealt with the stamp placed on his thinking by the Anarchism of his youth. This omission can only be justified by the subject of the book, his contribution to Marxist literary thinking, which will be understood all the better if we keep this background in mind while reading through it.

And we should also be aware of the audiences for which Serge wrote the majority of the essays here. *Clarté* was specifically designed to win over the left intellectuals in France to the cause of the Russian Revolution. A second group of reviews was commissioned by Martinet and Parijanine for *L'Humanité*, the newspaper of the Communist Party. A large number of French writers were involved in the enquiry into 'proletarian literature' undertaken by *Monde* magazine, which printed the third collection of Serge's literary articles. So these were very much live issues, discussed in far wider circles than such questions generally are today.

*   *   *   *   *

All that remains now is to thank those whose efforts have made this collection more coherent than it might have been. In first place comes Ian Birchall, whose patience has been tried, and his sense of humour tickled, in correcting the translations. Without his help, and that of the International Institute in Amsterdam, the documentation would have been much poorer. I have repeatedly drawn upon the expertise of Brian Pearce in the field of Russian language and literature. The book could never have appeared in the first place without the support of Richard Greeman. Mike Jones and a work friend, Claire Smith, have been an invaluable aid in German matters. Dave Renton has also been generous with his help, and our thanks must go to the editors of *International Socialism* for permission to publish Peter Sedgwick's moving translation of 'Twice Met'. Finally, Paul Flewers has been generous with his time in preparing it all for the printer. Any surviving errors are the responsibility of the translator alone.

Al Richardson

Notes

1. E.g. V. N. Voloshinov, *Marxism and the Philosophy of Language*, 1929 (English translation, Matejna and Titunik, New York and London, 1973); M. Lifshitz, *The Philosophy of Art of Karl Marx*, 1933 (English translation, New York Critics Group, 1938, reprinted by Pluto, London, 1973); S.S. Prawer, *Karl Marx and World Literature*, Oxford U.P., 1976; Raymond Williams, *Marxism and Literature*, Oxford U.P., 1977.
2. *The Communist Manifesto*, 1848, in the new translation in Hal Draper, *The Adventures of the Communist Manifesto*, Berkeley, California, 1994, pp.111, 115.
3. Op. cit, p.129.
4. Op. cit., pp.147, 157, 151.
5. Marx and Engels, *The Holy Family*, 1844, English translation Moscow, 1975, p.140.
6. Karl Marx, *Capital*, vol.i, Harmondsworth, 1976, p.168. Post festum means 'after the feast', i.e., after the event (Latin).
7. Op. cit., n.5 above, p.118.
8. Op. cit., p.59.
9. Karl Marx, *Theories of Surplus Value*, 1862–63, vol.i, Moscow, n.d., p.389.
10. Op. cit., n.9 above, pp.276–7. Marx does not explain this in full, but the reasons behind his arguments can be found in the *Grundrisse* (English translation by Martin Nicolaus, Harmondsworth, 1974, pp.110–1). Since they could not have been known to Serge, it is extraordinary how closely he echoes them in his remarks about the epic poetry of the revolutionary period in Russia (below, pp.274).
11. Karl Marx, *Capital*, vol.iii, Moscow, 1962, p.39. Cf. also *Capital*, vol.i, Moscow, 1958, p.589, n.1, Plekhanov, *The Development of the Monist Theory of History*, 1895, reprinted Moscow, 1972, pp.211–2, and Serge below, p. 87.
12. Karl Marx, Letter to Lassalle, 19 April 1859, translated in full in Prawer, op. cit., n.1 above, pp.213–6. We know that this correspondence was available in Russia at the time Serge was writing (A. K. Voronsky, *Art as the Cognition of Life*, Mehring books, 1998, p.108).
13. Karl Marx, *The Eighteenth Brumaire of Louis Bonaparte*, 1852, Moscow, 1977, pp.40–1, 43.
14. K. Kautsky, *The Materialist Conception of History*, 1927, English translation, New Haven, 1988, p.489.

15. K. Kautsky, *Thomas More and His Utopia*, 1888, English translation, London, 1927, pp.2, 15.
16. Op. cit., p.62. Cf. K. Kautsky, *The Materialist Conception of History*, p.173.
17. K. Kautsky, 'The Intellectuals and the Workers', *Neue Zeit*, vol.xxii, no.4, 1903, pp.101–3; English translation in *Fourth International*, vol.vii, no.4 (whole no.65), April 1946, pp.125–6.
18. Op. cit., n.14 above, p.397.
19. Paul Lafargue, *Socialism and the Intellectuals*, 1900, English translation *Labor News*, New York, 1967, pp.29, 38, 18, 27. For this last remark, cf. Serge, p. [***] below [***Refer to section in book on the position of the encyclopaedists at the courts of the enlightened despots***], and Prawer, op. cit. n.1 above, p.271.
20. Op. cit., n.19 above, p.30.
21. G. V. Plekhanov, *The Role of the Individual in History*, 1898, English edition, London, 1976, p.49.
22. G.V. Plekhanov, *The Development of the Monist View of History*, 1895, English edition, Moscow, 1972, pp.175–7.
23. Op. cit., pp.191–2.
24. G. V. Plekhanov, 'Art and Social Life', 1912–1913, *Plekhanov: Selected Philosophical Works*, vol.v, Moscow, 1981, p.657.
25. G.V. Plekhanov, *Fundamental Problems of Marxism*, 1908 (ed. Riazanov), English translation, London, 1941, pp.75–6.
26. Op. cit., n.22 above, p.190.
27. Op. cit., n.25 above, p.76.
28. Op. cit., n.22 above, p.181.
29. Op. cit., p.232.
30. Op. cit., n.24 above, pp.644, 646.
31. N. K. Krupskaya adds Lermontov and Nekrasov to this list: 'Ilyich's Favourite Books', in *Lenin On Culture and Cultural Revolution*, Moscow, 1970, pp.223–30.
32. V. I. Lenin, 'L. N. Tolstoy', 16 November 1910; 'L. N. Tolstoy and the Modern Labour Movement', 28 November 1910, *Collected Works*, vol.xvi, Moscow, 1963, pp.323, 332.
33. V. I. Lenin, 'Lev Tolstoi and His Epoch', 22 January 1911, *Collected Works*, vol.xvii, Moscow, 1963, pp.51–2.
34. V. I. Lenin, 'What the 'Friends of the People' Are and How They Fight the Social Democrats', 1894, *Collected Works*, vol.i, pp.280–2, 271. Lenin also approved of Chernyshevsky's adherence to Feuerbach's materialism ('Materialism and Empiriocriticism', May 1909, *Collected Works*, vol.xiv, Moscow, 1962, pp.359–60).
35. V. I. Lenin, 'From Narodnism to Marxism', 24 January 1905, *Collected Works*, vol.viii, Moscow, 1977, p.85; 'A Great Beginning', 28 June 1919, *Collected Works*, vol.xxix, Moscow, 1965, pp.424–5.
36. V. I. Lenin, Letter to Maxim Gorky, 31 July, 1919, *Collected Works*, vol.xxxv, Moscow, 1966, p.411; 'Report on the Attitude of the Proletariat to Petty-Bourgeois Democrats', 27 November, 1918, *Collected Works*, vol.xxviii, Moscow, 1965, pp.213–4. It should be remembered that when Lenin refers to 'capitalist culture' he makes no differentiation between science and the arts.
37. V. I. Lenin, 'On the Significance of Militant Materialism', 12 March 1922, *Collected Works*, vol.xxxiii, Moscow, 1966, p.230; 'The Tasks of the Youth Leagues', 2 October 1920, *Collected Works*, vol.xxxi, Moscow, 1966, p.287. Lenin advocated translating the classics of anti-clerical literature into cheap, popular editions to encourage literacy among the peasants.
38. V. I. Lenin, 'On Proletarian Culture', 8 October 1920, *Collected Works*, vol.xxxi, Moscow 1966, p.317; 'Speech of Greeting at the First All-Russia Congress on Adult Education', 6 May 1919, *Collected Works*, vol.xxix, Moscow, 1965, p.80; cf. 'Rough Draft of a Resolution on Proletarian Culture', 9 October 1920, *Collected Works*, vol.xlii, Moscow, 1969, p.217. The best general survey

of Serge's own views about the problem of proletarian literature is that made by Ian Birchall, 'Proletarian Culture', in *The Ideas of Victor Serge: A Life as a Work of Art, Critique*, nos.28–9, 1997, pp.75–98.

39. V. I. Lenin, 'Better Fewer, But Better', 2 March 1923, *Collected Works*, vol.xxxiii, Moscow, 1966, p.487.

40. N. K. Krupskaya, 'Ilyich's Favourite Books', op. cit., n.31 above, pp.227, 229; Maxim Gorky, *Days With Lenin*, London, n.d., p.59; V. I. Lenin, 'To the Editorial Board of *Pravda*', 25 May 1913, *Collected Works*, vol.xxv, Moscow, 1966, pp.99–100; 'To Demyan Bedny', 5 December 1912, *Collected Works*, vol.xliii, Moscow, 1977, p.311.

41. Op. cit., n.31 above, p.227; Maxim Gorky, *Days With Lenin*, London, n.d., p.59.

42. V. I. Lenin, Letter to A. V. Lunacharsky, 6 May 1921, *Collected Works*, vol.xlv, Moscow, 1976, pp.138–89; A. V. Lunacharsky, 'Lenin and the Arts', 1924, in *Lenin Through the Eyes of Lunacharsky*, Moscow, 1981, pp.149,151–2. Of course, there was no question of suppressing the work. Lenin suggested a smaller print-run of 1500.

43. N. K. Krupskaya, op. cit., n.31 above, p.228; op. cit., n.42 above, p.152.

44. E.g. *Fourth International*, vol.i, no.3, Autumn/Winter 1964–5, pp.105–111; *Revolutionary History*, vol.vii, no.2, 1999, pp.3–34,52–62, 83–98; Paul N. Siegel (ed.), *Leon Trotsky on Literature and Art*, New York, 1977, pp.63–91, 127–166; *Marxist Review*, vol.xv, no.1, January 2000, pp.23–29.

45. L. D. Trotsky, 'On the Intelligentsia', March 1912, in *Culture and Revolution in the Thought of Leon Trotsky*, *Revolutionary History*, vol.vii, no.2, 1999, pp.89–90.

46. Op. cit., p.91.

47. Op. cit., p.97.

48. L. D. Trotsky, 'The Intelligentsia and Socialism', *Sovremmeny Mir*, 1910, translated by Brian Pearce, London 1974, pp.6,7,14–5 (reprinted from *Fourth International*, vol.i, no.3, Autumn/Winter 1964–5, pp.105–11).

49. L. D. Trotsky, 'Tolstoy: Poet and Rebel', *Neue Zeit*, 15 September 1908, Leon Trotsky on Literature and Art, New York, 1977, pp.133, 135 and 130.

50. Cf. also L. D. Trotsky, 'Class and Art', 9 May, 1924, in *Fourth International*, vol.iv, no.2, July 1967, pp.51–60, reprinted in *Leon Trotsky on Literature and Art*, New York, 1977, pp.63–82. Even if he did accept Trotsky's general theoretical arguments against the possibility of a transitional proletarian culture in general, Serge looked upon *proletcult* itself with toleration and sympathy, and was not opposed to it in principle as Trotsky was. And even Trotsky qualified his views to some extent later. Cf. Maurice Parijanine, 'Interview on 'Proletarian Literature',' April 1932, in *Writings of Leon Trotsky*, 1932, New York, 1973, pp.347–8.

51. L. D. Trotsky, 'Culture and the Little White Bull', January 1909, op. cit., n.44 above, p.33.

52. Serge's examples of Ryleev, Pushkin and Lermontov as heroes of anti-Czarist resistance (p.57, below) are clearly taken from Luxemburg's 'Life of Korolenko', 1918, *International Socialist Review*, vol.xxx, no.1 (whole no.190), January/February, 1969, p.12

53. Op. cit., n.52 above, pp.12 and 13.

54. Rosa Luxemburg, 'Letter to Sophie Liebknecht', 18th February, 1917, in *Letters from Prison*, translated by Eden and Cedar Paul, London, 1946, p.12.

55. Op. cit., n.53 above, p.13.

56. Rosa Luxemburg, 'Gleb Uspensky' (unsigned article), *Leipziger Volkszeitung*, no.80, 9th April, 1902.

57. Rosa Luxemburg, 'Tolstois Nachlass', *Die Neue Zeit*, 1912/13, *Gesammelte Werke*, vol.iii, Berlin, 1973, pp.189–90.

58. A. V. Lunacharsky, 'Theses on the Problems of Marxist Criticism', 1928, in Anatoly

Lunacharsky: *On Literature and Art*, Moscow, 1973, pp.11, 10.

59. A. V. Lunacharsky, 'Alexander Pushkin', 1922, op. cit., n.58 above, p.76.

60. Op. cit., n.58 above, p.14.

61. Op. cit., n.59 above, p.75.

62. A. V. Lunacharsky, 'Alexander Blok', 1932, op. cit., n.58 above, pp.168, 133, 159.

63. A. V. Lunacharsky, 'Maxim Gorky', 1932, op. cit., n.58 above, p.171; *Lenin Through the Eyes of Lunacharsky*, Moscow, 1981.

64. A. V. Lunacharsky, 'Vladimir Mayakovsky, Innovator', 1931, op. cit., n.58 above, p.201; L. D. Trotsky, 'The Suicide of Vladimir Mayakovsky', May 1930, in *Leon Trotsky on Literature and Art*, New York, 1977, pp.174–8. Lunacharsky had been an old comrade of Trotsky in the Mezhrayontsi, and had also written a very sympathetic portrait of him in his *Revolutionary Silhouettes*, a book which did not even include Stalin.

65. Alexander Constantinovich Voronsky, *Art as the Cognition of Life: Selected Writings, 1911–1936*, translated by Frederick S. Choate, Mehring Books, Michigan, 1998, pp.147–171, 77–93, 124–132.

66. 'Art as the Cognition of Life, and the Contemporary World', 1923; op. cit., pp.111, 116.

67. Op. cit., p.114.

68. 'Sharp Phrases and the Classics', 1923; op. cit., n.66 above, p.81.

69. Op. cit., p.82.

Part One

The Theory of Proletarian Literature

The Impotence of the Intellectuals[1]

The Intellectuals in the Face of the Imperialist War

The cannonade of 1914 killed off a good many illusions. I would like to recall one in order to make clear that it is dead, that of the power of the intellectuals and of culture.

People are still wasting time looking for minute responsibilities during this anniversary. This would not be utterly useless if they were looking for them in good faith. For the system – what can be called the capitalist set-up – only moves when it makes men move. And these are the men responsible – the heads of industry, the imperialist plutocrats, the rulers and *the intellectuals*.

By what singular favour has the crime of the latter been forgotten, by the very people who blame the others? Why, on the occasion of this bloody anniversary,[2] in any appeal to memory and action, alongside financiers, ministers, monarchs, generals and working-class leaders – all of them murderers – have the intellectuals not been included?

Before the killing there was still the illusion that intellectual culture made up an international *human heritage*, whose guardians were the intellectuals; that the power of thought did not stop at frontiers; and that *freedom of thought* had purified an elite of *good workers* from complicity in the most repugnant of social crimes. Did not this dead illusion attempt to come back to life the morning after the war, when the signatories of a *Declaration of the Independence of Thought* collected around Romain Rolland?[3]

If moral responsibility is to be assigned to the extent of the development of insight, isn't the greatest that of the intellectuals?

Nothing was done without them. Every betrayal was theirs too. All surrender in the face of the force of imperialist arms, and all the stupidity and savagery was theirs. Scientists invented poisonous gases. Jurists justified using them, like the use of coloured troops, and like all the atrocities. Literary men put out the communiqué, held censorship scissors, pronounced the indictments of court martials, and poisoned the intelligence of the peoples. In August 1914 the German intellectuals signed the *Manifesto of the 93*.[4] French intellectuals banned Wagner and *boche* science, and branded the Teutonic race with the apocalyptic sign of the beast.[5] Intellectuals could be found in every country to committing the worst scientific abuses in the service of hatred devoted to the prosaic conquest of colonial markets. Remember what was written on both sides of the trenches about the particular shape of the enemy's skull.

The bankruptcy of Christianity, pacifism, socialism and anarchism: it is always the intellectuals who have abdicated. The betrayal of the working-class movement by the Second International was essentially carried out by the opportunist intellectuals who made up the leading caste of Socialism before the war. Wilsonism,[6] which banished the possibility of the social revolution and aborted the peace – another variety of poisonous gas – was invented by the intellectuals. The Russian Revolution – the real one – drew the fire of and was defamed by the intellectuals at its birth. The majority of the great names of Russian science and literature condemned it. The high mandarinate of the Sorbonne and Oxford cursed it yet again. From the tranquility of their working desks Bertrand Russell and Romain Rolland condemned the dictatorship,[7] without which the Russian commune would have died the same death as the other one ...

On an Article by G. Duhamel[8]

An instalment of the magazine *Europe* (15 July) – which is very much, so I believe, the most advanced French magazine[9] – reminds me of these things.

In it Albert Crémieux[10] (*After Ten Years*) deplores the bankruptcy of the intellectuals of Europe in the face of history. '*We would have wanted, to round off the ten years, to provide... a precious commemoration and a free confession*'. '*This plan has not materialised. The majority of those we approached ended up slipping away ...*'

It could not have been otherwise. And only G. Duhamel, *without fear and without rashness*, pronounced his judgement on the war. This bankruptcy has a very valuable social meaning. The judgement of one man alone is symbolic.

'The actual object of my thoughts', writes Duhamel, *'is the following: can thinking reconcile its cause with violence?*

'I no longer believe it ... Thinking takes place on one level, and armed force on another. Thinking has its instruments, and its victories. By associating itself with violence, it denies itself and decays'.

The enormity of such phrases quietly drawn up at a time of trenches, blockades, famines and uprisings that have run up against the wall of the Dawes Plan[11] is so great that it doesn't immediately become evident. Thinking, thinking? What thinking? The disembodied thinking of what fleshly humans – the poor or the rich?

It is only a word, and a lying word at that. There is no disembodied thought. There are only men on the earth who labour to live and others who live off the labour of others. There is no other thinking than that of these men. Cultivating ideas is only accessible to those who have the leisure, the requisite education and the knowledge that can only be acquired at monetary expense, by those who, in one way or another, benefit from the exploitation of crowds of workers condemned to ignorance and thoughtlessness.

The war was not the price paid for violence against thinking. The war was only a phase – and moreover a normal one, as the permanence of armaments and the state of *latent war* which has followed the conclusion of peace proves – in the life of a society based upon the exploitation of one class by another.

In this society, all armies, including those of the intellect, are in the hands of the owners, deployed against the workers, and violence is never separate from thinking. The educator takes part in preparing the citizen in the same way as the NCO. The pacifist philosopher prepares for war no less effectively than the general staff's chemist. The one shapes the brains of the men who will be soldiers. The other shapes death for them with grenades like children's toys.

The factory worker, if he does not want to relive the experience of the trenches, must disregard the philosopher and learn how to use grenades. For him, *thinking and violence* only operate on the same level: that of the order to mobilise. This level has nothing metaphysical about it. The dark outline of an execution post provides him with a particularly concrete way of looking at it.

'I am not trying to pacify the world. I want to pacify myself', Duhamel again writes. *'I refuse to look on war as a conflict of races, doctrines or economic interests. The*

war is a matter between myself and me. Limiting and extending the problem, I have only one further plan: to deny agreement and collaboration with war in any circumstances.'

It is a very noble solution very much to one's liking, in spite of the slightly jarring refrain of *me, me, me*, to preserve very preciously the purity of his conscience as a writer, while someone is pressuring, imprisoning, deporting, starving and machine gunning all the races somewhere in the wide world for economic interests disguised by doctrines which no longer fool anyone ...

Culture as the Servant of the Bourgeoisie

I hasten to add: I do not doubt the deep sincerity of this great writer. Nor have I forgotten the courageous revolts – however incomplete they might have been! – of some of the intellectuals against the war, the sincerity of impulses condemned to complete impotence, and the individual courage – moreover, very rare – a completely wasteful expense, generous revolts destined to serve the very cause which they wanted to combat ...

In the Middle Ages, so they say, science was the servant of theology. At the present time – the age of the plutocracies – culture is the servant of the bourgeoisie. All thinking – *apart from that of the proletariat* – serves, whatever its twists, to justify and perpetuate the domination of Capital over Labour. What appear to be the bravest *oppositional* ideologies produced by the culture of the controlling classes are only by definition the most ingenious expedients of these classes' instinct for self-preservation.

By their sensitivity, by the very forms of their thought, by their erudition, by their love for a culture of which they are the privileged captives, and by their material and moral position within the capitalist system, the intellectuals are, in many different respects, prisoners of the old world. Escape – and we know of some good examples of it – is possible, but infinitely difficult for them.

That is why, in these last ten years of war and revolution, they have failed in all that the best among them believed to be their mission. The world will not be changed, and war will not be killed off by engineers, lawyers, educators and artists; but the proletariat themselves will change them, by establishing the peace of the world through the victory of its thinking and the violence inseparable from it.

Notes

1. Translated from *La Vie Ouvrière*, 6th year, no.274, 22 August, 1924 (translator's note).
2. i.e. the tenth anniversary of the outbreak of the First World War (translator's note).
3. Romain Rolland (1866–1944) was a famous French novelist who opposed the First World War on a pacifist basis and took refuge in Switzerland, where he wrote *Au-dessus de la mêlée*. His *Declaration of the Independence of Thought* (1919) was signed by Benedetto Croce, Jane Addams, Bertrand Russell, Israel Zangwill, Stefan Zweig, and others (translator's note).
4. *The Aufruf an die Kulturwelt*, otherwise known as the *Manifesto of the 93*, was a nationalist document signed by a group of German intellectuals published in French and German in Paris in 1915, along with replies from the French (translator's note).
5. Richard Wagner (1813–1883) was a German composer of romantic nationalistic music. *Boche* was a racist term used by the French for the Germans in both world wars; the mark of the beast in the Apocalypse (*Revelation* xiii, v.16) was a symbol of the imperial cult of the Roman Empire, and hence, by extension, the worship of any evil imperial power (translator's note).
6. Woodrow Wilson (1856–1924) was the liberal Democrat President of the USA who brought his country into the First World War, one of the major architects of the Versailles Peace, and the founder of the League of Nations (translator's note).
7. Bertrand Russell (1872–1970) was a British empiricist philosopher who visited the Soviet Union just after the Revolution and criticised it in *The Theory and Practice of Bolshevism* (1920). Romain Rolland also criticised the Revolution in his *Clérambault, or One Against All – History of a Free Conscience During the War* (1920) (translator's note).
8. Georges Duhamel (1884–1966) was a 'unanimist' writer (translator's note).
9. *Clarté* is not an advanced magazine; it is a revolutionary magazine (author's note).
10. Albert Crémieux (1899–1967) was a novelist and a member of the French Communist Party until 1929, when he worked on *L'Humanité* (translator's note).
11. The Dawes Plan, so named after Charles Dawes (1865–1951), the Republican Vice President who was the chairman of the Committee that worked it out in 1924, was a scheme for regulating German reparations payments, in which the USA made short-term loans to Germany, which paid them in reparations to France and Belgium, which paid them in debts to Britain, which then returned them as debt payments to the USA. It thus created a money circle by which the whole of Europe was subjected to American financial interets, and, by temporarily stabilising the German economy, brought an end to the revolutionary ferment there in 1923. Cf. Victor Serge, *Witness to the German Revolution*, Redwood Books, London, 2000 (translator's note).

Intellectual Life in Russia: Is a Proletarian Literature Possible?[1]

The 1922 Literary Renaissance

The Civil War ended in 1921, with the introduction of the N.E.P. Lenin's about turn put a stop to the chaotic peasant Thermidor which was portended by the Kronstadt, Tambov and Volga uprisings.[2] 1921 was the year of the great famine. Wrangel was still holding out in the Crimea, but the end of the year brought peace.[3] 1921 was the year of the literary rebirth. 'Never did we have so many young writers, and so rich in promise', Maxim Gorky was to say later.[4] I have described already this new generation of Russian writers in various reports in *Clarté*. The Serapion Brotherhood of Boris Pilnyak, Vsevolod Ivanov, A. Yakovlev, N. Nikitin and N. Tikhonov, which is best associated with the Russian peasantry, was coming into notice at the same time as the young proletarian writers.[5] In June 1923 the journal *Na Postu* (*On Guard*) appeared in Moscow,[6] and the struggle for a proletarian literature was on.

To tell the truth, it was only being taken up again, but with surprising energy. At the height of the Civil War and Intervention during the heroic years of 1918–21, *proletcults*[7] had fought keenly for proletarian culture, set up literary circles in the smallest villages, smothered town walls with posters, created poets, staged plays, elaborated theses, put on courses, and even founded an international committee which survived for a short while. It was a premature attempt, an ambitious plan, but far too utopian. Its failure was obvious. For what cultural work was possible at a time when every member of the party in the was army surviving on two hundred grams of black bread a day with three kippers a week? Nonetheless, setting up *proletcults* was very useful. It is good that at such times class war fighters should devote a part of their thinking to great cultural projects. And the *proletcults* did train young poets: Alexand-rovsky, Kirillov, Vassily Kazin and Obradovich.[8]

Such is the Russian people's capacity for creation that by the end of one year of peace an entirely new literature had arisen in the capitals, bringing several names straightaway into public view. It was indeed revolutionary literature, but ambiguous, capable of very sharp turns, sometimes pointing in a mystical direction, at others towards a sort of neo-nationalism, but more often towards bourgeois thinking that was neither proletarian nor Communist. This was sur-prising. Communist writers, still reeling under the impact of other struggles that had barely ended, immediately declared war on the leanings of the new lit-erature. The journal *On Guard* was their organ of struggle.[9]

On Guard: Communist Criticism

We should say straightaway that this was one of the best and most representa-tive of the Russian journals, clearly presented, easy to read, and rigorously ide-ologically consistent in its stance. Its aim can be summed up as being to 'Bolshevise' the new literature. Issues 2–3 bore these lines on the dust jacket in bold type :

> In literature we are declaring implacable war upon lying petty bourgeois distortions of the revolution; we will tirelessly condemn petty bourgeois literary deviations among us; we will establish and support proletarian literature.
>
> For this is the only way to carry on our party's glorious tradition.

Another manifesto states that the journal 'has the aim of a revolutionary-Marxist criticism of literature today' and 'a merciless struggle against those lit-erary tendencies and groupings which, either openly or disguised in revolutionary terms, take their inspiration from reactionary ideas'.

This was posing the question with admirable clarity and the necessary stark-ness. There is a time for smashing windows, those of eternal bourgeois hypocrisy in particular, such as the old lie of art for art's sake, when in fact there could only be real intellectual culture for the property owning classes; the old idea that thinking and literature were alien to politics, when in fact no one can escape from his social class, and when the whole caboodle of our ideas and words belongs to a society whose *determining laws* are commodity production and wage labour; the outmoded democratic idea of the wandering intellectual, borne aloft on printed paper wings above the class struggle. These might go on for a long time whilst Europe is decaying, but they must no longer be allowed to fool anybody on land won by the Revolution.

Now the speciality of Russian writers immediately after the Revolution was to avoid taking sides. 'If Russia evolves towards bourgeois democracy', I wrote in *Clarté* two years ago, 'they will in ten years become polished littérateurs. But if Russia makes progress towards Socialism, they will become Communist writers. They will be shifted about by the tide.' And Zorin the Communist[10] said to me: 'You are quite right, except that in the first case it wouldn't take ten years: ten weeks would be enough.' The ideological wavering of Pilnyak (the most representative among them) required a reply. The Communist writers supplied it, and it was a real literary battle, closely linked to the class struggle then taking place in Russia.

On Guard was above all a journal of criticism, destructive and partisan ... Nothing was spared. On account of his eternal sourness and obstinate defence of the old intellectuals Sosnovsky[11] described Gorky in it as 'the old hawk who has become a hedgehog'. 'The poetic counter-revolution' of the poet Maximilian Voloschin[12] was quite rightly condemned. Pilnyak, Ehrenburg[13] and Nikitin were labelled slanderers of the Revolution. Mayakovsky got a right old thrashing for his proletarian futurist pretensions, Alexandra Kollontai for her free love novels, Lunacharsky for his plays, and the state publishers for their clumsy editing.[14] A sort of 'little anthology of Bolshevik put-downs' was published which was a very enjoyable read.

Some of the critical studies in this magazine do not seem to me to be ideal examples of their type, such as the Marxist analysis (i.e. from a class viewpoint) of Anna Akhmatova's love poetry by G. Lelevich,[15] but I should mention Libedinsky's lively study of *The Writer's Personality*.[16]

This movement had all the vices of its virtues. It tended to outrageous exaggeration of what were sound and legitimate claims. Caricature often became niggling, and debate dried up. Disappointingly schematic articles were published (e.g. J. Libedinsky's *Subjects Waiting for Authors*). The polemic directed at A. Voronsky, the editor of *Krasnaya Nov*, an old Communist writer who had contributed a great deal to the literary rebirth in 1922, was every bit as heated as a real political conflict. The Moscow Association of Proletarian Writers supporting *On Guard* demanded that the Party intervene and lay down a sort of 'literary protectionism'. It boasted in its theses of 'an artistic, ideological and formal programme which must become the basis for the further development of proletarian literature'.[17]

The Association posited 'proletarian literature as the opposite of bourgeois literature', defining it as 'the revolutionary Marxist world view'. *On Guard* asked the Party for 'rational and tactical leadership in art ...'

Other Communist Opinions (N. Bukharin and A. Voronsky)

Here we are at the very centre of the debate. The most reasonable replies to this tendency appear to have been drawn up by N. Bukharin,[18] whom nobody would accuse of the free and easy attitude of the old liberalism even in literature. 'We must have a peasant literature', says Bukharin (obviously, in a country where farmers make up ninety-five percent of the population!), and 'don't forget that a cultural problem differs from a military problem in that it cannot be solved by the mere use of force'.

Proletarian literature has to win out by criticism and competition, and not by restrictive measures against its opponent: we must realise at last that our proletarian writers have to write books, and not theses. One good book is far more persuasive than twenty platforms. This is the essence of good sense talking. And, moreover, 'giving up free competition is the best way of killing off young proletarian literature'.

The Pilnyaks and the Vsevolod Ivanovs who spring from rural Russia and voice its vacillations and confused thinking must not be subjected to 'cudgel blows' – at least, not all the time; they should rather be influenced, and if possible won over ... And finally, Bukharin draws our attention to the danger of setting up organisations of writers with structures copied from the Party and the army. Freedom and a range of groups and tendencies are necessary in the world of artistic creativity, and the Party should limit itself to giving very general directives to Communists.

In the proposals he submitted to the Central Committee of the Russian Communist Party in the spring of 1924 A. Voronsky ascribed the crisis in Russian literature as mainly due to the N.E.P.[19] The revolutionary romanticism that was still very much alive two years before had come to an end. Bohemianism had come back along with free trade. 'We have lost one of our most talented poets before our very eyes, corrupted by Bohemianism', wrote Voronsky, referring to Serge Yesenin.[20] Young writers now have a hard life. Young proletarian writers have to put up with the contrast between the N.E.P. and their aspirations. They are working in deep material hardship. The suicide of one of them – N. Kuznetsov[21] – very much underlines the meaning of many poems. B. Kovynev,[22] for example, says quite simply:

> Yonder Ballerinas are dancing,
> And hearts are filled with violets
> While I shiver at the window
> Fists tightly clenched, fists tightly clenched.

All too truly, in our opinion, Voronsky accuses the proletarian literature of the groups and magazines (*October* and *Young Guard*) of immersing themselves in 'sacred imagery', 'official optimism' and 'bureaucratic cliché'.

Proletarian Writers: *October*

I have before me issues nos. 1 and 2 (May and August 1924) of *October*, the journal of the Moscow Association of Proletarian Writers. Whereas criticism of proletarian writers in *On Guard* appears to be very strong and well-founded, here their output seems meagre to us. The poets (Ivan Doronin, *At War*, Bezymensky, *War in Stages*, and A. Gvozdev, *Fragments on the War*[23]) are good. We might say that they are still romantic about the Civil War, as shown by the subjects themselves. They do not know how to restrain themselves, to be concise, to polish their work; all too often their poems are too long, too diffuse, and too uneven. But they are lively and very striking, with high flights of lyricism. We have already had occasion to comment that during the Revolution poetry was far richer than prose. And prose works are still weak, far too weak, now. In his *At the Workbenches* A. Philippov goes on at great length about the factory.[24] He appears to have minutely catalogued the conversation topics and trivial jokes of a certain number of factory workers over an entire week with far too much patience. And yet he has carefully cut out of the conversations around the workbench practically everything that does not accord with his preconceived schema, the swearing, coarse language and bizarre jokes that you are most likely to hear at work in a country as devastated as the Soviet Union. To sum up, the rigmarole is as irritating as a pastoral idyll. We are only drawing attention to it because it is so typical. It is seriously devoted writers, imprisoned in preconceived ideas, and obviously obsessed with theses and schemas, who are ending up with these flops. A. Tarassov-Rodionov, the writer of *Chocolate*, a dramatic short story of which we will talk later, attempted a major composition about the heroic year of 1918, *Linev*.[25] It was an utter failure.

This is not good proletarian literature, because it is not good literature at all (in spite of a few successful pages). The same is true of J. Libedinsky, who a short while ago wrote *The Week*, one of the best works, perhaps even the best, of young Russian literature. *Tomorrow*, his story about the German Revolution which appeared in *Young Guard*, is obviously so wide of the mark that even the author openly admitted it was a failure.[26] The characters in these two stories are hopelessly conventional, and have all the appearance of marching out stiffly from a discussion about AgitProp. In *Linev* there is a French officer who is a counter-revolutionary because he has been brainwashed with the principles of political economy of ... Frédéric Bastiat.[27] There is obviously no shortage of counter-revolutionaries in France and elsewhere, but I do not think that Frédéric Bastiat still exercises so great an influence over them ... We get living proof here of an appallingly abstract process of literary creation. The writer is working with this simplistic reasoning: French, Radical, middle classes, free market, Bastiat. The character is a tailor's dummy stylishly dressed up.

The Association of Proletarian Writers rightly condemned in its theses the exclusive cult of form of the so-called 'formalist' literary school set up in Leningrad by V. Shklovsky, Professor Eichenbaum, etc.,[28] the verbal acrobatics of the futurists, and the bombast of *The Forge* (*Kuznitza*) proletarian group,[29] which dreamed, not without real talent, of ... a cosmic revolution; it appeals to the writer 'not to cultivate bourgeois forms of art, but to master them in order to create new forms', and to espouse 'monumental' compositions that deal mainly with proletarian life ... Ideas that are doubtless correct in themselves abound in these theories, but even the best theories require meaningful adapting to concrete reality. Is it possible, in vast rural Russia, where the towns are islands of advanced civilisation, for a young writer who has just *come out of the workshop* to *transcend* the expertise of the methods of bourgeois art? Maybe, in a few isolated cases, after fifteen years of struggling, with good luck. Does a literary apprenticeship start off with great monumental compositions? In short, it seems to us to be very dangerous to subject the creative efforts of young men newly awakening to literary life to such pure theories.

Achievements

However, there are some great successes to be picked out in the pages of *October*. You must look for them, and know how to read them. They are hidden away at the ends of the volumes under the unasuming heading of 'notes'. Here we learn quite simply that the *October* group will soon be publishing twelve booklets of verse, or that the Workers' Spring group (50 of them) has been applying itself 'to intensive work of late'. Let us pick some of it out. 'What has been read: 15 plays, 76 short stories, 261 poems and 20 lectures, in 96 evening meetings where 450 writers took part'. Don't mock the statistical brevity. Remember that two thirds of the workers here are trudging through winter in the snows of Russia with holes in their boots. They aren't going off to the café. They are working and writing with the pure simplicity of children determined to mature. The *Vagranka* group was set up on Rogojsko-Simonovsky Avenue (Moscow) by 16 worker correspondents of magazines. An old Bolshevik writer, Perekati-Polé, blind and as poor as can be, and quite forgotten, brings them all together in his comfortless flat and teaches them verse rhythms and prose. There are not enough chairs: they have to sit round in a circle on the wooden floor. It is true that the workers in this small literary fraternity, who come in stinking of coal tar, machine oil and swarf, are still very inexperienced; but don't you think as I do that the very existence of this literary circle alone is an event of the highest importance, and that all things considered it is rather more more promising for the future of human culture than any refined literary salon would be in Paris? An association of as yet unpublished proletarian writers was formed in Tsaritsyn, among them a locksmith, a lathe operator, a cook and some unskilled labourers; neither Pierre Hamp[30] nor Gorky would sneer at that. We know that the Soviet press has for some years been encouraging the efforts of its worker, peasant, soldier and sailor correspondents. There are thousands of them. Obscurantism hunts them down in backward rural areas and kills them off. You should know that there is an entire literature by Russian Communist youth: noteworthy poets like Bezymensky, Doronin and A. Zharov, interesting prose writers (Seifullina, Artem Veselyi), and critics and partisan writers of undisputable quality (Averbach).[31]

M. Frédéric Lefèvre, interviewing the English novelist Swinnerton[32] in a recent issue of *Nouvelles Littéraires*, asked him if it was possible for a poor man to get published in London. 'It is well nigh impossible', the novelist replied, 'for a man who is both poor and has the additional disadvantage of coming from the provinces ...' But in Moscow, Tsaritsyn, Tver or Tashkent a poor man can get published. A joiner or a bargee can write for the daily paper of the province or the capital, and if they have something worthwhile to say, they can be confident that they will receive nothing but encouragement for it.

Let us suppose that the work of these worker correspondents, small groups and Communist youth, the harvest of the awakening of an entire people, goes on for another fifteen years. What fruits will it not bring us! The superiority of the Russian proletarians over their brethren in the civilised countries of the old West is already obvious. When an entire generation has grown up in this work atmosphere, conscious of the duty to master culture, with a real possibility of succeeding in it, since they have already been successful in the class struggle, we will have a proletarian literature with something powerfully fresh about it.

Lenin's generation laid down the foundations for this. Several names stand out and ought to be noticed in a chapter about literary successes. Demyan Biedny is the inexhaustible creator of down-to-earth popular poetry. We should look for the living face of Russia today in the critique of manners undertaken by such masters of proletarian journalism as Sosnovsky and M. Koltsov,[33] and not in interminable factory stories dreamed up in accordance with an official ideal.

The Problem of a Proletarian Culture

Do these harbingers and beginnings justify waiting for a proletarian culture?

In *Literature and Revolution* L. D. Trotsky gives a reply to this much-debated question that appears definitive to us, with one reservation. Culture is the work of centuries. Will the proletariat, whose dictatorship can only be a short transitory period of history full of work and struggle, have the time to elaborate a culture of its own?

> It is legitimate to doubt this, because the years of social revolution will be years of fierce class struggles in which destruction will occupy more room than new construction ...[34]

But after victory?

> As the new regime will be more and more protected ... as the conditions for cultural creation will become more favourable, the proletariat will be more and more dissolved into a Socialist community and will free itself from its class characteristics and thus cease to be a proletariat ...
> The proletariat acquires power for the purpose of doing away forever with class culture and to make way for human culture.[35]

This is very much our view. The development of any intellectual culture takes for granted stable production, a high level of technique, well-being, leisure and time. In a society where exploitation would be banned, with a superior work organisation and a very advanced technique, conditions of comfort and leisure for all would be necessary for it. On the other hand the importance of the *time* factor would diminish. The collective effort and activity of the masses in civilisational work would take us to unhoped-for heights ... But the revolutionary era, the era of the transition from capitalism to Socialism, which began at two points, on 2 August 1914 and the 7 November 1917, will go on for decades, or even half a century (why not?). From where we are now to then, workers' republics will only be beleaguered fortresses, in whose life the arts will only take the same sort of second place as is accorded them in capitalist societies.

L. D. Trotsky even finds the words 'proletarian literature' dangerous, since they 'erroneously compress the culture of the future into the narrow limits of the present day'.[36] These words, it seems to us, answer to a need of the transi-

tional epoch, which is satisfied by new values to a certain extent. Several generations of workers are likely not to know any other times. They must fight above
all. They will have much to destroy and suffer : the world has to be refashioned.
But like the armies of old, they will have their bards, their story tellers, their
musicians and their philosophers. And it is all the more true since in order to
win the proletariat must be led by real leaders, thinkers and strategists, who,
following the examples of Marx and Lenin, will have absorbed the essence of
modern culture: it needs its *own* great intellectuals. It needs lesser men as well,
for lesser but vital tasks. But the main thing is that both of them are very much
its own, its servants. The revolutionary work it is achieving thus has a cultural
value in and of itself. In this historically limited sense there will be, and there
already is, a culture of the militant proletariat.

Notes

1. Translated from *Clarté*, no.lxxii (4th year), 1 March, 1925, pp.121–4. Another English translation of this
   article, by Anna Aschenbach, appears in J. Ehrmann (ed.), *Literature and Revolution*, Beacon Press, Boston
   Mass., 1970, pp.137–45. The Maspero French edition of 1976 contains the following note: 'Documentation:
   On Guard, a magazine of literary criticism, Moscow, nos.1–5, 1923–24; *October*, the journal of the Moscow
   Association of Proletarian Writers, nos.1–2, 1924; 'Literature and Art', The Declaration of Eight Communist
   Writers, *Pravda*, February 1924; *Young Guard*, a Communist magazine, Moscow, various issues; L. D. Trotsky,
   Literature and Revolution; A. Voronsky, *On Literature* (Theses presented to the Central Committee of the
   Russian Communist Party); *Arbeiter Literatur*, nos.5–6, Vienna, June 1924, and various articles; N. Bukharin,
   'Our Policy as Regards Art', *Searchlight*, no.10 (32), 1924; Demyan Biedny, 'On Proletarian Literature',
   Pravda, January 1925' (author's note). The English translation of Trotsky's *Literature and Revolution* was
   reprinted by the University of Michigan Press in 1960 and by Redwords in 1991. Alexander Constantinovich
   Voronsky (1884–1943) was a veteran revolutionary, literary critic and writer, and a supporter of the Left
   Opposition. He wrote *Art as the Cognition of Life and the Contemporary World* (1924), recently published in
   English translation along with other valuable articles by Mehring Books (Michigan, 1998). He was arrested
   and executed during the Terror. Cf. also Claude Kastler, *Alexandre Voronski, 1884–1943, Un Bolshevik fou de
   littérature*; 'Alexandre Voronski dans la première révolution russe', *Cahiers du Mouvement Ouvrier*, no.17,
   April/May 2002, pp.19–27. Demyan Biedny (Efim A. Pridvorov, 1883–1945) was a leading Russian poet
   (translator's note).
2. Thermidor 1794 was when the Jacobins were overthrown, and the reaction against the French Revolution
   began. It came to be used by revolutionaries as a general term applied to the period of the retreat of any
   revolution. Cf. Martyn Hudson, 'Trotsky and the Thermidorean Chapter' and 'Jacobinism and the Soviet
   Thermidor', *Weekly Worker*, 28th February and 7th March, 2002. There was a major peasant revolt against the
   Bolshevik government in Tambov and a mutiny of the fleet base at Kronstadt in 1921 (translator's note).
3. Baron Pyotr Wrangel (1878–1928) advanced upon the Bolsheviks from the South whilst the Poles were
   attacking from the West. After the Poles had signed an armistice with the Bolsheviks in 1920 he retreated to
   the Crimea, and tried to fortify the Perekop isthmus. When Stalin and Frunze broke through he evacuated
   the peninsula on 10–14 November 1920 (translator's note).

4. Alexei Maximovich Peshkov, known as Maxim Gorky (1868–1936) was a great Russian writer. He opposed the Bolshevik seizure of power in 1917 and afterwards emigrated, but returned to the Soviet Union in 1931. Serge met him still in Russia in 1919. He held a poor opinion of his collaboration with the regime (*Memoirs of a Revolutionary*, Oxford, 1975, pp.268–9), but the account there differs significantly from that in *The Revolution in Danger* (London, 1997, pp.27–8) written at the time (translator's note).

5. Boris Andreyevich Vogau, called Pilnyak (1894–1937) was a writer of symbolist short stories and novels including *Naked Year* (1922), a collection of impressions taken from life in a provincial town soon after the Russian revolution (English translation by Alec Brown, New York, 1928). He first got into trouble with the regime in his *Tale of the Unextinguished Moon* (1926; English translation by Brian Pearce in Michael Glenny (ed.), *Novy Mir, 1925–1967*, 1972)) which was a thinly disguised account of the suspicious death of Frunze in an operation. Then he fell under suspicion in 1929 for writing *Mahogany*, which contained an idealistic portrait of a Trotskyist, and was removed as Chairman of the All-Russian Union of Writers. He made his peace with the regime for a while by praising the first 5-year plan in *The Volga Falls to the Caspian Sea* (1930; English translation 1931), but perished in the purges (Serge, *Memoirs*, pp.269–70). He was posthumously rehabilitated, but a selection of his works did not reappear in print until 1976. Nevertheless, Serge was a close friend of Pilnyak, who greatly influenced his writing style (Richard Greeman, 'The Novel of the Revolution', in Susan Weissman (ed.), *The Ideas of Victor Serge, Critique*, nos.28–9, Glasgow, 1997, pp.61–3). Vsevolod Vyacheslavovich Ivanov (1895–1963) was a prose writer famous for his naturalistic writing. He fought in the Russian Civil War and wrote vivid stories about it (*Partisan Stories*, 1921, and *Armoured Train No.1469*, 1922). He joined the Serapion Fraternity in 1920. He reworked *Armoured Train 14-69* in 1927 because he had been severely criticised for neglecting the part played by the Communist Party in the partisan movement, made his peace with the regime, and went on to write party novels. Alexander Stepanovich Trifonov-Yakovlev (1886–1953), was a novelist. His best known work, *Povol'niki* (1923) is about the revolution in the Volga region. Nikolai Nikolayevich Nikitin (1895–1963) was a Russian writer who joined the Serapion Fraternity in 1921. His first short story was *Fort Vomit* (1922). Nikolai Semyonovich Tikhonov (1896–1979) was a poet and prose writer who took part in the revolution and the Civil War, about which he published collections of poetry (*The Horde*, 1922, and *Mead*, 1922). He joined the Serapion Fraternity, so-called after the hermit Serapion in a tale by E. T. A. Hoffmann, in the early 1920s. For Serge's views on the Serapion Fraternity (*Serapionovy Braty*a), cf. *Memoirs*, p.165 (translator's note).

6. *On Guard* (1923–1925) was followed by *On Literary Guard* (1926–1932) (translator's note).

7. *Proletcult* was a movement to form a proletarian culture, originally headed by A. A. Bogdanov. It took its name from the First Conference of Proletarian-Cultural Organisations held in Petrograd before the Revolution on the 16–19 October 1917, which issued the journal *Proleterskaya kultura* from 23 July 1918 onwards. Lenin opposed it, and the Party pronounced against it in 1920. Serge briefly refers to it in *Year One of the Russian Revolution*, London, 1972, p.361, and *From Lenin to Stalin*, New York, 1973, p.118 (translator's note).

8. Vasily Dmitriyevich Alexandrovsky (1897–1934) was a poet who celebrated the worker through abstract images, active in the *Proletcult* in Moscow in 1918–9, and then with *Kuznitsa*; Vladimir Timofeevich Kirillov (1890–1943) was a Russian poet who took part in the February and October Revolutions, and was active in *Proletcult*. His collections include *Verses* (1918) and *25th October* (1922). Vasili Vasiliyevich Kazin (1898–1981) was the founder of *Kuznitsa* (*The Forge*), and was among the first to bring out the theme of labour into Russian poetry in *Worker's May* (1922). Sergei Alexandrovich Obradovich (1892–1956) was a poet, also a supporter of *proletcult* and *Kuznitsa* and head of the literary section of *Pravda*. His poem *October* came out in 1922 (translator's note).

9. A footnote in the Maspero edition adds here : 'Published under the direction of Boris Volin, G. Lelevich and Semyon Rodov, with the collaboration of L. Averbach, L. Sosnovsky, I. Vardin, J. Libedinsky, A. Tarasov-Rodionov, etc.'

10. Serge S. Zorin was a member of the Petrograd Committee of the Communist Party and a supporter of Zinoviev. But the context here suggests that this is a typesetting mistake for Alexander I. Zonin (1901–1962),

a literary critic who joined the Bolsheviks during the Civil War and wrote for *October* and *On Guard* (translator's note).

11. Lev Semionovich Sosnovsky (1886–1937) was a popular Bolshevik journalist, and later a staunch supporter of the Left Opposition. His capitulation to Stalin in 1934 did not prevent him from being shot afterwards (translator's note).

12. Maximilian Alexandrovich Voloschin (1877–1932) was a Russian symbolist poet, translator and painter, who opposed the revolution, but remained in Russia. The symbolists were inspired by the teaching of Vladimir Solovyov. Their most outstanding poet was Blok (translator's note).

13. Ilya Grigoryevich Ehrenburg (1891–1967) was a prominent Russian novelist, poet, journalist and short story writer who left Russia for western Europe in 1921, but returned later on. He was afterwards notorious for his reporting on the Popular Front in Spain and France in 1936–40 as correspondent for *Izvestia* (translator's note).

14. Vladimir Vladimirovich Mayakovsky (1893–1930) was Russia's leading revolutionary poet (*Ode to Revolution*, 1918, and *Left March*, 1918), as well as being a theatre writer and a designer of posters and cartoons. He joined the R.S.D.L.P. in 1908, and was repeatedly imprisoned under the Tsar. He shot himself in 1930. Serge translated his *26th–27th February 1917* into French in 1931 cf. *Memoirs*, pp.267–8; Viktor Shklovsky, *Mayakovsky and His Circle*, London 1974. Alexandra Mikhailovna Demontovich Kollontai (1872–1952), a feminist icon, had been a Menshevik before 1915, and her early submission to Stalin gave her the rare distinction of surviving the purges. The references in the text are to her preposterous writings, three of which appear in Cathy Porter (ed.), *The Love of Worker Bees* (London, 1977). For Serge's attitude to Kollontai, cf. *Memoirs*, p.205. Anatoly Vasilievich Lunacharsky (1875–1933) was Commissar for Culture in the Bolshevik government, and the foremost proponent of *Proletcult*. Cf. Anatoly Lunacharsky, *Faust and Other Plays*, London, 1923; *On Literature and Art*, Moscow, 1965, A Yeramov, *A. Lunacharsky*, Moscow, 1975. Futurism was an artistic movement which began in Italy before the First World War, and was for a while very popular among the workers there. But after the War most of its leading spirits became Fascists. Futurism sought to express the urgency of modern life and rebelled against all traditions (translator's note).

15. Anna Andreyevna Gorenko, known as Akhamatova (1889–1966) was Russia's woman poet. Her husband was implicated in the Tagantsev affair and executed in 1921, and after 1923 no more of her poetry books were published until 1940. In 1946 she was denounced by Zhdanov, Stalin's dictator of the arts, as 'part nun part harlot', and was criticised by the Central Committee of the C.P.S.U. Cf. Roberta Reeder (ed.), *The Complete Poems of Anna Akhmatova*, Edinburgh, 1992. Lelevich was the pseudonym of Labori Gilelevich Kalmanson (1901–1937), a poet and critic, who was accused of being a supporter of the Joint Opposition, and arrested. He was posthumously rehabilitated (translator's note).

16. Yuri N. Libedinsky (1898–1959) was a leader of the Russian Association of Proletarian Writers (RAPP). He was the author of *The Week* (1922), which touched upon the excesses of the Cheka, which Serge reviewed in *Clarté* (no.43, 1923, pp.388–9; English translation, London, 1923). For Serge's attitude to him, cf. Ian Birchall, 'Proletarian Culture', in Susan Weissman (ed.), *The Ideas of Victor Serge*, *Critique*, nos.28–29, Glasgow, 1997, pp.86–7 (translator's note).

17. *Platform of the First Conference of Moscow Proletarian Writers*, 1923 (author's note).

18. Nikolai Bukharin (1888–1938) was the author of numerous works on Marxist theory, and head of the Comintern after Stalin had ousted Zinoviev. His article, 'The Proletariat and Questions of Artistic Policy' was published in *Krasnaya Nov*, no.4, 1925. He was a defendant in the Third Moscow Trial (translator's note).

19. Alexander Voronsky, 'On Proletarian Art and the Artistic Policy of Our Party', *Krasnaya Nov*, no.vii, 1923; English translation in *Art as the Cognition of Life*, Mehring Books, Michigan, 1998, p.152. *Krasnaya Nov* (*Red Virgin Soil*) was edited by Voronsky until 1927 (translator's note).

20. Sergei Alexandrovich Yesenin (1895–1925) came from a family of Old Believers, but welcomed the Russian Revolution. He signed the Imagist Manifesto in 1919, and was married to Isadora Duncan. He wrote *Inoniya*

(*Otherland*, 1918), a utopian vision, and a poetic drama about *Pugachev* (1920–1). He committed suicide by hanging himself in his hotel room (cf. *Memoirs*, p.195 (translator's note).

21. Nikolai Kuznetsov (1904–1924) was a proletarian poet who committed suicide early in the N.E.P. (translator's note).

22. It has proved impossible to trace B. Kovynev. Perhaps it is a misprint for the name of the poet Mikhail Yakovlevich Kozyrev (1892–) (translator's note).

23. Ivan Ivanovich Doronin (1900–1978) was a Tula factory worker who attended *Proletcult* classes, published his first poem in 1919, joined the C.P.S.U. in 1920, and supported *October*. Alexander I. Bezymensky (1898–1973) was a dramatic author, the writer of *The Shot* (1930). He was later to become known as a writer of verse on governmental policy in the pages of *Pravda*, but fell under a cloud in the 1930s, only to reemerge during the Khruschev period in order to oppose the rehabilitation of other literary figures. Alexei Alexandrovich Gvozdev (1887–1939) was a theatrical and literary scholar and critic (translator's note).

24. Boris Andreyevich Philippov (1905–1991) was a writer of short stories, with a prodigious output. He was arrested in 1927, 1929 and 1936, and escaped from the USSR. during the Second World War through Germany to the USA, where he lectured until his retirement (translator's note).

25. Alexander Ignatievich Tarasov-Rodionov (1885–1938) organised the *October* group, and published his controversial *Chocolate* in 1922 (English translation, London, 1933). He was arrested during the purges, and posthumously rehabilitated (translator's note).

26. Libedinsky published *Tomorrow* in 1923, and *The Week* in 1922, an English translation of which by Arthur Ransome was published in London in 1923. It was reviewed by Serge in *Clarté*, no.xliii, 11th January, 1923, pp.387–9 (cf. below, p. 222) (translator's note).

27. Claude-Frédéric Bastiat (1801–1850) was a French economist and politician, an advocate of free trade influenced by Richard Cobden. Marx called him 'the most superficial and therefore the most adequate representative of the apologetic of vulgar economy' (Afterword to the 2nd German edition of *Capital*, vol.i, Moscow, 1958, p.16), while Plekhanov called him 'a garrulous dwarf' ('Art and Social Life', 1912–3, in *Selected Philosophical Works*, vol.v, Moscow, 1981, p.655). His opinions were long outmoded by 1925 (translator's note).

28. Viktor Borisovich Shklovsky (1893–1984) was the leading theorist of Futurism and the founder of Formalism, which he expounded in his *On the Theory of Prose* (1925). He was later awarded the Red Banner of Labour. Professor Boris Mikhailovich Eichenbaum (1886–1959) was a leading formalist critic and literary scholar. He was denounced in 1946 for supporting Akhmatova, and disappeared from the literary scene until his death.The formalists were members of a critical school which declared form to be the essence of poetry, determining the content. The formalist critics concentrated upon a close analysis of the sound and meaning of the words in poetry. They constituted the leading critical opponents of Marxism at the time. Cf. Victor Erlich, *Russian Formalism: History-Doctrine*, The Hague, 1969 (translator's note).

29. *Kuznitza* was a literary journal which carried on a campaign against those writers who did not fully support Communist aims, and supported *Proletcult* (translator's note).

30. Henri Bourillon, known as Pierre Hamp (1876–1962) was a French writer and journalist, who began his life as a pastrycook's apprentice. He described his early life in *Mes Métiers* (1931) (translator's note).

31. Alexander Alexeyevich Zharov (1904–1984), was a poet and a member of the Communist Youth who wrote in support of the Russian Revolution in the style of Mayakovsky and Blok. Lidia N. Seifullina (1889–1954) is famous for writing *Humus* (1922) and *The Iron Stream* (1924). Artem Veselyi (N. I. Kochkurov, 1899–1939) depicted the revolution in an abstract and formal manner. Leopold Leonodovich Averbach (1903–1939), a literary critic and theorist, was Secretary of the Association of Proletarian authors. He was implicated in the fall of Yagoda, arrested in 1937, denounced in the 1938 purge, and executed. Cf. *Memoirs*, 1975, pp.264–5 (translator's note).

32. Frédéric Lefèvre (1889–1949) was a French novelist, essayist and journalist. Frank Arthur Swinnerton (1884–1982) was a publisher's assistant and writer of 42 novels, along with reviews, comments, etc. He was

largely instrumental in launching Everyman's Library for J. M. Dent (translator's note).

33. Mikhail Efimovich Fridland, called Koltsov (1898–1940) was a journalist and a pupil of Sosnovsky who went over to Stalin earlier. He reported for *Pravda* on the Spanish Civil War, but was arrested in 1938 and later executed (translator's note).

34. L. D. Trotsky, *Literature and Revolution*, Michigan U. P., 1960, p.185 (translator's note).

35. Op. cit., pp.185–6 (translator's note).

36. Op. cit., p.205 (translator's note).

Proletarian Literature?[1]

1. Do you believe that artistic and literary creation has to be a purely individual affair? Don't you think that it should or must reflect the great movements that determine the economic and social development of humanity?

2. Do you believe that a literature and an art exist which express the aspirations of the working class? Who are, in your opinion, its main representatives?

1. France has over twelve million proletarians but does not have a proletarian literature. The overwhelming majority of the proletarians of the world exist *outside* literature, just as they are outside all higher culture. It hits you in the face in the present circumstances that 'good literature', 'good behaviour', the sciences and the arts are almost exclusively the property of the comfortably off or the rich classes. Then we can talk about the part played by individuality in the creation of literature, and indeed of other such lofty subjects: there is no more elegant way of scorning the workers.

There are not, and cannot be working class writers in capitalist society; a training in the writer's craft is incompatible with factory work, which involves eight hours a day to gain a mediocre living.

There are not and cannot be literary figures writing for proletarians, because as a general rule they do not buy books. Today's book (at present 12 francs) is at an unaffordable price for the majority of the workers. It is therefore written for the middle classes or the rich. So by definition writers only do it to amuse well fed people. They no doubt have no qualms of conscience about this, but that hardly matters!

There are some writers – just as bourgeois or petty bourgeois as the rest of them – who are successful at exploiting the feelings of the man in the street.

They sometimes depict the proletarian. They can be of some use to the proletariat; but far more often they taint it with the radical bourgeoisie's ways of feeling and thinking about things.

There are writers allied with the Communist Party, or who sympathise with the working class movement. Their works are, with few exceptions, no less completely alien to the working class, for there is nothing more difficult than intellectual or cultural liberation. Feeling, thinking, talent, ways of expression, and the intellectuals themselves are moulded by bourgeois culture: even if they go over to the working class, and even if they understand how imprisoned they are, they cannot get away from it. Their *political* consciousness is therefore in advance of their deep identity as artists. Cultural influences from the past still prevail in literature in the USSR ten years after the October Revolution. The most noteworthy books that have come out this year (Maxim Gorky, *The Life of Klim Samgin*, Constantine Fedin, *The Brothers*[2]) are in no way proletarian.

2. A working class that has become conscious of itself nonetheless does have its own ways of feeling, of understanding life, of suffering, of laughing and of fighting; it has its way of thinking about society, the state, the laws, work and the family; it has, in a word, its world view and its historic mission. But until now all this has only been expressed to a limited extent for political ends in the class struggle. One could easily imagine a literature that expresses this proletarian feeling about life. It would find a limited audience among the workers; it does not make its authors rich; it would, on the other hand, be far more powerful than that which goes from closets to sofas, from Bourget to Morand![3] A proletarian literature is *possible*. In capitalist countries it could be the work of writers who have very much come over to share the life of the revolutionary proletariat. (These writers, except under very exceptional circumstances, usually have far better things to do than to write novels ... Let us note this vicious circle).

In Soviet lands where it made its beginnings, it is the work of young proletarians who have become intellectuals (or, if you prefer, young intellectuals who have emerged from the proletariat).

Some writers who are at a distance from the proletariat sometimes express in certain works or on particular pages a feeling and a view about man and life that is very close to that felt by the proletariat when it is on the move. It even happens that non-Communist writers express it in an infinitely better way than writers who are members of our party. Thus Vaillant-Couturier's *Le Bal des aveugles*[4] belongs to the furthest removed literature possible by the sentimental and sensual individualism it displays on every page. Yet on the other hand such recent works as *Autrui* by René Arcos, *5000*, by D. Braga, *40ᵉ étage*, by Luc Durtain, and *Codine*, by Panaït Istrati,[5] are to a considerable extent imbued with the sort of ideas and feelings that will only triumph along with the proletariat: feelings about collective life (it is not true that man has to be alone), the joy of life in honest effort and struggle, and a relationship between man and machine civilisation.

Here I cannot refrain from mentioning two great Americans under the same heading: Sinclair Lewis, who in *Babbitt*[6] has so admirably shown the bourgeois of middle America trapped in the dead end of his opulent technical civilisation; and John Dos Passos, who, in *Manhattan Transfer*,[7] gives a powerful impression of social dynamism (nor should we forget their forerunners, such as Whitman, Zola and Verhaeren ...)[8]

3. The same problem is posed under the rule of the dictatorship of the proletariat in rather different ways. Where has there been a proletarian culture? Culture is the work of the dominant classes elaborated over centuries, or decades at least. But the proletariat is working towards the abolition of social classes. For as long as the struggle continues, the requirements of the class war will absorb all its energies. L. Trotsky has very thoroughly analysed these questions in a book which has unfortunately not been translated into French, *Literature and Revolution*:[9] 'in its essence, the dictatorship of the proletariat is not an organization for the production of the culture of a new society, but a revolutionary and military system struggling for it'.[10] In these conditions the proletariat can only more or less adapt bourgeois culture to its needs. When the struggle is over, and the class division of society has been abolished, there will no longer be a proletariat. The newborn culture will be truly human. It is therefore only in a very restricted sense that it is possible to talk about proletarian culture and literature ...[11]

Notes

1. Interview undertaken by Augustin Habaru for the journal *Monde*, no.22, 3 November 1928, p.10 (note to Maspero edition). Augustin Habaru (1898–1944) was a journalist and Communist militant (translator's note).
2. *The Life of Klim Samgin* was a monumental epic novel in four parts published between 1925 and 1936, of which the fourth part was never completed. Constantine Alexandrovich Fedin (1892–1977) was a Red Army journalist and volunteer who joined the Serapion Fraternity in 1921, and tried to create a unity between Russia's national traditions and the new revolutionary art. His novel *The Brothers*, was published in 1927–8. He was later head of the Soviet Writers' Union and was appointed an academician and a Hero of Socialist Labour (translator's note).
3. Paul Bourget (1852–1935) was a French novelist and poet. Paul Morand (1888–1976) was the author of such novels as *Le Flagellant de Séville* and *La Folle Amoureuse*. To begin with he expressed libertarian views, but later served as Vichy ambassador to Switzerland (translator's note).
4. Paul Vaillant-Couturier (1892–1937) had opposed the First World War and joined the early French Communist Party. He later became a notorious slanderer of the Left Opposition and a defender of the Moscow Trials as editor of *L'Humanité*. Cf. *Memoirs*, pp.222–3, 242 (translator's note).
5. René Arcos (1881–1959) was a French poet and writer, who published *Autrui* in 1926; Dominique Braga was a French journalist and writer, who published *5000, récit sportif*, in 1924; André Nepveu, called Luc Durtain (1881–1959), was a French writer and journalist who published *40ᵉ étage* in 1927; Panaït Istrati (1884–1935) was a Romanian writer who wrote in French, and was known as the 'Balkan Gorky'. He supported the Russian Revolution, and later sympathised with the Left Opposition, but was broken by his experiences, and died in Romania. *Codine* was published in 1926. For Serge's remarks about him, cf. *Memoirs*, pp.278–9 (translator's note).
6. Harry Sinclair Lewis (1885–1951) was a novelist who satirised the small town complacency of American life. His book *Babbitt*, published in 1922, described a businessman completely drained of all his individuality (translator's note).
7. John Roderigo Dos Passos (1896–1970) was an American novelist. His *Manhattan Transfer* (1925) gives a view of the metropolis by shifting back and forth over the lives of over a dozen characters in a jerky, nervous, impressionistic style, and Serge criticised it for its impressionism. But Serge was greatly influenced by Dos Passos (*Memoirs*, p.263) (translator's note).
8. Walt Whitman (1819–1892), was an American journalist, essayist and poet. His *Drum Taps* and *Sequel to Drum Taps* (1865) are collections of poems expressing the horrors of war. Émile Zola (1840–1902) is famous for his *Germinal* (1885) describing life in a mining community. Émile Verhaeren (1855–1916) was the foremost Belgian poet and writer of short stories. He particularly addressed the social problems of modern times in *Les Villages illusoires* and *Les Villes tentaculaires* (1895) (translator's note).
9. Since published by Éditions Julliard, 'new literature' collection, Paris, 1964 (note to Maspero edition).
10. L. D. Trotsky, *Literature and Revolution*, Michigan U.P., 1960, p.190 (translator's note).
11. Victor Serge ends his reply to the interview by repeating the conclusion of the text *Is a Proletarian Literature Possible?*, above, p. 46.

The Intellectuals and the Revolution[1]

One At the Turning Point

The investigation opened up by *Monde* into proletarian literature poses in one of the clearest ways the problem of the attitude of the intellectuals towards the proletarian revolution (the only one that is both possible and necessary in our time).

On this topic the experience of Russia provides a rich documentation that is barely understood in the West. I will try to summarise it in a few overall views.

Under the old order the majority of the intellectuals were on the whole revolutionaries. The reactionary attitude of the regime brought together the most moderate liberals and the most radical of the petty bourgeoisie. The old bourgeoisie itself suffocated under the old edifice of the empire, caste-ridden and so wormeaten, heavy and old that it everywhere hindered the development of capitalism; the middle classes who provided the great majority of the intelligentsia felt doomed to mediocrity with no way out. The healthiest and best of the youth grew up inspired by a feeling of revolt which on several occasions brought them together with the proletariat. Well before revolutionary workers appeared on the scene it was the intellectuals belonging to the middle classes who declared a war to the death on the autocracy and round about 1860 gave the Russian Revolution its first leaders, its first heroes and its first traditions.

Of all the intellectuals, it is the writer who is called upon to express most clearly the aspirations of the social classes educated enough to become conscious of themselves. In the immense prison that the Russian Empire was – where the abolition of serfdom, more formal than real, dates from 1861[2] – the writer's voice was the only one that could make itself heard, and not very loudly, moreover, by a fairly large public. Censorship and its cohorts of imbeciles, official corruption, imprisonment, exile, work camps and public insult, inflicted upon the best thinkers and writers for over a century, were in the end to create a very different type of literary man from his western brethren, scarcely inclined to thought games of art for art's sake, but rather inspired by his social mission. The literary history of Russia is a life of martyrs. The poet Ryleev, implicated in the Decembrist conspiracy of 1825[3] was hanged. Pushkin and Lermontov, who were to create the grandeur of Russian poetry, experienced exile and the bitterness of a crushing yoke, and were both killed in duels,[4] and Chernyshevsky, a critic and publicist dear to an entire generation, spent twenty-one years in Siberia (1864–1885) having being subjected to the frightening ceremony of a public execution.[5] Dostoyevsky, who in his youth had been a member of a St Petersburg circle where they read Saint-Simon and Fourier, dragged out ten years in chains in the *House of the Dead*.[6]

In the oppressive atmosphere of the last thirty years of the old regime Russian literature rose to an admirable and sorrowful power. An entire country which wanted to live, which rose towards life, and which struggled in a confused way, painfully straining with all its immense strength towards the future, expressed itself through giants like Schedrin[7] and Dostoyevsky and in the works of the generation of Count Tolstoy[8] and the barefoot Gorky. There was no writer worthy of the name who did not try to be a revolutionary in his own way. Leonid Andreyev built up an incredible case for the prosecution, in which the problems of superstition, hunger, the death penalty and the terror are frighteningly posed, and gave shelter to a Bolshevik Central Committee.[9] Vladimir Korolenko, one of the most humane humourists of our time, to his very last day (he died in 1922) remained 'at the service of the people'.[10]

Tolstoy, excommunicated because he was one of the rare authentic Christians of our time, in the blackest days of the reaction signed his *I Cannot be Silent*, and denounced the 'Genghis Khan provided with a telegraph'.[11] Gorky went through prison, and collaborated with Lenin the émigré ... The Chertkovs, Kuprins, Merezhkovskys, Sologubs and Chirikovs right up to 1917 remained at the head of a literary movement that announced, prepared and waited for the Revolution ...[12]

At one point in the Revolution the petty bourgeoisie hoped to win. 'One morning in March 1917 the Petrograd workers, pushed to the limit by the sense-less slaughters of Galicia, the Carpathians, Poland, Volhynia and many other places,[13] overthrew the wormeaten edifice of the autocracy. In fact it collapsed by itself. The reports of the Petrograd police chiefs in the last days of the old regime announced the catastrophe every day. The working people shouldered it aside. Then a Prince Lvov, a Rodzianko, a Milyukov and a Kerensky, parlia-mentarians trained by the Duma, were seen coming onto the scene, believing that they were destined to resume the succession of the Stolypins and the Sturmers, and began by trying to save the monarchy.[14] It was the dream of a great constitutionally-minded bourgeoisie who were joyfully welcoming the coming of the power of money. The petty bourgeoisie did not allow it to be realised. It wanted a republic. It flooded into and practically in an instant took over the Socialist Revolutionary Party, whose ideologists and orators knew very well how to interpret its aspirations. The rule of businessmen, lawyers and a 'very advanced' and enlightened bourgeoisie was naturally about to begin. At the side of, or a little underneath the national flag, the red flag was freely waved about to please the people, the red shading agreeeably towards pink. They were to be Socialists – and even Socialist Revolutionaries[15] – that means that much was said, at great length, eloquently and seriously, of giving the land to the peas-ants – just like they went on about socialisation in Germany. And the Right's war was also to go on – not without the hope of gaining the Dardanelles.'[16]

For a few troubled months the Russian intellectuals cherished the hope of setting up a radical democracy modelled upon the Third French Republic[17] – (social classes have the ideal they deserve) – but the proletarian revolution annihilated this beautiful dream.

From one day to the next a magical transformation took place! The urban middle classes, revolutionary but yesterday, passed over completely to the counter-revolution in an instant. The intelligentsia were no exception to the rule. It was their second bankruptcy since the days of August 1914 and the wartime psychosis. As in 1914, the tremendous advent disorientated and blind-ed them: since then they have been starkly revealed, not as servants of 'the world conscience' (this magnificent talk is only good for peacetime), but of the capitalist class. The whole of Russian literature, all the press, and the entire intelligentsia almost without exception rose up against the proletariat.

The poetess Zinaida Hippius,[18] who organised a salon of advanced literature in Petrograd,[19] where Alexander Blok's[20] symbolism encountered Merezhkovsky's anarchistic mysticism, dedicated this *Song without Words* to the Bolsheviks:

> How clear a curse
> Weighs down on these senseless people!
> But the hour of punishment
> Will not be a noisy one.
>
> Let us have no requests for revenge
> No cries of celebration
> The noose is ready
> Let us hang them quietly.

When poetry came down from the summits of art to intervene in the class struggle it cast anathema on the proletariat and set up a gallows in the refined soul of a poetess.

Two With the Stronger

The day after the October Revolution the entire Russian intelligentsia, which had previously laid claim to revolutionary democracy and Socialism, along with the whole of the middle classes, passed over to the counter-revolution.

The seizure of power by the workers – that they themselves believed ought to be sharing power with the bourgeoisie – appeared to them to be so stupid an adventure and so criminal an usurpation that from then on anything was permitted to put an end to 'Bolshevik anarchy'. Technicians, state employees, supervisory staff, doctors and even peaceable people replied to the formation of the Soviet Republic with a strike; their children, the entire youth of the well-off classes, took up arms, plotted, and got ready for the Civil War. The ministries were left empty. The municipal administrations were left empty. Departmental heads, supervisors and engineers left; and they did not return for weeks and months. They left the towns to rot, without supplies, water and electricity! '*We will not work with the Bolsheviks!*' But the insurrectionary workers were able to do the lot. At the end of a few weeks – or a few months – in view of the failure of this counter-revolutionary strike, supervisors and technicians asked to be able to work in order to launch a period of sabotage.

These conflicts at the start of the Revolution are very much forgotten now. Let us not be afraid to remember them. It would be dangerous for the working class to forget lessons that cost it so dearly. And it is no more untimely to remember those intellectuals who wanted to serve the revolution. I have the magazines and books in front of me from that time (1917–1919). Two days after the proletarian insurrection Zinaida Hippius, the writer of the *Song Without Words* devoted to the Bolsheviks ('Let us hang them quietly'), correctly drawing attention to the disarray and humiliation of the radical petty bourgeoisie, wrote:

> Tied up, spat on, we are lying in every corner; sailors' spit shows on our faces.

To sharpen the contrast, shall I recall the tone of her wartime verses?

> What is frightening and intolerable is that no one looks forward to tomorrow (1916).

'Petrograd', she now writes, 'is a deep and dark pit'.

> The triumph of Bolshevism was the end of humanity ...

Leonid Andreyev, the writer of *Red Laugh* and *The Seven That Were Hanged*, who took refuge with the White riflemen in Finland, before his death wrote *S.O.S*, an appeal for help for the perishing and devastated Russian fatherland, appealing for intervention by everyone.[21] Kuprin and Merezhkovsky kept quiet because they had not been able to cross the border in time: they made up for it in the emigration later.

Others hesitated painfully. Maxim Gorky, who was the moving spirit behind a great St Petersburg Socialist daily paper, *Novaya Zhizn*, bemoaned 'the pitiless experience of Lenin and Trotsky, and denounced the anarchy Bolshevism unleashed'. Ilya Ehrenburg, who has since come back to us, published his *Plea for Russia* 'crucified by the proletariat' in 1918. I am only here quoting those names that are more or less known in the West.

It was the poets who were the first to get a grip on understanding the greatness of the men and events, and that a new era had begun in the pitiless struggles in which the others could only see and only wanted to see miseries, suffering, evils and absurdities. Perhaps their poetic intuition predisposed them to understand the activity of the masses better when this activity, breaking all the normal constraints, explodes in tumult, sacrifices and upsurges. Are they perhaps more calculating and more detached from their own class? Perhaps in the end we might look for an explanation of this fact in the influence exercised over them by the Left Socialist Revolutionaries.[22] Whatever it was, they understood the October Revolution in their own way from the start and soon supplied it with remarkable works. It is an interesting thing that it was by way of the Christian tradition that they came to understand the October Revolution, the rebirth of the Christ people, the coming of new times, the onset of *The Scythians on the West* (Blok).[23] The great Symbolist Alexander Blok, a pupil of the mystic Solovyev[24] wrote *The Twelve*, one of the most characteristic works of these years. Twelve Red Guards making their way in the dark night and snow across a terrified town leave behind them the blood of a woman 'crowned with white roses, invisible and invulnerable, with Jesus Christ going before them'.[25] Serge Yesenin, at the dawn of his career recited in the Moscow taverns :

> Bearer of a new law
> With neither cross nor suffering
> Someone holds in heaven
> The rainbow like an arch.
> Rejoice, O Zion
> Let your light shine!
> A new Nazareth
> Arises for the sleeping one ...

Nicholas Kluyev, a descendant and continuator of the Old Believers from the

North mixed together in his praise of Lenin legends from Karelia with that of the Gospel.[26] The Symbolist André Biely[27] announced the birth of the Third International at the same time as Christ's resurrection. The humanist Valery Briusov[28] joined up with 'the barbarians to found a new culture'. The Futurist Mayakovsky recited in the workers' clubs ...

Literary people gave the poets a wide berth. They refused to shake hands with the author of *The Twelve*.[29]

It was only a year after the October insurrection, when the proletariat had got control of the sabotage, created the Red Army, won the Civil War and overcome the conspiracies with terror, and when the German Revolution tore up the Brest Litovsk peace treaty,[30] strikingly confirming the foresight of the Bolsheviks, that a fairly numerous minority of the intelligentsia began to go over to the Revolution. Maxim Gorky came over to it at the end of 1918. Officers, engineers and scholars placed themselves at the disposal of the proletarian state.

The middle classes who had fought the newborn Revolution so bitterly submitted to the victorious Revolution. They had taken the side of the stronger.

Three The Lesson of a Shipwreck

It is still impossible, even after ten years, to pass judgement on the attitude of the intellectuals towards the Revolution and the repercussions of it in the domain of culture. All we have said about the writers basically applies to the intelligentsia as a whole. The proletarian revolution of October 1917 was a complete break. The writers (and this was the overwhelming majority of them) who had joined the counter-revolution before the coming to power of the workers remained in the emigration. Cut off from their native soil, they neither could nor wanted to understand anything of the immense transformation of the country, and linking their fate ever more closely to the vanquished, decimated and demoralised possessing classes, they were themselves condemned to sterility. Defeats can be bloody for the working classes; like all defeats they bring demoralisation along with them; but history is working for us; the working class that has won out on part of the globe feels itself growing all over the universe; the very blood it has shed fertilises the soil beneath its steps, its dead become heroes, martyrs and examples to follow; it sees traces of future victories in all its defeats. On the other hand the defeat of the Russian bourgeoisie in 1917 seems to have been as complete and irreparable as that of the French aristocracy in 1789–93. A class rising towards the future recovers from its wounds like a man at the height of his strength; a class in decline succumbs to them as an old man is exhausted by a minor loss of blood.

The glorious shedding of the blood of the Parisian Communards[31] fertilised Russian soil half a century later; the blood of Louis XVI and Du Barry, the blood of hangman Nicholas II and Kolchak is worth nothing.[32] Those intellectuals who linked their fate with that of the Russian bourgeoisie, which were defeated twice over, on the battlefields of the Civil War as well as in their very soul, and whilst today belonging to a White emigration that can be reckoned at almost two million people, have not within eleven years trained a single new writer of renown, a single remarkable scholar or one first rank publicist! We only find old names in the White press. Milyukov, Souvarine, Kuskova, Prokopovich and Burtsev[33] – that dates it. These people cut a sorry figure, just like ghosts. They have come out of the graves of the old order. Alongside them writers like Kuprin, Bunin, Merezhkovsky and Artybashev[34] have in ten years added nothing to already powerful works. (I do not wish to say that nothing has been printed, but that is a different matter altogether). The passing of Russian literature to the side of the counter-revolution in 1917 was in some respects a suicide.

Lenin spoke brutally in September 1918 at a time when, threatened by the proletarian dictatorship, that the whole of civilised society was waiting for the advent of a general, with typical petty bourgeois incredulity and an astonishing lack of understanding.[35] The most advanced thinkers looked no further than rule by the sword. The intelligentsia, trained in bourgeois culture, would not admit that the proletariat could win. Was it not by definition an inferior class (and, precisely because of this, it was necessary 'to think kindly about it ...')? They were ignorant of proletarian thinking, which during these times had attained a powerful maturity. Very much taken up with the old ideologies, ingenious and attractive edifices where they live, in the most prosaic sense of the word, they were as contemptuously ignorant of 'Marxist doctinairianism' and its 'schemas' of hateful economic determinism as are the majority of intellectuals in the West today. Even in their rebellions against bourgeois thought, like

Flaubert and Anatole France,[36] they proceed from bourgeois thinking. Their internal *imprisonment* was all the more absolute the more they believed themselves to be 'freer', more 'advanced', more 'Socialist' or more 'Anarchist'. Their idealist and literary, specifically bourgeois understanding of the democratic revolution completely blinded them to the reality of the proletarian revolution. In it they only saw chaos, instincts unleashed, culture ruined, nameless violence and a negation of the rule of law ...

And it was all that, but it was also much more. A new principle of order was taking shape in the chaos, a new man, the Communist revolutionary, 'the man in a leather tunic' of our young novelists (Pilnyak, Fedin)[37] little by little triumphed over the unleashed instincts, violence was consciously strengthened to do away with all violence, and old law codes were burned, but the new laws inscribed upon all the buildings, without anybody even thinking about it, were the rediscovered words of the Apostle Paul at the start of the Christian revolution: 'If any would not work, neither should he eat'.[38] Only to understand these important facts, over and above superficial impressions and day to day matters, it would have been necessary not to have your eyes blindfolded by bourgeois culture.

Individual good faith only aggravated the mistakes of the Russian intelligentsia. Their collapse contains an infinitely tragic lesson to which we may as well draw the attention of the intellectuals of the West, inclined as they themselves all too often are to condemn the violence of the proletariat, smile at 'Marxist' 'dogmatism', place themselves 'above the social conflict', and defend the superior values of we know not what disembodied 'thinking' (which all too often in practice happens to be represented by excellent writers in the habit of living in countries where there are bourgeois police and prisons). We saw our most advanced and most Socialist intellectuals appeal to the foreign soldiery against the workers of their own country. Under the protection of British bayonets, Chaikovsky, a white haired old Socialist, presided over a government of firing squads at Archangel;[39] an intrepid old liberal (Burtsev) opened the most poisonous counter-revolutionary den in Paris; the author of *The Duel, The Shulammite* and *The Pit* (Kuprin)[40] wrote up portraits of the leaders of the revolution in apocalyptic style as born criminals, the monstrous products of social hysteria ...; a master novelist (Bunin) declared: 'I only saw in the Revolution a pig's snout' ... There were intellectuals – and Socialists! – in all the White general staffs that were ravaging Russia, in all the ephemeral governments set up on the orders of foreign corporals, and in all the cock-eyed undertakings launched against the great Russian Commune. They dragged themselves through every mire. Their punishment has been utter sterility.

At the beginning of the proletarian revolution the Russian petty bourgeoisie – with the intellectuals at its head – committed an incalculable error. It wanted to be with the strongest, and was deceived. Moulded by bourgeois culture, it could not imagine that the proletariat could be the strongest. It did untold damage to the country and brought about its own political and moral suicide. Such is the lesson of the collapse of the Russian 'intelligentsia' in 1917–18. Would that this hard lesson could be understood by some of them ...

Four The Literary Renaissance of 1922–1923

A people fighting for survival and a man who earns his bread by the sweat of his brow are rarely interested in literature. From 1918 to 1921 revolutionary Russia was fighting the threats to its existence every day, and every day paid for its bread in blood. The majority of its literary people had emigrated: they ate their bread abroad and demanded that Russian blood be shed in the name of order and idealism. Little by little those who remained came round: hunger gripped their stomachs and doubts and reservations ravaged their minds. They condemned the terror, but admired the Bolsheviks' will to survive. Comparing the Whites with the Reds, they came to the conclusion that the Reds were the better – and the stronger. Some of them frequented the *proletcults* – the circles of proletarian culture – where André Biely was teaching poetry to the young workers. Small circles of young men with hollow cheeks wearing the grey greatcoat of the Red Army came together in the evening in very cold (but gold-panelled) rooms around poets and prose writers such as Gumilev and Zamyatin,[41] who stoically taught them the art of writing.

This was the time of the barbed wire fence around Russia, the death of the weak, the conspiracies, the allied intervention, and the war where no prisoners were taken. Capitalist civilisation had placed the rebellious Russian proletariat outside the law. This time left us no books. The only real literature of the time dealt with fronts and factories, famine and power: it consists of speeches and writings by the revolutionary leaders. Poets published a few verse booklets, such as Yesenin and his friends the 'Imagists' and the proletarian poets. A civic poetry was born. Each day Demyan Biedny provided the major newspapers with often excellent contemporary rhymes. His inspiration, so he said, was 'at the disposal of the Central Committee'. *Proletcults* trained a certain number of proletarian poets who, in spite of a few successes, soon appeared to be dominated by a new stereotype. The factory, the machine, iron, the proletarian, the new life and the red flag provided the subject matter for poetic elaboration with monotonous ease. The great enthusiasms of the day were translated into hyperbole: the conquest of the sun, gaining the stars, cosmic revolution ...

Literary life – like all intellectual life – was reduced to its simplest expression. But let us remember that the need to create it was nonetheless felt, and that it was never completely interrupted. Scholars worn out with hunger continued their work all the same in libraries deprived of heat through the great frosts. This heroism shows how deeply adapted the intellectual is to his social function, an adaptation which is one of the components of culture's tenacious vitality.

The New Economic Policy – the N.E.P. – in 1921 was marked by a return to free trade and an acceptance of private enterprise within certain limits. It brought peace to the countryside after the Civil War. The recovery of the country was astonishing. In less than a year food supplies, transport, everything was transformed and want came to an end, in spite of a great famine – in this case caused by a natural calamity in the Volga regions. The almost total halt in production and the general famine of 1919–20 had been caused by the blockade, foreign intervention and the conflict between town and country (the towns could provide nothing for the countryside in exchange for the wheat they required to live on). The year 1922, the first year of peace in which Russia ate its fill, saw intellectual activity reborn over an utterly desolated terrain. The opponents of historical materialism would do well, if they were not usually incapable of looking at reality except through the prism of old idealist doctrine, to regard this great recent fact with some attention. The literary production of the land of Dostoyevsky, interrupted during the years of famine, was reborn from the time food supply was reorganised. In spite of the hard privation imposed upon the masses, the Revolution had been a prodigious development of energy. It had sharply called to life, i.e. to creative activity, those social classes which until then had been condemned to passivity. The proletariat had had to improvise, and then in all haste train thousands of leaders, administrators, production leaders, creators and leaders of armies, teachers, and those mass educators called agitators. Organising the Soviet state continued to drain peoples' energies, but the middle classes in the cities took less of a direct part in it than the proletariat, and tended to take up a position in Soviet society analagous to the one they occupied in bourgeois society. In higher education the proletariat strove to train out of workers' sons and Civil War fighters the intellectuals and technicians it greatly needed: the petty bourgeoisie was partly eliminated. It installed itself in the administration, and its young talents found a wide field of activity that was more or less free in literature.

For these different reasons the first years of the N.E.P. were marked by a real literary renaissance.

Five **The Flowering**

Entire galaxies of young writers sprang up in Russia round about 1922–23, while men belonging to the previous generation applied themselves to writing completely differently from before. An inner change took place within them. After hesitations, struggles and crises of conscience, they moved closer to the dictatorship of the proletariat or came over to it. We should here mention Veresaev, who described in a good novel the drama experienced by a number of intellectuals attached to the liberal traditions (*At a Turning Point*),[42] the poet Maximilian Volochin, the old Socialist Revolutionary André Sobol,[43] who could never quite fit in and who committed suicide in 1926, and a novelist of real talent who is far too little known in the West, Vladimir Lidin.[44] The émigré Alexis Tolstoy returned from abroad.[45]

The Serapion Brothers' circle came to the fore in Leningrad where a little study group took shape around the prose writer Zamyatin and Viktor Shklovsky, later one of the masters of the 'Formalist' school (for whom form was the main thing in works of art). These were new men shaped by the storm. All these have since remained in the first or second rank in Russian literature: the novelist Constantine Fedin (*Cities and Years*[46]), the short story writers Nicholas Nikitin (*Fort Kvotny, Outright Theft*[47]) and M. Slonimsky,[48] the humourist

Zoshchenko,[49] the poetess Elizabeth Polonskaya,[50] Benjamin Kaverin, who was to write a beautiful story about banditry (*The End of a Gang*[51]), Vsevolod Ivanov, the epic story writer of the the Siberian peasants (*The Partisans, The Armoured Train*), and the poet N. Tikhonov. All were young and all had experienced famine. Each had carried out the Revolution in his own way, Fedin in the Red Army, agitation and the Party, and Tikhonov sword in hand in the Red Cavalry. At twenty-five years old Nikitin wrote: 'in four years I was a clerk, a docker, a rickshaw driver, a soldier, a military instructor, a soviet functionary, a meetings arranger, the director of an agitational service, a forrager, a saboteur, etc.' The biographies of these young literary men alone would make up a particularly lively book. They amount to an enormous human experience.

At the same time Boris Pilnyak was publishing a series of stories one after the other with an impressionistic lyricism describing 'the storm' over 'the old Russian land', and a great book which is like a synthesis of his former works, *The Naked Year*. He was twenty years old and was living in the provinces. Leonid Leonov (*The Badgers*[52]) and Y. Tynyanov (*Kyukhlya*, the story of a Decembrist[53]) appeared.

A Siberian schoolteacher of Tatar origin, Lidia Seifullina, achieved fame with some remarkable novels about the passionate life of the people of her country. Isaac Babel, a young Jew who had shortly before been a soldier in 'the First Mounted Army', wrote *Red Cavalry*.[54]

All these newcomers who sprang from the revolution only wanted to follow it in their own way, and not without misgivings. They claimed to be Soviet, but apolitical. They were not Communists. Trotsky, in an excellent work of criticism in which he drew up a balance sheet of this flowering (*Literature and Revolution*) called them 'fellow travellers of the revolution'. This very true label has stuck.

Much less remarkable in form and style, but sharper thinking, and more conscious of the aims of the revolution, appeared proletarian writers who had come out of the factories and workshops. Fyodor Gladkov, a convict's son, provided us with *Cement*:[55] Dmitry Furmanov, whom death took from us while still young, provided us with *Chapayev* and *The Rebellion*,[56] short but strong slices of the Civil War. On the same note Y. Libedinsky provided us with *The Week*, and S. Semyonov with *Hunger*.[57] Old Serafimovich was preparing *The Iron Flood*.[58]

Proletarian criticism, which very quickly became sharp and penetrating, saw the light of day with Voronsky, Lelevich and Gorbachev.[59] A. Neverov, a peasant writer who came to Communism, supplied *Tashkent, The City of Bread*.[60]

A talented young woman who had previously been a fighter on the fronts of the Civil War, Larissa Reissner, who died in 1926, published her diaries (*The Front* and *Afghanistan*), packed with colour and the best of revolutionary romanticism.[61]

I. Sadofev, Alexander Zharov[62] and Bezymensky pioneered proletarian poetry, a name also adopted by the older group of the Forge (*Kuznitsa*) with Gerasimov, Kirillov, Sannikov[63] and Obradovich and, under different labels, the Futurist poets (Mayakovsky, Tretiakov, Aseyev and Boris Pasternak;[64] the two latter are today overtaking the two former).

Communist criticism has rightly condemned how inclined the 'fellow travellers' were to psychology, individualism, sensuality and intellectualism, and their reservations as regards the life of the masses and Socialism.

On the other hand we must agree that the Association of Proletarian Writers has written too many theses and not quite so many good novels, and that some of the working-class writers all too often fall into a new stereotype; novels that end up with people coming out of factories or making cavalry charges singing the *Internationale* are neither necessarily good, nor are they necessarily imbued with proletarian thinking ...

This time of literary flourishing, which coincided exactly with the period of industrial reconstruction that returned production to its pre-war levels, went on for about three years (1922–1925). Young Soviet literature was enthusiastically finding its way. Heated conflicts divided it between extremists and moderates. There was even an 'internal emigration'[65] in it quite clearly hostile to the regime. But all the tendencies were rich in talent, and all the talents seemed destined for a promising future. Full of youthful vigour, tremendously enriched by the experience of a revolution which, through its unceasing appeals to the masses, had renewed human language, habits and psychology as regards ideas about the individual, society, the family, and life and death, Soviet literature on the whole provided the world with a sheaf of undeniably strong works, and promised yet more ...

Six Depression

The suicides of Sergei Yesenin (December 1925) and André Sobol (beginning of 1926) – two people who would not fit in – seemed to open up a crisis in Soviet literature, which has never been as rich since. We are hard put in these five years to note the appearance of half a dozen truly notable names.

The intensely realistic historical novel as composed by Alexis Chapygin (*Stenka Razin*) and scrupulously stylistically by I. Tynyanov (*The Death of Vazir Mukhta*) has enjoyed a certain vogue.[66] But ought we not rather to see in this one more way of avoiding the present? When the ground is on fire beneath our feet history becomes completely neutral territory.

The more or less realistic and psychological novel of sorts about Soviet manners that has been very well received by the wider public has brought us some painful surprises. The most widely read novelists have set about studying the old threefold game in all its aspects: the husband, the wife and the lover. Ten years after the Revolution a story about adultery conforms to the bourgeois patterns that have for so long been inflicted upon us. This is significant proof of the tenacity of the old habits among the middle classes. S. Semyonov, a proletarian writer, has dealt with the same subject in an undeniably successful novel (*Natalia Tarpova*[67]), but it does not noticeably differ from the other works of this type. The regressive significance of this literature was all the more obvious because of the naturalism of a young writer attempting to describe some of the wretched aspects of the behaviour of the Communist youth – free love – and who, in contrast, added the appropriate colour to his compilation (S. Malashkin, *The Moon from the Right*[68]). Malashkin caused a scandal.

Among the new writers we should note M. Ognev (*The Diary of Kostia Riabtsev*, about a Soviet schoolboy), Fadeyev (*The Nineteen*, a novel about the Civil War), M. Sholokhov, whose *Tales of the Don* is being talked about at the moment, and M. Selvinsky, who from the very start has been called a master of Russian verse, with his *Epic of Ulialiaev*.[69]

However, neither the proletarian literary figures nor the revolution's 'fellow travellers' have surpassed the level of their previous works. It should rather be noted with regard to both of them that there has been something of a collapse in creative strength. Proletarian extremism has disappeared, along with the eclectic tendency it rose up against. There is a shortage of new men, and a shortage of strong works; the Communist Party's most favoured critics recently denounced in the magazine *Chitatel y Pissatel* (*Reader and Writer*) published by the state publishing house the 'Right-Wing Danger' that in their opinion has become threatening in Soviet literature. In a majority of recent works attributed to the 'fellow travellers' they emphasised that Communists are represented in an unfavourable light.

The two most important works of last year were Constantine Fedin's novel *The Brothers*, whose high literary value is undeniable, but which can be criticised for counterposing art and the social struggle in a spirit foreign to the proletariat, and *The Life of Klim Samgin* by Maxim Gorky, which is also not in line with present day preoccupations.

To sum up, it seems to me to be legitimate to talk about a crisis. There is far too much marking time. 'Right Danger?' No doubt about it. But this danger *must be* everywhere in an immense peasant country – of small private landholding, in other words – and must make itself felt in literature as everywhere else. But it does not date from yesterday, and if it is on the increase today, or appearing to increase, it relates to a whole heap of other social factors. And on the other hand, how has it come about that proletarian literature in the course of these last few years has not known how to draw the country's attention to it, and by a counter-stroke lessen the influence of non-proletarian literature? To be able to sketch out a response to these questions it is necessary to make a deep study of the present phase in the development of Soviet society.

In a country just overturned by the proletarian revolution – ten or twelve years are not much on the scale of history – where the class struggle has been resumed under new and often hypocritical and crafty forms, with the foundations of the Soviet state barely established, the middle classes, including the intellectuals (even those of proletarian origin and convictions) which form part of it must, to the extent to which the difficulties the dictatorship of the proletariat comes up against are more or less great, or more or less controllable, feel a strong pull in the opposite direction. The subordination of intellectual life to economic and political life is much more immediate there than in capitalist countries. And Soviet literature reflects all too well in its present depressed state the precariousness of a situation in which problems altogether greater than those of art are making such a demand upon the country's energies.

Notes

1. Translated from *Monde*, 9 March, 30 March, 20 April and 1 June 1929 (translator's note).
2. Tsar Alexander II abolished serfdom in 1861, but in such circumstances that the peasants were little better off, and loaded down with debt (translator's note).
3. The Decembrists were young officers who initiated an attempted coup d'état in 1825, encouraged by the Tsar's brother with the promise of a constitution. The historical poet Kondratii Fyodorovich Ryleev (1795–1826), their de facto leader, was hanged on 15 July 1826 (translator's note).
4. Alexander Sergeyevich Pushkin (1799–1837) was a poet, playwright and novelist, famous for *Eugene Onegin* (1833). He suffered banishment between 1820 and 1826, and was mortally wounded in a duel defending his wife's honour, forced upon him by his influential enemies. Mikhail Yuriyevich Lermontov (1814–1841) was a novelist, poet and playwright whose most famous poem was *The Demon*. He was killed in a duel, provoked by his enemies, by another officer, N. S. Martynov at a spa in Piatigorsk on 27 July 1841 (translator's note).
5. Nikolay Gavrilovich Chernyshevsky (1828–1889) protested over the terms of the emancipation of the serfs, and was jailed in the Peter-Paul Fortress in 1862–3. In 1864 he was sentenced to 7 years' hard labour for writing *What is to be Done?* (translator's note).
6. Fyodor Mikhailovich Dostoyevsky (1821–1881) was one of Russia's foremost novelists, the author of *Crime and Punishment* (1866) and *The Brothers Karamazov* (1879–80). He was arrested along with the rest of the Petrashevsky Circle in 1849, sentenced to death, and a mock execution was staged, but he was reprieved and sent off to penal servitude in Omsk (1850–1854). Claude Henri de Rouvry, Comte de Saint-Simon (1760–1825) was a French utopian thinker; François Marie Charles Fourier (1772–1837) was the founder of the French school of utopian Socialists (translator's note).
7. Mikhail Yegrafovich Saltykov-Schedrin (1826–1889) was a famous Russian novelist, editor and publicist (translator's note).
8. Lev Nikolayevich, Count Tolstoy (1828–1910) is famous for writing *War and Peace* (1865–9) and *Anna Karenina* (1875–7) (translator's note).
9. Leonid Nikolayevich Andreyev (1871–1919) was a well-known Russian novelist, and a friend of Maxim Gorky. After the Russian Revolution he moved to Finland, from where he launched attacks upon 'Communist dictatorship' (translator's note).
10. Vladimir Galaktionovich Korolenko (1853–1921) was a well-known Russian short story writer (translator's note).
11. Tolstoy's essay, *Ne mogu molchat* (*I Cannot be Silent*) was published in 1908 (English translation by W. Gareth Jones, Bristol, 1989). Temujin (1162–1227), the leader of one of the Mongol clans, was proclaimed Genghis Khan, ruler of all the Mongols, in 1206, and thereafter embarked upon a programme of world conquest. His victories were marked by savage massacres (translator's note).
12. Vladimir Grigoryevich Chertkov (1854–1936) was a publisher and friend of Tolstoy, whose works he edited after his death. Alexander Ivanovich Kuprin (1870–1938) was a friend of Chekhov. He supported the Whites during the Civil War, and denounced the Bolsheviks from abroad. Dmitry Sergeyevich Merezhkovsky (1865–1941) was a Russian poet, novelist and political thinker with Christian-Anarchist leanings. To begin with he collaborated with the Petrograd Soviet, but then crossed over to Poland and denounced the regime. Fyodor Kuzmich Sologub (Fyodor Teternikov, 1863–1927) was a Symbolist poet, short story writer, novelist and dramatist. He remained in the Soviet Union after the Revolution, and was Chairman of the Leningrad Union of Writers at the time of his death. Eugene Nikolayevich Chirikov (1864–1947) was a novelist and playwrite who condemned the tsarist regime's anti-Semitism in his play *Jews* (1904) and the poverty in the countryside in *Peasants* (1906) (translator's note).
13. The Russian armies were very badly mauled in the fighting on the Eastern front in the First World War, against the Austrians in Galicia, the Carpathians and Volhynia in the South, and against the Germans in Poland in the North (translator's note).

14. The Liberal Prince George E. Lvov (1861–1925) headed the Provisional Government in Russia until 7 July 1917. Mikhail V. Rodzianko (1859–1924) was leader of the Octobrist Party and President of the Duma. Pavel Nikolayevich Milyukov (1859–1943) was the leader of the Cadet Party. Both were in Prince Lvov's cabinet in 1917. Alexander Fyodorovich Kerensky (1881–1970) was the last Prime Minister of the Provisional Government overthrown by the Bolsheviks in 1917. The Duma was a representative assembly elected by class voting granted by the Tsar to head off the 1905 revolution in Russia. Count Pyotr Arkadyevich Stolypin (1862–1911) was the Tsar's Chief Minister and Minister of Finance during the period of reaction following the suppression of the 1905 uprising. B. V. Sturmer (1848–1917) was Chairman of the Council of Ministers, Minister of Foreign Affairs and Minister of the Interior in 1916 (translator's note).
15. The Party of the Socialist Revolutionaries (SRs) was the main party of the Russian peasantry led by V. Chernov, founded in 1901 (translator's note).
16. Victor Serge, 'The Middle Classes in the Russian Revolution', *Clarté*, 1923 (author's note). As Minister for Foreign Affairs, Milyukov had issued a declaration in March 1917 that Russia would 'unreservedly adhere to her agreements with the Allies', including the secret treaty that would give Russia access to the Mediterranean through the Dardanelles at the end of the war (translator's note).
17. The Third Republic was set up in France in September 1870, and ruled after the smashing of the Paris Commune until replaced by the Vichy regime in 1940 (translator's note).
18. Zinaida Hippius (1869–1945) was a poet who married Merezhkovsky in 1889. She wrote manifestos for the SRs in 1917 (translator's note).
19. On Hippius' literary circle during the First World War, cf. Temira Pachmuss, *Zinaida Hippius: An Intellectual Profile*, Southern Illinois U.P., 1971, pp.188–9. Hippius opposed the First World War to begin with, but then came round to supporting it (translator's note).
20. Alexander Blok (1880–1921) was a Symbolist poet who supported the Russian Revolution (translator's note).
21. Leonid Andreyev's *Red Laugh* was republished in Minsk in 1984. *The Seven That Were Hanged* came out in 1908 (English translation, New York, 1958). *S. O. S. : Au Secours*, was published in Paris in 1919 (translator's note).
22. The Second Congress of the SRs early in April 1917 split between the Right, who supported Russia continuing the First World War, and the Left, who opposed it and demanded that land be given to the peasants. The Left allied with the Bolsheviks in the Revolution, and to begin with shared power with them (translator's note).
23. Blok's *Skify* (*The Scythians*) was published in Petrograd in 1918 (English translation in *Alexander Blok: Selected Poems*, Progress Publishers, Moscow, pp.319–322) (translator's note).
24. Vladimir Sergeyevich Solovyev (1853–1900) was a mystical philosopher who tried to combine dialectical thinking with what he regarded as the divine purpose in his book *The Meaning of Love* (1894; English translation, 1946) (translator's note).
25. 'In a chaplet of white roses
    Stepping through the pearly snowdust
    Shrouded in the snowy mist
    In the distance – Jesus Christ'.
    Alexander Blok: Selected Poems, Progress Publishers, Moscow, 1981, p.318). Blok's *The Twelve* (*Dvenadsat*) came out in 1918 (English translation along with *The Scythians* by Jack Lindsay, London, 1982). Cf. S. Hackel, *The Poet and the Revolution: Aleksandr Blok's 'The Twelve'*, Oxford U.P., 1975 (translator's note).
26. Nicholas Alexeyevich Kluyev (1884–1937) published poetry using religious imagery, such as *The Song of the Sun Bearer*. The Old Believers (Staroveri) were those led by the Archpriest Avvakum who refused to accept the liturgical reforms of the Patriarch Nikon of Moscow (1652–1658). They later split into several sects which set up settler communities all over Russia, and only benefited from religious toleration by the edict of 17 April 1905 (translator's note).

27. André Biely (Boris Nikolayevich Bugaev, 1880–1934) was a leading Symbolist poet and novelist. The reference here is probably to his *Christ is Risen*, published in the same year as the foundation of the Third (Communist) International (March 1919) (translator's note).

28. Valery Yakovlevich Briusov (1873–1924) was a poet, novelist and critic, the author of *The Republic of the Southern Cross* (translator's note).

29. Merezhkovsky regarded *The Twelve* as a betrayal of culture (Anatoly Lunacharsky, 'Alexander Blok', 1932, in *Anatoly Lunacharsky: On Literature and Art*, Moscow 1973, p.161) (translator's note).

30. The mutiny in the German High Seas Fleet in 1918 and the revolutionary disturbances that followed it led to Germany's request for an armistice and an end to the First World War, thereby losing the massive gains she had made in Eastern Europe at the expense of Russia at the Treaty of Brest-Litovsk signed seven months earlier. Lenin had prophesied that if Germany lost the wider war the Treaty would become null and void (translator's note).

31. The collapse of France in the Franco-Prussian War allowed the working class to administer Paris, where they proclaimed the Paris Commune in 1871. The Versaillais troops entered the city after a month-long siege on 21 May 1871, and in the week of reprisals that followed some 30,000 were killed (translator's note).

32. Louis XVI Capet, king of France (1774–1793) was first dethroned by the French Revolution, and then guillotined on 21 January 1793. Marie-Jeanne Bécu, Madame Du Barry (1746–1793) was the last of Louis XV's mistresses to play a significant role in court life. Accused of intriguing to restore the monarchy, she was guillotined during the Terror. Nicholas II Romanov, the last Tsar of Russia (1894–1917), was shot by the Bolsheviks at Ekaterinburg in July 1918. Admiral Alexander Vasilyevich Kolchak (1873–1920) led the White Guard attack upon the Soviet state from the Far East during the Russian Civil War, and proclaimed himself 'supreme ruler' of Russia. He was shot by the Bolsheviks after the surrender of Irkutsk in February 1920 (translator's note).

33. It is uncertain who is meant by Souvarine;. It is unlikely that it is a reference to Boris Souvarine, who was only breaking with Trotsky at this time. Nor can it have been have been the old Russian reactionary A. S. Suvorin, who died before the First World War. Yekaterina Dmitryevna Kuskova (1869–1958), the wife of Prokopovich, was a friend of Gorky who wrote *Credo*, the manifesto of the Economists opposed by Lenin during the early years of the R.S.D.L.P. She was arrested in 1922 for using the All-Russian Committee for Aid to the Starving as a cover for anti-governmental activities, was expelled from the USSR., and wrote for anti-Soviet journals in the emigration. S. N. Prokopovich (1866–1957) had been a supporter of the Economist trend in the R.S.D.L.P. and was minister of Food and Supplies in the Provisional government. He was banished from the USSR and carried on anti-Bolshevik propaganda in the emigration. Vladimir Lyovich Burtsev (1862–1942) was a Narodnik publisher famous for exposing hundreds of Tsarist agents infiltrated into the revolutionary movement, including Azef. He fled to Paris during the Revolution, and edited *Common Cause* attacking the Bolshevik regime (translator's note).

34. Ivan Alexeyevich Bunin (1870–1953) was a novelist, part of the circle around Maxim Gorky, who emigrated to Paris in 1920. Mikhail Petrovich Artybashev (1878–1927) preached an Anarchistic individualism that was very influential among the Russian intelligentsia before the First World War (translator's note).

35. This is not a direct quote from Lenin, but a summary of his views in the autumn of 1918, as is clear from Serge's *Year One of the Russian Revolution*, written at the same time as this essay (English translation, London, 1972, pp. 359–60 and 418, n.17) (translator's note).

36. Gustave Flaubert (1821–1880) was a major French novelist, author of *Madame Bovary* (1857) and *Salammbô* (1862). Anatole France was the pen name of Jacques Anatole François Thibault (1844–1924), a great French writer and freethinker. His *Penguin Island* (1908) is a satire upon human history (translator's note).

37. Cf. below, p. 208.

38. II Thessalonians iii.10. Cf. Lenin's remarks in 'On the Famine', 22 May 1918, *Collected Works*, vol.xxvii, Moscow, 1965, pp.391–2 (translator's note).

39. Nicholas Vasiliyevich Chaikovsky (1850–1926), the son of a provincial civil servant, founded one of the first Narodnik circles in St. Petersburg in 1869, and was active in the cooperative movement. The Socialist Revolutionaries and Cadets dominated the White government set up under him with British support in Archangel in 1918 (translator's note).
40. Kuprin published *The Duel* in 1905 (English translation, New York, 1961) and *The Shulammite* and *The Pit* in 1908. He emigrated to Paris in 1919 (translator's note).
41. Nikolai Stepanovich Gumilev (1886–1921) was an acmeist poet who returned to Russia after the Revolution. Eugene I. Zamyatin (1884–1937) was a writer who supported the Bolsheviks and lived in Britain during the First World War. He was a leading writer of the Serapion fraternity, but emigrated to France in 1932, and died in Paris (translator's note).
42. Vikenty V. Smidovich, called Veresaev (1867–1945) was a poet, prose writer and literary critic. *At a Turning Point* was a novella published by Veresaev in 1902 (translator's note).
43. Andrei Mikhailovich Sobol (1888–1926) was a Russian novelist, the author of *The Freak Show* (translator's note).
44. Vladimir Lidin was the pseudonym of G. Gomberg (1894–1979), a Russian novelist and short story writer (translator's note).
45. Alexei Nikolayevich Tolstoy (1882–1945) was a novelist, poet and playwright who fought in the Red Army during the Civil War, but emigrated to Paris in 1919. Upon his return to Russia 10 years later he became one of the most celebrated Russian writers, which disgusted Serge (*Destiny of a Revolution*, London, 1937, pp.53–4) (translator's note).
46. Fedin's *Goroda i gody* (*Cities and Years*) was published in 1924 (English translation by Michael Scammell, New York,1962) (translator's note).
47. *Kvotny* means vomit (translator's note).
48. Mikhail Leonidovich Slonimsky (1897–1972) was a short story writer influenced by Zamyatin who joined the Serapion Fraternity. His best known collection is *The Sixth Rifle Regiment* (1922) (translator's note).
49. Mikhail M. Zoshchenko (1895–1958), also a member of the Serapion Fraternity, was a popular short story writer who fought in the First World War and with the Red Cavalry in 1918. He was denounced by Zhdanov in 1946 and expelled from the Union of Soviet Writers, but was rehabilitated after Stalin's death (translator's note).
50. Elizaveta Grigoryevna Polonskaya (1890–1969) was a poetess, translator and army doctor (translator's note).
51. Kaverin was the pseudonym of Benjamin Alexandrovich Zilberg (1902–1989), an orientalist who joined the Serapion Fraternity. *The End of a Gang*, a novel about the Leningrad underworld, was published in 1926 (translator's note).
52. Leon Maximovich Leonov (1899–1994) first rose to prominence by publishing *The End of the Little Man* and *The Badgers* in 1924 (translator's note).
53. Yuri Nikolayevich Tynyanov (1894–1943) was a historical novelist. *Kyukhlya*, his first work (1925) was set in the Decembrist conspiracy (translator's note).
54. Isaac Emmanuelovich Babel (1894–1940) had served in Budyenny's cavalry during the war with Poland in 1920, and *Red Cavalry* (*Konarmia*), based upon his experiences as a supply officer, was published in 1924 (English translation in *Isaac Babel: Collected Stories*, Harmondsworth, 1974, pp.37–174). He reteated into silence after 1934, but was arrested in May 1939, accused of 'Trotskyism', and sent to Siberia after a 20 minute trial, where he was shot in January 1940. He was rehabilitated after Stalin's death. Cf. David King, *The Commissar Vanishes*, Edinburgh, 1997, p.164; *The Complete Works of Isaac Babel*, translated by Peter Constantine, London, 2002 (translator's note).
55. Fyodor Vassilievich Gladkov (1883–1958) was a Russian writer who published *Cement* in 1925 (English translation by A. S. Arthur and C. A. Ashleigh, London, 1929). Serge translated and published it in France in 1928 (translator's note).

56. Dmitry Andreyevich Furmanov (1891–1926) was a popular novelist. His *Chapayev*, a tale about a guerrilla leader in the Russian Civil War, came out in Moscow in 1923 (English translation, London, 1935), and *The Rebellion* in 1925 (translator's note).

57. Sergei Alexandrovich Semyonov (1899–1968) was a short story writer of proletarian origin and a supporter of *Kuznitsa* who had joined the Bolsheviks in 1917. His novel in diary form, *Golod (Hunger)* was published in 1922 (translator's note).

58. Alexander S. Serafimovich Popov (1863–1943) was a prose writer and journalist, a member of the *Znanie* group and head of the literary section of *Izvestia*. For Serge's reviews of *The Iron Flood*, cf. below, pp. 274 and 283 (translator's note).

59. Georgy Efimovich Gorbachev (1897–1942) was a literary critic who to begin with collaborated with *On Guard*, but then left to form the Federation of Soviet Writers (translator's note).

60. Neverov was the pseudonym of Alexander Sergeyevich Skobelev (1886–1923). His *Tashkent gorod khlebny (Tashkent, The City of Bread)*, a story about two boys driven from their homes by famine who make their way to the city, was published in 1923 (English translation, *City of Bread*, New York, 1927) (translator's note).

61. Larissa Reissner (1895–1926) was a writer and poet married to Fyodor Raskolnikov, the leader of the Bolshevik sailors in the Kronstadt fleet base, who fought with great bravery during the Civil War along the Volga. Her letters were collected into a book, *The Front*, of which only an extract has appeared in English (Svyazhsk, in *Fourth International*, vol.iv, no.6, June 1943, pp.184–189, reproduced in *Leon Trotsky: The Man and His Work*, New York, 1969, pp.112–118. Cf. Cathy Porter, *Larissa Reisner*, London, 1988, pp.53–92 (translator's note).

62. Ilya Ivanovich Sadofev (1889–1965) was a worker poet. His first collection, *Dynamo Verses*, ran into six editions (translator's note).

63. Mikhail Prokofievich Gerasimov (1889–1939) was a romantic poet and a supporter of *Kuznitsa*. Grigory Alexandrovich Sannikov (1899–1969) had fought in the Russian Civil War. His first collection of verses, *Lyric Poetry*, came out in 1921. He was one of *Kuznitsa*'s organisers (translator's note).

64. Sergei M. Tretiakov (1892–1937) was a Futurist writer, playwright and critic shot during the purges. Nikolai Nikolayevich Aseyev (1889–1963) was a Futurist poet and a friend of Mayakovsky. In 1923 he founded the 'Left Front', which published the journal *Lef*. He was later decorated with the Order of Lenin and the Stalin Prize. Boris L. Pasternak (1890–1960) was a Futurist poet and prose writer, later famous for writing *Dr Zhivago* (1955) (translator's note).

65. The term 'internal emigrés of the revolution' was first popularised by Trotsky (*Literature and Revolution*, Michigan U.P., 1960. p.28) (translator's note).

66. Alexei Pavlovich Chapygin (1870–1937) was a writer of peasant origin who began his work before the Russian revolution. *Stenka Razin,* his most well known work, came out in 1927. Stepan Timofeyevich (Stenka) Razin (c.1630–1671) led a major revolt of the Cossacks and peasants on Russia's South-Eastern frontier in 1670–1, and his memory had been revered by the peasants ever since. Tynyanov's novel *The Death of Vazir Mukhtar* was published in 1927–28. 'Vazir Mukhtar' was the title of the Russian ambassador in Iran, and the novel is based on the life of Alexander Sergeyovich Griboyedov (1795–1829), a writer and diplomat who sympathised with the Decembrists, who was killed in a riot on a diplomatic mission in Teheran (English translation by A. Brown, *Death and Diplomacy in Persia*, 1938) (translator's note).

67. Semyonov's *Natalia Tarpova* was published in 1927 (translator's note).

68. Sergei Ivanovich Malashkin (1888–) caused a stir when his novella *Luna s pravoy storony (The Moon from the Right)* was published in 1926, and it was often reprinted and much translated. Its story about a Young Communist group of twenty-two who all share the same woman demonstrated both the alienation of the party elite from the population at large and the disintegration of the moral values of society (translator's note).

69. Nikolai Ognev was the pseudonym of Mikhail G. Rozanov (1888–1938), a Constructivist who had been a revolutionary before the First World War. *The Diary of Kostya Riabtsev* came out between 1926 and 1927.

Fadeyev was the pseudonym of Alexander Alexandrovich Bulgya (1901–1956), who joined the Communist Party in 1918. His first work, *Razgrom*, about 19 red guerrillas trapped between the Whites and the Japanese during the Civil War, was published in 1927 (English translation by R. D. Charques, *The Nineteen*, 1929). Mikhail Alexandrovich Sholokhov (1905–1984) joined the Red Army in 1920. His collection of short stories, *Donskie rassky* (*Tales of the Don*) was published in 1926 (English translation, 1961). *Quiet Flows the Don* followed in 1934. The poet and plywright Ilya (Karl) Lvovich Selvinsky (1899–1968) published his *Ulialiaevschina* (*The Epic of Ulialiaev*) in 1927 (translator's note).

Literature and Revolution[1]

The aim of this essay appears a limited one only to a superficial observer. Literature is only one of the elements of culture in general. It is therefore necessary to pose the entire problem of culture and the revolution, to study the role of the intelligentsia in the class struggle, and to dwell at some length on the workers' movement. But, difficult and hazardous as this might well be, we must assign ourselves more limited tasks. I have nonetheless not hesitated to exceed the limits of my subject in order to deal with it better.

I have restricted myself to discussing some recent works, in order the better to bring this work into line with a collection of investigations and works which little by little are clarifying the contours of the new literature. To my deep regret, it has been impossible for me to get hold of several works from which I would have been happy to profit: for even when the writers or devoted friends sent them to me, the books did not always arrive. Hence the often all too obvious inadequacy of my documentation.

Leningrad, February, 1932

One The Writer's Situation

A very interesting study could be made of the situation of the man of letters in different historical periods. Let us not go back too far: during the Great Century[2] the main aim of men of letters was to provide the courts with higher forms of amusement than could be offered by jesters. On the eve of the French Revolution 'an ancient tradition required a court to have skillful orators, entertaining in their brilliant conversation, and shedding lustre on the prince who maintained them; they were therefore part of the luxury that had to surround rich people'. Georges Sorel, from whom I have taken these lines, highlights in several revealing pages the humiliating role of the Encyclopaedists, Diderot[3] and Voltaire, in the eighteenth century courts. Obviously, they owe their historical reputation to other reasons. It was Voltaire, the enemy of the church, the author of *Candide*, and the defender of the Chevalier de la Barre, whose fame lived on rather than Catherine II's flatterer.[4] But Voltaire was both. He had to earn a living. The writers of the victorious bourgeoisie – far more powerful at the time than the proletariat of today is in five sixths of the world – in spite of the revolutionary mission they accomplished so well, despite everything, did not escape the role that has fallen to artists at all times, of amusing the powerful. Whilst entertaining an aristocracy that was doomed (but which did not realise it), they thought for the advancing Third Estate, awakened its consciousness, furnished it with intellectual weapons, and provided it with an ideology. Therein lay their greatness.[5]

Has the writer's situation changed very much in one and a half centuries? Today's writer depends upon a public with which he communicates through the intermediary of the bookshop. The 'public', inasmuch as it is more or less visible, appears under two different forms: there is the public which reads, and the public which buys. The writer depends directly upon the buying public. It has been an established custom for some years now of publishing those works that are most appreciated by this public in luxurious editions, with a handsome return for both author and publisher, but hardly intended to be read, since they are often in the most inconvenient format. The bibliophile, a profitable person for the stylish littérateur, is naturally not a great reader; he is the owner of collections of classics with uncut pages ... What public buys a new book? Its usual price in France is more or less equivalent to half a day's wages for a skilled worker. A new book is even dearer in Germany, Britain and the United States. This fact alone shows that it is aimed at the middle classes and at the bourgeoisie. An entire vast reading public, without whose support no popular writer can exist, which cannot buy new books, is grouped around libraries and book clubs.

It is the preferences of the buying public that make up what can be called in fashionable terms the literary climate. The writer scorned by this public will not succeed, or will only succeed with great difficulty, in reaching the reading public of the poorer classes, which in any case exercises no influence over the press and the magazines.[6] Literature sticks to those groupings upon which to a great extent its literary reputation depends – a precondition for the existence of the writer – the judgement of narrow but rich, or at least comfortable circles. Claudel and Valéry, Duhamel and Giraudoux, Margueritte and Barbusse,[7] with their different circulations, depend upon publics between which there are no deeply divided frontiers, and which are not socially very different; and even the freedom they have acquired is to be explained by their deep agreement with certain social classes.

Even the writer who is welcomed by the buying public, certain circles of the possessing classes in other words, most often cannot live solely by his pen. The success gained by a Remarque[8] every ten years is perhaps an exception to this rule, and this is confirmed even more strikingly by lesser successes which must be called 'bestsellers'. Here literature becomes, in a cruel phrase, the 'literary situation'. A publisher who does not baulk at the expense of an American publication launches a new book in the same way as M. Babbitt launches a new toothpaste. A good publicity agent has to be able to make this calculation without any effort at all: so much for the profit, so much for advertising, so much for promotion, so much for the print run, so much for the 'success'. We see this in the business world; and here the writer is listed like a racehorse or a boxer. The way he has to live by his trade implies the opposite of what he wants to do.

The writer often has to rely upon a second profession. The closer this is to literature, the more the control exercised over him by the manufacturers of printed paper becomes obvious. Journalism provides the novelist with an employer; this employer is always a capitalist in the service of a section of the possessing classes. From then on the writer must have a bent, or at least a political nuance appropriate to his patron, or he must look for another way of earning his living. What goes on in the milieu does the rest; writers derive their opinions from their interests.

All this is known from of old. A publisher receives two manuscripts of equal value at the same time (hypothetically: their real value cannot be equal). In one of them there is the Gentleman, the Lady and the Lover, palaces, bars, love going along with luxury, and the wit (caustic, obviously, but conventional) of the intelligent Parisian who has fed well; and in the other the hardship of living, work, broken love, the gray houses of Charonne, the seething life of the crowd, the subversive liveliness (also Parisian) of a Vallès[9] for whom 'all waistcoats are too big' ... which of these two books will be accepted, or accepted first? Which, when published, will sell the most? Which will be read by the critic, flattered by the magazines, and win the book awards? – the less human of the two. This is what appeals to the taste of the comfortable public. It is what is done, after the manner of old, to entertain the rich.

Which of the two writers will be able to survive? The one who amuses the rich.

And that is the problem. A dead end.

Two And There Are Thirty Million Proletarians!

A calculation that should make us giddy, without giving us too high an opinion of the spirit of the age, would be about the French novels published over twenty years dealing with love among human beings. Count the number of marquises, petty bourgeois, viscounts and gigolos; reducing to figures the numbers of sentimental complications before the war and of perversions after it; and estimating the amount of bidet water required to wash away this literature, and the density and force of the flow it would need ...

Let us put it alongside some quite different figures.

France today amounts to fourteen million proletarians, thirty million along with their families. That makes fourteen million men according to the Biblical law – the only divine law that has been enforced since the creation of the world – who gain their bread by the sweat of their brows.[10] The only thing these figures add up to is the word 'masses', an overwhelming word. Then we might ask: how many books were written for these millions of people, talking about their existence, 'analysing their internal life' – for they must have one, after all – to show them to themselves, to enlighten them, to amuse them?[11] (Yes, to amuse them, other than by describing sleeping with the prostitute or the handsome Brazilian dancer).

How many works about miners have come out since *Germinal*? France has 500,000 miners who count towards her greatness! Novelists have gone looking for exoticism and adventures to New Guinea, Chad, Siam, along the Amur River, among the Papuans, the Caribs, and the Topinambous, even on the moon.

But they have not discovered the poor people of Amiens; the textile workers working at home; the Breton fishermen – though it's a pretty setting – and the same for the dockers, for are there only bars in the ports? With very little effort they might have found, among millions of hitherto ignored souls, love stories, adventure stories, and yet other stories involving love, adventure and much more – they would find something to supply all the genres, to dispel all melancholy, to revise all the old governing clichés, to awaken life's tragic feeling, and to find fresh reasons for living. But they found nothing. And the reason? Look above. The publisher would begin to ruin himself with such discoveries. The buying public would not pay, dammit! For it would show it things very unpleasant to know when you are having an easy time of it! Don't we read to forget such things? Thirty million workers occupy less of a place in French literature than the 'Faubourg Saint-Germain'. The thirty thousand dead of the Commune, whose living memory played so important a part during the Russian Revolution, have only inspired a few works among French writers which are barely obtainable today.[12] Literature is better acquainted with pederasts than producers. To be accepted requires an income and a car in the traditional novel; the only exception to this rule is the feminine personnel devoted to the pleasure of the men in the car.

Three Changing the Tone

Prewar literature was of a more 'advanced' tone than that of today.

Radicalism won hearts, even in the ministries, for obvious reasons. Europe had enjoyed capitalist peace since 1871. In forty-three years there had only been deep social convulsions in Spain (a democratic revolution defeated in 1874) and in Russia (a democratic revolution defeated in 1905). Far from shaking the Third Republic, the crises of Boulangism and the Dreyfus affair[13] had strengthened it by the victory of the bourgeoisie and the republican petty bourgeoisie over agrarian and aristocratic reaction. Since the bloodletting inflicted upon the Parisian proletariat in 1871, the second decimation of the working-class districts in less than twenty-five years,[14] the bourgeoisie felt itself secure. The drive to mechanisation that went along with colonial expansion and the expansion of international commerce opened up an era of prosperity. Darwinism made evolution into a natural law; positivism, augmented by faith in science, provided a reassuring doctrine of progress. Socialism itself, transformed into parliamentarism, reformism or pacifism, cutting Marx's texts to remove the dictatorship of the proletariat, disavowing violence, and substituting evolution for revolution, disarmed the proletariat; to be more exact, it was disarming the proletariat at the very time when the Essen and Creusot foundries were casting cannon for the Great War, and it was aware it was doing so. The literature of the day, which on the whole was guided by the best representatives of cultured society, could afford generous aspirations, and give itself wayward aims. Intelligent tyrants allowed poets to sing freedom at their table. Even the vigour of the working class movement – and here I am mainly thinking of the combative syndicalism of Griffuelhes, Pouget, Pataud and Yvetot[15] – far from threatening the regime in the present, stimulated its vitality all the more, as Sorel saw all too clearly. Zola and Anatole France were the time's most representative writers.

The general tone of literature today is very different. Paul Morand – *Rien que la terre!* – goes along the coasts of Italy, and seeing Fascism gives him hope, for he is full of doubts about France, Europe, the planet and himself: 'Four years have sufficed for it to be reborn (Mussolini's Italy), new, modern, well organised, preferring deeds to words [...] I can hear Paul Valéry telling me that the Greeks and the Romans showed us how to deal with the monsters from Asia.' Is it as easy as that? M. Paul Morand is not alone. Many writers are taking note of the need to marshal thinking in defence of capitalism. Drieu La Rochelle dreams of a 'young right'. Montherlant writes affectionately to Romain Rolland, whom he admires: 'It does not need too much imagination to conceive of circumstances in which it would be my duty to order you to be shot [...] Several reasons would justify me in doing so' (*Europe*, 15th February 1926). There is reaction and pessimism[16] among some people and despair and questions about suicide along a path that is in no way proletarian, with a final (final?) coming over to the revolution among others, the surrealist group.

Four At a Dead End

Literature finds itself in the same dead end as the social sciences, since its development has become contrary to the interests of the ruling classes. Marx proved this as regards political economy from 1872 onwards in the second preface to *Capital*: 'Insofar as Political Economy remains within that (sc. bourgeois) horizon, insofar, i.e., as the capitalist regime is looked upon as the absolutely final form of social production, instead of as a passing historical phase of its evolution, Political Economy can remain a science only so long as the class struggle is latent or manifests itself only in isolated and sporadic phenomena.' But when the class struggle hotted up, 'in place of disinterested inquirers, there were hired prize-fighters; in place of genuine scientific research, the bad conscience and the evil intent of apologetic'.[17] A literature that asked the great questions of modern life, that was interested in the future of the world, that understood work and the workers, that in other words had discovered the hitherto unknown nine tenths of society – which did not limit itself to describing the world, but now and again might think about changing it, in a word, was active and no longer passive, would appeal to all human potentialities, and would respond to every spiritual need instead of confining itself to amusing the rich; even independently of the intentions of its creators, a literature of this sort would be tremendously revolutionary. Its development from then on would be contrary to the interests of the possessing classes. That is why this literature is being born at great cost, lagging far behind events; the scanty elements that go to make it up are often vegetating in old flowerbeds kept at the sort of temperature that requires energetic pushes from dwarf plants intended for interior ornament ...

But since 2 August 1914 pebbles of a fair size have not ceased raining across the plots of the old flowerbed. The average Frenchman is no longer ignorant of share prices on Wall Street, of how the Five Year Plan is being put into operation in the USSR, the fall of the British pound, racist agitation in Germany, and many other factors that appear to be equally distant from his bedroom, which exercise a noticeable influence over his personal life, sometimes quite marked. Is he going to allow himself to be forever served with the eternal romantic novel,[18] about the good man who is worried, the beautiful woman who does not know what she wants, or the deep thinker who asks why he does not know what he wants? There are some indications that reveal other aspirations within him. Writers have opened up a persistent enquiry about the world since the War. The fashion for cosmopolitanism, travels and translations corresponds to the great changes public psychology has undergone in which catastrophic events have sharply revealed the interdependence of all human beings, and the global nature of civilisation. And the fashion for romanticised lives is no less significant, in spite of all the criticisms that can be legitimately made of a hybrid genre where literary invention is obstructed by the search for truth and obstructs it in turn. For it bears witness to the desire, even if a lazy one, to rediscover life, struggles and problems, through the man of action. In both cases it is a matter of substituting a semi-documentary reality for decrepit fictions. The powerlessness of art must have become very great for the reader to end up asking the writer to make a romance out of Baedeker or the life of Monsieur Thiers.[19] But the reader is right.

Five It Is Time to Take Note of the Revolution

It has been fifteen years since the revolution overturned the world. Three empires crashed in 1917–18: Russia, Germany and Austria. Four revolutions were defeated from 1918 to 1923, in Finland, Hungary, Germany and Bulgaria; a preventative counter-revolution triumphed in Italy out of a failed revolution; a Socialist revolution was aborted in Austria; Spain ended up sadly with a military dictatorship. The dictatorship of the proletariat has gone on for over fourteen years in the USSR. There have been the Chinese Revolution, the revolutionary ferment in India,[20] and political instability in Latin America. Finally there has been a general crisis in the most stable capitalist countries. In this ailing universe it is true that France forms a sort of oasis, but it is neither reassuring nor durable. The cold winds of crisis are extending towards the oasis. The feeling that the system requires a radical change has surfaced even among the bourgeoisie. Balkanised and bankrupt Europe, condemned to unemployment, ruled by financiers, politicians, policemen and adventurers, in its insecurity multiplies military alliances, security pacts and disarmament negotiations, and uses the cream of its fortune for manufacturing gas, planes, submarines, supertanks, and extra-rapid machine guns. It is time to look at where all this is leading.

The worst of the writer's betrayals is not what M. Benda has denounced.[21] In twenty years on three decisive occasions the intellectuals showed a hopeless blindness: faced with the world war of 1914–1918, when only a few men could be found around Romain Rolland to raise a protest on behalf of the European intelligentsia against imperialism; in 1917–1920, by their failure to understand the proletarian revolution; and in our days, by their disarray in the presence of the crisis, their ignorance of the revolution, and by their inability, even when they went over to it, to see their way through its contradictions.

These defects are no doubt linked to the social position of the middle classes, doomed to vacillate between the bourgeoisie and the proletariat. It is also connected with the present weakness of the revolutionary proletariat. If the proletariat had been equal to its task in at least three great countries it would be preparing to take power today: in Britain, in Germany, and in Spain.[22] But *no such thing* has occurred. Reaction has the advantage. Left standing, pedestrian democracy falls back, and, through ignorance, weakness or self-interest, often ends up stupidly helping reaction. Forced to make a choice between hazarding a workers' revolution and the threat of reaction, German Social Democracy never hesitated. When its duty was to shoot Ludendorff, it allowed Liebknecht to be murdered.[23] It is continuing to play this dangerous game. Perhaps tomorrow we will know if it is capable of going right to the end with it, to its suicide, in other words. The bourgeois and petty bourgeois intellectuals, 'who have raised themselves to the level of comprehending theoretically the historical movement as a whole', and 'have gone over to the proletariat'[24] share the mistakes of this indecisive democracy, or, failing to find any support, look for a way of taking part, in an isolation all the more painful and demoralising because to be able to exist it always has to come to terms with the system.

Technicians make up the cadres of the capitalist system; with the exception of the poor and subordinate personnel whom revolutionaries must not despise, the liberal professions are attached by a web of links to the bourgeoisie; the University fulfils a rigorously defined task in its service; under its various forms it maintains the traditions of bourgeois culture. Specialisation narrows the horizons of every profession. The engineer, the lawyer, the entomologist and the mathematician find it easy to live outside their specialities in the ideas of everybody else, in other words in a rag bag of ideas as worn out as old coins that have been in circulation for a very long time. It requires very great upheavals to draw them out of this condition, as shown by the Russian Revolution. In this respect writers form a privileged group among intellectuals, more likely than the others to provide the proletariat with allies or helpers. They do not belong to the industrial high command, they have avoided narrow specialisations, and to a limited degree they have escaped the caste spirit of the bar and the university mandarinate; they have, if they so desire, a more direct contact with the masses in the preoccupations to which their messages respond. The masses look to them for decisions, ideas, examples, even advice; the masses are expecting them to express what they do not know how to express for themselves. The great writer of the epoch or the hour speaks for the millions of men who have no voice.

Obviously, I am forgetting neither snobbery nor literary fashion, nor the ridiculous infatuation peculiar to so many 'men of letters'; but we have now got to the point at which the writer has to chose his own future; from now on we are only interested in those who wish to serve something higher than themselves.

Six The Ideological Function of the Writer

The great writers of a period are always its prophets, and occasionally its apostles. For example Balzac, some of whose novels are theses of such bourgeois naivety that they seem to be strangely satirical to us: look at *César Birotteau* or *Le Martyr de la boutique*, or, better still, *Thèse sur la probité du petit commerçant*.[25] Balzac put together his works with passionate conviction, at a time when the bourgeoisie was transforming the world in its own image. Even the smallest virtues of the victorious class had nothing ridiculous about them then – shall I give the names of his contemporaries – Whitman, Zola, Tolstoy, Rolland? There is something apostolic about these four, and this is perhaps what makes them great. There is something of the moralist and the preacher about Anatole France, Barrès and Gide,[26] in a word, in every influential writer.

The writer fulfils an ideological function. It can be said that there are two sorts of writers: those who entertain the rich and those who speak for the crowd.[27] In reality, which is often contradictory, the two men are often only one, but one or the other has to come out on top. Nothing would be more erroneous than to deduce from this that a political meaning penetrates, or has to penetrate, every work, which by definition would lead us straight to sanctifying didactic works. Didactic works, in the usual meaning of the word, are often, by definition, works of inferior quality, and are as a result not up to their task. Confusing agitation, propaganda and literature is equally disastrous to all three forms of intellectual activity and social action (and yet in particular cases they can be powerfully combined in various ways). The unique value of the novel comes from the fact that it presents to man something other than political slogans or demands; ways of feeling, coming alive in our deepest feelings, understanding the other person and understanding ourselves, loving and becoming passionate about it; it goes without saying, let us emphasise, that these ways of living, which, when they arise in our minds, are clothed in the form of an ideology, necessarily correspond to the written or unwritten credo of particular social classes; but it is in an indirect and distant way, apparently loose and invisible to all but the analyst. The Russians have a rather curt but striking expression about it: 'The writer is an organiser of the psychic.' It is a poor organiser who shouts at us; 'Come on, I am going to make you understand how to think and how to feel!' To begin with, it is a little pretentious; and even if the problem of wounded pride does not arise, you must be very lacking in critical spirit for this little declaration not to make you antagonistic. This is inferior didactic literature.

Another aspect of this sort of inferiority concerns the writer himself. He is involved in his idea, he knows where he wants to lead you, and therefore where he has to go. He is no longer in charge of releasing his creative faculties and following them with his eyes closed – for example, closed to the particular political contingencies of the day, but open, marvellously open to the vast universe, like the eyes of Rimbaud![28] The mechanisms of artistic creativity are far from being completely understood by us. In any case, it is certain that for many artists a complete attempt to subordinate creative activity, where a number of unconscious and subconscious factors come into play, to a rigorously conscious direction, would result in an awkward impoverishment of his work and personality. Would the book gain in clarity of ideas what it has lost in spontaneity, human complexity, deep sincerity, and rich contradictions? In some cases, perhaps. But the charm and effect of a work of literature come precisely from the intimate contact between reader and author, at levels where the purely intellectual language of ideas is no longer enough, a sort of sharing that cannot be attained other than by a work of art; by weakening the ways this sharing takes place, we weaken everything; I do not see what can be gained by this, although I understand all too well that the politician prefers above all others novels that are based on the articles of his programme. But this politician is a very shortsighted being characterised by his inability to subordinate his own interests to vaster and more durable ones; I would contrast him with the proletarian policy for which a vigorous and vital work, permeated by a revolutionary if diffuse spirit, even a work tainted with all that petty doctrinaires so bitterly denounce under the label of 'ideological deviations' is worth more, and is more useful to us than another, which meets all the requirements of propaganda, but which is bereft of the inexpressible and indefinable element that strikes deep into you, turns you inside out, and ignites within you the little warming flame of deep feeling.[29] An example is Helen Grace Carlisle's novel, *Mother's Cry*, of which Magdeleine Paz has provided a French translation, *Chair de ma chair*.[30] I know of few recent books cast from so pure a metal; it reminds me of the tragic bronzes of Constantin Meunier;[31] when we follow it step by step, explained in language all the more fascinating because it has all the mistakes and all the awkwardness of the real language of a poor woman from New York, and follow the development of this destiny right to the end, we have something of the inhuman weight of the skyscraper on our shoulders ... I showed this to a young doctrinaire having, alas, something of the politician about him, and this is the gist of what he said to me: 'Note that this book is very petty bourgeois in spirit; American capitalism is not condemned in it; a tone of resignation mingled with hope holds sway in it to the end, showing that the author has not shed all her illusions in American democracy; like its characters, it has not found the way of the party ...', etc. He must be very limited not to be able to see that precisely by abstaining from formulating an explicit condemnation of American capitalism, and even by showing how completely this system has succeeded in so shaping the spirit of an exploited woman that she can conceive of nothing outside of it, the writer is showing – perhaps in spite of her own very real democratic illusions – with an unequalled force, the grip American civilisation has over the exploited.

Seven Thinking About Man

What, therefore, is necessary for the writer to be able to speak today to the masses, to make a contribution to the formation of minds, as a citizen of our time? To leave chatter behind, and look at the reality of a civilisation admirable in its potentialities, but revolting, repugnant and catastrophic in its effects. To see man at the mercy of social struggles, wars, deceptive prosperity, crises, famines, terrors, dictatorships and armaments, the human ant making his way beneath buildings, the galley slave working on the line, the masked man preparing infernal gases for the next war, man more deceived than savages are by their witch doctors opening his 'daily paper of important information' in the morning, man occasionally happy to eat his fill and make love on this great pilotless boat that often seems so close to sinking ... To think about man! Ask him about causes, take part, 'descend into the fight'. Descend? But is this to descend? Descend from where? From what painted cardboard plinth? It is much better to get up from a miserable role into the struggle.

This does not necessarily mean becoming revolutionary; but any disinterested thinking about man's future from this time onwards draws close in a way to the revolutionaries – at least if we do not start out from a reactionary standpoint, in which case we would be obeying the social imperative of the conservative classes. It matters little to us where the writer stops in his search for a solution to the human problem; if his attempt is honest, even if he does no more than pose the problem, he will do immensely useful work. Revolutionaries will often reproach him for not seeing clearly enough, for being the plaything of illusions entertained by the ruling classes, for being to a more or less annoying degree a prisoner and transmitter of their ideology, and this may well be true; some will blame him angrily for bringing confusion into the ideas of the working class, and this might even be true, but it would be much less damaging than not saying it at all, as is usual, if the revolutionaries are on guard. Let us fear confusion in ideas less than sterility and a void. The thinking of the proletariat is vigorous enough not to shy away from ideological conflicts, a variety of mistakes, investigations, illusions and first attempts; but it does need to take hold of people and to lodge itself in brains, and for the petty bourgeois writer, in traditional terms, to become eternal, and to make a contribution, it is sufficient, for example, for him to be fired by a real feeling for justice, upon which only the vaguest idealistic socialism could be based in politics. The organisations of the proletariat will not ask of him instruction in the class struggle, militants will notice the obscurities and defects in his thought, but for all that they will welcome him as a valuable ally.

'From all that has been written, I only love what has been written with one's own blood,' says Nietzsche.[32] What is romantic in this declaration of passionate sincerity does not seem to me to be out of place at a time when the need for revolutionary romanticism arises and makes itself felt. The sincerity of a work is one of the necessary conditions for it to have an impact. Proletarian literature will not come into existence either by the efforts, however persevering, of bureaucratic organisations or conferences; the finest motions, thought up in the atmosphere of the wisest doctrine by the most zealous propaganda authorities cannot produce a good book[33] *if passionate sincerity is not involved in it.*

Proletarian literature will be the spontaneous work of writers won over to the revolutionary proletariat. The usual division between emotional life, culturally created by the past, in other words, and conviction will be sufficiently reduced among them for them to be able to reach the fulness of expression that comes from a deep agreement between subconscious aspirations, feeling, everything that goes to make up passion, and thought. Proletarian work cannot be defined otherwise than by its *quality.* Only writers who are used to looking at the world from the angle of proletarian thought, and who are henceforth incapable, whatever their individual origins, of separating their interests from those of the proletariat, imbued with the very rich revolutionary traditions of our times, whatever subjects they deal with, their state of mind or even their ideological variations, are capable of producing proletarian works – and they will be that only to the extent to which they are themselves proletarian revolutionaries.

Eight Internal Imprisonment

The most serious thing for a writer is his *internal imprisonment.*

Emmanuel Berl announces the *death of bourgeois thought.* That is going faster than we need; something that kills so effectively is not dead. Pamphlets permit exaggerated expressions, and Berl is right to denounce the inherent weakness of a literature that is at a dead end, greatly inferior as a whole to bourgeois thinking in its more essential forms.[34]

Without disparaging the pamphlet, we do not intend to bury our opponent verbally before having beaten him, above all if he is an opponent who annoys us, corrupts our people, and imposes on us by his language his ways of thought and feeling and still shows evidence of redoubtable energy.

We see the world through the categories of thought formed by capitalist culture. Contact between man and reality is not direct, or even between man and himself, since categories formed by society interpose themselves between them. 'Man has lost himself' (Marx). The sciences which deal with things that are furthest away from man, astronomy, physics and mathematics are the most objective. Whenever man is approached, this distortion, elusive to begin with, enormous at the end, strikes us. It is in the language, just as there is an entire primitive mythology in words when we say 'the wind blows' and 'the wave leaps', we continue to use expressions that transmit the animism of our ancestors. Similarly we end up being duped by capitalist mythology when we are formulating the simplest ideas. Here are the first lines of *The Surrealist Manifesto* (André Breton): 'So far does belief go in life.' We should not read too much into the word belief, such as results from the Christian past within us, we should not get hung up over the unhealthy idea of a *belief* in life. The third line reads, 'Man, the definitive dreamer ...' What mythology is richer than that of the word 'dreamer' here added to *definitive* by a static and abstract concept of man, such as was loved by the classical postivism of the nineteenth century, or by an intellectual concept of ideal entities? The Surrealist writer only has at his disposal an assortment of ideas and words shaped by a thinking that is the opposite of his own. Even his attempts to escape the bourgeois thought of today from which he comes, and by which he is moulded, have something about them that is heroic and comic at the same time.[35] Pick out at random a few phrases in any other book; think about the terms for a while, and you will discover there, without having to resort to deep investigation, notions obviously marked by successive imprints, like old stamps obliterated by several franking marks – the most recent mark being that of bourgeois society. By implacable selection and ceaseless remodelling, drawing upon all the resources of the collective, of the individual, the conscious, the unconscious, of repression, sublimation, imitation and a utilitarian dialectic, society has shaped our ideas. Bergson brought out that 'intelligence to begin with aims at creation', 'it aims at human action upon the concrete'.[36] Even at its birth it is connected with work. Marx's excellent chapter on *commodity fetishism*,[37] with the insights it reveals on some of the fundamental ideas of modern man, notably on the idea of freedom, should be quoted here in its entirety. Present day thought as shaped by capitalism often has something inherently anti-dialectical about it, above all French thought that is nourished by Cartesianism and Positivism,[38] and so is fixed in its expression

with a clarity that is perhaps incompatible with the dynamism and contradictions of what is *real*. Hence, no doubt to an extent, the unpopularity of Marx and
his successors in France.

The intellectual can only free himself from this internal imprisonment in
the extent to which he absorbs the ideology of the proletariat. So he has to join
the one class 'whose aim and historic activities are traced in a tangible and
irrevocable manner in the conditions of its existence as well as in the entire
organisation of bourgeois society', and which can, and must, by liberating itself,
free humanity. This joining is extremely difficult. How do we shake off the spiritual yoke of the old bourgeois humanism when Socialism itself is dominated
by it? The struggle of a few courageous spirits against the shadowy ideas that
they bear within themselves has something tragic about it.

Nine Our Crisis

The existence of a powerful revolutionary workers' movement ought greatly to
help the intellectuals in this engagement combined with escape. They should
cast off the old man by making themselves 'servants of the proletariat', far better servants inasmuch as they have better adapted themselves to the revolutionary class, than all the more unfaithful servants, the more dangerous inasmuch
as they are more deeply imbued with what is specifically bourgeois in modern
culture. French revolutionary syndicalism, having learned from the pre-war
parliamentary corruption, persuaded the working class to mistrust the intelligentsia; Bolshevism does not have a very different attitude with regard to them.
But everything depends upon the working class movement; if it were mature, it
would have nothing to fear from a few foreign influences; on the contrary, it
would know how to use even unstable allies, and even temporary 'fellow travellers';[39] it would train its own intellectuals and it would have its own literature.
Let us agree that the situation in this respect is a bad one. In the great crisis of
capitalism there is a crisis of the revolution. What is occuring in Germany at the
time of writing is still not that most merited revolution one might conceive of,
it is the Hitlerite counter-revolution. The French working class is still below the
level of fighting spirit that was its own in the great times of pre-war revolutionary syndicalism. Spain's splendid revolutionary syndicalism, entangled in its
old anarchistic formulae, has not succeeded to the advantage of the proletariat

in preventing the stabilisation of a bourgeois republic; in no part of the West does Communism seem to have found or broken a way through. The proletarian party, the supreme revolutionary instrument as conceived and hammered out in Russia by Lenin, has still not been forged, to tell the truth, in the Western countries, with the exception of Germany, where it appears to be clearly unequal to its tasks.

In these circumstances the intellectuals might very well exert a pernicious influence over the revolutionary workers; the formation of a revolutionary *intelligentsia* is compromised; revolutionary literature is condemned to circulate in the ideological circle of the middle classes; the creation of a proletarian literature is made particularly difficult. Let us not delude ourselves. Nothing is more alien to proletarian realism than the fear of looking things in the face. We are not afraid of breaking with any imposed optimism, because we are going ahead with a confidence in the future which in the darkest hours breaks all the shackles of pessimism. Those Communists who are in Mussolini's prisons magnificently embody the heroism of the proletariat and its confidence in the future. The Gramscis and the Terracinis[40] know that they may amount to nothing at the moment, that tomorrow they may well be murdered, and that they may never again see the light of day; but they understand history's inexorable laws, they know how parades end – as we knew in the days when most of Europe was hoping for its salvation from the advance of the Cossacks on Berlin that the Russian Empire was doomed; as Lenin and a few others affirmed in 1914, war was being transformed into revolution; like so many others who have been persecuted, defeated and exiled ... We see at the height of capitalism the germs of its decomposition and death; and in our weakness of today we see our power of tomorrow springing up.

Ten Concerning a Workerist Theory

The intellectuals can render the proletariat immense services; the part that they will play in creating a proletarian literature will be no minor one. Here I feel it necessary to refute a *workerist* conception originating in French revolutionary syndicalism springing from a legitimate suspicion of petty bourgeois intellectuals, and in Russian Bolshevism from the attitude of the intellectuals in the presence of the proletarian revolution of 1917–1919. 'Poets, thinkers and artists, the proletariat can expect nothing from them in direct help ... the poets, thinkers and artists of the revolution can only be born from the victorious revolutionary proletariat' (Pierre Naville[41]). Lenin – whom I am quoting because he is right, and not in order to call upon him as an authority – was of an opposite view. He pointed out: 'By their social status, the founders of modern scientific socialism, Marx and Engels, themselves belonged to the bourgeois intelligentsia.' He envisaged Communist propaganda and agitation 'among all classes of the population' and insisted upon the necessity of profiting fully from 'the best representatives of the younger generation of the educated classes coming over to us'.[42] Let us not forget the teams of great militants that the intellectuals provided for the Russian revolution. Does the working class origin of an intellectual, on the other hand, lessen his internal imprisonment for him? It rather seems that the self-taught person, in a good many cases, in more inclined than the other intellectuals to fall into the traps of bourgeois culture.

Eleven Is a Proletarian Culture Possible?

A glance at the experience of the Russian Revolution will allow us to ask the main practical questions relating to our subject.

Under the old regime, the Russian intellectuals generally seemed to be revolutionaries. Their part in the first battles against the autocracy was very great. But with the seizure of power by the proletariat, along with the majority of the middle classes, they turned against the new revolution, for their ideal did not go beyond bourgeois democracy. It was the middle classes who paid almost all the price of the civil war against the soviets; they bitterly defended the cause of a bourgeoisie that was quite incapable of defending itself. A few poets were the first to rally to the proletarian order. The coming over of the intellectuals was made all the more difficult because the revolution they had put at risk had mishandled them. A soviet *intelligentsia* of those who came over and of young people only began to be created after 1921, when the New Economic Policy based upon concessions to the petty bourgeoisie,[43] which, along with peace, led to a certain prosperity, allowed them the long-term hope of bourgeoisifying the regime. In two years (1921–1923) we saw the birth of an entire new literature rich in talent, quickly enriched with books, revolutionary in a confused sort of way, but not at all Socialist. This is the generation of Pilnyak, Fedin, Vsevolod Ivanov, Leonov and Gladkov, who now set the tone of Soviet Russian literature.

In the enthusiasm at the start of the revolution Communists dreamed of building a proletarian culture. Lenin, on the other hand, insisted upon the necessity of assimilating the intellectual heritage of the bourgeoisie and of ensuring the valuable cooperation of the intellectuals whom capitalism had educated. Trotsky poses the question in all its breadth: 'Will the proletariat have enough time to create a "proletarian culture"? In contrast to the régime of the slave owners and of the feudal lords and of the bourgeoisie, the proletariat regards its dictatorship as a brief period of transition. When we wish to denounce the all-too-optimistic views about the transition to Socialism, we point out that the period of the social revolution, on a world scale, will last not months and not years, but decades – decades, but not centuries, and certainly not thousands of years. Can the proletariat in this time create a new culture? It is legitimate to doubt this, because the years of social revolution will be years of fierce class struggles in which destruction will occupy more room than new construction. At any rate, the energy of the proletariat itself will be spent mainly in conquering power, in retaining and strengthening it and in applying it to the most urgent needs of existence and of further struggle.' But once peace has been attained and victory assured 'as the conditions for cultural creation will become more favourable, the proletariat will be more and more dissolved into a Socialist community and will free itself from its class characteristics and thus cease to be a proletariat. In other words, there can be no question of the creation of a new culture, that is, of construction on a large historic scale during the period of dictatorship. The cultural reconstruction which will begin when the need of the iron grip of a dictatorship unparalleled in history will have disappeared, will not have a class character ...'[44] That is Marx's concept as well: 'The proletariat [...] is compelled as proletariat to abolish itself and thereby its opposite, private property, which determines its existence'; 'when the proletariat is victorious, it by no means becomes the absolute side of society, for it is victorious only by abolishing itself and its opposite'.[45] The victorious proletariat is building a classless society, the first *truly human* society in history.

The art of the revolutionary epoch needs 'a new understanding'. It 'inevitably reflects all the contradictions of a revolutionary social system, should not be confused with socialist art for which no basis has as yet been made'.[46]

Once we accept these reservations, 'These words [proletarian literature or culture] [...] answer to the needs of the transitional epoch, which is satisfied with new values to a certain extent. Several generations of workers are likely not to know any other times. They must fight above all. They will have much to destroy and suffer: the world has to be refashioned. But like the armies of old, they will have their bards, their story tellers, their musicians and their philosophers. And it is all the more true since in order to win the proletariat must be led by real leaders, thinkers and strategists, who, following the examples of Marx and Lenin, will have absorbed the essence of modern culture: it needs its *own* great intellectuals. It needs lesser men as well, for lesser but vital tasks. But the main thing is that both of them are very much its own, its servants. The revolutionary work it is achieving thus has a cultural value in and of itself. In this historically limited sense there will be, and there already is, a culture of the militant proletariat.'[47]

Twelve The 'Literary Policy' of the Communist Party of the USSR

On 1 July 1925 the Central Committee of the Communist Party of the Soviet Union adopted a resolution on the party's literary policy, of which this is a summary:

> The materialist dialectic penetrates into completely new fields (biology, psychology, and the natural sciences in general). *The conquest of positions in the field of imaginative literature must sooner or later become an accomplished fact.*
>
> One must remember, however, that this task is infinitely more complex than other tasks [...] for even within the framework of capitalist society the working class could prepare itself for the victorious revolution, build its cadres of fighters and leaders and forge its magnificent ideological arsenal of political struggle. But it could not work on questions of the natural sciences or technology, any more than it could, as a class which is culturally oppressed, develop its own imaginative literature, its own artistic forms, and its own style. If the proletariat already has at hand infallible criteria for the social and political content of any literary work, then it does not yet have definite answers to all questions regarding artistic form.

For these reasons, the resolution recommends Communists to consider the 'fellow travellers', more or less sympathetic non-proletarian writers, as 'qualified specialists', and to take account of their feelings. We should attempt to make easier 'their transition [...] to the side of Communist ideology', and whilst we should struggle against anti-Communist tendencies among them ('which are now extremely insignificant'), and oppose the formation of an ideology of the new bourgeoisie among those who have come over to us, we should show ourselves 'tolerant of intermediate ideological forms'.

The party will encourage proletarian authors to the utmost, not without putting them on their guard against 'Communist conceit, the most debilitaing phenomenon'. 'Precisely because it sees in them the future ideological leader of Soviet literature, the party must fight wholeheartedly against a light-minded and negligent attitude towards the old cultural heritage, as well as towards specialists of the artistic world. In like manner, the position which underestimates the very importance of the struggle for the ideological hegemony of the proletarian writers deserves condemnation ... The party should also fight against attempts to create a purely hothouse "proletarian literature"; it must broadly embrace phenomena in all their complexity; it must not be confined to a single factory; it must be the literature not of a guild but of a great fighting class which leads millions of peasants ...'

Criticism is to give proof of proletarian intransigence, to uncover the objective social meaning of works, mercilessly to denounce manifestations of counter-revolutionary thinking, but also 'to show the greatest tact, caution and tolerance towards all those literary strata which might march alongside the proletariat ...' 'Communist criticism must drive out of circulation the tone of literary command. Only when it relies on its *ideological superiority* will this criticism have profound educational significance. Marxist criticism must resolutely drive from its midst any pretentious, semi-literate and self-satisfied Communist conceit.' It must 'learn ...'

The party has come out in favour of free competition between literary schools, and 'any other resolution of the problem would be formal and bureaucratic'. The party refuses to confer on a group, whatever it might be, a monopoly in publication: 'the party cannot grant a monopoly to any of the groups, even the most proletarian in its ideological content: this would signify the ruin of proletarian literature most of all'. The party proclaimed the necessity of 'eradicating attempts at makeshift and incompetent administrative interference in literature'. Finally, the party invited writers to break with aristocratic prejudices and throw open to the masses the heritage of the great masters.

It is an altogether excellent resolution.[48]

Since 1925 literary life has experienced the vicissitudes of all social struggles; to explain this it is necessary to go over again the history of the dictatorship of the proletariat in the course of the six years that have gone by. The Soviet press today considers that the hegemony of proletarian literature has been attained; the erstwhile 'fellow travellers' have all declared themselves without exception to be resolute Socialists and supporters of the general line of the party; nonetheless, every week the press condemns the anti-proletarian character of new books that are quickly disowned by their authors. Altogether very few new names have come to notice, and there have been no first rate works, or there are only a very small number of them. We shall see that Soviet literature displays to the onlooker – and by this I mean to the revolutionary proletarian who is looking at it – obvious gaps, and some of the annoying awkwardness warned against by the Communist Party's resolution. Thus last November *Pravda* was criticising the faults of the Russian Association of Proletarian Writers, which had often lost sight of the fact that it formed 'a literary and educative organisation, and not a ruling and administrative one'.[49] The Association soon met, condemned its own mistakes, and quickly gave itself a new 'line'.

Thirteen Schemas

The general orientation today imposed upon Soviet literature is hostile to psychology; it wants a social and not a psychological literature, of action and not of introspection, militant and not contemplative or analytical, of propaganda and not discussion, of agreement and not of research. Because a group of writers have supported the need to understand and create in every man, 'a living human being', this 'slogan' is seen as a reactionary attempt to undermine the morale of the class; it is not a question of understanding the enemy, to be specific, the pope, the comfortable or rich peasant, or the idealist professor, it is a question of struggling against him. They want a utilitarian and even a specialised literature, a present day one, devoted to great political campaigns, to the Red Army, to the Communist Youth, and to the collectivisation of agriculture: a literature for agitation and vigorously orthodox propaganda. There is a very strong inclination to consider that 'whoever is not *unreservedly* with us is against us', and therefore counter-revolutionary. These ideas only show their weakness when they are applied.

We saw some years ago in a good Soviet film for which Meyerhold's contribution should have guaranteed success (*The White Eagle*);[50] a governor, a worthy man in private life, who despite himself had to give the order to fire on a working class demonstration, and then suffered remorse about it. The critic declared this film detestable. From his point of view the governor obviously had to be a brute in uniform, had to open fire happily, and then enjoy remembering it ... Now both types exist in nature, I mean in the nature of military governors, but, apart from the fact that it is manifestly absurd to pretend to suppress all psychology, in order only to depict bourgeois as odious according to your taste, is not the propaganda effect far greater, on a higher level, and more likely to win over hard to please or simply newly awakened minds, by showing the man in thrall to his job, the good governor in spite of himself carrying out the vilest needs of the regime? Will someone object that what is important is to inculcate class hatred into the mass of onlookers? The hatred we require is that of the system; it is too easy to direct responsibility for the system onto individuals, an old trick of conservatives who want to limit themselves to a change of personnel. Moreover, rather than appeal to sentiments and instincts perhaps useful at certain times of social conflict, it would be better for us to guide the workers towards a higher level of class consciousness.

'My standpoint', says Marx, 'from which the evolution of the economic formation of society is viewed as a process of natural history, can less than any other make the individual responsible for relations whose creature he socially remains, however much he may subjectively raise himself above them.'[51]

In the same context of ideas, a Leningrad magazine criticised a young writer for giving a character who was a Communist oppositionist some sympathetic traits. Does he have to have been bowlegged, crosseyed, stammering and deceitful? Such stupidity has the opposite effect.

The same magazine criticised Alexis Tolstoy for having created the character of a Cheka officer[52] without 'showing the real Bolshevik Cheka officer in him'. I expect the orthodox press to blame Barbusse and Léon Werth[53] for not 'showing the real French soldier' in their books about the war. In both examples the aim is to impose utilitarian schemas upon the writer. If someone replies to me, as so often happens, 'we should condemn schemas that are useful to the bourgeoisie and adopt those of use to the proletariat', I see precisely in that an indication of a harmful way of thinking for proletarian art. Procedure cannot be identical between it and bourgeois art, above all in expressions about what is useful, *in other words, the most bourgeois*! We do not have to take up all the spiritual, or supposedly spiritual, weapons of the bourgeoisie. It needs the lying of stupefying conventions and brain washing. Let us leave them to it! Our needs are the opposite because our natures and our ends are opposite.

Obviously we can, when using convenient simplifications, use general terms such as the Worker, the Bolshevik, the Cheka Officer, and the Red Soldier, on condition that we do not draw abstract types from them in order to use them as ideal models; for it is an essential condition for a work of art not to substitute conventional beings for men of flesh and blood.

I do not intend to deny all literary value – restricted in its use – to useful schemas. Caricature has its charm, and is undeniably useful for propaganda. Books in which we see the Real-Marxist-Proletarian overcome the typical hesitations of the Petty-Bourgeois-Intellectual-Individualist and triumph over the Fat-Bourgeois-Liberal-Reactionary-And-Fascist (with eight gold teeth, a pot belly and a cigar) after the appropriate setbacks on page 250, could, on condition that the writers really had talent, become great simplistic frescoes with exaggerated contours, idealistic and caricatural at the same time, with a powerful effect; I am prepared to admit this, even though all the attempts I have seen of this type are far from being that. But even if they rise to this stature, works such as these cannot be the main ones in a literature associated with social change. They should take their place at the side of or below different works intended to interest, inspire, explain, reveal and educate men with more complex requirements, too concerned for truth, too grounded in reality, and too concerned to understand people to limit themselves to elementary and even rudimentary symbolism.

Fourteen **From the Schema to the False Idea**

I have just read a Russian story whose hero is a driver. I should say, he is The Driver par excellence: he only lives for the garage. There are no other characters except good or bad drivers; even half of the bad ones become good ones at the end. The author tells us that his character is thinking about Socialism; let us believe it on his say-so. A dramatic writer[54] maintains that the only real life a worker has is in the factory. I personally interject here: I have never seen workers of this sort in the USSR. It is the triumph of the conventional, and, moreover, a convention based upon a false idea that has nothing Socialist about it, *the idea that the producer exists for production.* The proletarian idea is the exact opposite. To reduce the worker to existing only in his capacity in the factory, even if you allow the factory an intense and interesting collective life, (collective life as a result of production, yet again, but here the question is posed differently) is, we must admit, to deprive social man of an enormous part of his value, and to suppress essential aspects of his life as an individual – love, family, fatherhood; it is, I repeat, creating a type of worker who does not exist, whom Socialism does not need. Socialism needs workers who are fully human, who enjoy life, in the factory as elsewhere, but elsewhere as in the factory. Surely everyone must know that. So why do we have works like this? To a young worker, 'fed-up with ideology', who wrote to him that he wanted 'to enjoy himself' ('Instead of embracing the tractor, I want the peasant to embrace the peasant woman, I want fields where grass grows instead of nails'), Gorky himself replied: '*Enjoying yourself* is the parasites' oldest motto: "let others work, so that we can enjoy ourselves".'[55] This disturbing response to a most natural request betrays an underlying idea of production for production's sake. The opposite reminds me of Lafargue's beautiful pamphlet: *The Right to be Lazy,*[56] the strongest demand that has ever been made for the right to leisure. The aim of Socialism is to rediscover the man inside the producer.

At the end of the summer of 1931 Russia's proletarian writers gave themselves the task of 'making known the labour heroes of the shock brigades'. The *Literary Gazette* published lists of writers, for the most part unknown, moreover, who attached themselves to large factories in order to praise their heroes. At the same time sculptors modelled statues of these selected workers, and engravings reproduced their portraits on postage stamps. Nothing would be more fitting than to understand work as a fresh honour, according to Pierre Hamp's remark – and this is so even under the capitalist system, for as far as we are concerned there is no greater figure than the Worker – nothing can be more desirable, so it seems, than to set out in a documentary essay, a novel or a short story, the traits of those true heroes who are making the Five Year Plan[57] an amazing revolutionary reality, often amid the harshest privations. Only this method is to be allowed: there is to be no psychology, isn't that so? The general idea is laid down; the general type is also laid down; the result is laid down; he receives the Order of Lenin. It is all preordained, and from that comes the disastrous result. No living, in other words real, literature can emerge from so artificial a construct. Can your hero be a bad husband? A believer? An Oppositionist? An alcoholic? A fighter in his bad days? Can anyone quote a single example of this sort among the portraits published? No; he has to be a 'Hero of Labour' from the roots of his hair to the soles of his feet; and if he isn't in the party, he is on the point of joining it ... The most insignificant character in Hamp or Poulaille (*Daily Bread*)[58] is a million times more human.

And so we saw appear on stage in one of Moscow's best theatres, in a play by Nicholas Nikitin, *The Line of Fire*, a well-written play very well staged by Tairov (1931),[59] an engineer-saboteur who was so perfect an example of his type, from his gaiters to his beard, that I was straightaway reminded of the stereotype of a deliberate black traitor, with bushy eyebrows and waistcoat, that I so often saw appear a long time ago on stage at Belleville. It is easy to judge the distance from reality; real saboteurs corresponded so little to this portrayal that for years they were to inspire confidence in the most able leaders of the Soviet economy.

The danger of these schemas is that they disarm the intelligence and falsify ideas. The conventional image imprinted on the brain one day prevents us from understanding reality. Art loses the wealth and variety of life. It avoids creative mistakes only to fall into the error of sterility. So the very dialectic of life, that constant interplay of contradictions that mingle, create and wear each other out, which deny themselves, destroy themselves and are reborn, escapes it.[60]

Fifteen Writers and Proletarians

The examples I have given, far from being exceptional, are typical in their banality. (Moreover, what I have said of them can be read from the pens of the leaders of the Soviet literary organisations; they repeat it from time to time without succeeding in improving it, which proves that the problem is deep-rooted). The same schematic spirit seems to have inspired the recent attempts to 'proletarianise' literary man. The year 1930 was that of the Writers' Brigades. Groups of writers were paid by the month by the industrial enterprises, with travel expenses and signed contracts for documentary works, to go all over the country and carry out agitation. Thousands of writers must have taken part in this movement, which must have cost a fair bit and didn't produce a single note-worthy book. So the project was abandoned. There was, however, behind this initiative an interesting idea, that of squads of writers working in direct contact with production.

A little later another campaign began. The shock brigade workers them-selves were invited to 'enter literature'. Those workers who belong to shock brigades commit themselves to take on particularly difficult work; even if we admit that these brigades very much represent the workers' elite, which cannot be completely true, for the good worker does not need to make special agree-ments to do as much as he can, can these workers, who expend the greatest amount of energy in the factory, and who have the least strength and leisure to spare, seriously think of becoming writers? In other words, are you talking about additionally training them in a new skill more difficult than several oth-ers, requiring just as conscientious an application as the others, years of prepa-ration, a general education, time, leisure – not to mention the talent to do so ...? Some enthusiastic Russian writers have nonetheless already today greeted the workers from the shock brigades as 'masters of literature'. This is the verbal diarrhoea of intellectuals who are too alien to working class consciousness to be able to allow themselves to judge seriously. The miner knows that he can't turn himself into a mason.

(Yet again, this originates in a true idea; it is undeniable that the working class contains innumerable talents that only lack culture and the opportunity to express themselves. It is up to the working class society to awaken them and provide them with both. But mechanical application of a correct idea can only end in a laughable result. Is there any need to recall what great contemporary writers came from the proletariat, or even lower down? There are the Americans O. Henry and Jack London, the Englishman Joseph Conrad, the Russian Gorky, the Frenchman Pierre Hamp, the Norwegian Knut Hamsun,[61] and Istrati the Romanian. I have limited myself to recognised names, universally known. Conrad, a Pole by origin, only learned English on British ships when he was twenty years old; Istrati also did not learn French, his language as a writer, until quite later on).

A noticeable impoverishment results from all this: literature always lags behind social life, even when it incessantly claims by means of its organs and conferences its willingness to catch up with it. But on no occasion, as far as I am aware, have the writers denounced evils, abuses, mistakes or dangers *before* the official organs of the press (as for denouncing them afterwards, what could be easier?); on not a single occasion have they advocated a solution, an improvement or an initiative *before* the official organs of the press (and as for approving of them subsequently, what merit do you see in that?). Historic reversals like the Chinese Revolution of 1927, even if the Russians are better informed about it than any other European people, have not produced among us the equivalent of Malraux's *Conquérants*, even when there have been far more Russians in China than Frenchmen, Russians who are far better equipped to understand the events.[62] Here we are putting our finger on the root of the problem: it is too embarassing a subject for many ideological reasons. For the same reason, talented writers prefer to deal with historical subjects.

Sixteen Proletarian Thinking and the Fear of Error

The causes of this state of affairs lie further back than in a no doubt over-excessive administrative control; they derive from far too narrow a concept of what literature is and from a horror of heresy that ends up in a fear of of all variety, all variation, all seeking, and even of any new fashion, however limited its novelty, of reformulating first principles or accepted ideas. Is error, therefore, quite so great a danger in works of inspiration?

It would seem that the materialist dialectic would help us to understand that, in the incessant battle for scientific truth, error is always more or less mixed up with it, and does not always play the dire role that we are inclined to ascribe to it after the event. Firstly, there is no such thing as *complete* error. Science is not a finished product, 'Marxism is not a dogma, but a guide to action' (how they love to repeat that in Russia, and with good reason!), and even the activity of a successful proletarian party is of necessity tainted with empiricism, mistakes, trial and error, and deviations of various types; it would be ridiculous to make a rigid and linear idea of it. And finally truth, our proletarian truth, isn't it necessary that it should develop unceasingly by everone's efforts, by productive emulation, research, discussion and fraternal struggle? The conferences of our organisations can lay down the line on matters of doctrine that initiate activity and are conditioned by it; this is necessary, for what is above all important to us in transforming society, is efficiency in action. We do not need to ask them to lay down the line on matters of philosophy, on the scientific method, on art or on history, unless we want to return to the dogmatic traditions of the councils of the Roman Church. A universal machine for creating the truth has yet to be invented – and it is not for us, revolutionary Marxists, to dream of doing so ...

Can we therefore demand from literature an ideological orthodoxy that is impossible in the scientific and political spheres? A great political party has to defend its thinking against disintegrative influences, to maintain its internal balance, and to struggle against elements of decomposition that arise within it, above all when it is exercising power and holding a monopoly of it – that is understandable; but is it necessary to apply to other spheres of intellectual life, in science and the arts, the methods by which it maintains a sound political intransigence (given that these methods may be excellent, which we do not have to decide here)?

The value of a doctrine cannot be considered in the absolute, in disregard of all circumstances; truth cannot be possessed separately from the intelligence, talent, honesty and individual and social activity of the one who has it; otherwise we end up with dogma. For some of the Church Fathers the least of the Christians were far greater than the greatest of the pagans; but for us revolutionaries of today, a great idealist, a man of science or a writer, however far removed he may be in his spiritual background from the dialectical materialism of Feuerbach,[63] Marx, Engels and Lenin – an Albert Einstein, a Nicolai,[64] or a Romain Rolland – is infinitely more valuable than a mediocre materialist freshly turned out of college, and at best good for ... I really know not what ... The latter's philosophy is superior to idealism in itself; but when the great idealist comes to the proletariat he throws into the balance a treasury of human experience, of culture, of knowledge, and of talent, all the wealth that humanity in our century has deposited within him – whereas our mediocre person ... The reader will excuse me for stressing things that are so obvious by using images that are offensive to common sense. It is necessary, because I cannot do otherwise: the reader is requested to believe that I am trying to explain myself in all this with the utmost moderation. Some time ago Lenin wrote to Gorky, 'I believe that an artist can glean much that is useful to him from philosophy of all kinds [...] I absolutely agree that in matters that concern the art of writing you are the best judge, and that in deriving *this* kind of views both from your artistic experience *and from philosophy, even if idealistic philosophy*, you can arrive at conclusions that will be of tremendous benefit to the workers' party.'[65] It is nonetheless true that all too often we see the letter preferred to the spirit, and mediocrity steeped in the repetition of approved formulae preferred over honest and searching intelligence, and consequently inclined to 'deviations'. The magazines have yet again stated that there is only place in the Soviet Union for rigorously Marxist criticism. In my opinion this is the only scientific criticism. But is this a sufficiently good reason for preferring to a Sainte-Beuve a young editor of the literary page in *L'Humanité*? This young editor and I may well be on the same side of the barricades, and the great critic might well be on the other: but it is the former whom we would rather ask in order to interpret Goethe.[66]

Finally, as to the rule: 'All who are not completely in agreement with us are against us' – is this true? It is as fake as a twenty-franc pearl. All revolutionaries know all too well how often in the struggle they have needed the support of men who in several respects are far removed from their views. It starts off with individual help, offered out of sympathy for an exile, and ends up with the work of the specialists in the Red Army and in industrialisation. And will people reply to me by saying that we cannot do without the engineer or the artillery officer, whereas we can very well do without the petty bourgeois writer and the syndicalist militant? I say that these two cannot be written off without resulting in an awful impoverishment.

As opposed to deviations in individual thinking, the proletariat in power has more to fear from mediocre going through the motions, disguise, and crafty imitation of its language, its ideas and its values, the entire vast forgery of a proletarian culture based upon the minimum, 'don't make a fuss, we must conform', and 'we can get along well enough ourselves'! Mechanical search for a rigorous orthodoxy will end up by making the wrong choice. Here are two authors: the one is full of vigour, devoted to the revolution, which he understands in his own way, a real artist, intent on defending in several respects indirectly, as is often the case in a novel, ideas that we might consider erroneous – and let us, in order to exaggerate the case, make him a follower of Freud in psychology, of Bergson in philosophy, or of Sorel in sociology;[67] and another, anxious to please, with nothing to stick up for apart from his petty personal position: who cannot see that the second will *adapt* better to all the demands made upon him, and that bureaucratic intransigence will end up getting rid of the former? The Socialist society that is being formed should fear this passive or self interested adaptation which, in the great struggles to come, can very easily be turned against it. It must train its citizens in *civic courage*. A man who does not energetically or stoically defend his opinions, according to the circumstances, will never be either a real revolutionary, a worthwhile writer, or a good citizen of the republics of labour.

And sterility is more to be feared than ideological errors. Our intransigence of thought can only win out in struggle: not in a void.

Seventeen The Problem of Intellectual Exchange

Like all intellectual life, literature is more and more tending to be international. The great writer is the one whose influence radiates throughout the world. A book that makes its mark is one that is translated. Literature is introducing a constant exchange of messages between generations, classes, countries, races and continents – an exchange that is not yet big enough for our liking, but which is going to get bigger. Here an important role must be assigned to new literature, I mean to say, of a revolutionary and proletarian inspiration. Shouldn't it concern itself with proclaiming across frontiers bristling with barbed wire the European spirit, the brotherhood of races, and working class internationalism – the only perfected form of the European spirit? It is inconceivable that such a literature could survive without very vigorous international exchanges. But as regards this also, on one very important point, the situation is bad, and Soviet literature suffers from it worst of all. Its communications with the rest of the world are very weak and sporadic. It is almost entirely ignorant of literary life abroad. There does not exist in the entire Soviet Union a single bookshop selling new books in foreign languages; nor even a library which possesses a complete collection of the main foreign journals. Apart from a few sporadic reports intended for a restricted public of administrators, not a single publication really follows the international literary movement.

For some years[68] foreign authors have only been rarely translated, and the paper shortage is not the only reason for this state of affairs. There is a tendency to regard bourgeois or petty bourgeois literature as useless, if not pernicious – the latter adjective being applied to the avant-garde writers of the capitalist world. The schematism of simplistic criticisms, themselves beneath all criticism, which can finish off an author for you in two words with a priceless self-confidence, does the rest.[69] I do not have to show how stupid this tendency is. Here I find, magnified, the insane fear of error, and the fear, hardly more justified, of the intellectual influence of rich classes abroad.

In the narrower circle of proletarian culture the situation is even worse; it is here that the fear of error bears its bitterest fruits. Intellectual exchanges, such as they are, become completely impossible, the official organs of the Communist parties being the only working class publications allowed into the Soviet Union. No direct communication can therefore be established between Soviet proletarian literature and the numerous proletarian groupings that, the world over, have always been the centres of working class culture, the laboratories where ideas and tactics are elaborated, and where militants are trained. These are centres full of contradictions, of weaknesses, and even of errors, oh yes! But they are living and irreplaceable centres. You are blind and demoralise them by ignoring them on the basis of preconceived ideas. If we add to what has gone before the often insurmountable difficulties of travel, we can get a more accurate idea of the enormous difficulty of intellectual exchanges between the literature of the USSR and new literature in other parts of the world. This is a serious problem, and I am only tracing out the main features of it.

Eighteen In Reply to an Ill-Disposed Reader

So great is the creativity of a socialist revolution (and the human experience that it infuses in a writer drawn by its lively grasp from self-contemplation, scholarly preoccupation, competition for literary prizes, etc.) that artistic production, in the two branches most necessary to the masses in these days, letters and the cinema, has from the very beginning in the USSR been greatly enriched for some years. The flavour of life, the quality of vital energy, the view of society, ideas about life, death, the future, the individual and the collective, have all more or less been modified. Compared with Western literature, which was enriched by the experience of the War, but to an infinitely lesser degree, for there the war was a catastrophe and not the beginning of a social renewal, a terrible setback for the people and not a titanic appeal for the energy of the masses, Soviet literature cut an impressive figure to begin with, in spite of a certain amount of formal imperfection, but otherwise came quite close to the great traditions of Russia. Dostoyevsky and Tolstoy, being preoccupied with their thinking, often neglected form. And such was the difference in tone between the West and the USSR that writers regarded in Russia as being quite close to counter-revolutionary passed as revolutionaries elsewhere, such as Pilnyak. These judgements were invalidated in both countries by opposing prejudices.

The evils that I have pointed have only worsened in the course of these latter years, but they were already making themselves felt by the influence of Soviet literature. Nearly all the Russian writers that have been translated today belong to the generation of 1922–1924; almost all the works known outside the USSR date back several years. We are now in the fourth and final year of the Five-Year Plan, and this grandiose phase in the revolution appears to be amazingly poor in literary works.[70]

For those who might be tempted to exploit these critical remarks against Communism, my reply is here already.

The bourgeoisie had centuries to develop itself, to grow, to seize power, and to build its civilisation. This was not done without mingling in the same streams the blood of kings as well as of plebeians. Before learning how to govern itself, it saw its republics strangled. Mercenaries dissolved its parliaments and imposed humiliating dictatorships upon it; that was yesterday. The history of its press and literature includes all too many inglorious pages that prevent its apologists from drawing serious argument from the difficulties encountered in developing a new literature in the first workers' republic. He who looks on in good faith cannot for a moment forget that we are witnessing an exceptionally courageous experiment by a young and still weak class, even in victory, moreover weighed down by a heavy inheritance.

Nineteen **The Double Duty**

In dealing with these questions I am guided by a rule that I believe to be indispensable for whoever wishes to serve the revolution: *the rule of double duty*. If literature wishes to accomplish its entire mission in our time it cannot close its eyes to the revolution's internal problems. Whether it be victorious or defeated, growing or falling back, preoccupying the vanguards of the working class or lying dormant in the spirits of the masses, the revolution is everywhere today; its defects are above all ours. It must therefore be defended at one and the same time against its external and its internal enemies, in other words, against the seeds of destruction that it bears within itself. The latter task is a very great one. In order to accomplish it, so it seems, we risk giving weapons to reaction and discouraging the indecisive; let us admit it; I maintain that the opposite risk, of inadvertently stuffing heads with rubbish and creating a revolutionary conformity that is as conventional and dishonest as any other, is far more serious. Workers who rise up against a bourgeois republic to begin with – i.e., not for long – always provide satisfaction for people of the extreme right. The activists who, while a Commune is being besieged, allow themselves to blame the incompetence of the leadership do not fail to be accused of playing the game of the Versaillais;[71] but when it comes down to it they are doing far less damage than the incompetence of the leadership. Let us adopt the active solution, the only one that is worthy of the proletariat, of looking truth in the face.

So it is necessary to deepen the idea of revolution; and if we say *yes* to it, it has to be a firm *yes*, neither vacillating nor holding back. At some times, the worst of them, the proletarian revolution must be defended in total; these are precisely the times in which we expect to see it make its most obvious mistakes, whether it be all sorts of abuses, popular violence, or terror with a ghastly visage; these are times of mortal danger, times of great surges of energy, pitiless times. Our duty here at least is simple, at least for free spirits and revolutionaries in other countries; however, in the country itself, our duty is always *double*, even if one of its facets *is much more important*; accepting all the responsibility never diminishes the pressing obligation every day to struggle against the evils from which the revolution is suffering; it is precisely that which takes up the intense activity of the millions of men who in the last analysis make up the revolution itself; each one every day in the great common action takes the initiative on his own, and does all that is possible on a host of questions. I am obedient to some important congress decision, even if I consider it to be stupid, for discipline is more necessary for public safety than my critical activity; but in the factory, the apartment block, the batallion and the committee, I must on every occasion react against ignorance, stupidity, brutality, unleashing of the instincts and dishonest self-interest. The result is that in the action itself your duty is always double, but its two aspects – the general defence and unceasing internal adjustment – vary in their importance and extent. When peace comes, and the revolution passes on to its work of construction, the struggle for internal reform obviously acquires a growing importance.

A phenomenon develops by virtue of its own internal contradictions. Sorel wrote of the French Revolution: 'The Revolution was soon to liquidate the Old Order by very often imitating the practices of the Old Order ...'[72] A revolution necessarily turns against the old regime the weapons it has wrenched from it. In a certain sense, *an opposite sense*, it continues it, it collects on the battlefield weapons it has in no way created, which are often contrary to its spirit, inevitably a host of contradictions ensue; we see Socialists who oppose the death penalty on principle resort to terror, antimilitarists form red armies, militants anxious to lead the state towards its disappearance become men of state, yesterday's political prisoners, whose greatest joy would have been to blow up jails, jealously guard their keys ... This must seem utterly incomprehensible for the petty bourgeois, stuffed with accepted ideas, and otherwise reduced to simple association of words, and they conclude that what the revolution achieves by the only means available, is because it denies itself, contradicts itself, and recommences the old cycle of history. Robert Louzon recently observed in *La Révolution prolétarienne* with what hitherto unheard-of weight the traditions of Russian history weigh down upon the Soviet Republic.[73] There is there – for this remark is strikingly true – a source of inevitable ills, to be combatted with such energy that the new regime will only succeed if it goes on to the end. The ten days that shook the world in October 1917 and the fourteen years that followed it came in history after three centuries of despotism.

A revolution is not made up of one homogeneous process, comparable to a waterfall: it is more a sum of a multitude of different movements, among which there are fortunate and unfortunate, revolutionary in the true sense of the word and reactionary, the healthy and the unhealthy. The impossibility of revolutionary conformity flows from this, *and the double duty*. By this I do not wish to say that a pseudo-revolutionary conformity cannot attempt to impose itself, but it would be in contradiction with the profound nature of the workers' revolution and could only succeed in imposing itself to the detriment of the latter.

When M. Julien Benda writes: 'It is nonetheless necessary to understand that the revolutionary idea, once it is achieved, ceases to be revolutionary, just as lava, when it hardens, ceases to be lava',[74] he is using a very deceptive metaphor. As if we can compare a historical process, which is by definition never finished, compare the flow of life itself to the hardening of lava! This is because M. Benda starts off from a typically *bourgeois* idea of the revolution. As far as the Third Estate is concerned, once power has been seized and order assured, it only remains to allow the popular lava to harden. When God had completed his work, he rested. Bourgeois society had been created for all eternity ... The ideologists of the Third Estate could not think otherwise, for the bourgeoisie in its periods of strength could not conceive of having successors. Quite different is the proletarian dialectic: the proletariat only wants to conquer in order to disappear: the dictatorship of the proletariat does not aspire to eternity; it believes that it is transitory, it desires its own end in order to make humanity pass 'from the regime of necessity to that of freedom'. We can see all too well where the bourgeois revolution ends; but the proletarian revolution does not come to an end; it desires to be permanent, according to Marx's words,[75] right up to the establishment of a society without classes and without frontiers. It is an ardent lava flow that continues on its way. And if it so happens that the lava becomes hardened, the revolution would not be 'achieved', M. Benda, it would be vanquished.

Those intellectuals who, in their desire to serve the revolution, allow themselves to go into a sort of revolutionary conformism, are in reality lacking in essential responsibility towards the revolution, testifying to the difficulty that they feel in uderstanding it, and showing thereby that they are still looking at it from the outside, as sympathetic onlookers, and not from the inside, as particpants. They are not up to their tasks. They are lacking in foresight, or in civil courage, according to the case. The thing that is least pardonable about a revolution is for it to compromise its own destiny. The position of the others, on the other hand, cannot be a happy one at certain times. Carrying out their double duty can put them between the hammer and the anvil. What should they do about it? Well – do their duty!

It may perhaps be objected that the intelligentsia are all too inclined to a certain anarchistic non-conformity, opposed to the effort of thinking along with millions of workers, hostile to proletarian discipline in action, to rigid class judgements, and to Marxism's subtle but vigorous clarity. This rebellious, petty bourgeois spirit, can only find an effective counterweight in *scrupulous* adherence to Marxism.

Twenty The French Revolutionary Tradition

It remains for me to define the main particulars of the literature that is in the process of formation, well defined by Henri Poulaille as that of the *New Age*. Its very wide range stretches, often by imperceptible gradations, from bourgeois humanism to proletarian humanism, and from 'advanced' literature to proletarian literature. It would be very absurd to attempt to classify men and books in rigid compartments. The writers of the old group of L'Abbaye, Duhamel, Romains, Arcos, Durtain and Vildrac[76] were far from being revolutionaries; but are we not in debt to them for having defined a quality of human feeling with an undeniable and deep revolutionary thrust? Are we not in debt to them for being the first to define this sense of the collective life possessed by every man, but which a century of insane individualism has ended up obliterating, to such an extent that it requires poets to rediscover it? Finally, let us not forget that in a society divided into classes, the humanist is very much in favour of the oppressed classes; he does not have to reveal the value of a man of the ruling classes, so highly esteemed outside himself; he recalls the human dignity of those whose masters very much want to forget now and then that they are men.

Poulaille has very well brought out what necessities oblige literature to renew itself, and in what sense this renewal has to go on. He has emphasised the role of the cinema and the radio in this change. He outlines a list of old and young, of pioneers and young teams. I will criticise him for being too narrowly focused on his subject, from which comes a certain disregard of social factors (ideology and politics) which have a crucial influence over the development of letters.[77] France has an entire revolutionary culture, an entire living spiritual tradition, capable, since its richness is undeniable, of 'inspiring the soul' towards a great literary movement. We must rediscover Proudhon,[78] open up Sorel again, and read Édouard Berth,[79] this amazing inspirer of proletarian ideas. We should also rediscover Guesde in his best times,[80] and the pamphleteer Lafargue. We should become acquainted with Reclus,[81] his clear thought and his sure science, his style as clear as his thought, and his passion for the Revolution! Let us go back to the sources of working-class energy in Babeuf, Blanqui, Varlin, the insurgents of Lyons, the Faubourg Saint-Antoine, and of the Commune.[82] Let us go back to the sources of proletarian literature in the French language in Vallès, bring a Coeurderoy out of oblivion, not allow a Darren or a Zo d'Axa to fall into it, write the history of a *Père peinard*, and understand an Albert Thierry.[83] An anthology of French revolutionary journalism that would draw on the forgotten Socialist, Anarchist, Syndicalist and Communist leaflets of early times would not be bereft of literary merit. Without being afraid of bringing together contradictory elements, I am deliberately only considering here the representatives of strictly working class, and strictly revolutionary thinking; then the horizon widens perhaps in an immeasurable way, and we would be led by Zola, Jaurès[84] and Verhaeren towards less strictly defined concepts.

This French revolutionary tradition has suffered for fifteen years from its conflict with Marxism; for its part, Communism, by having proved its myopia as regards this tradition, has not in France discovered what is necessary to win over the masses: a language and a style. The majority of French Communist writings, even the original ones, have something of the inevitable heaviness of translations, which contributes not a little to diminishing their effect.

I do not think that this tradition is necessarily hostile to Marxism, which has made massive borrowings from it; I believe that the French Communists, when they do not understand its importance, and that is often by a failure to confront it, are depriving themselves of the support of a great historic intellectual force, as well as committing a great error of principle; we have not come to substitute ouselves for those who have gone before us, but to take up their work again, and continue it; we feel that we are the Socialist heirs of all those who have fought, struggled and acted for and with the working class. Fertilised by the experience of the Germans and the Russians, this tradition should form the bedrock of the culture of French revolutionaries.

It is a matter of assimilating and continuing it, *critically*, and not *passively*.

Twenty-One The Production Novel: Hamp

Production will doubtless be called upon to take the dominant place in literature that it has already taken in politics, sociology, and even philosophy. Modern man recognises it as the basis of all social life. That is already an entire revolution in thought. It was Pierre Hamp, rather than Zola, who was interested in the miners and not in the mine, who made production enter the novel.[85]

Himself having come from the working class, Hamp takes as the subject of his story raw material which he follows from its appearance to its end: fish, caught at the start of *Marée fraîche*, and eaten in a great restaurant in the final pages; perfumes in the *Cantique des cantiques*; *Le Lin, La Laine*. The technical vocabulary, the speech of the craftsmen, the thoughts of the businessmen, the manufacturing cost, and the calculation of profit straightaway put literary language back in full contact with life. The machine – which extorts the labour of men in order to get money from them – rightly takes the place set aside in the classical novel for the 'thoughtful heart'. A new beauty is brutally revealed by these innovations. What today is being painfully attempted in the USSR, Hamp has already succeeded with *in his own sphere*. It is all the easier for us to give its due to this work which is for the most part because its weaknesses are strikingly apparent. The evolution of Pierre Hamp has severely damaged his talent. From *Le Rail* to his last works, little by little we see working-class power give way, in *La Peine des hommes*, to managerial control. Even the writer's language changes sadly. The trade union militants he describes in *Le Rail* on the occasion of the 1910 railwaymen's strike, are 'serious men, sobered by hard work', whose 'habit of too much thinking slowed down their speech'. In *Le Cantique des cantiques*, which belongs to the postwar period, a trade union 'leader' singing the *Internationale* is presented to us in these terms: 'He tossed out the solemn Socialist anthem in a cabaret tone'. We are led to believe that the writer has made his fortune between the two books.[86]

Not seeing, and being incapable of seeing the birth and strengthening of working-class consciousness, Hamp has subsituted professional consciousness for it, a restricted old concept created by craftsmen, which the management is concerned to encourage. In reality class consciousness destroys such professional consciousness to the extent that it has given rise to sabotage among French and American trade unionists ... and, during the social crises of 1918 to 1923, among Russian and German capitalists.[87] Hamp unreservedly admires the mechanism of capitalism, he is completely captivated by it, and it is surprising to see how a writer who sometimes knows how to make the workers speak in so true a spirit of class consciousness should allow himself complacently to be dazzled by praise of wealth: 'The church was full of millions' (the final scene of the rich marriage in *Le Lin*[88]). Nonetheless, a few beautiful pages of his work indubitably belong to proletarian literature. What went wrong with him that he failed to be its greatest protagonist today? By being backed up by the tradition of which I spoke. His workers live for capitalism, whereas in reality they want to live for themselves. Something essential has been distorted.

Twenty-Two Proletarian Humanism

The elements of this are to be found to various extents in many writers; and by these elements I mean the collection of feelings and ideas springing from a proletarian view of life, as it formed in the working class movement, revolutionary struggles, the USSR, and among the thinkers, leaders and militants of the proletariat. And it is very much a question of a new humanism, mainly appearing as a new concept of man and the world, in which man is the essential value. There is nothing definitive or static in this concept which is destined to evolve along with the working class and suffer the consequences of the latter's failures and successes. We can therefore try to disentangle empirically its main features.

These features seem to me to be the following:

– an interest in production, based upon an understanding of its primordial role, its beauty and its grandeur;

– a preoccupation with the development of society; a knowledge of the fact that the future of the world can be decided when all its problems are put before humanity in unavoidable terms, that capitalism has come to the end of its span, and that the revolution is a reality;

– a concept of the relationship between man and technology (between man and machine) which attempts a complete reversal of these relations – workers being today *in thrall to the machine* when it is a matter for them of winning so that the machine will finally appear *at the service of the man*,[89] in relation to what went before, a new, Socialist idea of the place of work and of the workers in life. From this point of view, 'populist' works, whose authors only see in the 'people' material for a more or less 'naturalistic' novel, belong to the most obsolete of the old literature; we can no longer today describe the workers solely from the outside, without bringing in the question of the socialist idea of work, as if we were describing a Canak tribe.

From here come a few other essential ideas:

– those of the relations between the individual and the collective – the contradiction, so often exploited by bourgeois philosophers, between the individual and society is on the way to being resolved; a feeling for collective life is taking shape to amplify, enrich and increase the individual;[90] we can glimpse a future in which the collective, far from restricting the individual, will assure him a complete development which will be a precondition for his own greatness; – a working-class spirit, in which are included rebellion, a critical sense, firmness of character, organisational spirit (devotion to the trade union or the party), an inclination to solidarity and internationalism, altogether all the elements of a new ethic and a new law.[91]

The proletarian humanism that is coming into existence takes up the heritage of bourgeois humanism, minus what bourgeois humanism takes in from utopianism, abstract and debilitating pacifism, false illusions about men and society, and decrepit and almost puerile idealism; we cannnot trust that 'progress' will come of its own accord, for tomorrow is really too dark; nor are we to have faith in the good will of the ruling classes, because we know that the laws of their own development exceed their control; nor should we allow pacifism at a time of great class wars which alone will allow us to put an end to capitalist suicidal wars and lead to peace through revolution; nor should we confound freedom with the development of human beings; nor should we profess the very noble but very powerless cult of 'the spirit', as if there existed a disembodied spirit soaring above human conflicts and miseries; nor should we trust in a 'revolt of conscience' which amounts to nothing unless it becomes incarnate among millions and millions of men ... But we intend to understand man, every man, in depth, to restore to him an understanding of his worth, working to disentangle modern civilisation from the barbarity of capitalism, and moving towards the future on real roads. Proletarian humanism, greater than the other[92] is true, virile, innovative and heroic.

But struggles within society, above all those of ideas, do not have the simplicity that we are accustomed to attribute to them. A struggle always has to do with association – even collaboration – interpenetration, and mutual enrichment. So the two opposing humanisms are often mixed up in the same circles, and among the same people. This interpenetration is not without its dangers for us, because we are, as we have seen, in many respects in the weaker circumstances. 'If we want to bring to the world principles of rejuvenation capable of rebuilding a completely decaying city, we must, very much like the Christians, maintain in Socialist ideology and action their completely intransigent character, and categorically refuse any invitation for us to *be incorporated*.' 'This heroic and revolutionary proletariat [...] can only accomplish its historic mission and promote an original and truly proletarian civilisation if it creates a philosophy on the same level as the great transformation of which it is the agent.' I fully subscribe to these lines by Édouard Berth,[93] on condition that by 'proletarian civilisation' he means the civilisation of free, human producers, in the fullest sense of the word, for which the working class struggles when it fights for the elimination of classes.

All these problems appear to be more complicated than they really are. Life is like that: whenever we wish to see clearly, we do see clearly. Everybody agrees about this: we can easily distinguish the true from the false, the just from the unjust, duty from advantage, and courage from servility. The oldest virtues today work for those who understand that transforming the world completely needs brave men. For them it is not a question (and what do the others matter to us?) of dreams or of profits; it is a question, in the practice of letters as in all the others, of feeling of use according to our means, to the revolution which is coming or is inevitably accomplished.

Many of the things of the present already belong to the past; even many of the things among what is being born already carry the mark of a dire past. Both of them cannot be defended. To talk about them we need the mentality of woodcutters. All that is sincere can be of use, providing it is not flabby or half-hearted. The time requires virile spirits. Its literature needs to be identified with life; it demands works that are acts, or justifications of acts, testimonies, appeals, examples ... The writer is taking his place among the millions of men on the march.

Some of them, the happiest of them because they have been the most resolute, will provide the proletariat and the mass vanguard with a literature for ardent combattants.

Notes

1. First published in 1932 in the *Cahiers bleus* series of the Librairie George Valois, and again by Maspero in 1976, from which this version has been translated. Serge describes how it came to be written in *Memoirs*, pp.262–6 (editor's note).

2. 'The Great Century' (*Grand Siècle*) refers to the 17th century, the age of Louis XIV, Racine, Molière and Descartes (translator's note).

3. Denis Diderot (1713–1784) was a philosopher of the French Enlightenment, the leader of the Encyclopaedists (editor's note).

4. François Marie Arouet de Voltaire (1694–1778) was a French philosopher famous for his opposition to obscurantism. When the Chevalier de la Barre was beheaded in July 1776 for insulting a religious procession and damaging a crucifix, Voltaire put himself at the head of the storm of public protest, and proposed that the *philosophes* show their disapproval by leaving France and emigrating to Cleves. Voltaire published *Candide* in 1759. Catherine II the Great was Tsaritsa of Russia, 1762–1796. Serge is mistaken here. It was Diderot, not Voltaire, who had the patronage of Catherine the Great. Voltaire's protector was Frederick II the Great of Prussia (editor's note).

5. Georges Sorel (*Les Illusions du progrès*, p.124 et seq.) tended not to recognise this role of the Encyclopaedists; Lenin was more fair (author's note). Georges Sorel (1847–1922) was a noted revolutionary writer with leanings towards voluntarism and syndicalism. *Les Illusions du progrès* was issued in 1908. Before the French Revolution France was constitutionally considered to consist of three estates, the clergy, the nobility, and everyone else. It was the Abbé Sieyès who pointed out in his famous pamphlet *What is the Third Estate?* (1789) that it made up the nation, though its representation in the States General mostly consisted of bourgeois, lawyers and professional men (translator's note).

6. The utter lack of interest, or even curiosity which such great bourgeois journals as *La Nouvelle Revue Française* show as regards the reader belonging to the lower classes of society has something amazing about it, and from an entirely different point of view, is even self defeating. These magazines obviously consider literature to be the monopoly of a small privileged elite. You can even feel it in their language (author's note).

7. Paul Claudel (1868–1955) was a poet, dramatist and literary critic, who later embarked upon a diplomatic career. Paul Valéry (1871–1945) was a poet, essayist and dramatic author. Jean Hippolyte Giraudoux (1882–1944), was a diplomat, writer and dramatic author. Victor Margueritte (1866–1942) was a French novelist. Henri Barbusse (1874–1935) was an influential writer who joined the Communist Party in 1923, and wrote a biography of Stalin; his *Le feu* (1916) was the most widely read novel about the First World War (translator's note).

8. Erich Maria Remarque (1898–1970) was a famous German novelist, the author of *All Quiet on the Western Front* (1929) (translator's note).

9. Jules Vallès (1832–1885), a supporter of Proudhon and the International, was a French novelist, the author of the *Jacques Vingtras* trilogy, and active in the Paris Commune (translator's note).

10. The 1921 census allows us to set out the following table for the social composition of the French population:

Active population (including foreigners)	20,000,000
Bourgeoisie	1,500,000
Middle Class (petty bourgeoisie, peasants, public employees and others)	4,500,000
Proletarians (workers, white collar workers, artisans and poor peasants)	14,000,000

(author's note).
The biblical reference is to Genesis iii, v.19 (translator's note).

11. Enlightening and amusing them: all of Paul Bourget's work is strictly didactic. In his best pages Paul Morand noticeably responds to a desire to amuse his reader. And in a slightly different sense we might well say that Gide and Proust enlighten the reader by expanding his intellectual experience (author's note). André Gide (1869–1951) was a famous left wing poet, novelist, essayist and dramatic author. He played an honourable part in the campaign to secure Serge's release from the USSR. Cf. *Memoirs*, pp.318–9; Bill Marshall, *Victor Serge: The Uses of Dissent*, Providence, 1992, pp.15, 90; Richard Greeman, 'The Victor Serge Affair and the French Literary Left', *Revolutionary History*, vol.v, no.3, Autumn 1994, pp.156–60; Susan Weissman, *Victor Serge: The Course is Set on Hope*, London, 2001, pp.162–3. For Serge's attitude to Gide, cf. Marshall, op. cit., pp.89–95. The most well-known work of Marcel Proust (1871–1922) is *A la recherche du temps perdu* (1913–1927) (translator's note).

12. I only know three of them: Vallès' *L'Insurgé*, P. and V. Margueritte's *La Commune* (1904), and Léon Cladel's *I.N.R.I.*, recently published by Librarie Valois booksellers. We should note that Vallès' work has not been republished for many years. It is very much the case that the bourgeois spirit of the book trade prevents even advanced publishers from republishing the communard, which could be an excellent undertaking. But there is much to be said on this aspect of the question. The working class parties in France take in several million voters; the different trade union organisations organise about a million members; the Socialist Party, the Communist Party and the syndicalist and libertarian groups represent altogether some hundred thousand militants – and I believe that the militant worker, with his enquiring mind, his independence of character and his active temperament, a fighter, in other words, with a feel for reality, is a human type of the highest value. Behind these formations are, the masses properly so-called, is a reservoir as vast as an ocean. There is an entire literary public ready there waiting, for which we can and must work, write and publish, an entire very capable public, if we could but know how to win its interest, and make its literature alive, this seems indisputable to me. And if its publishers have not yet appeared, that is due in the first place to the pressure exercised upon them by the bourgeois book trade, which is very touchy as regards anything that is really revolutionary. The difficulty of bringing to life working class publishing houses such as the heroic Librairie du Travail is due to their lack of resources for starting up, and perhaps even more to the unfortunate sectarian spirit of the working class organisations. Zola's abiding success shows what possibilities remain open for a popular literature, in the proletarian sense of the word (author's note) Léon Alphenian Cladel (1835–1892) was a French novelist (translator's note).

13. Boulangism takes its name from General Georges Boulanger (1837–1891), who helped suppress the Paris Commune, and later attempted to set up a right wing government in France. The Dreyfus Affair was an outbreak of virulent anti-Semitism which resulted from the unjust conviction in 1894 of a Jewish officer, Alfred Dreyfus (1859–1935) of spying for the Germans (translator's note).

14. The strengthening of the Second Republic was the June Days of 1848; the strengthening of the Third Republic was the bloody week of May 1871 (author's note). The Second Republic (1848–1852) was a brief interlude between the restored monarchy and the Second Empire; the Third Republic took power and

smashed the Paris Commune, ruling (1870–1940) until it was replaced by the Vichy regime in the Second World War (translator's note).

15. Jean Victor Griffuelhes (1874–1922) was a great strike leader elected General Secretary of the C.G.T. in 1901, who led the struggle for the 8-hour day. Jean Joseph Pouget (1860–1931), was an anarcho-syndicalist militant and publicist. Émile Pataud (1869–1935) was the General Secretary of the electricians' union, and an advocate of direct action. Georges Louis François Yvetot (1868–1942) was a typesetter and an anarcho-syndicalist militant, arrested on several occasions for his opposition to militarism (translator's note).

16. Again, in the same work by Paul Morand we find these lines: 'One day in the future [...] the Chinese and the Negroes will come to fight over the good lands with us: there will be a racial struggle for the best climates, just as there is a class struggle for the possession of wealth. If before then someone doesn't invent scientific scourges and artificial floods we can expect a number of world struggles [...] we might as well enter a monastery' (author's note). Pierre Drieu La Rochelle (1893–1945) was a French poet and novelist, who collaborated with the Nazis and committed suicide at the liberation. Henri de Montherlant (1895–1972) was a novelist and a master of French literary style. Romain Rolland was famous for his pacifism during the First World War. He was later a notorious Stalinist fellow-traveller. For Serge's relations with Rolland, cf. Bill Marshall, *Victor Serge: The Uses of Dissent*, Providence, 1992, pp.81–3 (translator's note).

17. Karl Marx, 'Afterword to the Second German Edition', *Capital*, vol.i, Moscow, 1958, pp.14–15 (translator's note).

18. I do not wish to speak ill of the novel of the couple, built as it is upon an eternal theme: but this theme must take its proper place among those that are more vast; at all moments in their existence the man and the woman depend upon social life; bourgeois literature, when it pretends to ignore this dependence, falsifies and impoverishes the image it gives us of reality; for the real world it substitutes a world as conventional as the old opera scenery. On the other hand Soviet Russian literature can take no pride in not having produced in ten years a single romantic novel worth remarking about: this only goes to show that it is not responding to all the needs of society (author's note).

19. Baedeker was a well-known series of very detailed and well-researched guidebooks to different countries popular in the 1920s; Louis Adolphe Thiers (1797–1877) was the French historian and politician who suppressed the Paris Commune and became President of the Republic (1871–1873) (translator's note).

20. A general strike in Finland was followed by a premature uprising on 27 January 1918, which was suppressed by General Mannerheim with the help of German troops, and thousands were massacred. The Hungarian Soviet Republic was formed in March 1919 and crushed by a Romanian invasion in the following August. The Spartacist uprising in Germany was smashed in January 1919, an ideal situation for seizing power was let slip during the Kapp Putsch of 1920, and further botched uprisings took place in 1921 and 1923. Cf. 'Germany 1918–23', *Revolutionary History*, vol.v, no.2, Spring, 1994. Alexander Tsankov seized power in Bulgaria in a coup in 1923 and set up a military dictatorship, and an abortive Communist insurrection failed to dislodge him. Large scale factory occupations in Italy during the 'Red Year' of 1920 failed to produce a revolutionary result, and Mussolini came to power after the March on Rome in 1922. Don Miguel Primo de Rivera seized power in a coup in 1923, and ran Spain as a military dictatorship until 1930. Workers' councils and the Schutzbund, a workers' militia, had been set up at the end of the war in Austria, but the influence of Austrian Social Democracy resulted in the formation of a bourgeois republic. A clash between the Schutzbund and the government in 1927 led to a general strike, but again this did not produce a revolutionary solution (translator's note).

21. *La Trahison des clercs* (1927) was the title of a book advocating non-commitment by Julien Benda (1867–1956), a novelist, essayist and journalist (English edition, *The Great Betrayal*, 1928) (translator's note).

22. The British General strike took place in May, 1926. The leaders of the General Council of the T.U.C. called off the strike without receiving guarantees for the miners, who were starved back to work some months later (translator's note).

23. Erich Ludendorff (1865–1937) was Quartermaster-General of the German army, and virtual dictator of Germany during 1916–8. He later marched with Hitler during the Beer Hall Putsch of 1923. Karl Liebknecht (1871–1919) was murdered by Freikorps with the connivance of the Social Democratic government during the suppression of the Spartacist uprising (translator's note).

24. 'Just as ... at an earlier period, a section of the nobility went over to the bourgeoisie ...' (Karl Marx and Frederick Engels, *The Communist Manifesto*) (author's note). (Allen and Unwin edition, 1948, p.138) (translator's note).

25. Honoré de Balzac (1799–1850) is best known for his *Comédie humaine* (1842–1848), a 17-volume collection of his novels and tales. He published *César Birotteau* in 1837. For a Marxist view of his work, cf. V. Grib, *Balzac*, New York, 1937 (translator's note).

26. Maurice Barrès (1862–1923) was a novelist, political writer, journalist and member of the French Chamber of Deputies (translator's note).

27. I am deliberately not using the words 'masses' or 'classes' here, which appear to be more exact to lovers of pseudo-Marxist schematism. The relations between intellectual circles and the categories of production are far from being so direct as imagined by simplifiers who often find nothing easier than to suppress difficulties with dogma. Obviously, this method has nothing in common with Marxist analysis (author's note).

28. Arthur Rimbaud (1854–1891) was a French poet, said by the Stalinists to have volunteered to fight for the Paris Commune (translator's note).

29. The point of view of criticism should be studied separately. A penetrating and combative criticism which does not content itself with highlighting the merits of the work, should take some time over its ideological weaknesses. Criticism of this sort seems to me to be a necessity for the development of a revolutionary literature (author's note).

30. Helen Grace Carlisle (1898–1968) published *Mother's Cry* in 1930. Magdeleine Marx Paz (1889–1973) was a French civil liberties activist, at that time supporting the struggle of the Left Opposition. Her French translation of *Mother's Cry* was published in Paris in 1934 (translator's note).

31. Constantin Meunier (1831–1905) was a notable French engraver, painter and sculptor (translator's note).

32. Friedrich Nietzsche (1844–1900) was a famous German philosopher, the author of *Thus Spoke Zarathustra* (1883–5). During his anarchist youth Serge was greatly attracted to his thought, and published 'Critical Essays on Nietzsche' in *Tierra y Libertad*, 18th December, 1917. For his influence upon Serge, cf. Bill Marshall, *Victor Serge: The Uses of Dissent*, Providence, 1992, pp.42–7 (translator's note).

33. It would be easy for them, it is true, to give birth to many bad ones – and to throttle some good ones, if circumstances allow, but this would not make up for it (author's note).

34. It is very wrong to reduce bourgeois thinking to literature, or even to philosophy; for it is neither by literature nor by philosophy that the bourgeoisie maintains its domination over the world, it is by constant activity, in line with subtle, ingenious and inventive thinking, sharpened by the desire for power with which it is connected. Which men incarnated the bourgeois thinking of Germany after the war? Writers like Heinrich Mann, Thomas Mann, Ludwig, von Unruh, and Remarque? Philosophers, like Spengler? Isn't it rather a Hugo Stinnes, a Walter Rathenau, a Helfferich, a Cuno, a Schacht, and the Hugenbergs, Thyssens, Klöckners and Krupps, who ought not to be considered as individual thinkers here, but as a thinking class represented by individuals? They pull the strings, and the ideologists set themselves to express it; and this is only one of their methods of domination. I am taking my example from Germany, where bourgeois literature lags so obviously behind the needs of the bourgeoisie, but real bourgeois thought is no worse off (author's note). Heinrich Mann (1871–1950) was a famous German novelist, who left Germany when Hitler came to power. Thomas Mann (1875–1955), his younger brother, was also a great wroter, influenced by Nietzsche and Schopenhauer. Emil Ludwig (1881–1945) was a German biographer and author of over 90 plays, novels and poems. Fritz von Unruh (1885–1970) was a former army officer who wrote books of pacifist idealism, such as *Opfergang* (1916), based upon Verdun. Oswald Spengler (1880–1936) was the author of *The Decline of the West*

(1918–22), an essay in the philosophy of history. Cf. H. Stuart Hughes, *Oswald Spengler*, 1952. Hugo Stinnes (1870–1924) was a German industrialist, often called 'the Kaiser of business', with extensive holdings in coal, steel, hotels, electricity supply, newspapers, shipping lines and banks. Walter Rathenau (1867–1922) organised Germany's war economy during the First World War, and was responsible for the economy afterwards. He was assassinated by a right-wing extremist. Karl Theodore Helfferich (1872–1924) was a banker and a supporter of the right-wing D.N.V.P., widely held responsible for the hyper-inflation in 1923. Wilhelm Carl Joseph Cuno (1876–1933) was director of the Hamburg-Amerika Line, and Chancellor of the Weimar Republic during the French invasion of the Ruhr in 1923. Hjalmar Schacht (1877–1970) was a German financial expert, who stabilised the currency at the end of 1923, and was later President of the Reichsbank and Minister for the Economy under Hitler. Alfred Hugenberg (1865–1951) was the chairman of the Krupp arms firm (1908–1918), and later leader of the right wing D.N.V.P. The Harzburg Front formed with the Nazis in 1929 greatly assisted Hitler's rise to power. Fritz Thyssen (1873–1951) was a prominent industrialist who began financing Hitler as early as 1923. Peter Klöckner (1865–1940) was a prominent German industrialist. Gustav Krupp von Bohlen und Harbach (1870–1950) was director of the Krupp works in Essen, Kiel, Magdeburg and Berlin. He played an important part in Hitler's reamarmament for the Second World War. For Serge's opinions about all these, cf. his journalistic writings on the crisis of 1923 collected together in *Witness to the German Revolution*, translated by Ian Birchall, London, 2000. Emmanuel Berl (1892–1976) was a French novelist, historian and journalist (translator's note).

35. I wrote about the Surrealists in a Soviet magazine in 1926: 'The main mistake of the Surrealists is to speak too easily of man in general, and to identify themselves, young intellectuals belonging to a petty bourgeoisie hammered by history in a bleeding capitalist country, a disturbed and debilitated bourgeois country, with modern man. This is an all too obvious egocentrism which would be ridiculous if it were not sad. The failed man, for whom suicide is the way out, to whom dreaming is an important resource and delirium a work of art, is only the result of certain limited constraints in modern France. He does not work. Millions of workers are toiling in this country, who are interested in reality, and do not dream of suicide – far from it – who prefer action to dreaming, for whom life as a word retains all its eternal powerful appeal, because they know or sense that it lies open before them to be attained' (author's note). André Breton (1896–1966) was a French poet, essayist and critic. His first *Surrealist Manifesto* was published in 1924. He later cooperated with Trotsky in writing *Towards a Free Revolutionary Art* (1938) (translator's note).

36. *Creative Evolution*, p.166 et seq. (author's note). Henri Louis Bergson (1859–1941) was a French philosopher, the author of *Time and Free Will: An Essay on the Immediate Data of Consciousness* (1888; English translation, 1910) and *Matter and Memory* (1896). Serge attended his lectures in Paris in 1909–10. For Bergson's influence upon Serge, cf. Bill Marshall, *Victor Serge: The Uses of Dissent*, Providence, 1992, pp.36–8 (translator's note).

37. Karl Marx, 'The Fetishism of Commodities and the Secret Thereof', *Capital*, Moscow 1958, vol.i, part i, chapter i, section 4, pp.71–83 (translator's note).

38. Cartesianism takes its name from the famous French philosopher and mathematician René Descartes (1596–1650), whose *Discourse on Method* was published in 1637. He is the originator of the proposition 'I think, therefore I am'. Positivism means the rejection of value judgements in social science, restricting itself to observable facts and relationships (translator's note).

39. The term 'fellow travellers' was first used for the creative writers favourable to the revolution by L. D. Trotsky (translator's note).

40. Antonio Gramsci (1891–1937) was the Italian Communist Party's major theorist, jailed by Mussolini in 1928; Umberto Terracini (1895–1983) was also a leader of the Italian Communist Party, and on the Presidium of the Comintern. He was imprisoned by Mussolini in 1926. Cf. *Memoirs*, pp.186–7 (translator's note).

41. *Les Intellectuels et la révolution*, Gallimard, 1927, p.128. I think that Pierre Naville long ago went beyond the positions of this book (author's note). Pierre Naville (1904–1993) was an early leader of the Surrealists, and of the French Trotskyists for many years. An extract from his book *Trotsky Vivant* (1975) giving his views on art

and literature appears in *Revolutionary History*, vol.vii, no.2, 1999, pp.140–45 (translator's note).

42. V. I. Lenin, 'What is to be Done?', March 1902, *Collected Works*, vol.v, Moscow, 1977, pp.375, 422 and 429 (translator's note).

43. The New Economic Policy (1921–8) introduced a free market in agricultural produce and private ownership of light industry (translator's note).

44. L. D. Trotsky, *Literature and Revolution*, Michigan U.P., 1960, pp.184–5 (translator's note).

45. Karl Marx, *The Holy Family, or, Critique of Critical Criticis*m, Moscow, 1975, pp.43–4 (translator's note).

46. L. D. Trotsky, *Literature and Revolution*, Michigan U.P., 1960, p.229 (translator's note).

47. Victor Serge, 'Is a Proletarian Literature Possible?', *Clarté*, no.lxxii, 1st March, 1925 (author's note).

48. 'On Party Policy in the Realm of Imaginative Literature', Resolution of the Central Committee of the RKP(b), 18th June, 1925, *Pravda*, 1st July, 1925. English translation, Alexander Voronsky, *Art as the Cognition of Life*, Mehring Books, Michigan 1998, pp.445–7 The resolution was written by Bukharin (translator's note).

49. *Pravda*, 24th November, 1931 (author's note).

50. Vsevolod Emilyevich Meyerhold (1874–1940) was Russia's foremost theatrical producer. His theatre was closed down, and he was tortured and shot by the NKVD. Cf. below, pp. 333–35 (translator's note).

51. Karl Marx, 'Preface to the First German Edition', *Capital*, vol.i, Moscow, 1958, p.10 (translator's note).

52. The Cheka (Extraordinary Commission for Struggle Against Sabotage and Counter-Revolution) was the Soviet state security service set up in December 1917. It was later expanded into the G.P.U./N.K.V.D. which carried out the mass murders under Stalin. For Serge's attitude to Alexei Tolstoy's defence of this, cf. *Memoirs*, pp.270–1; John Manson, 'The Carnets' in Susan Weissman (ed.), *The Ideas of Victor Serge*, *Critique*, nos.28–29, Glasgow, 1997, p.237 (translator's note).

53. Léon Werth (1878–1955) was a writer, art critic and journalist. He wrote the preface to Serge's novel *The Case of Comrade Tulayev* when it was published in Paris after his death in 1948 (translator's note).

54. Churkin, *The Shock Brigades* (author's note). Nikolai Nikolayevich Churkin (1869–1964) was a folklorist and composer, the writer of *The Liberation of Labour* (1922) (translator's note).

55. *Pravda*, 20 December, 1931 (author's note).

56. Paul Lafargue (1842–1911), Karl Marx's son-in-law, wrote *The Right to be Lazy* in Sainte-Pélagie Prison in 1883 (latest English edition, Chicago, 1975) (translator's note).

57. The first 5-year Plan (1928–32) attempted to modernise the USSR. by the methods of forced industrialisation and the militarisation of labour. Cf. Boris Souvarine, 'The Five Year Plan', in *What Became of the Revolution*, London, 2001, pp.90–129 (translator's note).

58. Henry Poulaille (1896–1980) was a prominent French essayist and novelist, who published *Daily Bread* in 1931. He played a prominent part in the campaign to release Serge from captivity in the Soviet Union. For Serge's relations with him, cf. Ian Birchall in Susan Weissman (ed.), *The Ideas of Victor Serge*, *Critique*, nos.28–29, Glasgow, 1997, pp.92–4 (translator's note).

59. As regards this title, it just shows how disadvantageous and false it is to use a military concept for production, even by hinting at it in the vocabulary. Production is not war, Socialist industrialisation is not the firing line (the term will do for capitalist industrialisation, that great devourer of human beings), and the worker is not a soldier. Production and war require different forms of organisation, different methods, and different human qualities (author's note). Alexander Yakovlevich Tairov (1885–1950) was a leading Soviet stage director (translator's note).

60. I cannot help quoting some lines by Romain Rolland here: 'Whatever the work undertaken [...] there are only two arts in the world: that which takes life as its point of departure, and that which takes convention as its point of departure'. And again: 'We have to fight bravely for truth in politics. It is no less necessary to defend it in art. The one is not distinct from the other. The source of justice is not the heart, sentimental feeling: it is intelligence, and the clarity of intelligence. The health of intelligence is important in the highest degree both for action and the Revolution' (*The Idealist Poison*, to Charles Péguy, July 1900, reprinted in *Europe*, 15th

February 1926 (author's note). Charles Péguy (1873–1914) was a poet and essayist, who ran a socialist bookshop before his rise to fame (translator's note).

61. O. Henry was the pen name of William Sydney Porter (1862–1910), the writer of *Voice of the City* (1908) and *Strictly Business* (1908); Jack London (1876–1916) is best known for his novels *Iron Heel* and *White Fang*; Joseph Conrad (Jozef Teodor Konrad Korzeniowski, 1857–1924) was a Polish writer, famous for writing *Lord Jim* (1900); Knut Hamsun (Knut Pederson, 1859–1952) was a Norwegian novelist, poet and dramatist; in *Growth of the Soil* (1920) he advocated a back-to-nature philosophy (translator's note).

62. There are different aspects of, and different values in a book. The *Conquerors* whom Malraux describes are Nietzschean dilettanti living off a revolution, who have almost nothing in common with proletarian revolutionaries. I do not wish to say that such people are not to be met with in revolutions; they take in everybody, and the part played by adventurers is not a negligible one. But today's revolutionary is Lenin's 'professional revolutionary', a 'party man', a Bolshevik, the *militant* of the Latin countries, and Garine is a thousand miles removed from such men – Malraux is completely alien to the proletarian idea of the revolution; and on closer analysis, his ideas perhaps reveal themselves to be hostile to it: very much bourgeois. But by bringing us the *feeling* of the Canton street, by revealing to us certain aspects of the Chinese masses that he has been able to see and make us see, and by the intense insight he gives us into the drama of everyday life, his book is precious; and I am not talking about its purely literary value, which is obvious (author's note). Serge was on the Committee set up by the Russian Left Opposition to investigate the failure of the Chinese Revolution, and later published his findings in France ('The Class Struggle in the Chinese Revolution', *Revolutionary History*, vol.v, no.3, Autumn 1994, pp.54–141). André Malraux (1901–1976) published the first of his novels on the Chinese Revolution, *Les conquérants*, in 1929 (English translation, *The Conquerors*, 1929 (translator's note).

63. Ludwig Feuerbach (1804–1872) was a Hegelian thinker who greatly influenced Marx (translator's note).

64. Albert Einstein (1879–1955) was the originator of the General Theory of Relativity. Christophe Friedrich Nicolai (1733–1811) was a great German novelist, historian, philosopher and literary critic, a friend of Lessing and Moses Mendelssohn (translator's note).

65. V. I. Lenin, 'Letter to A. M. Gorky', 25th February 1908, *Collected Works*, vol.xii, Moscow, 1962, p.450 (translator's note).

66. Charles Augustin Sainte-Beuve (1804–1869) was one of France's great men of letters. He dealt with the German poet Johann Wolfgang von Goethe (1749–1832) in his *Portraits allemands* (published posthumously, 1923) (translator's note).

67. Sigmund Freud (1856–1939) was a pioneer in the development of psychological method, noted for his *Studies in Hysteria* (1895). Serge studied Freud whilst he was in Vienna (*Memoirs*, p.190) (translator's note).

68. In contrast with the previous period: up until 1928 an enormous amount was translated (author's note).

69. One critic, incidentally, in the Moscow *Literary Gazette* of 26 January 1932, described Jean Giono as an ideologist of the *kulaks* (rich peasants) (!), which relieves him of the burden of any further proof …(author's note). Jean Giono (1895–1970) was a French novelist and dramatic author (translator's note).

70. By way of an example I only wish to notice three interesting books on industrialisation: *Thirst*, by Leonid Leonov, *The Volga Falls to the Caspian Sea*, by Boris Pilnyak, and *Hydrocentral*, by Marietta Shaginyan (author's note). Marietta Sergeyevna Shaginyan (1888–1982) wrote *Hydrocentral* in 1930–1, which was translated into French by Serge and published in Paris in 1933, even though he had a low opinion of her work (*Memoirs*, p,272). She had earlier been criticised in *Na Postu* for her book *The Adventure of a Lady from Society* (1923) (translator's note).

71. The National Government which made war on the Paris Commune sat at Versailles, and the term 'Versaillais' came to mean any counter-revolutionary. Before they could mobilise their army against the Commune, Eudes and Duval, who were Blanquists, unsuccessfully tried to persuade the Central Committee of the Commune to attack the National Government (translator's note).

72. *Les illusions du progrès*, p.118 (author's note).
73. Robert Louzon (1882–1976) was a French anarcho-syndicalist who joined the French Communist Party, which he left along with Monatte and Rosmer when they were expelled for supporting the Left Opposition. He edited *La Révolution prolétarienne* from 1925 onwards. Cf. Robert Louzon, *China: Three Thousand Years of History, Fifty Years of Revolution*, London, 1998, pp.i–ii (translator's note).
74. 'Scholies', in *La Nouvelle Revue française*, 1st November, 1929 (author's note).
75. Karl Marx, 'Address of the Central Authority to the Communist League', April 1850, in Max Eastman (ed.), *Capital and other Writings of Karl Marx*, New York, 1932, p.367 (translator's note).
76. L'Abbaye was the name adopted by a group of 'Unanimist' writers, including Jules Romains, the pen name of Louis Henri Jean Farigoule (1885–1972), René Arcos (1881–1959), Luc Durtain (1881–1959), and Vildrac, the pen name of Charles Messager (1882–1971). They later supported the Committee for the Liberation of Victor Serge after his imprisonment in the USSR. (translator's note).
77. Henry Poulaille, *Nouvel Âge Littéraire*. One of the merits of this book is to bring together a host of different texts on our subject, almost impossible to find, of which some are remarkable, for example, the pages of Martinet on class art (author's note). Poulaille's literary manifesto, *The New Literary Age* was published in 1930. Marcel Martinet (1887–1944) was a writer, trade unionist and cultural editor of *L'Humanité* in 1921–4, who later supported the committee formed to secure Serge's release from the USSR. For Martinet's views on proletarian culture, cf. Ian Birchall, 'Des Marteaux matériels', in *French Studies*, vol.xliv, no.3, July 1990, pp.303–5, 308 and 'Proletarian Culture', in Susan Weissmann (ed.), *The Ideas of Victor Serge*, *Critique* nos.28–9, Glasgow, 1997, pp.79–80, 89–91. Something to look forward to is George Paizis' *Marcel Martinet: The Forgotten Revolutionary*, due to be published by Philomel Publishers in 2005 (translator's note).
78. Pierre Joseph Proudhon (1809–1865) was a French social theorist, one of the founders of Anarchism, and author of *The Philosophy of Poverty* (1846), against which Marx wrote his *Poverty of Philosophy* (1847) (translator's note).
79. Camille Berth, called Édouard Darville (1875–1939) was a journalist and theoretician of the workers' movement (translator's note).
80. Mathieu Jules Bazile, called Guesde (1845–1922) was the leader of the 'Impossibilists', the left wing of French Socialism in the 1900s, but went over to the right and supported the First World War (translator's note).
81. Jean Jacques Élisée Reclus (1830–1905) was a French geographer, sociologist and theoretician of anarchism who was a member of the 1st International and took part in the Paris Commune. Serge had been friendly with him during his youth, when Reclus was a professor in Brussels. On Serge's attitude to Reclus, cf. Bill Marshall, *Victor Serge: The Uses of Dissent*, Providence, 1992, pp.34, 170 (translator's note).
82. François Noël 'Gracchus' Babeuf (1760–1797) was the leader of the Conspiracy of Equals during the French Revolution. Louis Auguste Blanqui (1805–1881) advocated the seizure of power by the working class by a conspiratorial elite. Cf. Maurice Dommanget, *Blanqui*, Paris, 1924; Alan B. Spitzer, *The Revolutionary Theories of Louis Auguste Blanqui*, New York, 1957. Louis Eugène Varlin (1839–1871), a bookbinder, and a supporter of Proudhon and the International, was shot for the part he played in the Paris Commune. A massive strike by the silk weavers of Lyons in 1831–4 led to riots and the erection of barricades in the streets. The army was drafted in and over 350 people were killed in the fighting. The political club of the skilled workers of the Faubourg Saint-Antoine was the backbone of the uprising of the Parisian workers in 1848–9, until it was smashed by Cavaignac's troops. The same district was equally combative in the rooftop fighting of 1830 and the Paris Commune (translator's note).
83. Jules Vallès (1832–1885) was a novelist and propagandist, the editor of the *Cri du peuple*, who was active in the Paris Commune; Ernest Coeurderoy (1826–1862) was a French republican, Socialist and anarchist who opposed authority and advocated internationalism in numerous books; George Darien (1862–1921) was a French radical writer; Zo d'Axa was the pen name of Alphonse Galland (1864–1930), a pamphleteer and magazine editor; *Père peinard* was the name of a militant workers' journal founded by Pouget, Albert Thierry

(1881–1915) was a teacher and moralist who supported the struggle of the working class (translator's note).

84. Jean Jaurès (1859–1914) was the leader of the French Socialist Party in parliament, a noted orator, and an opponent of the war. He was assassinated by a fanatic just before it broke out (translator's note).

85. Let us take note of the date when this happened. J.-M. Guyau wrote in 1897: 'According to certain aesthetes, such as MM. Ruskin and Sully-Prudhomme, human industry will become more and more incompatible with art'. Reflections follow that 'there is little that is aesthetic about iron roads', otherwise called railways ... (*Les Problèmes de l'aesthétique contemporaine*) (author's note). Jean-Marie Guyau (1854–1888) was a famous French philosopher. John Ruskin (1819–1900) was an English writer on art and culture. Sully-Prudhomme was the pen name of René François Armand Prudhomme (1839–1907), a French philosophical poet. Zola published *Germinal* in 1885 (translator's note).

86. Hamp brought out *Marée fraîche* in 1907, *Cantique des cantiques* in 1922, the 2nd edition of *Chercheurs d'or* in 1920, *La Laine* in 1931, and *Le Rail* in 1912 (translator's note).

87. Russian capitalists repeatedly closed down or sabotaged industry in order to overthrow the Bolshevik government during the Civil War; much the same happened in Germany during the hyperinflation of 1923. Cf. Victor Serge, *Year One of the Russian Revolution*, London, 1972, pp.92–4; *Witness to the German Revolution*, London, 2000, p.58 (translator's note).

88. Pierre Hamp published *Le Lin* in 1924 (translator's note).

89. Let us note the feeling that inspires books such as that of Georges Duhamel, *Scènes de la vie future*; I see in them more than a protest of the old humanism against Americanism, the ultimate in capitalist mechanisation. I greatly liked a novel by Luc Durtain, *Ma Kimbell*, because the relationship between man and machine is put there in the happiest light: here we see that a motor bike can provide happiness for the man who rides it, how the machine increases human possibilities, with what power and with what faithfulness it can serve him – and how he must know how to understand it (author's note).

90. Walt Whitman is the magnificent innovator in this respect – I have already referred to the work of the Unanimists. The little book of Dominique Braga, *5,000*, made an impression on me some years ago, by the strength with which he discovered association in competition, and by the community of existence that he revealed between the champion, his rivals and the stadium crowd (author's note).

91. Examples: *Le Pain quotidien* by Henri Poulaille is like an authentically proletarian work, obviously not just because working-class speech is reproduced with so much care or on account of the subject, which is entirely confined to a time in the life of some working class families (the subject, in this language, could be dealt with in a completely bourgeois manner), but on account of the *character* of the carpenter Magneux. I can say as much for the Collignon of Tristan Rémy (in *L'Ancien Tonnelier*). The books of Panaït Istrati, praising revolt and brotherhood, are ours because of this. I note in a little-known novel by Louis Hémon, *Battling Malone, pugiliste*, class feeling expressed with rare force (author's note). Tristan Rémy was the pen name of Rémy Despré (1897–1977), a French writer, historian and journalist. Louis Hémon (1880–1913) published *Battling Malone, pugiliste* in 1925 (translator's note).

92. Bourgeois humanism remains that of the white race. Only its most advanced representatives show an all-embracing sympathy towards the coloured races; even more is this a sign of progress towards proletarian humanism (author's note).

93. *Guerre des États ou Guerre des classes*, pp.155, 160 (author's note).

Remarks on Proletarian Literature[1]

Sincerity

How do we define a proletarian writer, if it is not by proletarian thinking? And as regards this thinking, it is itself defined every day by the struggle. It is all too obvious that a man can be authentically a proletarian in origin, to have spent years in the workshop, deal adequately with subjects drawn from factory life, and still be only a completely bourgeois writer. The class struggle supplies a mass of examples of the crossing over that allows the ablest men from the working class to become absorbed by the bourgeoisie, while an entire elite educated by the ruling classes came to place itself at the service of the proletariat. Noske, Mussolini and Hitler are of working-class origin;[2] Marx, Lenin, Lafargue, Guesde, Reclus, Jaurès and Sorel – only to mention those who are dead and as different as you could wish for – were of bourgeois or petty bourgeois origin. There is even crossing over in literature, though with not so many great names on the side of the proletariat, for refugees from the bourgeoisie generally prefer more direct revolutionary activity to that of the writer. I am emphasising this fact to refute the assertion, largely unfounded, according to which working-class correspondents for journals will be called upon to play an essential role in the formation of proletarian literature. Even in the USSR, where they have nonetheless profited from a privileged position for years, their work – the importance of which I would not dream of underestimating – has still not trained real writers, nor produced outstanding works. This is because there is a writer's craft as difficult to master as any other, and which requires at least as much of an apprenticeship. When you have more or less successfully gone through this apprenticeship, you cease to be a worker, and become an intellectual. And the relations between worker and newspapers can only play a fairly secondary role in training a writer, that of a stimulant, to begin with. The revolutionary press carries out too narrow a task (and all too often does it too badly) for it not to have a bad influence on its correspondents who, showing a talent for expressing themselves, were too exclusively subjected to its influence. The writer needs understanding and empathy hardly called for by minor journalism; nothing is more essential for him than intuition and imagination, qualities which militant journalism normally dispenses with.

There are doubtless among manual workers a host of talents which the new literature must tirelessly attempt to awaken; let us nonetheless avoid falling into a 'workerism' that has nothing to do with proletarian thinking. The working-class revolution does not have to flatter the workers; on the contrary, with an obstinacy that is a precondition for its success, it asks them to look clearly into and among themselves, as into the world, not to cover up their real weaknesses, and to know how to put into operation all their assistance and their energy in producing, defending and struggling for culture.

Workers who want to write can give proletarian literature precious support simply by saying what they have to say about their life experience. They should do this with the sole concern of being absolutely truthful and absolutely sincere, without fear of making mistakes, without imitating books, and without drawing their inspiration from learnt positions; they should know that human experience, expressed without regard for art or ideology, can attain an incomparable value and, by the truthfulness of a document founded on lived experience, attain the perfection of a new genre.

... Without regard for ideology, I said, which means without a preconceived desire to fall into line with a slogan or apply propaganda directives. Any such intention would unavoidably lead them to force certain notes, falsify others, and fall into an agitational stereotype with all the weight of their literary inexperience. The spontaneity of their attempt would be irreparably compromised. Let us be clearly understood. We are asking every worker to have the convictions of his class, to be a militant, and to throw himself into that revolutionary activity which, by leading to the liberation of mankind, gives a new meaning to life; we are asking him to think about the problems of Socialism, to distinguish between our groups, to weigh up and judge our theses, to educate, and in this way, by constant activity, to form and maintain the class feeling of the proletariat. He must therefore write with all his conviction, but also with all the spontaneity of his being.

It is a question of avoiding the most boring genres. Propaganda has its own requirements, about which, to be honest, we can only be inflexible. The requirements of literary expression are very different. Propaganda comes out of doctrine and tactics. Literary work comes from living experience and inner life. The former is the overwhelminly utilitarian product of the intelligence and will of the class. The latter, more detached, is the product, to a great extent spontaneous, of a throng of conscious and unconscious aspirations that have passed through the prism of the individual. Proletarian literature will only add a crucial element to the spiritual life of the working class (and hence provide invaluable assistance to the diffusion of proletarian thinking, i.e., to revolutionary propaganda in the best sense of the word) if, keeping itself well clear of all the shackles that will be suggested to it, it only imposes on the writer the rule of absolute sincerity towards his comrades and himself.

Solidarity

The strength of the working-class movement resides in its militants. The majority know how to express themselves – obviously, not in literature – often far better – when it is a question of what they know well; their trade, their industry, their trade union, their party or their region. There is not one who has not been active in struggles, on various grounds. Why have they not written about what they have experienced? For them it would often be a new way of continuing the work. They should always be on guard against two dangers: those of literary imitation and of agitation. Express yourself with simplicity, truth and sincerity, look for the finest exactitude, not 'make literature', steer clear of fine phrases, and not go in for romancing. Leave the novel to the writers whose trade it is. Be on guard against 'arranging things' in a sectarian spirit, group interest or desire for agitation. Tell yourself that you are one who is bearing witness, with all his passionate conviction, and also with all his honesty; take on board the idea that it is only in this way that the testimony will obtain the maximum effect.

Some militants are first-rate writers, and it is noteworthy that no one has dreamed of asking for a more lasting contribution from them than contemporary or historical writings and, in the same way, to proletarian literature. Could not a Pierre Monatte,[3] if he found the time to turn back from the road he has gone over, give us 'things seen' in his exemplary style that are much more attractive than imaginative works?

A novelist's testimony, very much subject to the same requirements, is of a different type, since he calls upon fiction to express human truth that is general and exploratory rather than documentary. I freely admit that we cannot, in our time, exclude from the arsenal of propaganda the 'hundred percent ideological' novel with a message, as I often try to say with great fairness, – I even hope that in the end it will come about that this sort of production of works of real value becomes fairly common in two or three countries. But let us beware of counting on it. Nothing would be more disastrous for proletarian literature than encouraging the creation of mediocre works which would only have an ephemeral existence with reference to the message and support of organisations. The proletarian novel needs real talent, good hard work, burning convictions, deep feelings and spontaneity; if it has a wealth of these, the rest – and that will be what the critics discover when analysing it and will call ideology – will come to it as a plus.

The revolutionary proletariat is split up between half a dozen tendencies and undercurrents. Inspired as it is by feeling rather than doctrine, and expressing opinions and ideas that are common to all the revolutionary tendencies – solidarity, rebellious spirit, organisational feeling, and the desire for social change – literary work does not reflect this division, but it can neither ignore it nor fail to feel it. It would be all the more stupid to go over again on the literary level party struggles that have often become demoralising, ending up with the unforgiveable mistake of allowing the same weapons to be used against us – let us say, for example, the same forms of polemic – as in the class struggle. Fraternal discussion, which is so necessary for forming proletarian thinking, would then give way to animosities which would at times make all conversation impossible between men who were basically devoted to the same cause. We see deep clefts yawning between working comrades. It would be more than stupid to set up groups of proletarian writers to give or refuse appointments, pronounce excommunications, to lay down commands, or to print diatribes ... And if a few people want to start out on this path, the most elementary wisdom dictates that we should firmly ignore their pathetic antics. Do we really want to create, defend and enrich a literature that will be ours? That means forming a milieu favourable for it to grow, a milieu in which the severity of criticism, the firmness of character and convictions, doctrinal intransigence and comradeship will help to shape both men and works. In a word, it means that solidarity must win out over division.

Leningrad, April, 1932   Victor Serge

Notes

1. Translated from *Monde*, no.206, 14 May, 1932 (translator's note).
2. Gustav Noske (1868–1946) was the right wing German Social Democrat who organised the suppression of the Spartacist revolt and was responsible for the murder of Luxemburg and Liebknecht. Serge is labouring a point here, since Hitler's father was a customs official, and whilst Mussolini's father was a worker, his mother was a schoolteacher (translator's note).
3. Pierre Monatte (1881–1960) was a proof-reader, a pioneer syndicalist, and an opponent of the First World War. Examples of his revolutionary journalism frequently appeared in *La Vie Ouvrière* (translator's note).

Part Two

A Chronicle of Intellectual Life in Soviet Russia

Chapter One[1]

We are beginning this section today, in which our readers will be kept in touch with the changes in ideas that are going on in Russia. In this first study our collaborator Victor Serge supplies an overview of intellectual activity in this country, that has for five years been cut off from the rest of the world.

No country since the dawn of European civilisation has been so harshly dealt with by all the others as Russia has. For some years to kill off the revolution the civilised world has sought Russia's destruction, and consequently the destruction of Russian thinking as well. Months went by in 1919 without a British or French magazine getting through to the land of Tolstoy. From 1918 to the end of 1921 there was no postal communication of any sort between Russia and the rest of the world. From 1918 to 1921 no book, no magazine and no product of European or American thinking came into Russia – unless by subterfuge or in exceptional circumstances. The blockade has created a void – a deadly one – around Russian thinking.

It has killed it off in quite other ways. Schools, universities, writers, the press and bookshops are short of paper, pencils, ink, the lot. There is not always even one pencil for an entire class of pupils. There is *almost never* any wood for heating, and in winter, whether it be for the writer or student (in cold averaging between 20 and 25 degrees), there is rarely any light during the evening to be able to read. Typhus, exhaustion and famine are decimating the Russian people, striking down above all those that are weakest and least able to survive, the children and the intellectuals ... (those that were most energetic and the strongest were falling on the battlefields of the civil war).

1919 and 1920 were years of deadly suffering. But whatever the darkness enfolding it, thought among the revolutionary people never failed for a minute. At the most difficult times in the civil war, when famine raged in the two capitals, research was kept up in the universities, discussion carried on in the workers' clubs, enthusiastic verses were publicly recited in the *Proletcult*, and writing went on. Writing was carried out by candlelight in ice cold rooms, hands numb with cold, on an empty stomach. Life was lived to the full. You thought deeply, because you had the obstinate desire to grasp and understand things. These things have to be remembered before we start casting a quick eye over Russia's intellectual life: the crime committed as regards the country, its terrible sufferings, and its unconquerable will to resist. They put its intellectual work in sharp relief.

This work was never cut off. But starting from the summer of 1921, when relations with Europe were picking up a bit again, and the civil war was ending, it has continued under slightly improved conditions. In 1922, after over a year of the New Economic Policy, of free trade and business, in other words, intellectual life was resumed with intense activity. We will only examine it in this article in a very summary fashion, in order to give a general overview of it. Let us say straight off that the mass of facts upon which we have to throw light overwhelms us. On this occasion we will not interest ourselves in the intellectual life of the Russian emigration, which itself is abstruse and relatively intense, for the only Russia that is really alive and matters is obviously the Russia of the revolution.

*   *   *   *   *

At first sight the Russian daily press appears to be very poor. It consists of no more than three daily papers in Moscow, the Communist Party's *Pravda* (*The Truth*), the Soviet's *Izvestia* (*The News*), and the Supreme Council of the Economy's *Ekonomicheskaya Zhizn* (*Economic Life*). We may well deplore the fact that the present hard times do not allow better and more varied information for the Soviet capital; but such as it is, sober and apparently one-sided, the soviet press is indubitably far superior to the mainstream press of the capitalist countries, whose freedom is always only that of the Northcliffes, the Bunau-Varillas and the Jean Dupuys,[2] and any variation in outlook that of their competitors. There is no advertising in the Soviet press, no reports paid for by foreign governments, no false information leaked by politicians or financiers, no sensational news items to appeal to the baser instincts of a degenerate public, no serial stories directed at poor people's stupidity in order to encourage it, and no wordy exchanges between people intending to influence public opinion ... But it is constantly preoccupied with teaching propaganda, self-criticism and revolutionary information. In each number there are three or four weighty and serious articles dealing with Socialism, intellectual life and production, and some pages about the factory, the working woman, young people and literature, with the keen collaboration of all the personnel of the revolution. And above all there is one noteworthy thing: how continual and severe the self-criticism of this press is, which tirelessly denounces the evils, abuses and mistakes of the transitional epoch.

The magazine press is very rich. In July–August it amounted in Moscow to no fewer than 53 journals (weeklies, monthlies and quarterlies) (2 bibliographical, 3 literary and artistic, 5 scientific, 15 economic and trade union, 11 military and 7 Communist), 8 in the provinces, and 16 in Petrograd. We should mention *Soviet Law*; the journal of R.I.L.U.; *Proletarian Student*; *Under the Banner of Marxism*;[3] *Military Science and the Revolution*; two important bibliographical magazines, *The Press and the Revolution* (Moscow) and *The Book and the Revolution* (Petrograd); two journals dealing with religious matters, *The Church and the Revolution* and *Science and Religion*; *Red Virgin Soil* (*Krasnaya Nov*), an important literary journal, *The New East*, published by the Oriental Studies Department of the Academy of Sciences, *The Bulletin of Foreign Literature*, five periodicals dealing with the history of the revolution (*Proletarian Revolution*, published by the Party, the semi-Menshevik *Voice of the Past*, *Prison and Exile*, the organ of the Former Political Prisoners, and *The Past*, published by the historian Shchegolev[4]), three organs of the Communist Youth, three artistic journals, fifteen specialist scientific journals published by the State Publishing House, and several economic magazines ... And we should note the especial attention devoted to bibliography, revolutionary history and economic life in Russia. A Russian magazine rarely has less than 100 pages, and the most important monthly or quarterly ones have between 300 and 400 pages each.

War Communism attempted the difficult policy of nationalising the book trade. The New [Economic] Policy has allowed private publishing houses to reopen. It has not meant that much more has been published, or even much better. But in view of the extremely precarious economic situation, an enormous amount of what sort of new books have been published?

I do not think that there is any other country in Europe where translations of foreign literature enjoy so much favour. We might mention among the more recent, M. Martinet's *La Nuit*,[5] translated into verse by the poet Serge

Gorodetsky;[6] R. Rolland's *Liluli*,[7] translated by the poet V. Briusov; the tales of Henri de Régnier,[8] translated by the poet Kuzmin;[9] Victor Hugo (*Quatre-vingt-treize*[10]), Upton Sinclair,[11] Walt Whitman, Camille Lemonnier,[12] Zola, B. Kellerman,[13] Jack London ... Kipling[14] ... Barbusse's *Le Couteau entre les dents*,[15] Pierre Brizon's *L'Histoire du Travail*,[16] and recent books by Keynes[17] and Norman Angell[18] have all come out. Finally, important scientific translations have been made, such as William James' *Psychology*.[19] On the occasion of Feuerbach's centenary the State Publishing House announced the appearance of his complete works, something that nobody in France has ever dreamed of doing.

Here are a few figures to summarise the production of the State Publishing House alone. Last March the State Publisher brought out in Moscow seventy-four works printed in 1,209,000 copies of about the size of six printer's sheets each. The press run of a book brought out by the State Publisher is rarely less than 10,000. The Academy of Sciences, the War Commissariat and the Cooperative Centre also have important publication services. There are also fifty private publishing houses. Sytin, the Russian 'bookselling king', has set up in business again.[20]

★　★　★　★　★

A quick glance over the range of new books will allow us to get to know what are the subjects that interest Russian thinking the most in the aftermath of the social revolution.

The complete works of Marx and Engels have been republished, as have those of Lenin, of which the fourteenth volume which has now appeared, dedicated to the interval between the two revolutions of March and October 1917, will remain a historic document of prime importance. The *Koloss* publishing house of the Left SRs in Petrograd has published SR classics by Lavrov and Mikhailovsky.[21] But among the great precursors of the revolution it is Bakunin[22] who is the main subject of passionate studies on the part of Communists. I. Steklov[23] has devoted a monumental biography to him which will have over a thousand pages when it is completed. V. Polonsky[24] is publishing a book on Bakunin's youth. The poet C. Fedin is writing a play, *Bakunin in Dresden*. Finally, Bakunin's *Confession* has appeared.[25] Professor Illinsky,[26] Vyacheslav

Polonsky and the anarchist writers Grossman-Roschin (*The Decline of a Great Soul*, Lectures[27]) and Borovoy[28] are commenting on it and explaining it with passion and fervour. Armand Ross ('Sazhin'[29]), one of Bakunin's last companions in struggle, is preparing his *Reminiscences*.

The history of the French Revolution and of the Paris Commune, widely popularised by a good hundred translations, has just been added to by several original works: Angelica Balabanova's *The Struggle against Hunger under the French Revolution*,[30] Dzhivelegov's *The Armies of the Revolution*,[31] I. Stepanov's *The Paris Commune and the Tactics of the Proletarian Revolution*,[32] and N. Lukin's *The Paris Commune*.[33] These last two works are above all important for pioneering the application of today's revolutionary Marxist point of view to the study of the events of 1871.

Communist theory is widely debated in the journals. But we should also note in this sphere the appearance of N. Bukharin's *Historical Materialism*.[34]

The thought of Kropotkin, who died in voluntary exile at Dimitrovo after three years' silence,[35] is very much alive. We should note his posthumous work, *Ethics*, which is based upon the model of *Mutual Aid*.[36] The magazine *The Past* (Petrograd) is devoting a volume of *Reminiscences* to him. The Kropotkin Committee and the Anarcho-Syndicalist bookshop of *Golos Truda* are publishing collections of articles devoted to his memory. His work has been added to by a study written in 1918 on *The Revolutionary Ideal in the Revolution*.[37]

Present day Russia has a cult of its great dead, and this is a psychological trait that is worth bearing in mind. Russia never wearies of examining their thought in greater depth, of studying their lives, with a burning desire for the truth. Of the new books that have come out in the course of these last few months, four are devoted to Korolenko, eleven to our great classical poet Pushkin, nine to the poet Nekrasov,[38] who was the first to express the suffering of the Russian people, six to Tolstoy, five or six to Dostoyevsky and as many to Alexander Blok.[39] Of these new contributions, some are of real value. The critic Chukovsky[40] has studied the life and work of Nekrasov in a totally scientific spirit. Paul Biriukov, N. N. Gusev and Victor Chertkov have provided reminiscences of Tolstoy, whose friends and followers they were.[41] V. Veresaev[42] and B. Eichenbaum have both portrayed him, the one as *Living Life*, and the other as *The Young Tolstoy*. A year has hardly gone by since Alexander Blok had passed away and already Chukovsky, André Biely and Beketova[43] have left a lasting memorial of him in their works.

Concerning the history of the Russian Revolution, L. Trotsky has published *1905*,[44] and the Socialist Revolutionary Mstislavskii *Five Days*, a moving account of the great days of 1917.[45] A publisher is bringing out the memoirs of Martov and Chernov.[46] Nor is the military art unrepresented by original works, such as N. Frunze, *New Military Doctrines*.[47] Bernhardi has just been translated[48] (Jaurès' *L'Armée nouvelle*[49] came out in 1919, at the height of the Civil War).

I will say no more about the poets: there are too many of them. Poetic production during the last quarter amounts to no less than some fifty booklets, but it does not appear to have added much to the heritage of contemporary Russian poetry. The criticism of poetry is much more innovative: there is the *Opoyaz* circle set up in Petrograd by V. Shklovsky (*The Development of the Subject in Poetry*) and B. Eichenbaum (*Sounds in Russian Verse*)[50] to apply scientific methods to the study of poetry.

Literature is being reborn. This is to such an extent that *Pravda* has set up a literary page and assigned as editor to it an old revolutionary literary figure, George Ustinov,[51] and in it Trotsky devotes to our writers some extensive pieces written in his best hand ... Space prevents me from giving here more than a few names of the newcomers whose talent asserts itself with undeniable vigour: B. Pilnyak (*Ivanda-Maria*), Vsevolod Ivanov (*Armoured Train no.14-69*), I. Slezkin (*Famine*) and A. Aroseyev.[52] It is a literature as extraordinary as the men themselves, who have gone through fire, cold, famine, typhus, the White Terror and the Red Terror, and who understand the whole torment of the revolution – and all its greatness. It is realistic, brutal, vivid and truthful ... Thanks to it, in any case, we have a literature that is powerfully *up-to-date*.

*   *   *   *   *

One small fact shows us with what careful interest European thinking is followed in Russia. Is the French reader acquainted with Spengler? I very much doubt it. The 'boche' thinker, whose work (*The Decline of the West*[53]) has given rise in Central Europe to an interest comparable to that once provoked by the rise of Nietzsche, seems to have remained unknown to a learned public among whom even Einstein has encountered disparagers. But in Russia, on the other hand, Oswald Spengler's thinking has evoked a powerful echo. A group of mystics (Berdiayev[54]) welcomes it with joy. Our comrades Pyatakov (who was in charge of the Revolutionary Tribunal in Moscow in the trial of the SRs[55]) and Preobrazhensky[56] have subjected it to severe criticism.

A country's intellectual life needs many centres where it can concentrate. In Russia, the paper shortage (the results of which were so severely felt that the Academy of Sciences has until now been unable to publish important new research) and the need for collective life springing from the years of shortage and blockade have gone towards giving a particularly intense vitality to groupings and organisations.

The number is as extensive as the variety of them. Workers' Faculties (*Rabfaks*) have just been added to the old universities, set up to make higher education accessible to workers who have only an elementary education. They are teaching at the moment 30,000 young workers. Alongside them are at work the Communist Universities of Moscow (Sverdlov[57]), Petrograd, Omsk, etc., which in two years are training revolutionary thinkers expert in the use of the Marxist dialectic, matured by the experience of fifty years' struggle. Finally, the Party is covering the country with a network of Communist schools (two levels of them), clubs and study circles, and at the top of this teaching set-up the Moscow Socialist Academy is applying itself to training highly qualified teaching personnel. This vast network of institutions was wholly created by the revolution and has been added to the old higher educational institutions of which not one, to my knowledge, has disappeared.

The learned societies, which did not stop working, have for a year now been moving to resume their normal level of activity. Conferences (of Medecine, Surgery, Egyptology and pure and applied Chemistry) have met. Scientific expeditions are radiating out from Moscow into the heart of the Pamirs and as far as the Arctic circle. The Academy of Sciences is sending geologists and zoologists to Mongolia. The Geographical Institute is exploring the Kara Sea. The Central Observatory is setting up stations in the Arctic Ocean. The Geographical Society is exploring the Malyguine Straits in the Siberian far north. An anthropological commission is studying Russia's industrial centres.

The literary circles in the capitals are grouped around the Press House, the

Society of Book-Lovers, the Bibliographical Society, the Bibliographical Research Centre, the (Moscow) Journalists' Institute, the Arts House, the Literary House, the Art Historical Institute, the (Petrograd) Living Voice Institute, and the scholarly and *proletcult* centres ... Present day literary circles, or at least one of them, have acquired a renown that seems to be well-deserved: that of the Serapion Brothers, a literary fraternity formed in Petrograd by the novelist Zamyatin *(Short Stories,* an *Essay on Herbert Wells*[58]), Zoshchenko, Lunts,[59] Pilnyak and Ivanov.

Patient and enthusiastic brains are at work even in towns lost in the depths of the steppes of immense Siberia. In Tomsk, Krasnoyarsk and Irkutsk the archives of the Decembrists are being subjected to study. Let us take one statistic: on the Yenissei 38 books were published in 1921 and 114 in 1920, and 7 journals have appeared there. In European Russia the State Booksellers have branches in Penza, Ryazan, Homel, Nizhni-Novgorod, Saratov and Odessa. The Soviets have their own publishing services in Smolensk and Tver. *A Museum Journal* comes out in Kazan that is known throughout Russia. A philosophical society has been set up in Rostov ...

★   ★   ★   ★   ★

... Is this factual round-up, however incomplete it may be, not already too long and too detailed? I hope that it will be enough to show to an impartial reader what enormous intellectual work is being accomplished in the country of the revolution – while it is being tormented by its brother countries – and all that is valuably new of what this work contains.

I will try in my next study to fill in the gaps of this one by showing a close-up of the new, revolutionary thinking in this intellectual life – as well as the old, conservative and reactionary thinking, struggling to survive. Because it is this struggle at present that makes up the real drama in Russian thinking.

Notes

1.   Translated from *Clarté*, 1922, pp.6–8 (translator's note).
2.   All these were famous manipulators of public opinion. Alfred Harmsworth, Baron Northcliffe (1865–1922) was the owner of *The Daily Mail, The Sunday Dispatch* and *The Daily Mirror*. Philippe-Jean Bunau-Varilla (1859–1940) engineered a nationalist uprising in Panama, which then appointed him Minister

Plenipotentiary, in which position he signed an agreement with the USA assuring American control over the cutting of the Panama Canal. Jean Dupuy (1844–1923) was a French right-wing politician and adventurer instrumental in the takeover of Vietnam (translator's note).

3. The journal *Under the Banner of Marxism* was set up in 1922 at the insistence of Vagarchak Ter-Vaganyan (translator's note)

4. Pavel Eliseyevich Shchegolev (1877–1931) wrote several books on the Decembrists and put together several documentary collections on the fall of the old regime (translator's note).

5. Marcel Martinet's *La Nuit* was published by Éditions Clarté in Paris in 1921 (translator's note).

6. Sergei Mitrofanich Gorodetsky (1884–1967) was a poet and a co-founder of the Poets' Guild and the Acmeist movement (translator's note).

7. Romain Rolland's *Liluli*, a 'farce tragique', was produced in 1919 (translator's note).

8. Henri François Joseph de Régnier (1864–1936) published his *Contes à soi-même* in Paris in 1894 (translator's note).

9. Mikhail Alexeyevich Kuzmin (1872–1936) was a poet, playwright and literary critic (translator's note).

10. Victor Hugo (1802–1885), the famous novelist, published *Quatre-vingt-treize* in 1874. The English edition, *Ninety-Three*, came out in the same year (translator's note).

11. Upton Sinclair (1878–1968) was a famous American novelist (translator's note).

12. Camille Lemonnier (1864–1913) was a French writer (translator's note).

13. Bernhard Kellermann (1879–1951) was a painter, writer and journalist, best known for his novel *Der Tunnel* (1913), which was translated into English as *The Tunnel* (1915). He became a prominent member of the Cultural League in East Germany after the Second World War (translator's note).

14. Rudyard Kipling (1865–1936) was a prominent English writer (translator's note).

15. Barbusse published his *Le Couteau entre le dents: aux intellectuels*, in Paris in 1921 (translator's note).

16. Pierre Brizon (1878–1923) published his *Histoire du travail et des travailleurs* in Paris in 1906 (translator's note).

17. John Maynard Keynes (1883–1946) was a British economist. His most famous book dealing with this period is his *Economic Consequences of the Peace* (1920) (translator's note).

18. Sir Ralph Norman Angell (1872–1967) was a pacifist before the First World War, famous for *The Great Illusion* (1910). During this time he wrote copiously in support of the League of Nations, as well as *Must Britain Travel the Moscow Road?* (London, 1926), an answer to Trotsky's *Where is Britain Going?* (translator's note).

19. William James (1842–1910) was an American psychologist and philosopher. His *Principles of Psychology* was published in New York in 1890 (translator's note).

20. Ivan Dmitriyevich Sytin (1851–1934) was a Russian publisher of Pushkin, Gogol and Tolstoy, especially active in educational publishing (translator's note).

21. Peter Lavrovich Lavrov (1823–1900) was a journalist and philosopher who supported the Narodniks; Nikolai Constantinovich Mikhailovsky (1842–1904) was a writer, critic and sociologist, and a leading ideologist of Russian Populism (translator's note).

22. Mikhail Alexandrovich Bakunin (1814–1876) was one of the theorists of Anarchism, and an opponent of Marx in the 1st International (translator's note).

23. Yuri Nakhamkes, called Steklov (1873–1941), a historian and the editor of *Izvestia*, had joined the Bolsheviks in 1903. His four volume biography of Bakunin came out in Moscow between 1920 and 1927, and another four volumes of Bakunin's *Works* between 1934 and 1936 (translator's note).

24. Vyacheslav Pavlovich Gusin, known as Polonsky (1886–1932) was a critic, journalist and historian who had been a Menshevik until 1919. During the Civil War he was in charge of the Literary and Publishing Department of the Political Administration of the Red Army. His book, *M. A. Bakunin: Life, Works and Thoughts*, came out in 1922, and the three volumes of his *Materials for a Biography of M. A. Bakunin* between 1923 and 1933 (translator's note).

25. Bakunin's *Confession*, 30,000 words long, was written to secure his release from the Peter and Paul Fortress

where he had been incarcerated by Tsar Nicholas I in 1851. It was discovered by the Bolsheviks in the imperial archives and published in 1921. Victor Serge deals with it in 'La Confession de Bakounine', *Bulletin Communiste*, vol.i, no.56, 23rd December 1921 (translator's note).

26. Professor Grigory Andreyevich Ilinsky (1876–1937) was a philologist and a scholar of Slavonic studies (translator's note).

27. Grossman-Roschin was an anarchist revolutionary who had been a supporter of 'motiveless terror' in 1906. He later became a leader of the *Golos Truda* syndicalist group, and cooperated with the Bolsheviks (translator's note).

28. Alexei A. Borovoy was an anarchist militant who persuaded the Anarchist Black Guard not to attempt a takeover of Moscow in 1918 (translator's note).

29. Armand Ross was the pseudonym of Michael Sazhin, who met Bakunin in Geneva in 1871 and supplied him with funds. They parted acrimoniously a few years later (translator's note).

30. Angelica Balabanova (1877–1936) supported the Communist International to begin with, but disapproved of the slanders directed against the Italian Socialist Party, which she rejoined after her expulsion from the Communist Party in 1924 (translator's note).

31. Alexei Karpovich Dzhivelegov (1875–1952) was a literary and theatre scholar and historian, specialising mainly in the Renaissance period (translator's note).

32. Ivan Ivanovich Skvortsov-Stepanov (1870–1928) was Deputy Chairman of the Editorial Board of the State Publishers in 1921, the author of a number of economic and historical works, and the translator of *Capital* into Russian (translator's note).

33. Nikolay Mikhailovich Lukin (1885–1940) was a newspaper editor and historian. The second edition of his *Parizkaya Kommuna, 1871* came out in Moscow in 1924 (translator's note).

34. Bukharin's *Historical Materialism: A System of Sociology* was published in Moscow and Petrograd in 1923. The first English translation came out in New York in 1925 (translator's note).

35. Serge describes Kropotkin's last days and funeral in *Memoirs of a Revolutionary*, Oxford University Press, 1975, pp.123–4 (translator's note).

36. Kropotkin's work on *Ethics* was never completed. The English translation by L. S. Friedland and J. R. Piroshnikoff entitled *Ethics: Origin and Development*, was published in New York in 1924; *Mutual Aid: A Factor of Evolution* first appeared in London in 1902, and was reprinted by Penguin Books in 1939 (translator's note).

37. A new edition of his *Memoirs of a Revolutionist* has just come out, annotated and revised by Kropotkin in the last year of his life (author's note). An English translation by James Allen Rogers was published in London in 1962. Kropotkin's *L'idée révolutionnaire dans la révolution* was published in Paris in 1913 (translator's note).

38. Nikolai Alexeyevich Nekrasov (1821–1878), a poet, journalist and literary critic, was a supporter of the Narodniks and a spokesman for the plight of the Russian peasantry, famous for his poem *Who is Happy in Russia?* (translator's note).

39. Blok had served as secretary to the Muravyev Commission for Investigating the Crimes of the Old Regime in 1917 (Translator's note).

40. Kornei Ivanovich Chukovsky was the pen name of Nikolay Ivanovich Korneichuk (1882–1969). His magnum opus on Nekrasov's *Literary Creativity* did not come out until 1952 (translator's note).

41. Pavel Ivanovich Biriukov (1860–1931) was famous for his 4-volume biography of Tolstoy published between 1921 and 1923; Nikolay Nikolayevich Gusev (1882–1967) was Tolstoy's personal secretary, and the editor of his *Collected Works* (translator's note).

42. Veresaev was famous for his studies of the classical Russian authors. His study of Tolstoy, *Zhivaya zhizn*, contrasts him with Dostoyevsky to Tolstoy's advantage (translator's note).

43. Maria Andreyevna Beketova was very closely acquainted with Blok, and published her study of him in 1922. Cf. Anatoly Lunacharsky, 'Alexander Blok', 1932, in *Lunacharsky On Art and Literature*, Moscow 1973, p.134.

44. The first draft of Trotsky's *1905* was written in 1908–1909 for a German edition that came out in Dresden. The

revised and expanded Russian version went through two printings in 1922 (English translation by Anya Bostock, New York, 1972) (translator's note).

45. Sergei Dmitriyevich Maslovsky, called Mstislavsky (1876–1943) was an SR who took part in the uprising in Moscow in 1905, and sided with the Bolsheviks in the Russian Revolution and the dissolution of the Constituent Assembly. His *Five Days Which Transformed Russia* was published in 1923 (English translation by Elizabeth Kristofovich Zelensky, London, 1988) (translator's note).

46. Julius Ossipovich Tsederbaum, known as Martov (1873–1923) was the leader of the Internationalist wing of the Mensheviks. His *Istoriya Rossiiskoi Sotzial-Demoktratii* (*The History of the Russian Social Democratic Labour Party*) came out in Moscow and Petrograd in 1923. Vladimir Mikhailovich Chernov (1876–1952) was the leader of the Socialist Revolutionaries. His *Mes tribulations en Russie soviétique* came out in Paris in 1921, and *The Great Russian Revolution*, translated into English by Philip E. Mosely was published in New Haven in 1936 (translator's note).

47. Mikhail Vasiliyevich Frunze (1888–1925) was a cavalry commander during the Russian Civil War, and succeeded Trotsky as War Commissar in 1925, but died in suspicious circumstances (translator's note).

48. Theodore Von Bernhardi (1803–1887) was a German military historian (translator's note).

49. Jaurès' *L'Armée Nouvelle* was published undated in 1910, and in a second edition after his death in 1915 (translator's note).

50. This was the so-called 'Formalist' school. Shklovsky developed the theory that literature developed by the continual substitution of themes, genres, styles and literary devices in its own logic. His essays on this were published in *Poetika* (1919) (translator's note).

51. Some slip of the pen has taken place here. The writer George Ustinov died in 1907. The reference is probably to Alexei Mikhailovich Ustinov (1879–1937) a Bolshevik party functionary and diplomat, or to N. Ustinov (*Izvestia*, 2 February, 1919) (translator's note).

52. Pilnyak's novel *Ivan da Maria* (*Ivan and Maria*) was published in Berlin in 1922. Ivanov's *Armoured Train No.14-69* was published in 1922 (English version translated by Keith Hammond in *Vsevolod Ivanov: Short Stories*, Raduga Publishers, Moscow, 1983, pp.243–373). Yuri L'vovich Slezkin (1887–1947) was a Russian novelist. Alexander Ya. Aroseyev (1890–1938) was a short story writer who joined the Bolsheviks in 1907 and wrote for Voronsky's *Red Virgin Soil*. He perished in the purges (translator's note).

53. 'Boche' was a pejorative term applied to Germans by the French in both world wars (translator's note).

54. Nikolay Alexandrovich Berdiayev (1874–1948) was a Russian historian and philosopher. He began as a 'legal marxist', but then moved over to religious mysticism (translator's note).

55. 34 SR leaders were put on trial in the spring of 1922 on charges going back to the beginning of the Civil War. Georgi Piatakov (1890–1937), who presided, was himself later one of the main defendants in the second Moscow trial, the Trial of the Seventeen (translator's note).

56. Yevgeny Alexandrovich Preobrazhensky (1886–1937) was a veteran Bolshevik and secretary of the C.P.S.U.(B) in 1919. He disappeared during the purges (translator's note).

57. Yakov M. Sverdlov (1885–1919) was an old Bolshevik who survived years in prison. He was Secretary of the Party Central Committee and President of the Council of Soviets. Upon his death in an influenza epidemic Moscow University was renamed in his honour (translator's note).

58. Herbert George Wells (1886–1946) was an English left-wing writer whose visit to the USSR. in 1920, when he interviewed Lenin, and the fair-minded way in which he described the problems of the new republic, aroused considerable interest among the Soviet intelligentsia (translator's note).

59. Lev Natanovich Lunts (1901–1924) was a Russian playwright (translator's note).

Chapter Two

The Russian Writers and the Revolution: Novelists, Poets, and Literary Circles: Is There a New Literature?[1]

I wish to make a quick sketch of Russian literature as it arose during the revolution for the readers of *Clarté*. Isn't it over-confident to presume to do this in a short article (such as you can write when you are a communist activist in 1922)? The reader is asked to take account in advance of the inevitable inadequacies of such an attempt. He will only find mentioned the greatest of the Russian writers and poets, those recognised for original and powerful work or of great fame. He will only find the thoughts and conclusions of a revolutionary who has not examined the facts from the viewpoint of literary criticism, but from the standpoint of the social change undertaken by red Russia, less concerned with the differences between schools than with a writer's attitude towards the terrible battle joined between an absurd world that is ending and a new world that is trying to be born.

Russian literature is obviously one of the world's greatest treasures. The young Russian people, which until the seventeenth century remained cut off from European culture – inheriting from paganism a number of admirable and charming legends, passionately Christian, subject to distant and very much conflicting influences – Byzantium, Iran, the Mongol civilisation, and then, so suddenly in its history, the Swedish (Charles XII) and Napoleonic invasions,[2] severely and implacably oppressed by despots who at the same time held on to their titles of Tsars – the Greek Caesars, with their despotic manners,[3] of Mongol Khans, with their autocratic law,[4] and with a church, whose heads they were[5] – at the mercy of servitude until after the middle of the nineteenth century, and ruled by the knout until 1917[6] – the simple, naive, melancholic and often savage and brutal Russian people, endowed with such musical sensitivity and so complex a soul (we should remember the songs of its sailors and soldiers, and the galaxy of great musicians it has given the world), the Russian people which, out of every cluster of poplars or fir trees scattered across the steppes, has carved out green, blue and golden turrets, decorated by its churches, has produced perhaps a unique literature.

I do not use this word lightly. From Dostoyevsky to Tolstoy and Gorky, and even in the work of our minor writers, Russian thought is dominated by the (often intolerable) agony of doubt and the power of affirmation. *Why do we live?* Tolstoy examined this question all his life. Andreyev wrote his symbolic tragedy the *Life of Man,*[7] and seemed bitterly to mock his own torment. Chekhov[8] and Gorky show us – the one petty bourgeois imbeciles, and the other vagabonds and outsiders haunted by the suffering of living without knowing why ... Artybashev ended up with suicide (*Breaking Point*).[9] Such is Russian questioning. *Revival*, that is the powerful affirmation. Irrational, you might say. What logical link is there between the question and the answer? It doesn't matter. Is life rational? What logical, or at least apparent link, is there between life and death? Revival, being reborn on a higher level, reviving without ceasing. Tolstoy writes *Resurrection,*[10] and, from being a dissipated official, becomes one of the clearest thinkers of his time; the vagabond Alexis Peshkov becomes Maxim Gorky – and Gorky describes how, day by day, through maternal love and revolutionary activity, an old woman worker who lived until she was sixty like a beast of the field was reborn (*Mother*). Before sinking into pessimism, Artybashev wrote his *Sanin,*[11] a real human resurrection, after the defeats of the revolution in 1905–06, with an individualism that reminds you of Whitman. Korolenko describes in a small masterpiece, how a human intelligence that appeared to be damned revives (*The Blind Musician*).[12] The seriousness of the question and the importance of the affirmation endow Russian literature with a *unique* meaning.

The influence it exercises is therefore legitimate. And, more than other people, revolutionaries need to understand it and to love it. For the question it asks amounts to an everlasting dissatisfaction, a contempt for mediocre cheerfulness, an ambition to spring out of a vegetative or purely animal existence as slaves or masters, in order finally to attain the human life whose justification can only rest in affirmations of higher energies, which are love, intelligence and creative will.

'*To be able to live,*' said the Russian poet C. Balmont,[13] '*the whole universe must be justified.*'

It seems to me that when we read a poem by Blok or a page by Razumnik,[14] to understand them better we must place them within the entirety of Russian culture.

So now they arrive at the long awaited, anticipated storm of the revolution, hoped for by the best minds of this culture. What is to become of the Russian writers in the revolution?

⋆   ⋆   ⋆   ⋆

All the pre-revolutionary writers were 'those who forecast a storm'.

Leonid Andreyev had written some very sad masterpieces inspired by the struggle for revolution: *The Governor, The Seven That Were Hanged*, and *King Hunger*, a tragedy that has now perhaps become the most relevant of the masterpieces of Russian literature. He had sketched out in *Sava* the broad lines of the struggle between the spirit of destruction and the religious spirit.[15] But Andreyev panicked in the face of its day to day realities when the revolution came. For a long time he had been inclined to lose faith in man, who as far as he was concerned was the human brute, whose intelligence was always overcome by his bestiality. When the Petrograd sailors and soldiers, forced beyond endurance by the harshest and cruelest disciplines that have ever held sway on ships or in barracks, subjected their officers to that implacable revenge that infuriated people have always kept for their oppressors, Andreyev did not see, and did not understand, that the violence of the people, however impulsive it might be, was the summary expression of the justice that the unhappy people had thirsted after for centuries. He believed it was the end of all civilisation. He wrote *S.O.S.*, the anti-Bolshevik appeal published by M. Burtsev[16] in thousands of copies. He became a 'White'.[17] Only a few days before dying alone in White Finland[18] did he begin to understand (letter to Burtsev, which the latter published) that civil war against the revolution was hopeless, and was shedding the blood of the Russian people to no avail.

A. Kuprin, whose *The Duel* and *The Shulammite* have just come out in French, with a pity which would not condemn any fault unless you had experienced and suffered it, had described the mediocrity of the garrison towns, and the sordid and banal horror of prostitution (*The Pit*). All he produced was imbued with contempt for the old society. The sole content of his books was the double light of kindness and pity upon all its victims alike. Now at the time when Yudenich[19] made his first attack on Petrograd in 1919, A. Kuprin, then living in Tsarkoye-

Selo, passed over to the Whites. Then, in Estonia, this 'Christian anarchist' (for so he described himself) edited a noxious little paper on behalf of the White General Staff. And then, in the Helsingfors newspapers and in *Common Cause*, he published 'portraits' of the Bolshevik leaders in a disgraceful style ...

During this time another 'mystical anarchist' and enemy of all violence, the gentle and wise Dmitry Merezhkovsky, the novelist, poet and philosopher, who gave us some definitive works on 'the brutal Tsars', was collaborating with the publications of the Petrograd Soviet. But as soon as he had crossed the Polish frontier he went on to denounce Bolshevism as the *Antichrist*, appealed in Warsaw for armed intervention against Russia, opposed aid for the starving, and abused Gorky for asking for this aid from all men of goodwill. Along with Merezhkovsky his wife, Z. Hippius, a poetess of great talent, dishonoured herself in the same fashion.[20]

Eugene Chirikov had described small town life, and the moral distress of the students and intellectuals suffocated under the weight of the old regime. Eugene Chirikov wrote pamphlets for General Denikin's propaganda office.[21]

Ivan Bunin, a great poet and great novelist, who published *The Man of San Francisco* and very recently *The Village* in France, also became one of Burtsev's collaborators. This artist, who in so striking a manner had depicted the misery, ignorance, enfeeblement and subjection of the people (Cf. *A Night Conversation, The Primer of Love, The Village*), who had once wanted to work by his art for the people's regeneration, an apparently simple but sentimental soul, but moreover always faithful to the prejudices of the 'nobility' to which he was proud to belong – he also recoiled in the face of the real, effective, murderous and life-giving revolution.[22] He abandoned his cause. He is reckoned among our enemies.

M. Artybashev (writer of *The Death of Ivan Lande, Sanin* and *Breaking Point*[23]) had been a Tolstoyan, then a heartbroken witness of the 1905 repression, which blighted his hopes, and then an individualist, only finally to arrive at a pessimism more bitter than that of a Leopardi or a Hartmann,[24] by advocating suicide. He had been broken even before the revolution. But this broken man would not dirty his hands by doing the work of reaction. He became silent. Last year he was living in poverty in Moscow.

Our gentle and lucid Korolenko, very old and greatly afflicted by physical infirmity, and by-passed by the events, could not accept the unavoidable inhumanity of the civil war, did good to those around him, and worked on to his last day, but he never wanted to leave the country of the revolution. He really belonged to the former generation, of whom only the Stoic poet and novelist Fyodor Sologub any longer remained. In 1921 Fyodor Sologub, whose art has long been recognised as outstanding, read to us in the Literary House in Petrograd some poems and chapters from his last book. I will never forget the smooth face of the old sage, and the hollow and tired voice reciting the lines where it was all a question of *suffering* and *waiting* – nor that on that day in one of the capitals of the civil war Fyodor Sologub read to us some pages on 'the reconciliation of the classes ...'

Only one of the great Russian prose writers of today, after many hesitations and many internal struggles joined the revolution completely. Obviously this was not without criticising it frequently and sharply. But it was whole-hearted. He has surpassed himself with his pages on Lenin.[25] In all that I have heard him say about the revolution and the future, Gorky (a pseudonym that means 'bitter'), while suffering all the sadness of the present time, has never lost sight of the immense 'global significance', to use one of his favourite expressions, of 'the revolutionary experience'. But how can I not say here that of all the writers I have just mentioned, Gorky is the only one who came from the people, not the proletariat, but from the *lumpenproletariat*, in other words the lowest depths of the declassed of labour who are situated in the hierarchy of capitalism even below the proletariat?

It cannot be denied that it is the class outlook (of the petty bourgeoisie) of the majority of the Russian writers that has been one of the main causes of their almost total inability to understand the revolution.

⋆　⋆　⋆　⋆　⋆

How can we explain why the poets understood it better? That is generally the case. The majority of the novelists were Whites. The poets, above all those who were only poets, were Reds, or else observed neutrality, hostile at times, but then distant and passive. In any case, the greatest Russian poets are with us. The Russian novel has still not noticed the revolution. No novel about attitudes during these terrible and great years has come out from 1917 to the present, and we do not even know of manuscripts. But poetry has been enriched with several masterpieces.

To begin with there is Alexander Blok's *The Twelve*, a poem about twelve Red Guards on a snowy night in November 1917, who 'are preceded by Jesus Christ, invisibly and invulnerably, crowned with white roses'.

There are the ten magnificent pages of our mystic André Biely, *Christ is Risen*. 'O Russia my country! You are the shining bride to whom everyone looks ... And I see my Russia triumphing over the Serpent'.[26] The divine Christ for André Biely is the railway worker whose head pierced by a bullet he sees rise in the car's headlights while the telegraph is transmitting from one end of the world to the other the words 'The Third International ...'

Still young, but already one of the foremost lyric poets on Russian soil, of which he is the son, Serge Yesenin is the author of *Inoniya*,[27] a poem whose form deliberately imitates the biblical prophets and ends with this announcement: 'A new saviour is coming into the world. Our strength is our faith. Our truth is within us.'

Nicolas Kluyev has also hymned the revolution (*The Song of the Sun Bearer*[28]). Kluyev, a Communist, is a peasant from the Ladoga[29] who only rarely comes to town. He wears the clothing that has been worn in the area for three or four centuries. He has a thorough knowledge of Russian, of Slavonic and of the language of the Karelian sagas. He takes his imagery from these old Nordic legends.

These four poets, Blok, Biely, Yesenin and Kluyev are Christian in inspiration; in talking about the revolution they borrow Bible and Gospel language; they are so profoundly imbued with Christian feeling that as far as they are concerned the social change that is putting down roots into the very renewed soul of man and of the crowds appears to them all like the resurrection of a Christ, as well as a fresh rebirth of the Christian era.

Two other great Russian poets, Valery Briusov and Serge Gorodetsky, who were renowned under the old order, have come over completely to the revolution. But in spite of a fairly extensive production and despite a respected talent, the revolution added nothing worthy of note to their work. We could say much the same about Constantine Balmont, who was the undisputed 'prince of poets' of Russian literature from 1910 to 1915, on whom the Russian émigré press heaped abuse last year because he refused to distance himself from favouring neutrality with regard to the Soviet regime. Ehrenburg, the most productive of the Berlin Russian writers, after describing in two booklets, where there are several pieces deserving to be put in an anthology, the tragedy of the revolution (as well as the 'crucifixion of the fatherland' by the Bolsheviks) ended up adopting a similar attitude.

This was also the attitude of most poets who were known under the old regime and who stayed in Russia – often with some reservations as to the very relative benevolence of their neutrality. Vyacheslav Ivanov, a delicate stylist, continued his learned researches into aesthetic and verbal music undisturbed. N. Gumilev (shot in August 1921 along with those implicated in the Tagantsev plot[30]), in spite of his very backward opinions on the right of might, on authority, and on how splendid the war was, always assumed a distant loyalty in the presence of the revolution. M. Kuzmin, the refined poet of bourgeois decadence (*Songs of Alexandria*) and Anna Akhmatova, perhaps the author of the most beautiful love poetry produced by modern Russian literature, are living in Petrograd, keeping to themselves, and stubbornly *refusing to be up-to-date*. And it would be unfair and pointless to ask any more of them. Obviously the bard of a decadent bourgeoisie cannot understand a revolution: let us be happy that they have enough detachment from the things of this world not to be completely antagonistic to it. And the heart of a woman in love beats during revolutions, just as it does at other times.

Mayakovsky must be accorded a place on his own. Mayakovsky, a futurist in whom criticism recognises a rich talent, who thinks of the technique of a poem almost like that of a poster, and, moreover, very much announcing with the voice, appeal and tone of a town crier, is the author of the only revolutionary work worthy of note, completely new in shape and form, and detached from any religious inspiration: 'One Hundred and Fifty Million'.[31] As a final touch he gave it to the public without signing it. The poem is about the 150,000,000 anonymous Russians who made the revolution. The *muzhik*[32] Ivan is the sole authentic incarnation of these 150,000,000 men. In some strong pages vehement as a Medieval epic Mayakovsky sets out the duel between Chicago and Moscow, and between Ivan and Wilson. Everything in it is mocking, epic, exaggerated, trivial and powerful. 'Even Wilson's underpants are interwoven with the subtlest poetic tenderness ...'

It remains that the revolution was understood by the poets and that it has enriched Russian poetry. Why? The answer to this question has been provided for us by André Biely: 'We are living an epic', wrote Biely: 'to be able to understand these times, hearts and minds must rise to the epic ...' The fact is that there is a profound lyricism in the revolution, that it is a new faith, and that at all times it teaches us to sacrifice the old, shrinking, outworn and outdated values for new values: the fact is that because it only reckons with the masses, it sometimes arouses an irresistible sense of greatness in the individual ...

★   ★   ★   ★

During the entire duration of the revolution literary circles in Petrograd and Moscow experienced a relatively intense internal life. I know the Petrograd ones best of all, which had two centres: *The Writers' House* and *The Arts House*. These houses provided for both the material and the intellectual needs of all those who, in the old capital, had hitherto lived by the pen. Cooperatives, restaurants, bookshops, libraries and conference and concert rooms packed every night could be found there. In addition there were in Moscow several noisy and colourful *Poets' cafés* (*The Imagists*, *The Domino*, etc.).

The *Writers' House* was the last resort of a world of journalists, gossip columnists, chroniclers, short story writers and scholars condemned by the proletarian revolution to premature retirement, in the face of which they were inconsolable. What could be the use, between 1918 and 1922, of gifts of the mind and an environment especially cultivated for many years for the amusement of the bourgeoisie? The revolution had brutally revealed the futility, or should we rather say, the uselessness of the impoverished and servile 'minor letters' which had previously been the ornament of the public of the Nevsky Prospect.

The whole of literary Petrograd came together for the evening meetings in these *Houses*. The music was good, and the verses generally at least passable. There were special nights, when Blok's serious voice resounded there. But you always felt a quite particular feeling in this milieu. Nothing of the tragedy of the time apparently got through to there. You found nothing of the anguished, bloody and violent life of the time in what was read, in what was said, in the measured gestures, in the kissing of hands or even in the language. You felt that you had suddenly been transported back to some years before. But once you came out of these salons into the street where soldiers were passing in rags, you sobered up, and returned to reality. The distinguishing mark of these literary circles during the revolutionary years was to remain behind the times, cut off from social life, and shut off from the wind of revolution.

Quite otherwise was the impression made by the poets in their cafés. It was very different, but hardly better. Poetry, whether Futurist or Dadaist,[33] reigned there, often reaching the heights of complete unintelligibility. All the street noises came in, only to form an indistinct cacophony. There, as among the imagists, arguments were sometimes 'shouted out'. Was art enriched amid this racket? I doubt it. And I very much fear that Yesenin demeaned his creative talent on more than one occasion.

To finish off this far too rapid outline of the literary circles, it remains for me to say a couple of words about *Proletcult*. Its poets have published some twenty booklets. Several of them (Kirillov, Alexandrovsky and Obradovich) are probably destined to leave behind a work worth remembering. But when taken as a whole their attempt to create a proletarian poetry has mainly produced banal verses, in which the factory, the factory chimney, the machine, the hammer and sickle and the red star are so many conventional clichés. Have the *Proletcult* poets confined their horizon too closely? I am inclined to accept this. Where on the other hand *Proletcult*'s role has been productive, is when it has devoted itself to awakening artistic feeling among the worker and peasant youth. As far as teaching them to create for themselves, we should say that in general it has still not succeeded. This is not meant as blame. The new writers, whom the revolutionary people need, cannot take shape in a few months amid the turmoil of the civil war.

★   ★   ★   ★

The great poverty of the Russian writers has often been talked about, and it has not always been exaggerated. Unfortunately, it ought to be said that the Russian intellectuals have not generally known how to lift their minds and hearts above day to day personal trivia. The black bread of the revolution has often seemed so bitter to them that they were willing to flatter (obviously, in a literary sense) the Gallifet[34] who would provide them with white bread. The poverty of the Russian writers has been terrible, because the poverty of the entire Russian people during the civil war was indescribable. But whereas the worker, the peasant and the Communist were fighting for the future, and accepted the privations stoically, the stock exchange gazette writer, henceforth deprived of all means of subsistence, since he was completely incapable of providing any useful work in a society that needed neither stock exchange nor 'financial press', flooded the foreign press with his complaints. Russian writers and learned men experienced cold, hunger and long winter nights without light; they sometimes had to cut and chop firewood for themselves (or do without at 30 degrees below freezing, and work hard to get their potatoes for the next day). That is true. But it is also true, even amid this great poverty, *that they were better off than the great majority of workers and Communists*. The Putilov engineer, to whom the Commune gave larger rations than to the retired journalist, did much rougher work, and had nothing to sell in order to live, since he had never had anything.

The writers almost always benefitted from privileged treatment on the part of the consumer cooperatives and the state. But even if famine wreaked cruel ravages among them, no doubt in proportion to those it did among the entirety of the population, it is above all among those whom long-established habits, or a certain want of practical ability (quite often to be found among highly thought of people) made a particular case; sometimes they allowed themselves to be cheated by more 'resourceful' colleagues. This annoying egotism on the part of certain elements did not prevent the rest of them from giving very tenacious daily practical proof of solidarity and *high morale*.

Even at the most difficult times in his life the Russian writer never lived as the Russian worker generally lives. But that is a fact that a philosopher as detached from the earth's benefits as Monsieur Merezhkovsky has never been able to reconcile himself with.

Kiev, May 1922   Victor Serge.

Notes

1. Translated from *Clarté*, no.17, 11 July, 1922, pp.387–90 (translator's note).
2. Russia had been excluded from the Baltic during the 17th century by the expansion of Sweden, which practically turned it into a Swedish lake. The Swedish threat was only removed by the defeat of Charles XII at Poltava in 1708. Napoleon captured Moscow in 1812, but suffered heavy losses in his winter retreat (translator's note).
3. Ivan III married Zoe (Sophia Palaeologina), a Byzantine princess, whilst the Byzantine Empire was being overrun by the Turks. From then on the Russian Tsars claimed to be the legitimate successors of the Byzantine empire, copying its despotism and aping its manners (translator's note).
4. The Mongol domination of Russia by the Golden Horde lasted from 1243 to 1462 (translator's note).
5. Vladimir, Prince of Novgorod and Kiev, made Orthodox Christianity the official religion of Russia in 988 A.D. There was a long tradition of Imperial control, generally known as 'Caesaropapism', in the Orthodox church, which went back to the time when Constantine the Great proclaimed himself 'equal of the apostles', and interfered in the church councils (translator's note).
6. Tsar Alexander II had emancipated the Russian serfs in 1861, but beating with the knout continued in the villages until the Russian Revolution (translator's note).
7. Andreyev's *The Life of Man* was published in 1906–8 (English translation, New York, 1915) (translator's note).
8. Anton Pavlovich Chekhov (1860–1904) was a well-known Russian writer of short stories (translator's note)
9. Artybashev's *Breaking Point* was published in 1910–2 (translator's note).
10. Tolstoy's *Resurrection* came out in 1899 (translator's note).
11. Artybashev's *Sanin*, about young people who speak freely about their sensual desires and espouse the principle of free love, was published in 1907 (English translation, London, 1914) (translator's note).
12. Korolenko's *The Blind Musician* was published in 1886 (English translation by Sergius Stepniak and William Westall, London, 1890) (translator's note).
13. Constantine Dmitryevich Balmont (1867–1943) was a noted Russian poet and a supporter of Modernism (translator's note).
14. Ivanov-Razumnik was the pen name of Razumnik Vasilievich Romanov (1878–1946), a philosopher and historian and a supporter of the SRs, and the author of a well-known *History of Russian Social Thought* (1907). Serge was the only Communist member of Razumnik's Free Philosophical Academy (translator's note).
15. Andreyev's *The Governor*, published in 1906, was about a governor who had ordered the violent suppression of some revolutionaries and was now awaiting certain assassination at the hands of their associates. *King Hunger* was published in 1907, and *Sava* (*Sashka Zhegulev*) in 1911 (translator's note).
16. Leonid Andreyev's *S. O. S.: Au Secours*, was published with a preface by Burtsev in Paris in 1919 (translator's note).
17. 'White' is a traditional term for counter-revolutionary, dating back to the royal colours of the French monarchy before the revolution (translator's note).
18. A general strike in Finland followed by a premature uprising on 27 January 1918 was suppressed by General Mannerheim with the help of German troops, and from then on Finland served as a base for attacks upon the USSR (translator's note).
19. Nikolai Yudenich (1862–1933) was a White general who began his first advance on Petrograd in Spring 1919 (translator's note).
20. Cf. The 'Appeal to Russian Soldiers', an attempt to undermine the Red Army during the Civil War, in Temira Pachmuss (ed.), *Between Paris and St. Petersburg: Selected Diaries of Zinaida Hippius*, Illinois U.P., Chicago, 1975, pp.242–3. Merezhkovsky's 'brutal tsars' was a series of novels, including one on Alexander I (translator's note).
21. General Anton Ivanovich Denikin (1872–1947) attacked the Bolsheviks from the Don and the Kuban during the Russian Civil War (translator's note).

22. Bunin's *A Night Conversation* (1915) is a rural story echoing Turgenev's *Bezhin Meadow* (English translation by Isabel Florence Hapgood published in *Fifteen Tales by Ivan Bunin*, London, 1924). *The Primer of Love* was published in 1915 (English translation, 1984) and *The Village* in 1910 (English translation, London, 1923) (translator's note).

23. Artybashev's *The Death of Ivan Lande* was published in 1902 (translator's note).

24. Giacomo Leopardi (1798–1837) was an Italian poet and philosopher, famous for writing the poem *Approach of Death* (1835); Karl Robert Eduard von Hartmann (1842–1906) was a German philosopher who adopted Schopenhauer's pessimistic view of the state of civilisation (translator's note).

25. Maxim Gorky's *Vladimir Lenin* was published in Russian in 1924, and in English translation in Edinburgh in 1967 (translator's note).

26. André Biely published *Christ is Risen* in 1918 (translator's note).

27. Serge Yesenin's *Inoniya* came out in 1918. The word is made up from *inoi*, 'other', by which he counterposes a new city to the religous polity of old Russia (translator's note).

28. Kluyev published *The Song of the Sun Bearer* in 1920 (translator's note).

29. Lake Ladoga lies in Karelia, between St Petersburg and the Finnish border (translator's note).

30. Nikolai Stepanovich Gumilev (1886–1921) was the main theorist of acmeism. Serge met him in Paris on their way to the USSR., where Gumilev intended to fight for the Whites in the Civil War. They became friends, and Serge later tried to intercede with the Cheka not to shoot him (*Memoirs*, pp.59–60 and 150) (translator's note).

31. Mayakovsky's *One Hundred and Fifty Million* came out in 1921 (translator's note).

32. A *muzhik* is a Russian peasant (translator's note).

33. Dadaism was a nihilist movement in the arts first pioneered by Tristan Tzara and others in Zurich in 1916 (translator's note).

34. General Gaston Alexandre Auguste, Marquis de Gallifet (1830–1909) was responsible for the massacres following the suppression of the Paris Commune (translator's note).

Chapter Three

Whites and Reds[1]

On the soil of Russia torn apart and upturned by the plough of the revolution much chaff is mixed up with the wheat that is starting to grow again. An unceasing and inexorable struggle is going on between what is wanting to grow and what does not want to disappear in all spheres of existence. This is particularly true in the realm of thought. The intellectual life of a period is always tightly conditioned by the essential relations that exist between classes, that is by the part they play in production and distribution. This first principle of historical materialism is most strongly illustrated by looking at intellectual life in Russia. There is the proletarian revolutionary state, in control of the main industry and transport system expropriated from the bourgeoisie, with a Communist Party exercising dictatorial power to lead the country towards Socialism: and private trade, privately owned industries, markets, a stock exchange, speculation, concessions, businessmen, shopkeepers, gold prospectors and parasites: every day these two worlds are confronting each other. No one is unaware that there can be no lasting peace between them. Strengthened by its success and confident of being the hope of the world, the revolution is counting on conquering the future. Strengthened by the apparently unshaken power of the dollar and of some of the capitalist states where it does not want to hear its old framework cracking, reaction is looking on closely, hoping and waiting. It is in no way inactive.

Even the Terror has not succeeded in annihilating its intellectual resistance. In the fifth year, 1922, this opposition has taken on the most diverse forms. At the start of the year a strike of the university teaching staff, which spread to the majority of the country's higher educational institutions, amounted to trying to drive shameful 'sovietism' out of higher education. The professors demanded 'autonomy', no more, no less. They objected to the preference allowed to worker-students. Then came the scientific conferences (particularly that of the doctors) which amounted to virtual political demonstrations: the old counter-revolutionary liberalism was calling the tune here. Students of proletarian origin in the universities felt that they were sometimes being treated like the plague. They had to react and get organised – isn't the N.E.P. (New

Economic Policy) the start of a return to the old capitalist system? Professor Ustryalov, a Cadet who noisily came over to the Soviet Republic, says it all: 'Bolshevism is changing, let us help it to change!'[2] This is the theme, with all the caution that prudence requires, that is producing an entire literature rapidly arising in the two capitals exhausted by the Civil War. Academician V. M. Bekhterev, a psychiatrist, has published an edifying work on *Collective Reflexology* in the manner of Lombroso.[3] Bolshevism? It is a collective psychosis, no more than that. This book is coming out in Petrograd, and the writer of it has been subsidised in various respects by the Commissariat of Public Education! Likewise in Petrograd two economic journals, *The Economist* and *Economic Rebirth* (since closed down) set themselves the aim of calling for the reconstruction of capitalist Europe. Professor Venediktov[4] one day announced in them that the proletarian state would inevitably be defeated in the mixed enterprises, where capitalists would swindle them quite openly. In the first number of *Economic Rebirth* one Zaitsev[5] asked: What is to be done with our railways? and concluded to start off with that we must grant a good part of them – for a start – to private industry. So here we have the policy of Stinnes and Mussolini being disseminated in Petrograd at the beginning of 1922! The economist Y. M. Stein[6] is full of the same sort of thing ...

The works of Oswald Spengler have just been translated. They contain a bold affirmation of imperialist teachings. They are providing the decapitated and dispossessed former Russian ruling classes with an explanation for their misfortune and a new reason to hope. The old religious philosopher Berdiayev and his friends J. M. Bukspan, F. A. Stepun and S. L. Frank have devoted an entire volume of essays to Spengler's revelations.[7] Vitalism[8] is being reborn in biology. And there are other occurences of the same sort! Right up to these last months practically eight tenths of the poetic and literary work published in Russia belongs to the *non-contemporary* category. Now being non-contemporary, taking refuge in an ivory tower, is another way of being counter-revolutionary without taking the risk of political action. Some of the great poets, whilst Red Russia was fighting from inside a fiery circle, restricted their creative activity to translating Henri de Régnier (Kuzmin), or were proclaiming in beautiful mystical sonnets that the Beast of the Apocalypse[9] would be overthrown (Fyodor Sologub).

In the street, such as the N.E.P. has made it, which has turned half of it over to petty traders, other phenomena no less dangerous demonstrate of the intellectual offensive of the forces of the past: dumbed-down cinema, the music hall, trivial literature that is titillating if not pornographic, and a spread of freshly published stories about dubious escapades. We can see that it is an offensive all along the line against the new thinking, in which all weapons are drawn upon. There is fashionable philosophy for the educated; economics for active people; 'art for art's sake' intended for the literary; idealism and mysticism (the subjects of innumerable lectures) for those who are hung up on nostalgia for the hereafter; the last but one film by *Fatty*, the licentious ditty, the 'Parisian' magazine for the passer-by – and what an atmosphere, and what teaching in the schools where the youth awakened by the revolution are going to be looking for their spiritual sustenance! ...

Zinoviev warned of the danger at the Twelfth Congress of the Russian Communist Party in a long detailed report: Radek[10] and Bukharin declared a counter-offensive by the Revolution in the domain of ideas. To tell the truth, the Russian Communists have never ceased being active and aggressive in this sphere. Only – and what more can we say – during the Civil War their blood was shed, all things considered, more than that of the old intellectuals of the previous regime, and they were less numerous to begin with. The Russian proletariat is short of educated men who know how to teach, to argue and to wield spiritual weapons. The present teaching staff in the universities is almost entirely from the pre-revolutionary period. The struggle was very unequal, in higher education above all. This explains why they resorted to repression: the recent exile of a certain amount of incurably reactionary intellectuals, whose senile ambitions had been emboldened by the N.E.P ...

Satire and Literary Criticism
Organising advanced elements among the professors (*the red professors*); educating new staff in higher education, recruited from among the young intellectuals (and as far as possible from among young educated proletarians); party educational work; organising communist students to take over the universities; creating and distributing innumerable communist periodicals; systematically defending the philosophy of materialism and the compulsory study of

Marxism; refuting opponents: such are the methods tirelessly put into operation by the Russian Revolution in the battle of ideas. Let us here remind ourselves of some important facts we have already mentioned: the appearance of
Bukharin's *Historical Materialism*, and half a dozen refutations of Spengler in
the magazines, moreover, the labours of Professor N. Pokrovsky, the author of a
Brief History of Russia,[11] devised in a rigorously Marxist spirit, effortlessly elim-
inating the poor historical textbooks about battles, which are still in use practically everywhere in Russia.

The new thinking still has two precious weapons barely known abroad: *satire*,
wielded by Demyan Biedny, and literary criticism, which Trotsky has just
enriched in a powerful book.[12]

Demyan Biedny – 'Poor Demyan, the evil-minded muzhik', as he has lately
described himself to please the N.E.P. profiteers – his only concession! –
employs the criticism of manners with inexhaustible spirit. He enjoys a popularity of the highest esteem. Contributing to the big Soviet dailies, every day for
years he has published in them rhyming couplets, among which excellent ones
can easily be found. Demyan Biedny has a feel for rhythm and popular language to the highest degree; all the rhythms of Russian verse are familiar to
him, like all the local expressions, and all the new, often meaty street turns of
phrase during these trying times. But what has earned him unequalled popularity among the public of simple, rough workers and fighters, is that he rarely
lets slip the occasion to say at the top of his voice, cleverly and amusingly, what
the people are thinking. There is no everyday absurdity he doesn't pick up, no
blemish he doesn't send up, and no disagreeable truth that sooner or later he
doesn't serve up 'to his Commissar friends'. Unfortunately, we think he is
untranslatable. Nobody has done more in Russia to fight bureaucratism, casti-
gate the bad Communists, and make a mockery of the profiteers of the New
Economic Policy. How can we give an idea of how it is done? Let us remind ourselves of his *Complaint about a Dead Mare* (1919–1920). The poor animal
dropped dead in front of the *Teo* (the Theatrical District); its carcass provided
the occasion for long and laborious negotiations between three Commissariats:
the Leather Centre demanded the hide, the bone centre the bones, and the
Supplies Department the rest of it ... Only when the bureaucrats had finally settled the matter, there no longer was a dead mare. The Cheka intervened to carry

out an enquiry and ascertained that the dogs had eaten it while the negotiations were going on ... Any comrade who has lived through this year of war, blockade and socialist construction and has done his simple revolutionary duty against all comers, would read this laughing out loud. Satire is a bit of revenge on the odious petty bourgeoisie who are already infesting the Soviet ministries.

Literature After October is the title of Trotsky's new book. *Pravda* has published long extracts from it. Trotsky studies the contemporary Russian writers one by one from the vantage point of revolutionary Marxism, drawing out of each of them the ideology that represents a social class. For there is no creation of human thought that is completely divorced from the class struggle; there is nothing in which revolutionary criticism cannot be fruitfully used; and the flame that lights up and burns must be openly displayed over the sanctuary of high literature. The new thinking has to free itself from the grip of a world that is on the way out and stagnating. On some of these pages Trotsky the critic becomes a polemicist and a pamphleteer. At times his style comes close to an extraordinary violence, precision and sharpness of expression: so cruel are some words that they cut as sharp as a lancet, and so summary are some judgments that they are like a bludgeon. Thus André Biely's anthroposophic *Epic*, an egocentric and overladen book, for the most part almost unreadable, merits a terrible and beautiful chapter that is one of the most fascinating.[13] He says it all about the revolutionary's indignation in the presence of those absorbed in contemplating *themselves* while the peoples are transforming the world. Elsewhere in fifteen lines what a demolition we see of the critic Chukovsky, who is anxious to demonstrate that Alexander Blok's *The Twelve* is a 'nationalist' poem![14] The craftily counter-revolutionary hack is laid hold of, tied up, stripped bare and thrown to the foot of the pillory. Alongside this unceasing hand to hand struggle with the class enemy there are periods of contemplation during which thinking spreads its wings and rises up. I would like to be able to quote a page here – in impeccably rhythmical language – on the poetry of the revolution.

The New Literature

In this battle that pits Reds and Whites against each other again, the new literature occupies imprecise, or even intentionally equivocal positions. But let us straightaway say that it is very rich. The year 1921–1922 saw a good dozen young talents arise or be awoken by the storm. But if we make an exception of the poet Mayakovsky, who, if his works are anything to go by, has been a communist for a long time, and who gave us his epic *One Hundred and Fifty Millions*, all the new ones avoid appearing to be political. Mayakovsky has just published *International Life*, an impressive fresco in which countries, masses, machines and the entire planet are seen through the electronic brain of the radio-telegraph. It is literature that at first sight has nothing 'literary' about it, simplified, a poem for reciting in a public square, with brutal imagery, dominated by the new feelings of love and understanding of technology, and a desire for social transformation, a 'planetary' way of looking at things – words dear to Maxim Gorky.

The Serapion Brothers have made a sensational entry into the lists with some collections of short stories, of which not one out of all of them is bereft of originality or talent. They most often describe the manners of the Revolution, without pretending to be realistic, but with a great deal of truth. Some completely different people have entered this fraternity, over which the influence of the novelist Zamyatin, a subtly counter-revolutionary observer with a style developed from British culture, has been great, including both a Constantine Fedin, who has just become a Communist, and a Vsevolod Ivanov, a red partisan from Siberia. What brings them together is above all, we think, a way of feeling and a very broad way of expressing it. Form is of enormous importance for them, though it is not always apparent. Their style is direct, without tedium, precise and violent (how many times have this latter word been written, and it is not by pure coincidence!), true in the sense that by ridding itself of slowness and inertia, it tries to reproduce the dynamism of life itself, visible in the smallest things. They are in the first instance Russians, free of foreign influences, having gone back to the sources of their people's originality. We can see this above all in their language, enriched by the speech of the village, the factory and the steppe. They often appear to be completely in the line of descent of Dostoyevsky and Tolstoy, of great Russian idealism, in other words. But what do they think of the revolution? In all their autobiographies they write with great and almost childish pride, how they have more or less been shot by the Whites, the Reds, or both of them, have been imprisoned, suffering from typhus, soldiers, wandering lecturers and agitators, as hungry, cold and heroic as are the

Russian people themselves (and that's banal), hence their feeling, and their new thinking. They have not been schooled in salons and five o'clock teas, thank God! They owe everything to the Revolution, and feel it. They accept it and they follow it, but they only confess their love for the new Russia; there is a neo-nationalism among them, which proves that they have not fully understood the Revolution. They are very careful to suspend judgement about Communism. 'My revolution is over!', exclaims C. Fedin. His revolution! We are sorry for this wretched revolutionary. They depict the Revolution in its everyday goings-on with an accuracy that is often painful. Let us imagine Flaubert describing a French village during the time of the Jacobins.[15] The work would be true to life. But would it tell the *whole* truth? There are essential things which we only see from higher up, by looking above and beyond the market place where Homais[16] is pontificating. For example, by describing the Civil War 'impartially' in too careful a detail, we risk painting a picture without light, which would especial-ly satisfy our enemies. Almost all these considerations equally apply to Boris Pilnyak, perhaps the greatest of the present day Russian writers, who far sur-passes the Serapion Brotherhood. Trotsky emphasises this in his essays: the majority of these writers are of peasant origin, or imbued with peasant think-ing, or pretending to be. In other words they do not understand the *whole* of the revolution in the workers' community.[17]

Vsevolod Ivanov has brought into Russian literature the harsh struggle of the Siberian muzhiks for freedom, the Khirgiz, the Yakuts,[18] the hunger, the snow, death – and above all the primitive grandeur of these unknown rebels who are without doubt among the greatest of this time. Pilnyak and Yakovlev have cre-ated a literature around famine. We should also mention Vladimir Lidin for his book *Stories of Many Days*,[19] where we see arising 'in the black night, blood, tor-ture, above years of torment, war, among lice, insults, hopes, banquets, prisons, elections and toasts – the October Revolution'.

We shall have to return to this new Russian literature. There will be great astonishment when it becomes known in Europe. All we wanted to do in this account was to notice it and briefly describe it – far too briefly. This will be enough for people to understand how deep is the gulf separating it from the drawing-room and bedroom literature whose sentimental complications are still so much in favour among the most educated public in old Europe.

A Little Note about Intellectual Activity in Russia

They are reconsidering reestablishing intellectual property rights. This ownership, so it appears, will be limited to the author and his direct heirs, and even to those for a substantially shorter time than was allowed for by the old legislation. Works considered useful to the public may be declared state property. The previous literary agreements made with foreign countries remain abolished.

A scholarly commission is preparing to publish an extensive work on *Contemporary Russian Culture* which will take in all the scientific work done in these last years. The public is complaining about the price of the book. Among new books we should mention Vera Figner, *Sealed Book* (the memoirs of a revolutionary who suffered twenty years in prison[20]); Preobrazhensky, *From the N.E.P. to Socialism*[21]; *In Memory of Those Who Died in the Revolution* (a biographical collection; *The October Revolution* (published by the Party Historical Commission; R. Rolland, *Theatre of the the Revolution*[22]; R. Kipling, *The Jungle Book*[23] (state publishing house); H. Roland-Holst, *Lyrical Dramas*[24]; A. Sologub-Teternikova, *Woman During the French Revolution*[25]; *The National Economy in 1922* (a documentary collection by the Supreme Council of the Economy); *A Marxist Reading Book* (in Ukranian); *Kharkov*, by S. I. Semkovsky[26] (Art Publishing House); *Portraits*, by I. Annenkov[27], an admirable series of a hundred contemporary portraits engraved in 1918–22.

An association of intellectuals has been formed in Moscow to study the problems of revolutionary culture (*October and Thought*). The Moscow Architectural Society has been set up again.

In the provinces the Kazan Poets' Union – a region ravaged by famine – is translating the Tatar poets. The poet Vyacheslav Ivanov is professor at the University of Baku.

Exploration and Research: Professor Ballod's[28] archaeological expedition in the Volga region has uncovered the ruins of Tatar cities from the fourteenth century providing evidence of a high cultural level.

Music: Unpublished works by Scriabin[29] and numerous monographs have been published (on Tchaikovsky,[30] Glazunov,[31] etc.). The orchestra without a conductor called the Symphonic Ensemble made its début in Moscow starting from 1 August.

Notes

1. Translated from *Clarté* no.28, 1 January 1923, pp.91–93 (translator's note).
2. Nikolay Vasilyevich Ustryalov (1890–1938) had been a supporter of the Cadets (Constitutional Democrats) and then a member of Kolchak's government, who edited *Smena Vekh (Change of Waymarks)*, a magazine that suggested that the Russia of the N.E.P. was on its way back to capitalism. His argument is summarised by Lenin, 'Political report of the Central Committee to the Eleventh Congress of the R.C.P.(B)', 27 March 1922, *Collected Works*, vol.xxxiii, Moscow, 1966, pp.286–7 (translator's note).
3. Vladimir Mikhailovich Bekhterev (1857–1927) was a psychiatrist and neuropathologist specialising in reflexology. Cesare Lombroso (1836–1909) was an Italian criminologist who held that criminal behaviour produced observable mental and physical traits in those habituated to it (translator's note).
4. Anatoly Vasilyevich Venediktov (1887–1959) was a jurist specialising in economic law (translator's note).
5. A. Zaitsev was an economist who wrote about mineral resources in Belorussia, agrarian questions, and Russian constitutional history (translator's note).
6. Y.M. Stein was the pseudonym of Ekaterina Mikhailovna Alexandrova (1864–1930), a Menshevik who specialised in the study of the cooperative movement and was later a functionary in the state trade union apparatus (translator's note).
7. Yakov Markovich Bukspan (1887–1939) was a lecturer in economic history. Fyodor Augustinovich Stepun (1884–1965) emigrated to Germany and became a professor of Sociology in Dresden. His main book on this subject, *Bolshevism and Christian Life*, was published much later, in 1959. Semyon Liudvigorich Frank (1877–1950) had been a Marxist in his youth, became a professor in Saratov, and also went over to a religious philosophy. He was deported from the USSR in 1922 (translator's note).
8. Vitalism is the theory that life does not owe its origins to chemical or physiological processes, but to some supposed life force (translator's note).
9. The Beast of the biblical Book of Revelation (xiii, vv.11–18) originally represented the persecuting power of the Roman Empire, but the image passed into Christian tradition as a symbol for any malignant political power (translator's note).
10. The Twelfth Congress of the C.P.S.U.(B) was held on 17–25 April 1923. Karl Bernhardovich Sobelsohn, known as Radek (1885–1939) began his career as a revolutionary in Poland and Germany, where he gained the censure of Rosa Luxemburg. He returned to Russia in 1918, where he became a noted propagandist for the regime. He was a supporter of the Left Opposition, but his subsequent capitulation to Stalin did not prevent him from being one of the main defendants in the Second Moscow Trial, that of the Seventeen, in 1937 (translator's note).
11. Mikhail Nikolayevich Pokrovsky (1868–1932) joined the R.S.D.L.P. in 1905, and was Chairman of the Moscow Soviet during the Russian Revolution. An English translation of his *Brief History of Russia* was published in London in 1933 (translator's note).
12. L. D. Trotsky, *Literature and Revolution* (English translation published by Ann Arbor, 1960, and Redwords, 1991) (translator's note).
13. This is not a question of the poet André Biely, and that seems a gap to me. For a very different judgement can be applied to several of his works (author's note). Trotsky discusses Biely's book in *Literature and Revolution*, Ann Arbor edition pp.46–55, Redwords edition pp.79–87 (translator's note).
14. L. D. Trotsky, op. cit., n.12 above, Ann Arbor edition pp.122–3, Redwords edition pp.153–55 (translator's note).
15. Flaubert was noted for his careful attention to detail. The Jacobins were the most radical of the leaders of the French Revolution, who controlled the country at the height of the Terror (translator's note).
16. Monsieur Homais was a Voltairean chemist, a typical local character who appears in Flaubert's *Madame Bovary* (translator's note).

17. L. D. Trotsky, op. cit., n.12 above, Ann Arbor edition pp.69–76, Redwords edition pp.102–109 (translator's note).
18. The Kirghiz are a Turkic people who inhabit a large area of southern Siberia; the Yakuts, another Turkic people, were the majority of the inhabitants of eastern Siberia during the time of the Russian Civil War (translator's note).
19. Lidin's *Stories of Many Days* was published in 1922 (translator's note).
20. Vera Nikolayevna Figner (1852–1942) was a heroic supporter of the Narodniks and the SRs who spent 20 years in the Schlusselburg Fortress for attempting to refound Narodnaya Volya. Three volumes of her memoirs, *Remembered Work*, were published in 1921–1922, and a French translation, *Mémoirs d'une révolutionnaire*, in Paris in 1930 (translator's note).
21. Preobrazhensky's *From the N.E.P. to Socialism* was published in 1922. An English translation by Brian Pearce came out in London in 1973 (translator's note).
22. Romain Rolland published *Théâtre de la Révolution*, a play, in 1909, but the first part, on the events of 14 July, was first performed on 21 March 1902 (translator's note).
23. Rudyard Kipling's *Jungle Books* were published in 1894 and 1895 (translator's note).
24. Henrietta Roland-Holst (1869–1952) was a Dutch left wing poet and political writer on the Executive of the Comintern at this time. She left the party in 1927 (translator's note).
25. Anastasia Nikolayevna (Chebotarevskaya) Sologub-Teternikova (1876–1921) was the wife of Fyodor Sologub. She committed suicide when her husband was denied permission to go abroad. Part i of *Woman in the French Revolution* was published posthumously in 1922 (translator's note).
26. Semyon Yulievich Bronstein, called Semkovsky (1882–1937) was a philosopher who worked with Trotsky in Vienna before the First World War, and then joined the Menshevik Central Committee, but went over to the Bolsheviks in 1920, after which he concentrated on scientific and literary research (translator's note).
27. Yuri Pavlovich Annenkov (1889–1974) was a Russian printer, author and graphic artist. He went abroad in 1924 (translator's note).
28. Professor Carl Ballod (1864–1933) was a German historian who wrote about Russian history (translator's note).
29. Alexander Nikolayevich Scriabin (1872–1915) was a composer of sonatas and concertos, particularly noted in revolutionary circles for *Prometheus* (1911). Molotov was a relative of his (translator's note).
30. Peter Ilich Tchaikovsky (1840–1893) has always been regarded as one of Russia's foremost composers (translator's note).
31. Alexander Constantinovich Glazunov (1865–1936) was one of Russia's major composers. He remained in the USSR after the Revolution, but left to live in Paris in 1928 (translator's note).

Chapter Four

The New Writer and the New Literature[1]

A woman is walking in the street. Her down-at-heel shoes are treading on spit. She sees her life in the spit. It has snowed that morning. Amid the splendour of the cold and light a sledge is carrying a young girl whose whispered name becomes a story in itself. A provincial doctor who has to look after idiots becomes like them. An old professor sees at the end of his days the futility and emptiness of his existence, and that there is nothing, nothing ... They have sold the *Cherry Orchard*, his family inheritance[2] ... Such are the subjects of Anton Chekhov's best stories, which we must always call to mind when we think about Russian literature and society under the old order. Mortal anxiety wanders over this literature, the expression of this society (there is a lot of suicide in Chekhov's plays). One of his masterpieces is, moreover, simply entitled *A Dreary Story*.[3] And if this feeling of boredom reaches its highest level of sharpness in Chekhov, he is no different from other writers about manners in the pre-revolutionary period. The petty bourgeois and intellectuals of Maxim Gorky's *Summer Folk*,[4] Kuprin's little garrisons and Leonid Andreyev's students and artists provide us with the same tragic impression of a useless existence. 'Rotting, thickly swathed in annoyance ...' (Verhaeren).

We understand all too well the social causes of this psychosis today: under the rule of the Holy Synod, the Okhrana[5] and a prematurely degenerated bourgeoisie, everything withered. The human spirit only had a very small number of ways out: revolutionary activity (that was the fate of energetic people, but it led straight to prison), mysticism and extravagance. Hardly keen, basically, to lose the material benefits all the same allowed them by this society, the majority of the intellectuals 'sought the ways of God' after the manner of Merezhkovsky, or were engulfed by contemplating the drama of their own impotence in the face of destiny (Andreyev, *The Life of Man*, *The Black Masks*[6]).

Nothing is more striking than the contrast between this literature – even though it is one of the richest – of a bourgeois society in decline with that of Red Russia in the year 1922.

* * * * *

At the end of 1921 there was still no new literature in Red Russia. Apart from the recognised works of a few poets (Blok, Biely, Yesenin, Mayakovsky and Kluyev) the revolution had still not contributed anything to literature. The tale, the short story and the novel seemed impossible. To be able to create the writer needs long periods to be able to take things in. The syntheses he creates are preceded by innumerable analyses. He can create *one peasant* only after penetrating the minds of thousands of peasants – the masses. On top of this, literary creativity is preceded by the crystallisation of social types. Now in 1918, 1919, 1920 and 1921 social types were not yet sufficiently fixed, or studied for long enough, for the writer to be in a position to recreate them. It had previously been easy to create a female and a male student talking with each other, an officer and an intellectual, a woman or a muzhik and a priest. But now he saw fresh students who had come out of the factory and were on their way to fight; the officer was dead or was sacking Novorossiisk;[7] the intellectual woman was spending her afternoons putting together oatcakes; the priest was selling eggs ... How do we make these unforseen personalities speak and act in a book, with every day being even more unexpected? What would the young Red commander who had previously been a mechanic in the Dynamo factory, or the young female apprentice agitator from Zhenotdel[8] (the Women's Section) think of the crafty 'bagman' who is secretly bringing into the city potatoes, and typhus along with them? The writer knew nothing about it. And in any case he would himself have been preoccupied with getting his own next day's potatoes ...

The old writer emigrated or, if he could not do this, joined the 'internal emigration'. Since the revolution, which had taken away his caste privileges, was imposing the same burdens upon him as upon the rest of the citizens, and was completely suppressing the sinecures he got for amusing idlers, he ended up hating it from the bottom of his soul. But hatred is not creative, above all when it is linked to an a priori utter inability to come to terms with a loss of privilege. From 1919 onwards, when people took up firm positions, it became obvious that one phase of intellectual life had ended in Russia, and that the older generation no longer had anything to contribute ...

The new people arrived in 1922. Along with the NEP? No. They came along with peace, the end of the Civil War, the end of the terror, and going back to work.

* * * * *

The new people are really new.

The poet Alexander Kusikov (*Towards Nothing*), a very good poet, and one of the youngest, freely recites some verses that begin in this way:

> Everywhere they are saying that I am a scoundrel
> A nasty and crafty Cherkess ...[9]

Is this Byronism[10] and vulgarity? Boasting? In no way. This Kuban cossack fought in the Civil War. A Red commander, he intervened in the middle of a pogrom pointing a revolver. He has seen the utmost human bestiality at work. Foul language does not frighten him, nor blows, and his very noticeable lack of morality does not rule out spiteful action, an eye for an eye and a tooth for a tooth, the rule of the class struggle is just as valid in the Caucasus as elsewhere. Kusikov is an authentic Red. Serge Yesenin, who is not at all a hooligan, it is true, writes *The Confessions of a Hooligan*, and notes on an autobiographical page: 'During the Revolution I travelled from the Arctic Sea to the Caspian and India, and from the Western borders to China' (we ought not to ask him in which rickety carts and broken down wagons, filled with typhus sufferers and thieves). 'The most beautiful year of my life was 1919. It was five degrees below zero in winter in our rooms.'[11] Vladimir Mayakovsky is not yet thirty years old: he was a Bolshevik at fifteen, in breach of the law at sixteen, and imprisoned for eleven months at seventeen. He described the war as having his heart turned over by a horrible repulsion. He made out the two revolutions of March and October to be the most natural things in the world: what was monstrous was that they should not have happened earlier. During the days of March 1917: 'Went with the cars to the Duma. Slipped into Rodzianko's office. Looked over Milyukov. He said nothing. But for some reason it seems to me that he hiccoughs when he speaks.Got fed up with them after an hour. Went away'.[12]

I have other short autobiographies of Russian writers to hand. Constantine Fedin, one of the Serapion Brothers, a little peasant from Saratov, still has the frightening memory of the pogroms from his infancy. A shop accountant and a student in Germany, and a civilian prisoner during the war, he gave himself body and soul to the Red October. At Syzran in the east, 'I was editor, manager, typesetter and proof reader of the local paper, and lecturer, chairman and secretary of the executive of the soviet, a volunteer in the Red cavalry, and a commissar ... That was my best year.'[13] In Petrograd, while they were fighting against Yudenich, this young poet was in the Bashkirian Division. During one journey he stayed 'thrice twenty-four hours in a railtruck full of sufferers from typhus...' Alexander Yakovlev, a writer of beautiful stories, himself also a revolutionary just emerging from adolescence, even had a narrow escape from the gallows. Joining up as a stretcher-bearer, he saw 'in less than an hour almost 20,000 choked by German gas'. 'I spent the winter of 1918–19 without taking off my clothes, my socks or my hat. Hunger swelled up my feet and hands. Both of the people closest to me died ...' André Sobol (*Freak Show*, *The Madman*, and *The Pullman Car*, things seen during the revolution) is thirty-four years old.[14] A Socialist Revolutionary, he was a convict in 1906, taken from one prison to another; then, having escaped in 1909, he passed through Switzerland, Rome, Brussels, Paris, Copenhagen, Nice, Munich and many other places. Having volunteered for the French army, he took part in the retreat from Serbia,[15] got back illegally to Russia in 1917, was beaten up by Bolshevik soldiers, fled during the October Revolution, was nearly shot by the Whites in the Ukraine, avoided having his throat cut in a pogrom – he is Jewish – in Odessa, and finally spent six months in a Cheka prison for being a counter-revolutionary ... He settled down in Moscow. I will go no further with these references, which are very typical. The Russian writer of today has experienced a great deal of hardship. He did not learn about 'life's epic venture' out of old books. Least of all is he a literateur, a snob or a coiner of phrases. He can talk about revolution knowing what it is. The great upheaval has made of him a new man. Here is a little detail to end up with that I find striking, that shows to what extent the new man has overcome intellectualism without thinking about it among these 'literary types'. Obviously, nothing is more precious to a writer than his thought, the work of his mind and hands, elaborated at great length, cherished, thought about, and held on to ... Eugene Lundberg, in his remarkable *Notes of a Writer* (1919–1921[16]) nonetheless describes so simply, in fifteen lines, how he lost in the most banal and accidental circumstances the results of four years' work, all his manuscripts from Siberia, his essays on Rabelais, Montaigne amd Pascal[17] ...

André Biely, as well, lost an entire volume of his works, a whole year's work, and talks about it in the same simple way. I see a sign of the times in these writer's detachment with regard to the 'precious things' of the world ...

⋆   ⋆   ⋆   ⋆   ⋆

Their style cannot even be compared with that of Chekhov. To start off with, they are far more Russian than the very cultivated, very European intellectuals from before the revolution. For having been of the common people during its terrible and magnificent years – which were, let us not forget it, those in which Red Russia found itself very closely cut off from all intellectual contact abroad – they have delved into the peasant vocabulary, discovered its riches, and tasted its strong flavour. Present-day literature shows a renewal of the language, enriched by returning to its roots in the speech of the masses, above all the rural masses. They make free use of the dialogue form. Vsevolod Ivanov writes an entire novel – but is it really a novel? – 'a slice of the life of my Kalmuk, Bashkir, Yakut and Great Russian brothers, the Red partisans of Siberia' – made out of dialogues of tiny phrases, short, cut and sudden; you are laconic when you are fighting in the *taiga*.[18] You are in the diametrical opposite of the salons where M. Marcel Proust holds forth! Their style is singularly direct, wastes no words, and is contemptuous of rhetoric. The Serapion Brothers have the great merit of cultivating their writing. They have achieved a beautifully realistic concision. If a Vsevolod Ivanov or a Pilnyak are sometimes diffuse, it is quite simply because they are still searching and groping; when they succeed, there is not a word too many, and everything is called by its own name. They have a noticeable aversion to psychological study. Their literature is one of action. Thought reveals itself above all in activity, obviously it does. In the best works (Pilnyak's *Naked Year*, for example) an extraordinary dynamism holds sway. The storm is everywhere, people, things and events are overturned, are driven along, are loosened up, and are mixed up together in a continual vibrating thrust. It is a literature of action, realistic, dynamic, with a direct style that relegates to second place the subjective topics of life, and almost ignores 'questions of conscience', the old Russian writer's usual theme, and takes no account of any moralism. It is a literature for new men, who, instead of dreaming, are determined to live: completely cured, so we might think, of intellectualism.

'*Why should we live?*' is also absent from it. Is this what you dream about when you have to work hard at digging a hole in the snow for somewhere to sleep? Mysticism is very, very much downplayed. Life is for grasping with both hands, palpably material. He who reads Tolstoy and Korolenko is to begin with shocked by the apparent lack of morality in these works and these men. I said apparent: because it is the lack of morality in nature that is everywhere pitiless, and tramples on our most sacred laws of good and evil, for it never loses sight of the supreme good: living. Listen: some partisans – in the remotest part of Siberia – have killed a couple of 'Whites' and have discovered his newborn infant, who was crying in the sledge. They get the infant fed by a Kirghiz woman, kidnapped for that purpose from her tribe. And because the Kirghiz woman cannot share her milk – there is not enough of it for two – these men sewed up the little Kirghiz in a sack and abandoned it in the steppe. There is only room for one here: and ours must survive! It is so cruel and so true, this mixture of charity and inexorability! (Vsevolod Ivanov, *The Child*[19]).

★　★　★　★　★

Vladimir Lidin writes: 'I was born in Moscow in 1918 like all those for whom Russia is a dream and a faith ...', and Yakovlev, 'now I see Russia reborn ...' Is he not mixing up the N.E.P. with rebirth? Did he see nothing being born earlier? Constantine Fedin writes, 'it seems that my revolution has ended. I have books and I write ...', and Yesenin jokes, 'I am not a Communist, I am more to the left.'

These writers, created by the revolution, are not in fact revolutionaries, or are only such (Pilnyak, Nikitin and Ivanov) in an instinctive or an incomplete manner. You are disappointed if you read them for you find no general ideas. They experienced the storm without trying to make sense of it, and without agreeing with it in all their consciousness. They have looked at its minor aspects very closely; but they have not penetrated its deep secret. Have they voluntarily abstained from all ideology or do they not possess one? No essential affirmation gives life to their works, however alive they may be in their particular context. Or else there is a pure and simple affirmation of the creative energy of

Bolshevism, a cry of admiration and no more (Pilnyak, *Naked Year*). These great talents are politically limited. A revolutionary used to grand vistas and the strong construction of Communist thought is unhappy to observe their doctrinal insufficiency.

Let us try to explain it. To begin with, these men are not proletarians, nor are they intellectuals assimilated by the proletariat: the latter don't have time to write stories. The idea of class is quite foreign to them: like the Socialist Revolutionaries they more freely speak about the 'people', a vague idea, which belongs to the old advanced liberalism. Not being assimilated by the revolutionary class, and never having understood how to think along with it, they remain subject to contrary influences. Their future depends upon it. Their literature is not that of a victorious proletarian revolution, nor that of a defeated revolution. It corresponds exactly to the transitional period. It will become what Russia will become. If it should – as some hope – evolve towards bourgeois democracy, these writers will be transformed without difficulty into good members of a 'Society of Moscow Writers', cleverly exploiting their memories of an eventful youth. But if the dictatorship of the proletariat leads Red Russia towards Communism, by adapting to their milieu little by little, in ten years they may be in tune with the period, and perhaps really revolutionaries ...

Once again, in the light of the experience in Russia, the intellectuals – writers and artists – appear to us not as the creators of new values, in the deep sense of the word, but as charged with expressing, passively and faithfully, the consequences of the class struggle in the inner life of the masses.

Memorandum

Among the new books: Arslan, *The New Turkey*. Jordanov, *The Balkans After the War*. V. Kriupin, *The Red Cockerel* (The Jacquerie). S. I. Wolfson, *Historical Materialism*. Sidorov, *The ABC of Communism*. L. Kamenev, *History of Housing*.[20] Historical Commission of the Communist Party, *The Mensheviks in the First Russian Revolution*. In Five Years – P. Kerzhentsev, *Principles of Organisation*.[21] A. Rykov, *The Economic Situation*.[22] *Historical Materialism* (Jaurès, Lafargue, Kautsky, Engels). J. Jaurès, *The Convention*. P. Rolland, *Les Amies*.[23] I Walls, *Walt Whitman and the World Crisis*. R. Hilferding, *Finance Capital*.[24] Numerous very luxurious artistic albums, Ostrumova-Lebedeva, *Petrograd*. Mitrokhin, *Graphic*

Art.[25] Pavlov, *Engraving.*[26] Konnenkov, *Works*. Pavlov, *Corners of Moscow*, etc., etc.
Magazines: In no.1 of *Red Archives* N. Pokrovsky is publishing all the documents concerning Russo-German relations from 1875 to 1914. New magazines: *Pedagogical Teaching* (Petrograd). *The Science of Nature in School, Teaching College, The Journal for the Study of Early Infancy, The Atheist, Notebooks of the Society of Scientific Marxists*. And *Krasnaya Nov* is publishing the works of Alexis Tolstoy and I. Ehrenburg.

Theatre – Alexandrovsky Theatre, Petrograd: they are rehearsing *The Diary of Satan* by Leonid Andreyev. Dramatic Theatre, Moscow – *Father Serge*, by Tolstoy. First Studio of the Moscow Arts Theatre – *King Lear* (Shakespeare), and *The Golden Book of Love* (Alexis Tolstoy). 30 December: 150th performance of Oscar Wildes's *Salome*[27] in the Kamerny Theatre in Moscow.

V. S.

Notes

1. Translated from *Clarté*, no.xxxi, 15 February 1923, pp.158–160 (translator's note).
2. Chekhov's *Cherry Orchard*, a play, came out in 1904 (translator's note).
3. Chekhov's *Skuchnaia istoriia* is variously translated into English as a 'dreary', 'boring' or 'tedious' story (translator's note).
4. Gorky's *Summer Folk* (1905) is a play that explores the essential futility of the lives of provincials (translator's note).
5. The Holy Synod was the department of state set up to regulate the affairs of the Russian Orthodox Church: it had extensive powers of censorship. The Okhrana was the tsarist secret police (translator's note).
6. Andreyev's play, *The Black Masks*, was translated into English by C. I. Meader and F. N. Scott, and published in *Three Plays: The Black Masks, The Life of Man and The Sabine Women*, New York, 1915 (translator's note).
7. *Novorossiisk* fell into Krasnov's hands early in the Civil War, and when he retreated there his army began to disintegrate (translator's note).
8. Zhenotdel was the Women's Section of the Communist Party set up in September 1919 by a directive of the Central Committee out of the previously existing Commissions for Propaganda Among Women Workers (translator's note).
9. Alexander Borisovich Kusikov (1896–1977) was a Futurist and Imagist poet who left Russia for Berlin in 1921, and then went on to Paris. (translator's note).
10. Byron (1788–1824) was a poet, chiefly appreciated in revolutionary circles for *Childe Harold* (1812–8) (translator's note).
11. Yesenin's *Confessions of a Hooligan* was translated by Charles Brasch and Peter Soskice in *Poems by Esenin*, Wellington, 1970, no.14, and by Geoffrey Thirley in *Fifty Poems by Sergei Essenin*, Cheadle Hulme, 1973, pp.45–7, but this autobiographical note was not included (translator's note).
12. V. Mayakovsky, 'I Myself', 1922, as translated by Alex Miller in *V. Mayakovsky, Selected Verse*, vol.i, Raduga 1985, p.40 (translator's note).
13. Fedin was on the Executive Committee of the Syzran Soviet for eight months, and while there edited a

newspaper and the journal *Otkliki*. He fled to Moscow when Denikin advanced on the town. He served in the Bashkirian division in the defence of Petrograd, and was assistant editor of the 7th Army's newspaper. Cf. K. Fedin, *Sobranie sochinenij y devjati tomax*, i, Moscow, 1959, p.12 (translator's note).

14. Sobol wrote *The Freak Show*, which was translated into English by Jenny Covan, New York, 1930. *The Pullman Car* is the longest story in his collection *The Wreckage*, published in 1923 (translator's note).

15. After Greece had entered the war the Allies promised to send aid to Serbia via Salonica in October 1915. However, only a third of the promised forces arrived, and these were defeated by the German, Austrian and Bulgarian armies, after which the front became deadlocked (translator's note).

16. Evgenny Germanovich Lundberg (1883–1965), a writer and literary critic, published *Notes of a Writer, 1917–20*, in 1922 (translator's note).

17. François Rabelais (1494–1553) was a great humanist and writer of comic fictions of the Renaissance period in France, whose exhuberant writing in *Pantagruel* (1532) and *Gargantua* (1534) held up the ideals of the feudal epoch to public ridicule. Michel de Montaigne (1533–1592) was a French writer famous for pioneering the essay as a literary form (translator's note).

18. The *taiga* is the marshy pine forest country of Siberia (translator's note).

19. Vsevolod Ivanov, *The Child*, translated by Helen Colacides in Krystyn Pomorska (ed.), *Fifty Years of Russian Prose*, vol.1, Cambridge Massachussetts, 1971, pp.82–91. This short story was first published in Petrograd in 1918 (translator's note).

20. Lev Borisovich Kamenev (Rosenfeld, 1883–1936) was the main Bolshevik leader who opposed the overthrow of the Provisional Government in 1917. He was murdered by Stalin after the first Moscow trial (translator's note).

21. Kerzhentsev was the pseudonym of Platon Mikhailovich Lebedev (1881–1940), a historian and supporter of the Bolsheviks from 1904 onwards. He was Assistant Editor of *Izvestia* in 1918, and Executive Director of ROSTA, the state telegraph agency, in 1919–20 (translator's note).

22. Alexei Ivanovich Rykov (1881–1938) was President of the National Economic Council in 1918. He later became a leader of the Right Opposition along with Bukharin, and was a defendant with him in the third Moscow Trial (translator's note).

23. Pierre Rolland was the pen name of Pierre Joseph Louis Jules le Loup de Sacy de Rolland (1877–) a French writer and dramatic author. (translator's note).

24. Rudolf Hilferding (1877–1941), an Austro-Marxist and a prominent theorist of the German SPD, published his *Finance Capital* in Vienna in 1910 (English edition, London, 1978) (translator's note).

25. Dmitry Isidorovich Mitrokhin (1883–1973) was a noted Russian graphic artists (translator's note).

26. Ivan Nikolayevich Pavlov (1872–1951) was a Russian artist and engraver (translator's note).

27. Oscar Wilde (1854–1900) brought out *Salome* in 1893. It was censored by the authorities for bringing unnatural passion into a Biblical theme (translator's note).

Chapter Five

Proletarian Literature[1]

'Advanced' thinking people still condemn the involvement of politics with the arts. Doesn't the artist have the 'sacred duty' not to take sides in the 'social conflict'? And there is no point in talking to them about proletarian literature. 'Free' thought claims not to give its allegiance to classes in struggle, and condemns 'all violence and all dictatorships'. Let us not waste time refuting these ideas yet again, which are so weak that they are only a trap, for in the final analysis they come down to an attachment to bourgeois thinking, under its liberal form, and to submission to the dictatorship of the bourgeoisie in its democratic form. This language – doubtless courageous and sincere at times – can really only belong to men who are comfortable with the old society, used to identifying culture with capitalism, and who find the violence of the bourgeoisie so natural that a policeman passing under their windows calls for no comment. Let us rather ask for the facts to decide on the impartiality of modern literature and thinking ...

Several tens of millions of proletarians the wide world over labour, and the whole of civilisation obviously rests upon their work. They are the world's builders. Nothing exists that has not been made by their hands. They are more numerous than the nations. But as opposed to the smallest of the nations, which in this instance are represented by their bourgeoisies, they have no intellectual culture of their own, no scholars, no artists, no writers and no poets. There is no country in the capitalist world where the working class freely takes part in intellectual life. Arts, literature and sciences are the exclusive inheritance of the possessing classes.

Do you doubt it?

Then name the French scholars, writers and poets educated by the working class! Quote the works inspired by work and the workers! Quote the works where the *thinking* of the workers stands out! You will be hard put to do it.

Just cast a glance over French literature (which in this respect is similar to that of the majority of other countries). The overwhelming majority of writers belong by origin, education and standard of living to the bourgeoisie or to the middle classes. The immense majority of their works are intended for the relaxation and intellectual culture of the well-off or rich classes. The 'best' works are exclusively intended for them; it is said hypocritically that they are aimed at 'the elite'. Some men can claim to be from the proletariat as far as their origins are concerned: they *came from* it.

The very few works in which the proletariat occasionally recognises its aspirations and rhythm of life are those of noble deserters who have come over to it from the enemy classes. They are rare. Its nourishment – and what a miserable pittance it is! – is all the time provided for it, wholesale and retail, by the popular press and the bourgeois bookshop, practically working factories as far as the masses are concerned. Poisoning the minds of the workers is powerfully organised.

★   ★   ★   ★   ★

The success of the October Revolution was necessary for intellectual culture to become accessible to the workers in a great European country. It is an experience that ought to make the reformists think: the proletariat can only grow, mature, be educated and create on its own behalf after it has won. It must win its right to a higher life through struggle. The Russians have won it.

They won it five years ago: the civil war started by the Allied military intervention came to an end in 1921. The Russians have only been working and thinking for five years, and with what difficulties! No country has ever been more put to the test than theirs. But the Revolution gave rise to such fruitful sowings; and a magnificent harvest has already been raised from them.

This country has universities full of workers and peasants. This country has hundreds and thousands of worker and peasant newspaper correspondents. This country has young – proletarian – scholars, and the country has a rich proletarian literature.

As early as 1922 Semyon Rodov,[2] himself a young Communist writer, collected together, in an *Anthology of Proletarian Writers* which appeared last year, the names of sixty *outstanding* prose writers and poets belonging to the Russian working class. In the revised edition the anthology contains a good hundred names.

The young proletarian literature has at its disposal several magazines (*Young*

Guard, October, On Literary Guard). It is enriched with a variety of varied talents in full vigour. Poetry is closer to action than any other literary form. And in any case don't all literatures begin with heroic poetry? Ours is no exception. It already includes two generations of poets who profoundly differ in their sources of inspiration: those from before and from after 1921. The former, now out of fashion (Kirillov, Alexandrovsky, Kazin, Gerasimov, Sadofev) was inspired by the romanticism of the heroic years; the latter (Bezymensky, Zharov, Utkin[3] and Sannikov) is looking for its heroic motifs in the reality of everyday life deprived of rhetoric, for elements of a new internal life and powerful agreement, both individual and collective.

Demyan Biedny, a writer of fables, a story teller and author of innumerable rhyming news sheets, whose popularity is immense, is close to Communist publicists such as Sosnovsky and Koltsov, who devote their many-sided talents as moralists, pamphleteers and story tellers to an unceasing denuciation of abuses.

The Marxist dialectic is used to critical thinking: literary criticism, as you might expect, is one of the strongest features of proletarian literature. It has a horror of eclecticism as empty; it spares nothing and no one; it is incisive, brutal, scathing and pitiless; the whole stubbornness of the revolution is found there. We ought to mention here Kogan, Raskolnikov, V. Poliansky, Boris Volin, G. Lelevich, S. Rodov, L. Averbach and G. Gorbachev.[4]

More numerous, the proletarian prose writers also have a less prominent profile. Novels and short stories rarely turn out well for them. They have doubtless not yet reached the necessary level of maturity: the novel is the height of literary creativity. Our record, however, is not negligible. There are the great epic compositions of old Serafimovich, *The Iron Flood*, *The Week* and *The Commissars*, of Yury Libedinsky, Fyodor Gladkov's *Cement*, the remarkable chronicles of the Civil War (*Chapayev* and *The Rebellion*) by Dmitry Furmanov – whom death took from us this year at the age of thirty-five – and there is S. Semyonov's terrifyingly realistic book *Hunger*. With only one exception these works all belong to young people. It would be all too easy to draw attention to their inadequacies. They are vivid, alive, strong and meaningful works in which a new and vital feeling for life is expressed.

No doubt *the other* Russian literature of today is richer as regards form and generally superior to ours. It benefits from the traditions of the Russian intelligentsia, experience going back for nearly a century, in other words, more preoccupied with form rather than content, and contemptuous of 'ideology' – and often inclining towards the well-worn paths of bourgeois literature. It is a literature for littérateurs in the old sense of the word: ours is a literature for revolutionaries. Give it ten years to prove itself, and we shall see what it is capable of. The gains produced by its first years of work sufficiently prove the intellectual fertility of the exploited classes – as soon as their chains fall from them.

Victor Serge   **Leningrad, August 1926.**

Notes

1. Translated from *L'Humanité*, 26 September 1926 (translator's note).
2. Semyon Abramovich Rodov (1893–1968) was a poet, literary theorist and translator, who worked with *Kuznitsa*, and then with *Na Postu* and *Oktyabr* (translator's note).
3. Osip P. Utkin (1903–1944), the son-in-law of Raskolnikov, was a poet and journalist who had served in the Red Army (translator's note).
4. Fyodor Fyodorovich Ilyin, called Raskolnikov (1892–1939) was a Bolshevik naval leader in the Civil War, which he describes in *Kronstadt and Petrograd in 1917* and *Tales of Sub-Lieutenant Ilyin* (English translations by Brian Pearce, 1982), later served as an ambassador and was also on the editorial board of *Young Guard* and *Red Virgin Soil*. Valerian Poliansky was the pseudonym of the Marxist literary critic Pavel Ivanovich Lebedev (1882–1948) Boris Mikhailovich Fradkin, called Volin (1886–1957), who joined the Bolsheviks in 1904, was appointed Editor of *Pravda* in 1918 and Assistant Editor of *Izvestia* in 1925. He was the author of several works on the history of Bolshevism (translator's note).

Chapter Six

On Literary Creation: Russian Writers Tell us How They Work[1]

Eighteen Soviet Russian writers have collected together some articles, the majority of them substantial, into a volume entitled *How We Write*.[2] If they were restricting themselves to developing publicity for themselves, as usual, we would not be talking about it; but they are doing far more, they are attempting to give the reader access to this inner laboratory, which is no less interesting after all than the laboratory of a physicist. They have been blamed for being willing to talk about themselves, a point of vanity that so easily identifies a man of letters and strikes such a disagreeably false note in the eyes of people for whom the 'literary affair' is something vain in itself, when it doesn't in some way serve much greater ends ... For an artist to attain some simplicity it needs real greatness or a revolutionary spirit just as rare.

This book deserves to be translated while the investigation should be continued. The people who began it rightly claim that they are working from the principle of work organisation. Intellectual work must receive the same scientific attention as any other. By his sustained, scrupulous, careful and hardworking character, living off his own efforts, the literary person who does not want to become one who just amuses idlers takes his place among the workers in the most serious sense of the word. In this sense a Zola is very much a great 'literary worker'. We should note, however, for it results in important differences in mental outlook, that a writer is closer to an artisan than a worker.

Gorky points out that he began to write in his twelfth year and that he had already been subjected to a 'profuse experience'. One of the first lines he wrote was this one, full of practical philosophy: 'Ah, life is happy; it's a pity there is nobody to fight'. No good can be done, he says, by treating men with cold detachment: 'The writer must love his human material, the living man, at least a little, or admire him as a subject ...' Zamyatin provides a remarkable description in miniature of the various states of thinking that in one way or another organise themselves in creative work. A deep and tense collaboration is set up between the conscious and the unconscious, of which neither are simple categories, but on the contrary are infinitely complicated in their forms and combinations. 'The most difficult thing is to start off, to leave the shore of the real for the dream.' Zamyatin points to the process of internal crystallisation which operates unconsciously in the mind and is an essential condition for creating. When, on the other hand, we start off from a thesis or an idea, we must 'hypnotise ourselves' to bring on this process.

Moreover, the procedures and the methods can vary quite markedly. If investigations of this type multiply, and above all if the writers consulted make the effort to respond to them with the requisite seriousness, material for a new classification can begin to be found in it: it can indubitably be seen that there are more or less pure and mixed mentalities. And however true Zamyatin's theory might be, it might well only be true, or characteristic of one type of writer.

The humourist Zoshchenko, so bitter and so serious in his sketches of stupidity, silly little things, banality and mediocrity, after having mentioned that he works best when 'things go by themselves', provides this definition of inspiration: 'It is the fortunate coming together of physical health, awakening, freshening of the nerves and self confidence that allows all the strengths of the personality to be concentrated ...' That seems too simple; we do not see enough of the mobilisation of the forces of the unconscious that makes the writer, starting off from what he observes, leave it to begin once more on a wholly different plane.

Tynyanov, the writer of fine historical novels, shows us that language and history are encumbered with a jumble of false, conventional and falsified notions; and that 'official documents can lie as much as people'. Distrust documents, dig into them, try to discover what they are hiding. 'I start where the document ends.' There is much to be said on this theme. Will the proceedings instituted some time ago by M. Norton Cru[3] against the war writers be taken up again from another angle: are non-literary documents more true? We might say that official documents about the War lie far more than those novelists who are the least concerned for the truth ... And here, about the relationship between the lie and literary imagination, is a curiously apt observation from Boris Pilnyak: 'My childhood took place between Mojaisk and Saratov; in Saratov I lied immeasurably about Mojaisk, and in Mojaisk I lied about Saratov, peopling the two towns with all I knew that was marvellous. I lied in order to organise nature and ideas in a way that appeared to me to be the best and most entertaining.'

Fedin and Shishkov pay attention to style: How musical the prose is, and how the rhythm of the style corresponds with that of the action or the subject. In his own way, each of these eighteen Russian writers seems to say well what appears to be the essential thing for them about a craft that is more imposed upon them than chosen. 'I write everything because I cannot but write' (Pilnyak). And yet we remain astonished, once we have closed the book, to find an immense gap in it. One essential factor in literary creation – conviction – is only valued by one of these 'literary artisans' – the Communist writer Libedinsky, in whom, morover, conviction is identified with his profession. On the part of Gorky, who was always a fighter in the highest sense of the word, it is only an omission. It is a disconcerting oversight on the part of the others.

Great literature, which excites the masses and contributes to forming consciousness, is always the work of writers moved by passionate convictions. We only have to recall Balzac, presenting the worship of gold when the victorious bourgeoisie was changing the world in its own image. Closer to us, Zola remains a giant, and among the Russians, from Dostoyevsky to Tolstoy, Korolenko and Gorky. We must not only want to explain, but to act – for we only explain forcefully when we do act – in order to produce more than merely books, however excellent. Periods of social calm can often be satisfied with analysts, painters and entertainers, but not ours! We live in the heavy atmosphere of the end of one world and the birth of another, and for twenty years we have seen wars, victorious revolutions, vanquished revolutions, terrors, famines, prosperity, crises, armaments and diplomatic comedies repeatedly beating against a civilisation admirable in its possibilities and revolting and repugnant in its effects. We must think of man, ground down by so many forces. The future is too dark for us to be sure of it, and it is with will, knowledge, and militant earnestness – in a word, with conviction – that today's writer needs to speak to the masses. He must bring them reasons for living – for struggling, in other words; he must, more exactly, reveal to them the reasons they already have. If a new literature must triumph over the sale of printed paper, it will be that which talks to the man of today of the cataclysms in a language appropriate to his needs: that which will help him to find a way out.

Victor Serge

Notes

1. Translated from *Monde*, 9 January 1932 (translator's note).
2. Publication of the Writers' Bookshop, Leningrad. The following have collaborated in this book: André Biely, Maxim Gorky, Eugene Zamyatin, Mikhail Zoshchenko, Benjamin Kaverin, Boris Lavrenyov, Yuri Libedinsky, Nicholas Nikitin, Boris Pilnyak, M. Slonimsky, Nicholas Tikhonov, Alexei Tolstoy, Yuri Tynyanov, Constantine Fedin, Olga Forsh, Alexei Chapygin and Vyacheslav Shishkov (author's note). Boris Andreyevich Lavrenyov (1891–1959) was a poet who began writing in 1913. His best known work is *The Forty-First* (1924), about a Red heroine in the Russian Civil War. Olga Dmitryevna Forsh (1875–1961) was a historical novelist. Her *Clad with Stone* (1927) is about the old terrorist movement against the Tsar. Vyacheslav Shishkov (1873–1945) was a novelist. His book *The Gang* (1923) is about a group of Old Believers who became revolutionary partisans in the Russian Civil War (translator's note).
3. Jean Norton Cru (1879–1949) was born of English and French parents and fought in the First World War. He collected testimonies from the soldiers at the front to prepare reliable materials for future historians. His *Témoins: essai d'analyse et de critique des souvenirs de combattants édités en français de 1915 à 1928* was published in Paris in 1929 (translator's note).

Part Three

Books and Writers

Alexander Blok[1]

The greatest of present day Russian poets, one of the magicians of word and thought, who best expressed the deep sense of the revolution, has just died. Alexander Blok died in Petrograd on Sunday, 7 August, in the morning. Russian literature will be in mourning for him for a long time. For he was indubitably among those three or four great lyric poets whom nature gives to a privileged people in a hundred years. Moreover, for many years, and without any mutual admiration society having hailed him as 'the prince of poets', he was very much the first, the most admired and the most loved of the master musicians of the Russian language.

He leaves a considerable and lasting work, almost exclusively poetic. His most admired books are called *Poems About the Beautiful Lady*, *The Unexpected Joy*, *The Snow Mask*, and *The Earth in Snow*, seemingly untranslatable titles, which already contain a bit of enchantment, very musical, mystical and charming at the same time, whose basic symbols were eternally united, and *The Rose and the Cross*, in which joy and flowers are etherealised by noble suffering – a martyr crowned with the most beautiful and sweet smelling flowers.[2]

His work is inspired by mysticism, very much original, avoiding all religous or conventional symbolism, but always concerned to reveal among ephemeral forms and images, in light, indecisive minor harmonies, or in vague illuminating touches, the intangible and inexpressible feeling that is love – sadly – and dreams of flying from 'the Unknown' towards the stars. Even though his mastery of the Russian language was almost perfect, he was never a virtuoso of verse, nor, properly speaking, a poet by trade. In his books we find neither patriotic song, chant, didactic poem nor material 'with a message' – with which the academicians and poet laureates of the West are unfortunately accustomed to disgracing themselves. Alexander Blok was only a singer, a very great singer, who experienced things as a poet and expressed his intimate emotion or dream as he felt it at the time.

And this is perhaps why it was granted to him to leave to Red October's revolutionary Russia two poems that are masterpieces, because they sum up, express and deeply praise the revolution: *The Twelve*, and *The Scythians*.

A French translation of *The Twelve* has recently appeared in *La Vie Ouvrière*. But the poet and musician of *The Rose and the Cross* is in reality untranslatable. *The Twelve* – twelve Red Guards of November 1917, clad in torn overcoats, armed with Austrian rifles, are going through the black night in the white snow. Above their heads a streamer rattles in the wind, bearing an inscription that is lost in the darkness: 'All Power to the Constituent Assembly' ... They go forward: their shots bursting out into the night are inexorably dispersing the shadows of the past. These are poor, rough, violent and sad men. One of them with a blow of his gun knocks onto the pavement his former girlfriend who is riding on a sledge in an officer's arms ... And on the snow behind them lies a spot of blood: but though they go on 'with powerful step', followed by a poor starving beast, these twelve do not know that 'invisible in the storm, safe from human harm, in a chaplet of white roses, stepping through the pearly snowdust, shrouded in the snowy mist, in the distance is – Jesus Christ'.[3]

They do not know that they are the twelve unknown bearers of a new Gospel, and that the ideal they are following without knowing it is invulnerable to their own shots ...

In this poem, in which each word, because it is so vibrant, carries so that it can be heard in the street, there are lines in which the revolution has practically framed its slogans by attaching them to the walls of its capitals:

> Bourgeois, bourgeois, you beware
> When we set the world on fire.[4]

And there is always a double vision of the revolution, poignant and powerful – the ideal and the revolution – reality.

By their rhythm and their flight, the vehement stanza of *The Scythians* recall certain passages from the *Châtiments* of Victor Hugo or the *Iambes* of Barbier.[5] Millions and millions of greedy barbaric Scythians, bursting with life in whom love burns and devours ('Yes, love! For you of Western lands and birth no longer know the blood our love enjoys'[6]) appeared, on the threshold of the future, to throw a fraternal appeal to the old world which resounds like a challenge:

> O Ancient World, awake! For the last time
> We call you to the ritual feast and fire

Of peace and brotherhood! For the last time
O hear the summons of the barbarian lyre!7

For if old Europe cannot understand the immense hope and the immense love that is arising from the breasts of the Scythians of the Urals and the Volga, it is towards Asia that they will turn – and so much the worse for the old Europe!

There is a deep meaning in the tragic warning of Alexander Blok. Europe did not reply to the rough but magnificent invitation of the 'barbarians' – the proletarians and muzhiks who made the revolution. It is they who are now calling the peoples of the East to them. If old bourgeois Europe knew so little of what the consequences of the awakening of the East might presage, what terrible disquiet will it not feel as regards the slightest tremors in India and Iran?

The author of *The Twelve* and *The Scythians* is connected by sympathy to the Left Socialist Revolutionary Party, in the Soviet from the time of the October Revolution, and whose legal organisation, having gone through a great deal of mistakes, is today trying to form a 'loyal opposition'. The truth is that Alexander Blok, who is barely acquainted with political affairs, understood the revolution as a poet – and understood it admirably.

He did not stop working in Petrograd. He had a job, for a long time, I believe, in the theatre section of the Commissariat of Public Education. He was a member of the bureau of the Writers' Union, and one of the founders of the Union of Poets, which took up the defence of the interests of the poets, considered as exercising a trade in the Republic comparable in every way to the others. He was very much interested in the Arts House, which is one of the centres of the intellectual life of Petrograd.

You could find him there quite often. Slender in appearance and well built, he had the stiff attitude and bearing of an Anglo-Saxon gentleman. His elongated clean shaven face, with firm lines, which slightly flushed at the least emotion, and the deep blue of his eyes, again reinforced the first impression, a trifle disconcerting, which produced the most lyrical and the most Russian of of our poets today. None of those who approached him in any way will forget his calm and warm voice, which always seemed to control his emotions, and his look, so blue, so timid, so distant and so gentle.

He died aged forty-one from a heart attack, complicated, so it seems, by the onset of scurvy due to the breakdown of an organism that years of privations had slowly destroyed. The living conditions of the milieu to which he belonged, even if they were generally noticeably better than those of the majority of the population, were nonetheless very hard by the time of the civil war, the blockade and the permanent famine. And the most noble natures are not those which best adapt to the new requirements of the struggle for life. It all too often happened, in Red Russia during the civil war and famine, that the best of the revolutionaries went to be killed at the front or on the barricades – while others slipped away – and that the best of the artists and scholars suffered the harshest privations stoically, while waves of 'intellectuals', clever saboteurs in all the Soviet institutions, 'managed to come out of it' remarkably well.

By this distressing selection in reverse, the war that had to be carried on – and still is being carried on, but more craftily – against Red Russia, was more than anything else the deliberate murder of the best. Artists, scholars, children – all that humanity has of the best and the richest for the future – have suffered the most in it. Poets died young in the country of the revolution, and hundreds of thousands of Russian children are, at the very time when Alexander Blok's eyes closed, a prey to famine.

People who begin great social changes have to pay this cruel price for the future of all people.

Petrograd, 8 August, 1921   Victor Serge

Notes

1. Translated from *La Vie Ouvrière*, 26 August, 1921. For Serge's reminiscences of Blok, cf. *Memoirs of a Revolutionary*, Oxford U.P., 1975, p.151 (translator's note).
2. Blok published his *Stikhi o Prekasnoy Dame* (*Poems About the Beautiful Lady*) in 1904, *Nezayannaya radost* (*The Unexpected Joy*) in 1906, *Snezhnaya maska* (*The Snow Mask*) in 1907 and *Zemlia v snegu* (*The Earth in Snow*), poems, in 1908. *Roza i krest* (*The Rose and the Cross*), a drama, was published in 1913 (translator's note).
3. *The Twelve*, as translated in *Alexander Blok: Selected Poems*, Progress Publishers, Moscow, 1981, pp.317–8 (translator's note).
4. Op. cit., p.310 (translator's note).
5. Victor Hugo's *Châtiments* (*Punishments*) was a book of poems published in 1853; Auguste Barbier (1805–1882) published his *Iambes* in 1832 (translator's note).
6. *The Scythians*, as translated in *Alexander Blok: Selected Poems*, Progress Publishers, Moscow, 1981, p.320 (translator's note).
7. Op. cit., p.322 (translator's note).

Vladimir Korolenko[1]

Vladimir Galaktionovich Korolonko has just died at Poltava (Ukraine) at the age of sixty-seven. Little known abroad, he was nonetheless one of the great Russian writers of the last thirty years and in a certain sense – the noblest! – the successor of Tolstoy. Like Tolstoy, Korolenko was an elevated and luminous mind. And 'a light has just gone out', an admirable life has just come to an end.

He came from a bourgeois family, in a country divided by old national hatreds – Ukrainians, Russians and Poles have persecuted each other for centuries – Korolenko as a child, by a personal effort, immediately withdrew from this poisoned atmosphere. At twenty he was a student in Moscow, at the agricultural school. Together with all the ardent intellectual youth of his day, he welcomed new ideas, which were still vague but which powerfully elevated minds. At this time students were already in the vanguard of the movement for emancipation. University disturbances continued and spread despite repression, and Korolenko took part in them. When he was twenty-two, the authorities exiled him to Vologda.

This exile, which marked a decisive break in the normal course of a bourgeois career, was a liberation. Korolenko did not wish to become an 'intellectual' of the type that there are so many of. Together with the elite of his generation, he envisaged a different social duty: going to the people, being one of the people oneself in order to work for emancipation. Korolenko became a shoemaker, earned his living the hard way by the work of his hands, lived with poor people, as their equal and their brother – but remained a tireless reader, sitting up very late every night poring over the works of human thought.

He was loved and he was listened to. He was 'very dangerous'. Portraits from his youth and later life always show him with the same calm, handsome face with regular features, bearded and with luxuriant hair, presenting an expression that was both solemn and peaceful. We should picture him thus, a bearded shoemaker with a gentle, steady gaze, who spoke in a deliberate manner and who was slowly accumulating a first-class standard of learning, a lucid consciousness, an uncompromising character. In Tsarist society he was a dangerous 'outsider', like a being from another planet. Exile in Vologda (then in Kronstadt) did not seem sufficient to subdue him. In 1879 he was sent to Vitka. From there to Siberia. From Siberia he was sent back to Perm. From Perm he was sent back to Siberia. Korolenko knew all the main routes of the frozen North of Russia and of Siberia, for he had travelled them on foot – or in rudimentary peasant carriages with his tools, his books, his notes, his small but precious luggage! In 1881 he was working on the railways, somewhere in Siberia. When Alexander III became Tsar, Korolenko refused to swear the oath of allegiance. This gesture, which had no purpose and could have no result other than to satisfy his own conscience, earned him the harshest exile, on the banks of the Lena, in a frozen waste amid the Yakuts. Patient and obstinate, Korolenko spent four years with these primitive people, sharing their labours, entering their way of thought, and learning to love them.

Exile thus took ten years out of his life. Dostoyevsky had spent as many years as a convict. From his convict days Dostoyevsky brought back an unforgettable book, *The House of the Dead*. Korolenko brought back from Siberia his travel notes, stories, tales and legends, a whole varied collection of work which could be called 'The Land of the Dead' – for the *taiga* (the Siberian outback) is an immense jailhouse of snow where men suffer, a thousand dead, tortured by a tenacious desire for resurrection.

On return from exile, in 1885, after the publication of his first story, *Makar's Dream*, Korolenko right away became one of the great Russian writers. Solitude and tribulation had ripened within him the soul of a poet. Moreover, he, better than anyone, knew the Russian people, the Russian character and the Russian territory. His language was not literary, but alive, drawn from the wells of popular thought, but polished by an honest mind and fortified with learning. Today his books are classics – and they will remain so. *In Bad Company*, *The Murmuring Forest*, a little masterpiece after the manner of *Pan*, by Knut Hamsun, but with the tragic evocation of serfdom in the Ukraine, the *Blind Musician*, his finest literary work of which Rosa Luxemburg has given us a German translation, his *Notes from Siberia*, and his *Short Stories*.

His entire work is profoundly social. The very reason that it enriches Russian literature is that it is no way 'literature' in the impoverished sense given to the term in certain bourgeois intellectual circles. Korolenko did not write in order to apply his style – though he had a perfect one – nor to get a place in an Academy, nor to win approval in the writings of the bourgeoisie, of dilettantes or of neurotics, nor in order to be a best-seller. He told of the suffering of human beings and of their painful but irresistible rise to inner illumination. From 1891 onwards the social task of the writer absorbed him so much that the story-teller and novelist gave way, for many years, to the journalist. 1891 was the year of the great famine. But Tsarism, far from calling on the civilised world to assist the starving *muzhiks*, wanted to keep this dishonourable calamity secret. Korolenko, in articles which deserve to be read and reread, made it known. When after the famine, cholera appeared, spreading unbelievable panic among the inhabitants, it took all Korolenko's moral authority to restore calm. And since then, every time a new scandal revealed to the world the deficiencies of the Tsarist regime, every time an injustice or an infamous act was committed, Vladimir Korolenko made his protest, in sober language, firm but gentle, persuasively. In his articles which certainly stigmatise and condemn relentlessly, there is never violent language of any sort. The good shoemaker of Vologda shakes his head and in a sedate, thoughtful voice he denounces *evil*. In this way he denounced the horrors of the Tsar's prisons, the shabby acts of anti-Semitism, the pogroms (in an unforgettable page from his work, *House No. 13*), torture, the malpractices of the police and of the officer caste ... So much so that, as historian of Russian life, he has preserved the memory of the martyrdom – the word is not too strong – of a great people.

His last years were wretched. Sickness, infirmity and domestic sorrows overwhelmed him. The spectacle of the civil war, which, in Lenin's words, is the harshest form of war, must have imposed very great suffering on this humanist and idealist. But he carried on working on his last book (*A History of My Contemporary*), carried on thinking, and pursuing in his province of the Ukraine his personal activity which was both utopian and beneficent. In a society shaken up by social revolution, he would have liked to be an agent of appeasement. He expressed his views on the Revolution in a series of friendly letters to Lunacharsky, which are still unpublished. In many respects he must have failed to understand it. But he never opposed it nor criticised it. Until his last day he remained faithful to his Russian soil. Doubtless, beyond the struggles of the present he could clearly catch sight of the future which the Revolution is aiming for.

The dominant character of his personality, beyond and above humanism, beyond and above faith in culture and in the future, beyond and above the Slav spirit, is unfailing goodness, which never despairs of humanity, however degraded and defeated it may appear. That was why Korolonko could describe with so much love the terrible outcasts of the main roads of Siberia. In them too his eyes could see the better man.

Events had left him behind. The present generation no longer has the time to read, nor to contemplate as he did. The Red Army needs commissars, the factory needs administrators! But it is no paradox to state that the great builders of Russian culture, who also number in the front ranks of those of modern culture – and notably the powerful tradition of social writers which begins with Dostoevsky, continues with Chernishevsky, Turgenev, Tolstoy and ends with Korolenko and Gorky – have, to a large extent, prepared the path of the men of the Revolution. They shaped revolutionary consciousness. They taught whole generations to hope, to wish, to believe that social transformation was possible. They kept alive holy indignation against the old world and gave an example. These pre-revolutionary writers can be profitably compared with the pitiable entertainers of the bourgeoisie who produce so-called 'literature' in the capitalist world. They enable us to understand the social mission of the writer. After them were to come, were able to come, the men with no less conscience, but with unrelenting will who transformed a society.

Kiev, 3 January 1922

---

1.   Translated from *Bulletin communiste*, vol. ii, no. 4, 26 January, 1922, pp. 72–3. (Translator's note)

Korolenko[1]

Korolenko is dead.[2] He is very little known in Europe. The announcement of his death caused his name to crop up in the newspapers (third page, five or ten lines). The broad public who never knew him will forget him tomorrow. Would that the revolutionaries could be less unconcerned, and less unjust! They should know that this great name is comparable with those of Tolstoy or Kropotkin. Vladimir Galaktionovich Korolenko was one of the great fashioners of modern Russian culture. His work is vast, rich and luminous. And he has just completed an admirable life. He did not call himself a 'revolutionary'. He remained alien to what is generally called 'politics'. But in order to understand Russian thought, the thought of the people who made the revolution, he is one of the great Russians with whom you should be acquainted.

Korolenko, a man of bourgeois origin, became a student. He wanted to devote himself to agriculture. Like the whole of his generation, he became enthusiastic about the new ideas then being revealed to the Russian youth. This youth was in perpetual effervescence. Student disturbances were followed by repression – often ferocious – and repression by disturbances. The era of revolutionary activity was about to open up. Gentle Korolenko, expelled from the Moscow agricultural school for bad attitude, was exiled to Vologda at the age of twenty-two, and then allowed to stay in Kronstadt under a regime of strict supervision. But he did not regret his ruined career. The Russian youth of that time, to which the revolution owes so much, hardly thought about careers – even liberal ones. Korolenko wanted to live by the work of his hands and live among the people. Entirely alone, he 'went to the masses' in his out of the way province, without anyone having to give him this order of command, and without looking for anything other than to satisfy his conscience. He became a shoemaker.

In 1879 came a new exile, in a far-off corner of the Viatka Gubernia, in the middle of the steppes. And that was only the beginning of his tribulations. This well-read shoemaker who travelled with notebooks, this gentle bearded innocent, stubborn and simple, upset the authorities everywhere. They felt the moral strength within him. From Viatka he was sent to Siberia. From Siberia he was sent on to Perm. From Perm he was sent back to Siberia. Years passed.

Korolenko understood, worked, and went on with his work, not as a writer, but as a man who had become completely alien to the society of his time, heroically out of touch, because he belonged to the future. He did not agitate, since it seems he did not belong to any organisation, and was not deeply involved in any programme: but he lived like a revolutionary.

In 1881 Korolenko became a railwayman in Siberia. As a railwayman, he refused the oath of allegiance to Tsar Alexander III[3] required of political exiles. You are tempted to smile. How can you describe this railwayman who repaired his own boots in the night, refusing the oath to the Tsar ... and where? – in a frozen hamlet of a few dozen inhabitants! Wasn't that a vain gesture? But it was a gesture which Luxemburg – who admired Korolenko – in some beautiful pages compared with that of Galileo defending the idea of the rotation of the globe in spite of the Inquisition.[4] 'Such "empty gestures",' wrote Rosa Luxemburg, 'in spite of their total insignificance in practice, are indispensable in our spiritual realm'.[5] Korolenko was here only obeying his conscience. He was therefore dangerous! This persistence in evil cost him the harshest exile, among the Yakuts, cut off from all contact with civilisation, in an icy region on the banks of the Lena. Korolenko spent four years there, living the life of the Yakut fishermen.[6]

When he returned from exile in 1885, he emerged as a writer, without having gone through the minor magazines, and without having frequented the literary circles and editorial offices, he became a powerful artist. No one knew the Russian people and the Siberian peoples better than he. The steppe, and the implacable Siberian *taiga*, where man is a wolf to man, trained him, in working alone, in thinking, and by continually exercising active kindness. Korolenko soon turned out to be a great writer, and won over the public – a public, moreover, which did not ask for decadent poetry, amorous psychology or cinematic stories.

Korolenko possessed a subtle language, of great purity and great richness. But he was completely alien to art for art's sake. He also – like Tolstoy in the second half of his life – was a powerful writer who did not want to be a literary man. He wrote to express the suffering of the men whose soul he had penetrated and to try to make them understand how to become a little better. He sowed hope. There was no lying in it: it was healthy, human, and often very sad hope. He described the life of the poor people of Siberia. To sum up, he rewrote, but outside exile, Dostoyevsky's *House of the Dead*.[7] Only it is more 'the Land of the Dead' – those who died badly and wanted to be resurrected. He wrote *The Murmuring Forest*,[8] a charming and tragic story. He wrote *The Blind Musician*, and this is perhaps his masterpiece, the day by day diary of a blind child who becomes a man and an artist, rich in inner light. He wrote short stories comparable with the best works in the Russian language, like the three pages of *Easter Eve*:[9] on a night full of stars and chimes two almost identical men are separated by a wall; a prisoner and a sentry. The call of the bells and of space and of dream and of life fill the spirit of the prisoner on this night. The man tries and succeeds in climbing over. He is free. Then the other, who is like him and is his brother, fires ... It needs no more than this: the common life of these two men and their common suffering is a world condemned.

But for Korolenko narrative and story were still merely literature. Social life required more immediate participation from the writer. Korolenko became a journalist. His press campaigns were to stir up everyone who thought in Russian society. A rural bourgeoisie cynical to the point of oblivion tried to deny the famine (1891[10]). Korolenko exposed it, with all his talent. Two years later cholera ascended the Volga, panicking the populations. Korolenko calmed them down, and brought help. And every month and every year since, this writer has risen up against every injustice and every social crime of the old regime, rarely as a polemicist, and never as a pamphleteer, but always with sober language which consistently comes down to just two notes: kindness and hope.

Korolenko denounced progoms, the cruelty of the policing system in the countryside, the atrocities in the prisons, the behaviour of the military caste, and anti-semitism. No one was more formidable to the regime. But his moral authority was nonetheless such that Tsarism did not dare to resort to such measures of repression as against Tolstoy.

Korolenko lived out his last years in the Ukraine, at Poltava, where friends of mine finally found him physically much weakened, sorely tried by domestic misfortunes and by having to witness the Civil War, but still active and faithful to himself. On the one hand he finished his last book, *A History of My Contemporary*;[11] on the other he tried to accomplish a modest task in his own milieu, to be a factor for peacemaking and serenity throughout the cruel times of the social war. About the revolution, whose horrors must have profoundly moved him, he wrote nothing publishable. But maintaining friendly relations with Lunacharsky, he wrote him a series of letters intending to serve as the basis for the discussion of ideas. Let us hope that they will be published soon. Whatever it was, the intellectual and moral experience of a Korolenko during the Revolution can only be of use to us.[12]

I seek to define the distinctive trait of his work. Was this interest, at the same time patient and passionate, which he bore for all things human, humanism? Was it idealism? Korolenko was intent on finding glimmers of the ideal in the souls of Siberian semi-savages as well as of the bandits of the *taiga*.[13] Was it faith in the future? That is what was foremost with him. But all this took second place to kindness. It was a purely Slav kindness, it seems to me, and all the more precious in Korolenko because it was defined neither by doctrinal formulae nor by theses. But it was all-pervasive. When he described 'Ivan, thirty-eight years old', a nameless tramp, who was a murderer, we feel that he forgave and loved him in every line because he basically saw in him an infinitely better man *whom society had killed* ...

The importance of a Tolstoy or a Kropotkin has been immense for modern culture. If some day, and in the manner he really deserves, his works cross the frontiers of Russia,[14] or if he only finds a biographer worthy of him, it seems to me that Korolenko's importance will be almost as considerable. His field of activity was limited to the immensity of Russia, doubtless on account of his purely Slav temperament. But we should not forget that he was one of the unchallenged masters of Russian thinking on the eve of the revolution. By his pen and his example Korolenko taught entire generations to protest incessantly against the old world, the necessity for taking part in the social struggle, and the duty to remain a free man at any cost. And it was not fruitless.

During the Civil War his thinking, his kindness, and his work itself – had we the time to read it! – appeared to recede into the past. Other men, of will, and kind in a very different way, even to the point of inexorable acts when higher interests required it – were necessary to accomplish the daunting ploughing up of a world: the revolution. But once this ploughing up is over, sooner or later, we will read Korolenko again for all the human enlightenment it contains. And in other countries, where there are 'literary gentlemen', 'poets', 'journalists' and 'intellectuals' who are happy to amuse a rotting bourgeoisie, we can make known to revolutionaries, using Korolenko's example, what it is to be a great authentic pre-revolutionary writer.

Victor Serge   (Kiev, 9 January, 1922)

Notes

1. Translated from *La Vie Ouvrière*, 13 January, 1922.
2. At Poltava (in the Ukraine) on 25 December, aged 67 (author's note).
3. The reign of Tsar Alexander III (1881–1894) marked a period of repression and reaction in Russian history (translator's note).
4. Galileo Galilei (1564–1642) was a mathematician, physicist and astronomer who was put under house arrest by the Papal Inquisition for teaching the Copernican theory of planetary rotation (translator's note).
5. Rosa Luxemburg, 'Life of Korolenko', July 1918, *International Socialist Review*, vol.xxx, no.1, January/February 1969, p.20 (translator's note).
6. Korolenko's first successful novel, *Son Makara (Makar's Dream)*, published in 1891, describes the life of the Yakuts (translator's note).
7. Dostoyevsky's *Zapiski iz mertvogo doma (House of the Dead)* was written in 1861–2 (English translation by David McDuff, Harmondsworth, 1985) (translator's note).
8. Korolenko published *Les shumit (The Murmuring Forest)* in 1886 (translator's note).
9. Korolenko's *Noch'in (Easter Eve)* was translated into English by William Frederick Armytage and published on pp.135–49 of *The Sanghalian Convict and Other Stories* (London, 1892) (translator's note).
10. This famine was so severe that it lasted for three years (1891–4) (translator's note).
11. Korolenko's *Istoriia Moego Sovremennika (A History of My Contemporary)*, a semi-autobiographical novel, was written from 1906 onwards and still incomplete when it was published in St. Petersburg in 1922 (English translation by Neil Parsons, Oxford U.P., 1972) (translator's note).
12. Korolenko's letters to Lunacharsky were not published in Russia until the adoption of Glasnost in the 1980s (translator's note).
13. The Siberian bush (author's note).
14. Rosa Luxemburg has translated *The Blind Musician* into German. I know of a French translation of the same work, but badly done and clumsily abbreviated (author's note). The translation to which Serge refers is that by R. Candiani which occupies part iii of *La Forêt murmure, contes d'Ukraine et de Sibérie, d'après texte russe*, Paris, 1895 (translator's note).

Boris Pilnyak[1]

Of the new Russian writers, Boris Pilnyak is one of the most typical and the most famous. His first book appeared in 1920 from the Moscow State Publishers. He only writes about the revolution. He is young. His name is to be found in all the journals of Moscow and Petrograd, as well as in the majority of the catalogues of Russian publications in Berlin. The fact is that even if he gives us nothing else, his work perhaps would remain the most evocative of the year 1922, from which dates the rebirth of Russian literature. This work is composed of a novel, *The Naked Year*, and of several collections of stories, *Manners*, *What is Mortal is Seductive*, *St Petersburg Tales*,[2] and *Ivan and Maria*. They make up two volumes and two pamphlets in total, but they take in *almost the entire revolution*.

At first sight Pilnyak's way of writing appears to be distinctive. Basically, it exactly conforms to the spirit of the time. He writes a bit like certain Futurist painters paint; and perhaps this isn't effortlessly; but it hardly matters. It does not seem to me that you could depict the Russian Revolution with the style and manner of a Balzac describing the sordid and monotonous life of Père Grandet,[3] or even in a detached tone, a style at the same time florid and chaste, with a formal harmony of details and wholes, such as Anatole France shows us in *The Gods Are Athirst*.[4] Those who come after us in a hundred years' time may well be able to talk about the October Revolution in this way, but we cannot, and Pilnyak cannot. The Revolution that broke all the old social habits also broke the all too conventional ones of literature. There is no story line to be followed in this Russian writer. There is no 'plot' (a poor thing, a poor word!). There are no distinctive, central personalities. There are crowds in movement – in which each is a world, an end in itself – events which overturn, cross over, mix up, overlap with each other, muliple lives that appear and disappear, all rare, unique and central, since they are human, and all of them insignificant in 'Russia, the snow storm, the Revolution', for the one thing that remains and matters is the country, the masses, the storm ... The typographical composition of Pilnyak's works has to be adapted to the text. The appearance of the pages is often bizarre. They show us an old priest among his icons, overwhelmed with the weight of sin; then the text suddenly breaks off and we hear passers-by in the street talking: then another break, and then we see a wolf that is going to die on the edge of the woods howling, hungry with shining teeth ... The interplay between images and texts makes different typographical alignments necessary. The reader is a little thrown off course (so how much harm must the likes of Bourget have done us!) But the final appearance is impressive. Pilnyak has been influenced, not without compulsion, may we say, by the stylistic masters of the end of the old regime, André Biely and Alexis Remizov,[5] but he only took from them their methods without the content, methods which he would have otherwise have had great difficulty in finding. He has so many things to say, to show and to take note of in his book that all limits are oppressive to him. Allow life to pass by, allow it to go wherever it wishes. Classicism is only worth anything in societies that have been stable for a long time. In *The Naked Year* we find no less than eight subjects extensively dealt with: the small town, the dying aristocracy, the 'members of religious sects', the Anarchists, the monastery, Train 57, the peasants, and the Bolsheviks. Nonetheless, in these books a great overall unity holds sway. It results from the totality of different or contrary dynamics, like a symphony – heroic. And Pilnyak, just like the musicians, uses *leitmotivs*.[6] This is still in line with a life whose rhythm often obstinately leads us to the same tasks, and often allows a terrible permanence to things. In *Ivan and Maria*, repeated on several occasions apparently quite extraneous to the narrative, is the mention of a miner, 'the black slave of international metallurgy' who has just gone to sleep, worn out with work, in his room. But how many idyllic or supremely psychological stories need this implacable reminder of reality as a counterpoint? The *leitmotiv* common to Pilnyak's whole work is the howl of the snow storm, which is what is most Russian in the life of the Russian land. Pilnyak's style is moreover often musical. The author doesn't disparage anything, but rushes to say things, to cry out, to shout ... Let us sum up: dynamism, simultaneism, realism – absolute, direct – rhythmic in its details and as a whole, such appear to us to be the dominant characteristics of his literary form. Let us also note a love for precise documentation, for a trace of authentic manners, for a phrase or a catchphrase picked up in the street and reproduced without explanation, like a historian does in his notebooks.

Pilnyak is only interested, so it seems, in the ways of the Revolution, above all in those of the province or the countryside. The usual setting for his stories is the small town (*Ryazan-the-Apple*), or Ordynin-Gorod (*The Naked Year*), which he knows so well. What, essentially, does he see there?

He sees the swamp of the past. Over what a swamp, stagnating for thousands of years, the revolutionary storm is passing! In the small town the little people were living like animals, between the counter, the well-provided table, the hot stable impregnated with sweat and filth, and under the icons. They were brutal, hard on the weak, inflexible towards the oppressed – the servant, the woman and child – egoistical, self-satisfied, ignorant and barbarous – for a thousand years. The war tore the young men from the stagnant little towns of the old regime. When Donat returned there he '*knew nothing of any order; Donat knew the old order, and he was out to do away with that old order. Donat had come to be busy – he hated the old order*'.[7] The horror of the past was revealed by the great shake-up of the war; here, pointed out in four lines, is one of the deep causes of the Revolution.

– In this stagnant swamp of the past those who had previously been the ones who dominated society have degenerated. Their blood is corrupted ever more shabbily: their spirit is debilitated: they feel weighing down on them what we Communists call the verdict of history. The syphilitic Ordynin princes, whose ancestors founded Ordynin-Gorod, reach the end of their degeneration. The old father is awaiting his end, shut up with holy images, with constant mortifications. Igor gets drunk, steals and sells the last clothing of his sisters for drink (we are in 1919). Boris is a young, second-rate and hard bourgeois who feels tainted. The old women slumber in stupidity, the young ones in depression; they feel nostalgia for the worldliness and debauches of former times (*The Naked Year*). In a short story entitled '1000 Years' the same theme comes up again in an abbreviated form. Princes Constantine and Fedor Vilyashev are looking at the small town from the very point where a thousand years earlier their ancestor, the conqueror, had halted. And nothing but despair speaks in them:

> A thousand years have passed ... famine, scurvy, typhus, sorrow brood over the countryside ... I feel utterly lost, Vilyashev. We are no good to anyone. Not so long ago our ancestors used to flog peasants in the stables and abduct maidens on their wedding nights. How I curse them! They are wild beasts![8]

They sense that they are finished, but that the land will live. At length, close to these *isbas*[9] where typhus holds sway, the young girls start to sing:

> That's good, that's sad. That will not die. That is admirably, strangely, terribly good ...

But what is *that*? It is the life of the land and the people to which the degenerate aristocracies can no longer contribute anything. Their desolate end is told with a minute care for the truth. Here, for example (*The Heirs*) an old general, with those closest to him, a student, and an entire bourgeois family, expropriated and hungry, sees

> Each barricaded and entrenched himself in his own room, with his own pot and samovar. They lived tedious, mean, malignant, worthless lives, execrating existence and the Revolution; they lived utterly apart from the turmoil that now replaced the placid even flow of the old regime; they were outside current events, and their thoughts forever turned back to the past, awaiting its return ...[10]

Impotent, and overwhelmed with petty miseries, they fight over cigarette ends.
   – Survivals from the past penetrate the weft of the present, creep into the rough habits of the Revolution, and reveal themselves after having been smashed. Disorientated people, idiots, mediocre fools and witches in the lost countryside where they tried to create a peasant commune, set up an absurd religious sect (*Ryazan-the Apple*) ...
   – In its furthest past Russia belongs to Asia. Pilnyak understands this and brings out its deeply Asiatc nature – which inspires Alexander Blok when he writes *The Scythians*, and which Lenin does not lose sight of when he announces the coming struggle of the oppressed peoples of Europe and Asia (Russia, China, India) against Western imperialism.[11] Soon there is on every page a reminder of the Pamirs, the heart of Asia, to which the small town is linked by an infinite number of strands (*Ivan and Maria*), then, in the *St Petersburg Tales*, the Chinese revolutions of two thousand years ago and yesterday and ours are woven together, the clash and confusion of destinies of the builder of the Great Wall of China, Shi Huang Di, who constructed feudalism and made himself

emperor, and of Peter the Great, the builder of St Petersburg, who tamed the nobles and made himself an autocrat.[12] I have often been struck by the obvious resemblances between Russian and Chinese things: in the Kremlin, the residence of the first Tsars, in the presence of the *terems*,[13] and in Petrograd, in the presence of the golden arrows of the Admiralty and the St. Peter and Paul Fortress, which made me think of those which the architects of the Far East often put on the tops of pagodas. One person says in the *St Petersburg Tales* 'Russia is going through an anarchistic revolt; it is being cured of the European sickness with which Peter the Great infected it ...' Another, in *The Naked Year*, says:

> The road of European culture led to the war ... Machine culture forgot about spiritual culture, the culture of the mind. Those who've ruled Russia for the last two centuries, since Peter, have been trying to adopt that culture. Russia ... was being stifled in that atmosphere. And the Revolution has opposed Russia to Europe. What is more – now, after the first days of the Revolution, Russia, in her life and her ways and her towns has gone back to the seventeenth century.[14]

Is this a retreat? No, it is a return of Russia back to itself. I am only pointing out those ideas whose influence upon Russia is not insignificant.

– The revolutionary storm has broken over this old Asiatic Russia. Pilnyak increasingly employs the Russian word *metel*[15] – a snow storm – whose fierce, wild poetry a foreigner cannot understand. Perhaps the best of his stories is that entitled 'Metel'.

> A man came quickly out of the storm ...
>   The snowflakes were spinning round, piling up, swirling over the plain, thousands of snowflakes ... It was a storm. Springing from it, the snowflakes were sweeping over thousands of versts, fields, woods, rivers, towns, dying, dying, dying in the fighting, the death rattle, the noise and the sobs ... Everything was white ...

And elsewhere:

> I was in the full blast of the storm and the wind. A froth of snow swept

round me and froze between my hands (*Ivan and Maria*).

The 'untitled' chapter Seven of *The Naked Year* is in fact only three words in Russian: 'Russia, the Revolution, the storm'. Here is distilled together the physical poetry of the essence of Russia – which again reminds me of Blok and *The Twelve* – and that of the Revolution, another storm. We never know if they ought to be distinguished in Pilnyak. I do not think so ...

– To the backward Asiatic nature of the old Russia, Pilnyak counterposes the new Russia he sees being born in the storm, which he clearly sees being born – and that is greatly to his credit. Listen to this snatch of conversation in a train:

> ... In one hundred and fifty years men will be nostalgic about present day Russia as being one of the finest manifestations of the human spirit – but my footwear is leaking, and I would rather spend a month abroad, eating in a good restaurant and drinking whisky ...

So speaks an engineer, 'thoughtfully'. Now in Pilnyak's work, as in the reality of the Revolution, the real creators of the present and the future are not the engineers. This brings us to the Bolsheviks.

Pilnyak flatters neither the Revolution nor the revolutionaries. Dark and nightmarish pages are not rare as far as he is concerned. There are in his books peasant women who pay soldiers with their bodies for places in the verminous train, crammed full of typhus sufferers, who are fleeing from the famine-stricken countryside. There is a hysterical Cheka woman who shoots her lover. There are peasants who are buying coffins in advance for their whole families: for hunger and typhus will not spare them, this they know. There are pages of real or far-fetched horror. People today still do not know what torment the Russian people have gone through; Pilnyak knows, and writes about it along with the blood. And it is precisely his hard duty to bear witness to the truth – perhaps he is even being too complaisant about it – as intellectuals so often do towards the ugly, which makes his testimony about Bolshevism so important and precious for us.

There is only one type of men who are staunch and firm in their work in the storm: the Bolsheviks:

In the nunnery, in the morning, in the Execcom ... there gathered, sign of the times, leather men in leather tunics (Bolsheviks!), everyone a standard leathern man, each of them hefty, and hair in curly ringlets sticking out on his neck from under a forage cap – but what more than anything else made them was the purpose in the tight-drawn muscles of the cheek, in the folds at the lips, in their rigid movements – the purpose and the insolent courage. The pick of the sluggish and twisted folk of Russia. And this wearing of leather tunics, too, was a good thing: no damping of these with psychology lemonade – there's what we're fixed on, there's what we know, and that's what we want, and that's the end of it.[16]

And here is one, seen from close up. And this is what they do, if I am permitted to quote it at great length:

Arkhip Arkhipov spent his days in the Execcom, filling in forms, and then he rushed about the town and the ironworks – attending councils and meetings and conferences. Whenever he wrote his eyebrows were tight drawn, and he held his pen like an axe. At meetings his pronunciations of foreign words was peculiar: he would say constant-irovat for constatirovat (to state a fact), any-gritchno for energitchno (energetic), something like saying phone for telephone, faction-irovat for function-irovat (to function) ... But more ridiculous still was Arkhip Arkhipov's getting up with the sun and swotting on the sly – at Kiselyov's *Algebra*, Kistiakovsky's *Economic Geography*, Granat's edition of *The History of Russia in the Nineteenth Century*, Marx's *Capital*, Ozerov's *Economics*, Weissmann's *Calculus, German Self-Taught*, and – and – a little dictionary by one Galkin, a dictionary of foreign words used in Russian'.[17]

   Leather tunics.
   Bolsheviks. Bolsheviks? Yes, Bolsheviks. That's what they're like.
   The Whites left in March. And in the first days of March an 'Expedition' (a commission) came down from Moscow to find out what factories and works were left after the Whites and the troublous times that had been. There were representatives of the O.T.K., and the K.L.M.U., the Metals Department, and the C.E.P.T.Y., and the C.E.P.E.K.A.P.E., and the Promburo, and the R.K.P., and the V.C.K.,[18] etc., all specialists – they held council in the chief town of the district,

and a decision was reached that as clearly as twice two is four the factories and works were in a worse than catastrophic state, that there were no
raw materials, no instruments, no labour, no fuel and that there could be
no question of letting them go. Out of the question! I, the author of this
book, was a member of that expedition, and the head of the expedition
was K., called Loukitch, after his father. When the order to be ready to
start went through the train (we were a detachment of rifles) I, the
author, thought we were off back to Moscow since there was nothing to
be done. But we went to the factories and ironworks because there's no
such thing as a thing that can't be done – because it's impossible not to
do. We went because Bolshevik K. Loukitch, non specialist, argued very
simply indeed. He argued that only if everything was done could there
be nothing to be done, and that man can do anything.

　　Bolsheviks – leather tunics.

　　Any-gritchno faction irovat (order to function enegetically), that's
what the Bolsheviks are. Get on with the job! And to hell with you all,
you sweety-tartish lemon-squashes!' (*The Naked Year*, Chapter Six).[19]

These energetic people are not only rebuilding the devastated factory with their
bare hands, they are by themselves creating a new life for themselves. When
Arkhipov's father, having learned that a cancer was condemning him to suffer
and die, comes to ask Bolshevik son 'Should I kill myself?', a very calm scene
happens between the two men. 'If I were you, father, I'd do it myself. You do
what you find best, father, what you think ... 'You, son, live, don't give up your
work, marry; have children, son ...'[20] They only exchange these words before
leaving each other, both of them firm and strong, the one to live and carry on his
work, and the other to fire a revolver shot into his mouth. Everything is strained
and sad in Pilnyak's work; but after this stoical page, there is one luminous
page. Two people appear in it, Bolsheviks, strong people, simple people,
because they have great inner strength. The man, Arkhipov, says to the woman,
Natalia, whom he is asking to become his companion:

　　'I'm busy all the time, what with the works and the committee and the
　　revolution ... As a lad I used to fall in love, well, and go the wrong way
　　with women. Then I got over that sort of thing. There's no nonsense in
　　me. We are working together, for one thing. And the kids we'll bring up

without any nonsense, as they should be brought up. I want intelligent children – and you're cleverer than I am. Well, and I'll school myself up a bit. We're both of us young and healthy'. Arkhipov lowered his face. Arkhipov bowed his head.[21]

She consents with the same simplicity. It might be said that these revolutionaries are afraid of letting go and relaxing the nerves and spirit, of letting two beings come close to each other to become a couple.

'Children, yes, that's the one thing'.
    'But I'm not a virgin!' And the man shrugs his shoulders. 'What matters is being human, the proper thing, the right thing!' ... 'Without love – yet loving!', she says. 'Oh, but there will be cosiness, and children, and – we shall do our tasks!' ... My dear, my own one, mine. No hypocrisy. No pain.
    Cosiness. Arkhipov came in without a word, and went through to his own room – in Galkin's little *Dictionary of Foreign Words Used in Russian* he tried, without succeeding, to find that word which, though it was a Russian word, he had never heard before ...[22]

Has the writer idealised these Bolsheviks? It does not appear so. Energy and the will to create a new life is paramount among them. But history proved this a long time ago. If, on the other hand, it is necessary to enter into a detached criticism, all we need say is that the simplicity of relations between man and woman – the frank companionship that there is between them and the love of children[23] are characteristic traits of the new Russian manners that cannot escape the notice of any observer.

'This', said Nietzsche, 'is the new nobility!'

Boris Pilnyak saw many other energetic people in 'the storm, the Revolution, Russia ...' But the Bolsheviks are the most upright and the most successful, and their victory lies in their simplicity, rationality and knowledge of the aims in view. (Among the others are distinguished in sharp relief the Anarchists – the Revolution's dissidents and lost children – and the sectarian Christians, church dissenters, backward survivals of an old revolution. This witness knows both of them quite closely since he had been a member of an Anarchist commune, whose short life he describes).

– These Russian Anarchists who came during the revolution fought on all the fronts, and cultivated the soil 'under the black flag of free men' on an expropriated princely estate, ardently profess a philosophy of force. Irina writes in her diary:

> Those robbers knew how to seize a right to life – they lived, too, and I bless them. To hell with anaemia. They knew how to get pleasure out of it without a thought of others' tears ...
>   What does it matter if they were plunderers!... To hell with humanism and ethics! – I want to experience everything that freedom and intelligence and instinct have given me ...[24]

'Only the strongest may survive'. Have I not heard this individualistic language of thieves on more than one occasion, in Russia and elsewhere?[25] They do not seek to lead the revolution, they abandon themselves to it, they rejoice in it:

> Natalia ... again felt sharply that for her the Revolution was bound up with happiness, a turbulent happiness, the happiness mingled with gnawing sorrow ...[26]

They work, love, dream and fight. And their adventure ends in *The Naked Year*, as so often it comes to an end in the Ukraine.[27] Harry, a farmer emigrant from America, comes to claim his share of the money 'expropriated at Ekaterinoslav'. Yuzik refuses him it. Shots crackle out in the night. Free men have killed free men. They have killed – for money – the beautiful young woman who felt the joy of the revolution so much. The 'black flag of free men' becomes a shroud for the young dead. And the Soviet sends a squad of red soldiers to occupy the abandoned commune. Pilnyak elsewhere writes:

> I lived in the libertarian commune of Pesky up to the day when the Anarchists were to shoot each other ...

– Have I succeeded in making people understand how strongly realistic this new writer is? To the extent to which his immediate view of things – concrete and partial – often works out wrongly for him in his understanding of the whole set-up.

This realist professes a sort of cult of energy, among men, among animals, and even in nature (*The Blizzard*). The most energetic people among men are revolutionaries, and among animals, they are the predators. Pilnyak freely mixes together the lives of wolves with the lives of men in the storm.

> ... In the wind and swirling of the snow, in the black night, one following the other, the snow very soon covering up their tracks, came the wolves, in a grey file, males, females, and the leader in front ... (*Ivan and Maria*).

Pilnyak published several stories dating from 1917–18, before the Revolution and at the start of it (*Things*, *The Blizzard*, *Death*, *Two Short Stories*), extremely peculiar in the radical contrast they represent compared with the entirety of his later work. The oldest, *Things*, is wholly in the grey, sad manner of Chekhov in his worst days: again the drama of the boredom of the insignificant life of a (petty bourgeois) woman. The others, far better, communicate the usual feeling in the literature of the pre-revolutionary period of a life without a future, incurably mediocre, which is all too aware of its mediocrity. If the storm had not arrived, the writer going on in this way would very likely have never added anything to Russian literature.

In all the originality of his talent, his dynamic view of things, the breadth of his outlook over limitless Russia, enriched by such a variety of suffering and of struggle, his revelation of the energy – formerly inaccessible to the intellectuals of the old order – Boris Pilnyak owes everything to the Revolution, all of it, even to the extent of his style, and his onomatopeia ... And yet we are all the more saddened by not finding in him anything more than intuitive insight and primitive admiration. What does this Revolution want? The reader who is alien to revolutionary thinking must feel obsessed by this question, once he has closed the book. What is the storm aiming at? The writer would perhaps reply, for he has seen in the immense expropriation of one class by another the disappearance of a feudal order incompatible with the steam engine, the dynamo, machine guns and rotary presses, the coming to power of the peasants, serfs for centuries, nothing but the unleashing of elemental forces. The absence of an ideology – I was going to say, of a conviction – takes the edge off his work. In other repects it is true that he confers a particular value upon it for us: the spontaneity and sincerity of his witness speak for themselves: the work, in form and content, shows how the revolution has penetrated a writer with its spirit who is not, as he admits, either a Communist or a revolutionary. (As a student in a College of Commerce Pilnyak only left his neck of the woods during the four heroic years of 1917–21 in order to stock up with potatoes and flour.) Pilnyak is *exclusively* interested in behaviour. Even so, he should not, so we think, ignore ideas which he well knows have an influence over behaviour. The ideology of a social class in struggle, victorious and then in power, reading between the lines, becomes a powerful factor in remodelling behaviour. The new writer does not possess all the means to do this. Rough, prickly, diffuse, hasty and badly balanced, nonetheless his work already makes up a great and beautiful poem dedicated to the Russian storm and to revolutionary energy.

Victor Serge   Kiev, 25 March 1923.

Notes

1. Translated from *Clarté*, no.xxxvi, 20 May 1923. It should be compared with Voronsky's analysis, 'Literary Silhouettes: Boris Pilnyak', in *Art as the Cognition of Life*, Michigan, 1998, pp.51–76. The date of Serge's essay was intended to give the impression that he was still in Russia, for he spent most of the year clandestinely in Berlin covering the Ruhr crisis in Germany for *Inprecorr* (Victor Serge, *Witness to the German Revolution*, London, 2000, p.viii) (translator's note).
2. Pilnyak's *St. Petersburg Tales* was published in Berlin in 1922 (translator's note)
3. Père Grandet is a miser in Balzac's *Eugénie Grandet*, published in 1833, whose obsession has devastating effects upon the lives of others. The novel is one of a series of minute observations of everyday life (translator's note).
4. Anatole France published *The Gods are Athirst* in 1912 (translator's note).
5. Alexei Mikhailovich Remizov (1877–1957) looked upon revolutionaries as fanatics and naive visionaries. He left Russia before the revolution. Pilnyak dedicated his *Third Metropolis* 'to A. M. Remizov, the master in whose workshop I was an apprentice' (translator's note).
6. *Leitmotiv* is the German word for a theme (translator's note).
7. Pilnyak, *The Naked Year*, translated by Alec Brown, New York, 1928, p.46 (translator's note).
8. Pilnyak, 'A Thousand Years', in *Tales of the Wilderness*, London, 1924, pp.53, 65 (translator's note).
9. *Isba* is a Russian word for a peasant hut or cottage (translator's note).
10. Pilnyak, 'The Heirs', in *Tales of the Wilderness*, London, 1924, p.196 (translator's note).
11. The end of his study on 'The Workers' Inspectorate', *Pravda*, March 1923 (author's note). V. I. Lenin, 'Better Fewer, but Better', 2 March 1923, *Collected Works*, vol.xxxiii, Moscow, 1966, p.500. Serge himself was a member of the sub-committee set up by the Left Opposition to frame a policy for the Chinese Revolution

('The Class Struggle in the Chinese Revolution', *Revolutionary History*, vol.v, no.3, Autumn 1994, pp.54–141) (translator's note).

12. King Ying Zhen of Qin (246–210 B.C.) eliminated the other warring states in China and proclaimed himself Shi Huang Di in 221 B.C (Robert Louzon, *China: Three Thousand Years of History, Fify Years of Revolution*, London, 1998, pp.21–3. It is, however, very doubtful if the system he imposed can be described as 'feudal'. Cf. pp.ii–iii). Peter I the Great (1682–1725) was the modernising Tsar who founded St. Petersburg in 1703 as 'a window to the West' (D. B. Riazanov, *Marx and Anglo-Russian Relations and Other Writings*, Francis Boutle, London, 2003, pp.103–26) (translator's note).

13. *Terem* is an archaistic term, Byzantine Greek in origin, for the upper room of a palace, or a room above a gateway (translator's note).

14. *The Naked Year*, English translation p.116 (translator's note).

15. *Metel* is Russian for a snowstorm, or blizzard (translator's note).

16. *The Naked Year*, English translation, pp.58–9 (translator's note).

17. *The Naked Year*, English translation, p.254. Andrei Petrovich Kiselyov (1852–1940) was a Russian mathematician and educator. His works became standard textbooks in Russian schools. Theodore Kistiakovsky (1868–) was a German sociologist of economic affairs. Ivan Khristoforovich Ozerov (1869–) was the author of several books on Russian economics, economic history, public finance and industrial development. Weissmann and Galkin appear to be fictitious characters: but Samuel Salmanovich Galkin (1897–1960) was a Jewish poet and playwright at this time (translator's note).

18. The O.T.K. was the Technical Inspection Section; the Promburo was the Industrial Bureau; RKP means the Russian Communist Party, and VCK (VTsIK) the All-Russia Central Executive Committee (translator's note).

19. *The Naked Year*, English translation, pp.254–5 (translator's note).

20. *The Naked Year*, English translation, pp.83–4 (translator's note).

21. *The Naked Year*, English translation, p.267 (translator's note).

22. *The Naked Year*, English translation, pp.269–70 (translator's note).

23. On various occasions Pilnyak explains (*The Blizzard, Two Stories, The Naked Year*), or more exactly, makes his heroines explain, the idea that 'motherhood is woman's only satisfaction', – 'what is most gentle in a woman's life' (*Two Stories*). This is not a question of an argument, as in Zola's *Fecundity*, but of an idea that frequently returns to the author's mind, which otherwise so negligently repeats itself. I emphasise this trait because it seems so Russian to me – V.S. (author's note). Zola's *Fecundity* was published in 1899 (translator's note).

24. *The Naked Year*, English translation, pp.178–9 (translator's note).

25. Serge had first hand experience of this through his acquaintance with the anarchist illegals in Paris before the First World War. Cf. Ezra, Brett and Mel, *The Truth About the Bonnot Gang*, Coptic Press, 1968, pp.8 and 13; Richard Parry, *The Bonnot Gang*, London, 1987 (translator's note).

26. *The Naked Year*, English translation, p.160 (translator's note).

27. Chapter V, 'The Death of the Commune', English translation, pp.208–213. The Ukraine was the focus of Anarchist activity in Russia, dominated for a considerable time by the peasant armies of Nestor Makhno, until it was reconquered by the Reds.Cf. E. Yaroslavsky, *History of Anarchism in Russia*, London, n.d., pp.60–81; Victor Peters, *Nestor Makhno: The Life of an Anarchist*, Winnipeg, 1971; Peter Arshinov, *History of the Makhnovist Movement, 1918–1921*, Detroit and Chicago, 1974; Voline, *The Unknown Revolution*, Montreal, 1975, pp.541–711; Paul Avrich, 'Nestor Makhno: The Man and the Myth', *Anarchist Portraits*, Princeton U.P., 1988, pp.111–24 (translator's note).

The Ideas of Boris Pilnyak[1]

Boris Pilnyak, one of the most remarkable of the young Russian writers of the present day, is beginning to be known to the French public. The N.R.F. has just published a translation of his masterful work, *The Naked Year*, which our comrade Léon Bazalgette has similarly commented upon here.[2] As early as 1923 we had discussed the work of Pilnyak at length with the readers of *Clarté*; *Clarté* and then *Europe* later published long extracts from it. The time seems to us to have come for defining the position of Boris Pilnyak within Russian literature, which is of necessity the literature of the revolution.

Pilnyak – is there any need to emphasise it? – is not a proletarian writer. He is one of the greatest, if not the greatest of the post-revolutionary writers, who adapted to the new order but were in no sense Communists, and are called in Russia 'fellow travellers'. And among them he has for a long time been placed on the right, though without his agreement.

In referring to these writers as 'fellow travellers' of the revolutionaries, I wrote elsewhere (*Clarté*, no.31, 1923): 'To begin with these men are not proletarians, nor are they intellectuals assimilated by the proletariat ... The idea of a class is quite foreign to them: like the Socialist Revolutionaries they prefer to speak about the "people", a vague idea, which belongs to the old advanced liberalism. Not being aligned with the revolutionary class, and never having understood how to think along with it, they remain subject to contrary influences. Their future depends upon it. Their literature is not that of a victorious proletarian revolution, nor that of a defeated revolution. It corresponds exactly to the transitional period. It will become what Russia will become. If it should – as some hope – evolve towards bourgeois democracy, these writers will be transformed without difficulty into good members of a 'Society of Moscow Men of Letters', cleverly exploiting their memories of an eventful youth. But if the dictatorship of the proletariat leads Red Russia towards Communism, by adapting to their milieu little by little, in ten years they may be in tune with the period, and perhaps really revolutionaries ...'[3]

But the dictatorship of the proletariat has not failed in its task since 1923 and these writers, and Boris Pilnyak in particular, have very much evolved towards the left. The journal of the Moscow proletarian writers, *Na literaturnom Postu* (*On Literary Guard*) nonetheless in its no.7–8 which appeared last November devoted a close study to Pilnyak signed by J. Lers, which ends in this way:

> We should consider Pilnyak as a representative of a literary ideology in
> the process of formation, belonging to the new bourgeoisie.

This is a brutal formulation, and no doubt a summary one, but it is not devoid of truth, and is very much in line with the views of the most varied Communist criticisms (Trotsky, Lelevich, Voronsky, Gorbachev and Kogan[4]), none of whom fail to recognise the writer's beautiful talent.

It should be correctly noted that Pilnyak belongs to rural Russia, which is neither the leading factor, nor the most conscious factor in the Revolution. Two very clear ideas in *The Naked Year* run through the whole of his work and allow us to understand what separates us from Pilnyak. Here they are:

– Russia is Asia.

– The Revolution is a storm, springing from elemental forces.

It is necessary, so it seems to me, to say this quite frankly. The first of these ideas, which is often taken up in Western Europe, as much by our friends as by our enemies, is radically false, and deeply contrary to Communist thinking. It is not a question, and this is self-evident, of talking about geography and ethnography; the beautiful themes that can be developed about the Volga, the Urals, the Pamirs and the heart of Asia are familiar to us. We are thinking about historical and political truth. For it is Socialist Russia, created by the proletarian revolution – otherwise described as headed by the proletariat – led by a party whose entire policy proceeds from scientific Socialism that is no doubt, in a certain sense, in its living work, the most European country in the world. European civilisation is characterised by its achievements in the experimental sciences, whose application to production has given rise to great mechanised industry. The thinkers and leaders of the capitalist system have good reason to refuse to apply their own methods of scientific investigation to social problems. The system of which they are the beneficiaries, its contradictions, its defects, its dangers and its limitations, is all too easily revealed by scientific criticism; for the class struggle appears in all its deep meaning in it, and we can see all too well on which side of the barricade the intelligence and truth are to be found which will save the future. But as long as the old 'European' thinking, the thinking of the worn out ruling classes, condemned to lie both to others and to itself in order to exist – hesitates between the old restrictive positivism, the old idealisms and the old religious mysticisms, only to end up sometimes agreeing with a Spengler by admitting to its own decline, as long as the thinking of *capitalist* Europe stumbles and betrays itself, the intellectual disciplines which were the greatness of European civilisation will be reborn, rejuvenated, refounded and enlarged only by the revolutionary dialectic of the proletariat. From now on Soviet society is characterised by rational and conscious organisation, on a plan for the whole of production; and this is very much the application of the scientific methods of European thought at its highest and most audacious level to the entirety of social life. However freely the bourgeoisie's experts might speak of a return by the Bolsheviks to the Scythian horde, as expressed by M. Grousset, the historian of Asia,[5] it is only one of the ploys at their disposal. For the USSR, and for Communism, it is European influence that is penetrating into Asia, no longer the influence of a European barbarism armed with the superior technology of alcohol, bibles and long range artillery, but that of a precise understanding of the play of social mechanisms such as Marx, Engels and Lenin gave us, themselves the beneficiaries of the whole of modern culture.

Shall we refute the idea of the revolution-storm so dear to Boris Pilnyak? Looked at from the outside by a foreign observer, the revolution might appear to be a prodigious unleashing of elemental forces. But if that is all it had been, it would have been limited to a primitive *jacquerie* which the possessing classes, sufficiently well organised, would in the end have been able to get under control. It is really a matter of a peasant revolution which was well and truly created in Russia, assisted, led, supported and guided by the proletarian movement. We believe that never before has the organisation, the consciousness and the will of the masses played so decisive a role as in the Russian Revolution. It is enough to convince yourself by studying the formation of the Bolshevik Party, starting from 1903, its deliberate march to power as defined by Lenin in March 1917, the careful preparation of the October uprising, and the further struggles up to the consistent capitalisation of today's USSR. But such a study would require a deep identification of the intellectual with the proletariat, and a desire on the part of the intellectual to become a mere servant of the proletariat.

A number of the young Russian writers originating in the Revolution, but linked by their social origins and their mentality to yesterday's educated classes, bourgeoisie, petty bourgeoisie – have remained very alien to Communism, and it could not be otherwise during the transitional epoch we are going through. That is why their glances turn more freely towards the past than to the future.

Victor Serge

Notes

1. Translated from *L'Humanité*, 25 May, 1927 (translator's note).
2. Léon Bazalgette (1873–1928) was a French writer on literature and the arts (translator's note).
3. Above, p. 170
4. Peter Semyonovich Kogan (1872–1932) was a literary historian and art critic, and a professor at the State University in Moscow. 3 volumes of his *Essays on the History of Recent Russian Literature* were published between 1908 and 1912 (translator's note).
5. René Grousset (1885–1952) was one of France's foremost orientalists, the author of a well known history of the Crusades and a classic survey of Chinese Art and Culture (translator's note).

Y. Libedinsky

Libidensky's *The Week*[1]

I live in a country where a French book is the rarest of the rare. The victory of French arms, paid for with one million seven hundred thousand young men's deaths has had the effect of opening up a gulf between the intellectual culture of the victors and that of the others, allies or enemies, who, (with the exception of the Russians), being poor, must be considered as vanquished. In fourteen European countries, Russia, Estonia, Latvia, Lithuania, Poland, Czechoslovakia, Germany, Austria, Hungary, Romania, Yugoslavia, Greece, Bulgaria and Turkey, inhabited by two hundred and seventy-eight million people, no one, as a general rule, can any longer buy a French book, or have access to a French journal. The high value of the franc has cut off French intellect as far as these countries are concerned; on the other hand the fall of the franc in relation to the dollar and the pound sterling has made intellectual works by Anglo-Saxons difficult of accesss for French intellectuals. So, in the universe of capitalism, the weight of coffers stands in the way of mental progress. Allow me, incidentally, to throw open this theme to those 'good European' intellectuals who are happy to place themselves 'above the social struggle'. I live in a country where a French book is the rarest of the rare. I only rarely receive as a result of chance those read by the wider French public, though always with keen curiosity. We are all of us so anxious, in this country of the revolution, where amid immense sufferings a new world is being born, to make the acquaintance of the latest works of Western intellect! I was in great joy the other day when a friend, who had come from Cairo –! – put on my table one of the new books, which, to judge from the press, has had a great success in France: Henri Béraud's *Martyre de l'obèse*.[2] A little later another piece of luck got for me the *Mercure de France* of 1 July, a book by Pierre Mille, one by Marcel Proust, and the pleasing book *Les Copains*, by Jules Romains ...[3] All these names are counted among the best; the success of all these works very much illustrates the average appearance of the literary works which nourish 'the wider French public' ... I already had on my table among the thinkers of the Revolution, our present day Russian writers, Pilnyak, Mayakovsky, Ehrenburg, Tarasov-Rodianov, Nikitin, Vsevolod Ivanov, Libedinsky and Veresaev. Among them I opened Henri Béraud, and then the

Mercure de France. I found here a story, very well told, it is true, about a fat man who did no more in his life than eat well, who only ever thought of winning the heart of 'the fair sex', and who felt no greater unhappiness than to feel ridiculous, who never, ever suspected that he was very much a poor imbecile, a banal product of the degeneration of an overfed, playboy and gently stupified social class, but who still thought that he was 'very witty' ... A writers' panel felt this book to be the best, on the level of Barbusse's *Feu*;[4] this fact cannot but be very symptomatic. In the *Mercure* I found an article on the Balkan crisis,[5] a general's opinion on the problem of Bacon-Shakespeare,[6] a medical contribution, a documentary novel, of which several hundreds come out a year, an article about Pierre Loti,[7] and an inept political survey on Russia signed by the ex-Socialist Alexinsky.[8] The educated readers of the *Mercure*, who might have improved their critical sense a little by some acquaintance with Rémy de Gourmont,[9] now allow themselves seriously to be offered 'Zinoviev *Affelbaum*' (yes, from the late name – garbled – of J. Martov, who was the most outstanding leader of Russian Menshevism[10]) 'the former agent of the Prussian General Staff' ... Their limited and stubborn bourgeois sentiment, blotting out all judgement among them, still allows them to hang on to the putrid anti-Bolshevik lies of 1917. More interesting, the article by Louis Carice about Pierre Loti shows me one who was, at the end of his life as a poet, a great writer belonging to the race and class of the fat man with whose martyrdom we are acquainted: a poor old man anxious to grow old and die, who strained to the utmost to *look good* a little more, who made himself up, who was ashamed to show his age to women, who was fearfully anxious to wear a uniform – and who understood nothing of the terrible drama of the war, who hadn't the slightest inkling of the end of the culture he had enriched, who didn't have a clue that there was a social and a human problem in it, and went off, desolate, into his own void, dead in reality since he had lost both sensual pleasure and the sweet melancholy that comes after it (for 'man is sad after making love ...'). The war came along breaking up empires, murdering nearly forty million human beings – among them how many geniuses! – and delivering a mortal blow to the old European civilisation; the revolution has just started up its duel with death over the ruins; a new form of state has arisen, unknown to all previous civilisations, the workers' state that wants an end to the state; a new order is being born among the terror and famine, taking in half of Europe and half of Asia. And placed between the two extremes of French – bourgeois – understanding, the one a nothing and the other a very great poet, the ridiculous fat and old man Pierre Loti – symbolising the whole class whose leisure they sustained – they seemed to be ignorant of all that ...

A company of red soldiers was passing under my windows singing:

> We are spreading over the world
> Labour's red flag! ...

I left there Pierre Loti, Pierre Mille, the unfortunate *Obèse* and even the pleasant kindly *Copains* of Jules Romains, and opened Yuri Libedinsky's little book, *The Week*.

★   ★   ★   ★   ★

This little book, which appeared a few months ago, very quickly took its place among the best of the year. Yuri Libedinsky is a young man, and this is his first work. He worked for the revolution at a local level. He is not a littérateur, or even a well read person: he has the episodic and incomplete education of young workers who love to read or the proletarian students who have laboured for four years while fighting on an empty stomach. He has a flat style. We can see that to write his account he took his model from the classical Russian writers of yester-year and had neither the time, nor perhaps the inclination to cultivate his own style. A book like this takes us back to the simplicity of the first works of all literature. The author wrote neither to sell it dear to a publisher, nor to advertise himself, nor to be flattered by a few journals, nor to appeal to polite society. He feels the primordial need, the source of all artistic creativity, to express what he has experienced, in other words seen, done and understood. Without embroidery, he takes all the elements of his work from the life of the milieu around him. The lake dweller, when he came back from hunting or fighting, felt the need to describe to his tribal assembly the exploits of those who did not return, and his own, the danger they confronted, the courage of the heroes, and the greatness of their victories. That man was the first poet and the first historian at one and the same time. Some of our young Russian writers returning from the battles of the revolution appear to be moved by the same primordial feelings. That is why they appear to us to be so rich in experience, energy and knowledge about the essential laws that govern human life – and so powerfully young.

Let us read *The Week*. The action takes place during a week in a small town in the middle of Russia in 1918–19 or 1920 (everything rings true in this story, and there were so many episodes of this sort!). The Communist branch of the district has met: a worker, the director of the provisions services of the local soviet has just reported news of the famine in detailed terms. The town is finished. The town will die of hunger. Follow this argument:

Only a single railtrack connects this little factory district to the important centres situated 500 kilometres away, and therefore a journey of twelve or fifteen hours. The town has no reserves. They were all used up during the war and the first months of the revolution. Far from being able to supply them, the neighbouring countryside itself is threatened with death from hunger. The peasants know that, turn sour, and direct their anger against the town. Banditry spreads. The roads are no longer safe; moreover the roads are disappearing, reclaimed by the steppe once human endeavour has given up. To bring grain from a province nearby the railway needs fuel. The coal has run out (the Whites have no doubt occupied the coalfield). It needs wood: and there isn't any around. *What can they do to avoid death?*

The whole problem of the Russian revolution is posed in these seven words. For years the entire Soviet Republic has been a city under siege. Nobody has come up with the idea of calling in question the dictatorship [of the proletariat] or of invoking great principles. One man, an old militant suffering from tuberculosis, gets up and proposes a solution:

There is a wood belonging to a monastery twelve versts – fifteen kilometres – from the town. It can be cut down. That will make the fuel. We can go looking for grain with this fuel. Where do we get the manpower from? The strongest are at the front, and all who remain in the town are those needed to do the work. *Let us requisition, willingly or by force, the ex-bourgeois population!*

But then we see another dire risk. There is only a weak garrison, a red battalion, in the town, plus a few of armed communists. Bandits, recruited from the backward and discontented countryside, led by old counter-revolutionary officers, or perhaps by the Anarchist Makhno or the ex Socialist Revolutionary

Antonov,[11] are prowling round about. If the requisition squads that are going to cut the wood are not guarded they risk being slaughtered. And if they are guarded the town, abandoned for three days by its garrison, risks being taken … Should they have the batallion leave the town? Should they wait for the famine, or take a risk? They discuss it. They decide on action. Famine is more dangerous than bandits: it kills more people more certainly. Let us go and chop down the wood!

I am passing over the details and character sketches. It is an impressive drama through the simplicity of its symbols, the rigorous logic of necessity, and the simple human will it shows resisting them everywhere, Russian truthfulness in detail and as a whole. A squad requisitioned from the bourgeois escorted by the red batallion goes off to chop the wood. The bandits launch themselves on the defenceless town where the shopkeepers, provoked by the requisitions, welcome them with joy. A treacherous Red officer leads their night foray towards the lodgings of some communists, and orders summary executions. Kobeiko, Simkov, and Martynov the intellectual – ashamed of his bourgeois origins – and the intellectual Klimin – who hesitates to fire even in self-defence – are slaughtered, surprised getting out of their beds, leaning over their books, or in the street while rushing to the party headquarters: twenty-nine are killed, which is all the town had of intelligent administrators, devoted teachers, and men who knew how to convey an ideal, set an example, and hand on the faith … They cut open the stomach of the Commissar of Supplies and pour a bushel of corn into it. You will find scenes of ferocity of this type in Balzac's *Chouans*.[12] All Chouans are all too like each other!

Twenty-nine communists have fallen, and the whole town is drenched in blood. But the requisition squad returns, bringing the wood. The red batallion reenters the town.

> 'The batallion should not have been made to leave the town', says Karaulov. 'I was right!'
> Gornik pauses. Then he speaks, as if lining up heavy stones on a wall:
> 'No, Karaulov, we were both wrong. Look: the wood has been brought in. Just think about it! That means seed corn to damp down the peasant revolts; it will be like water on the fire! Our comrades have not fallen in vain!'

It is hard to lose twenty-nine in this way – when we have barely fifty. It is hard, atrocious and absurd to see the best die like this. But that is the price that has to be paid in blood for the seed, and therefore the corn and bread, for peace, for the future, and for Communism. None of these men – and Russia has thousands and thousands of such men – has read Marcus Aurelius: but their *reasoned acceptance of the necessary sacrifice* reflects the greatness of spirit of the Stoics.[13] Here Y. Libedinsky is showing us one of the most important characteristics of the Bolsheviks.

Libedinsky is throwing us into the stark reality of the revolution. There is no lyricism where he is concerned, and none of the great sweeps of Pilnyak,[14] but always inflexible necessity, always reasoned acceptance, and always the inexorable will of men – of revolutionaries – which sometimes appears to be superhuman and sometimes even inhuman, since it is so great. An incidental chapter neatly poses the problem of cruelty in the revolution. By cruelty I mean the desire for or the act of inflicting a measure of random demoralisation upon an enemy you have to reduce to impotence or suppress (at a time of revolution, the only way of reducing an irreducible enemy to impotence is often to suppress him). This desire is absolutely alien, and even contrary to revolutionary thinking. But the brutal fact can result from circumstances. The young communist and Cheka man Surikov, inspired by the thought that 'you must know how to die when you exercise the right of life and death',[15] sent to supervise the killing in a rebellious village, confesses in his last letter to a friend that, completely revolutionary and utterly convinced as he is of the necessity for the terror, he has suffered by taking part in it.

'I pitied these men, I suffered for their suffering, but I know that the road to Communism goes by way of the death of the revolution's enemies. *I have changed my great pity into great hatred.*' Surikov takes part in the execution of five counter-revolutionaries on a very frosty night in the snow. The worst thing was to order these five men about to be shot to undress, and to see the five human forms at whom they had to fire shiver in the icy fog. Now each piece of clothing is precious; in this country reduced to extreme poverty – where we know what seed costs – in this Russian winter every tunic can save a life, or add to the strength of a fighter. Clothing cannot be wasted. Cruelty only results from poverty. This is a general truth. We have seen shipwrecked men reduced to cannibalism in this way. But quite different is the cruelty of counter-revolutionary pogroms. In Libedinsky's story the Chekist Surikov is buried alive by rebellious peasants. In a recent article Gorky describes similar examples of peasant cruelty during the civil war. It is basically connected with primitive savagery, through a general lack of culture; held back, fought against and finally brought under control by revolutionaries anxious to do their social duty and always preoccupied with lifting the level of the consciousness of the masses – but the very opposite of that cultivated, exploited, and scientifically operated by the military caste defending the old capitalist system: for it is encouraging the obscurantist cast of mind that is favourable to its plans. There is proof of this in the development of anti-semitism under all the White regimes in the South of Russia, in the terror of pogroms which the communist regime has everywhere effortlessly brought to an end.

'There is always the feeling of walking, along with some thousands of comrades, over a thin layer of ice, with furious water billowing underneath ready to drag down everything and sweep away everything', writes Libedinsky of one of his characters. How right he is! You have that feeling all the way through this book. We have had it in Russia for years. The little revolutionary town is lost in a boundless, backward and primitive countryside, infested with bandits. And the twenty-nine communists who went to their deaths and the twenty who were to survive are lost among the uncomprehending, the lazy, the weak, and the hostile. The communist workers' revolution in this peasant country is the work of a splendid minority, against whom on certain occasions, along with the 'delirious countryside', even the forces of nature, heavy frost, enduring famine and the vastness seem to be in alliance. Necessity forces harshness upon this minority, above all towards itself. Poverty sometimes changes this harshness into cruelty. It has to be inflexible, inexorable, calculating, disciplined, Stoic – and always thinking. It is that. And it wins out!

That is the story of the Russian revolution. This story with unlimited perspectives – and the great human problems to which it gives rise – is all contained in miniature in a story, the first work of a proletarian writer less than thirty years old.

This is powerful and invigorating literature. But if all you ask of a writer is not to make you think too much, and not to trouble your placid digestion, but only to entertain you whilst discretely reminding you that you are an honourable educated citizen of a Great Democracy Victorious in the War for Justice and all that stuff, don't read these writers, Sir. And don't read *Clarté* any more. Buy the *Mercure de France* instead.

Kiev, 15 July, 1923   Victor Serge

Notes

1. Translated from *Clarté*, no.xliii, 15 September, 1923, pp.387–9. The English translation, *A Week*, made by Arthur Ransome, was published in London in 1923 (translator's note).

2. Henri Béraud (1885–1958), a right wing French writer, published *Le Martyr de l'obèse* in Paris in 1922 (translator's note).

3. The *Mercure de France* was a Symbolist magazine; Pierre Mille (1864–1941) was an author of an anthology of contemporary French humour published in Paris in 1912; Jules Romains published *Les Copains* in 1913 (translator's note).

4. Barbusse published *Le Feu* in 1916 (translator's note).

5. Professor Tsankov seized power in a military coup in Bulgaria in June 1923, followed by an abortive communist uprising in September (translator's note).

6. The theory that Shakespeare's plays were really written by Sir Francis Bacon (1561–1626) has long been a literary curiosity (translator's note).

7. Julien Viaud, whose pen name was Pierre Loti (1850–1923) wrote travel books and novels (translator's note).

8. Grigory Alexeyevich Alexinsky (1879–?) was a member of the Second Duma who broke with the Bolsheviks, and in 1917 produced documents accusing Lenin of being implicated with the German General Staff. He became a propagandist for Wrangel during the Russian Civil War. Cf. Victor Serge, 'Lenin in 1917', *Revolutionary History*, vol.v, no.3, Autumn 1994, pp.20–1, and n.76, p.48 (translator's note).

9. Rémy de Gourmont (1858–1915), poet, novelist and essayist, founded the *Mercure de France* (translator's note).

10. Grigory Yevseyevich Radomysslsky, known to history as Zinoviev (1883–1936), a Bolshevik, has here been confused with Julius Ossipovich Tsederbaum, known as Martov (1873–1923), the leader of the Menshevik Internationalists (translator's note).

11. Nestor Ivanovich Makhno (1889–1934) was the leader of the peasant guerrillas in the Ukraine during the Russian Civil War who fought against both Whites and Reds; Alexander Stanislasovich Antonov (1889–1922) was the SR leader of the Tambov peasant uprising of 1921 (translator's note).

12. Balzac published his novel *Le Dernier Chouan, ou la Bretagne en 1800* in 1828. Its title was later shortened to *Les Chouans*. The Chouans were royalist insurgents in Brittany during the revolution, so-called after 'Chouan' (screech-owl), the nickname of Jean Cottereau (translator's note).

13. Marcus Aurelius, Roman Emperor (161–180 A.D.) was an adherent of the Stoic school of philosophy. His *Meditations*, written while campaigning against the Germans, preach accepting the dictates of necessity (translator's note).

14. Cf. the study of Boris Pilnyak in no.36 of *Clarté* (author's note).

15. This idea of responsibility, pushed to its limit and rightly emphasised, has not been rare. I personally know of two analogous cases – V.S. (author's note).

Yuri Libedinsky[1]

Yuri Libedinsky is twenty eight years old, with the slender shape and fine bony face of a young working class scholar of firm and combative convictions, a Communist past as a red soldier and writer, and an unceasing activity as a militant ... Fairness demands that he should be reckoned in the first rank among the founders of proletarian literature; in 1922 he published in Russia a first book of a singular power in which implacable and admirable necessity, the vital law of the Revolution, was described by a real revolutionary. This book, *The Week* – courageously sad – was a revelation. The proletariat on the march, at times in darkness and blood, deserves to have its own literature! *L'Humanité* has elsewhere provided in serialised form a fairly good translation of *The Week*, which I have also introduced to the readers of *Clarté*. It is a matter for some regret that a publisher could not be found in France who would offer this remarkable work to French working-class readers.

After *The Week* in 1923 Libedinsky wrote *Tomorrow*,[2] a work that we have to admit – along with the author himself – was a failure. Such are our new literary habits: to flatter each other is no part of the law. Criticism goes on vigorously among proletarian writers, often ungraciously, but always as comrades. And if they fall out – and they do fall out – it is over principles, and not over considerations of self esteem. 'My book miscarried', says Libedinsky simply, shaking his chestnut hair. And he writes as he speaks. If you, dear reader, know of a Parisian writer who has shown proof of critical feeling towards himself that is as severe and detached from petty vanity, have the goodness to show him to me! *Tomorrow* was not, however, a bad book. It is even a document which will often be looked at in the future. The first effects of the N.E.P. upon the Russian society produced by the October Revolution and the agonising and enthusiastic expectation of the German revolution form its twin subjects; in it the revolution appears between getting bogged down and starting up again. Great mastery would have been required to bring so broad a theme to a conclusion. Libedinsky's failure was neither surprising nor humiliating. The writer went back to work.

His third book, *The Commissars*, which came out this year,[3] shows great progress, great labour, and a persevering effort in a fresh furrow where it is a question of aiming straight and deep. Libedinsky here shows himself to be a

Communist writer of the first rank. Do not jump to the conclusion that he is preoccupied with arguing on behalf of the Party, or of social point-scoring by means of a novel. These are petty ways of going on to which he has no need to resort. No, he is Communist in all his thinking, in his whole life, and even in the forms his language takes. He does not envisage life employed in the service of the proletariat as spent within the Party; the only air he can breathe is in a great fraternal collectivity which is at one and the same time an immense spiritual family, a disciplined army, and an impressive assembly of thoughts perpetually at work, a society in the process of formation ... In it Libedinsky does not know how you pose the problem of the individual and society; all too often the old society opposed one man to all men; the new society growing up within us has already succeeded in strengthening both of them so well that life has taken on a new flavour in it.

There are, obviously, many Communists in the works of present day Russian literature; the writers *on the other side* have only succeeded at times in giving obviously powerful portraits of our militants, but the depth of their lives, or should I say its essence, is always created flawed. They describe the Communist as good *foreign* observers. Lidedinsky's success proves to us that to be able to describe the new man you have to be a new man yourself.

His theme is this. Now that the Civil War has ended, the Commissars who formerly led the Red Army in its daily exploits, in death or victory, are beginning to get used to the blessings of peace. But the Party is aware of this. Should it not strain its energies unceasingly, but combat slackening, to put to good use the days of peace? An organisation is set up at the centre of the military district for the Commissars, taking advantage of the peace, to perfect their education as Communists and soldiers.[4] Unfortunately, there is only one man who can organise these courses, and he is a worker whose lungs can only breathe with great difficulty, and whose brain is no longer up to it. This Joseph Mindlov knows how many ignorant people we have among us, and that the job is going to take up the last hours of his life, and the friend who has ordered him to do it in the name of the Party knows it also. There is a brief argument between them. Necessity rules both of them: both of them know their duty with inexorable understanding, however weak the flesh.

There are all types of men among the Commissars. Libedinsky's merit is not to fall into epic exaggeration. There is no trace of the superhuman. For these men, imbued with all the human weaknesses, it is a matter of combining in a way that will strengthen a common thought and will within them that will lift them above themselves and make good soldiers of their class out of them. It is no more than this: a tough task. Instinctive resistance has to be broken down – it will be so good to live now that we no longer have to fight: don't we have the right to rest on our dearly bought laurels? – in order to persuade, direct, drag along and clean up this battalion of young veterans of the Civil War, among whom there are now some black sheep ... This struggle fills up the whole book. How many living men, anxious to improve themselves, pass through it, and how many significant events? The Party is the mould in which this human material is moulded into such powerful shapes.

Libedinsky abounds in just the right expressions that only a real comrade could find. 'Vassiliev carried for months inside him the simple unexpressed thought that he was ready to throw away his life like a log on the brazier of the Revolution, for as long as the brazier continued to burn. But nobody took his life, and it seemed to him that the Revolution was over.'

Love, which holds sway in the traditional novel, has little place in this book, perhaps fifteen pages out of a hundred and seventy. For if love maintains an essential place in the life of the individual, there are yet greater forces in social life, with more imperious laws than it has, and more passionate themes than the eternal drama of man and woman. Think about changing the world, the architects of which we wish to be. Here each person has obligations to all: private life takes second place, and the revolution comes first. Contrary to what our individualistic (bourgeois) education leads us to believe, private life is only enriched and embellished by it. It is impoverished when it becomes an aim in itself: a man who only dreams about himself is a poor sort of man. But harmonised with the vast social activity of a revolutionary class ripened in noble struggles in the light of a great plan, made healthier by work, thinking, collective action and solidarity, individual life, let us not forget it, takes on a richness, a fertility, and an astonishing new health. Libedinsky knows how to describe with tragic and clear simplicity the drama of the revolutionary who meets a young woman with a wretched bourgeois mentality, and then the clear happiness of the man and woman as comrades who understand each other without even having to speak because a new life has risen between them with an equal strength.

This beautiful book is by no means perfect ... It errs in the first place by being too rich. Libedinsky ignores the art of being economical with his methods, his observations and his findings in order to draw from them what is of most advantage to him. He is extraordinary. *The Commissars* condenses the material for several volumes – in the same way as the compositions of the great progenitors who preceeded the masters of the Renaissance, it often includes the subject matter for several canvasses.

Leningrad, 26 October   Victor Serge

Notes

1. Translated from *L'Humanité*, 17 October, 1926 (translator's note).
2. *Tomorrow* was published in 1923 (translator's note).
3. *The Commissars* was published in 1925, which was presumably when Serge wrote the original review (translator's note).
4. This was a general directive from above. Cf. L. D. Trotsky, 'The Red Army, Seedbed of Enlightenment', *Pravda*, 27 May, 1923, in *Problems of Everyday Life*, New York, 1977, p.105 (translator's note).

Vsevolod Ivanov[1]

Vsevolod Ivanov has been nicknamed 'the new Gorky'. Without questioning the importance of his work and the youthful vigour of his talent, I do not find this an exact comparison. Gorky has provided a long career which is by no means ended. Vsevolod Ivanov is only just starting out. He is a young man, and his first stories only came out after the Revolution. Gorky is one of the masters of the Russian literary language. Vsevolod Ivanov's style is in the process of being formed. Gorky came up from the depths of society, which forever placed their stamp upon him. Gorky actually experienced the deep human misery he talks about. Vsevolod Ivanov is a young Siberian intellectual who has mostly observed the people and things he describes. The difference here between the two intellectuals seems to me to be an essential one. Moreover, such comparisons can only be lamentably arbitrary. But it has been said, and it shows just how successful Vsevolod Ivanov has been, and that is why I have put it on record.

Vsevolod Ivanov belongs to the half dozen new Russian writers whose work has added to the intellectual heritage of the Russian Revolution, and even more, of Europe today. It will one day be translated. It will be discovered as once Gorky and Andreyev were discovered, and as little by little our great Anton Chekhov, so by-passed by the new Russia, is being discovered in France today. We should understand that at a time when one of the most cultivated of the peoples of the old Europe is satisfying its leisure time with Henri Bordeaux, Pierre Benoît[2] and Victor Margueritte, young men who have come from the Siberian steppes in verminous peasant war trains to the ancient decorated towers of the Kremlin have enriched European letters with books that are a bit on the hasty side, but heavy with life and thought, as heavy as massive ingots of pure metal.

Vsevolod Ivanov is the author of several long stories: *Armoured Train no.14-69*, *The Coloured Winds*, *The Partisans*, and *The Skyblue Sands*, in all three volumes. He is about to publish a new novel. Until now he has only dealt with subjects invariably taken from the lives of Siberian peasants during the Civil War. He wrote *The Song of Things Done* by the Red partisans who carried out the revolution over a territory of over twelve million square kilometres (twenty-four times the size of France), in spite of betrayal by a great Socialist Party (the Socialist Revolutionary Party), in spite of the reactionary government of Admiral Kolchak, and in spite of Czechoslovak, American, French and Japanese interventions.

★　★　★　★　★

When we read Vsevolod Ivanov we feel as if we are being carried off in an express train across the Russian steppes. It is spring, after the melting of the snows. Everywhere there is space: lively and soft colours, pure blue skies, pure white of the clouds, pure green of the meadows, dull brown of the earth, the pale silver of the birch trees and the soft tones of the firs in the sunlight. Your throat constricts: you want to breathe more deeply. Your eyes are drunk with pure colours, and your spirit is intoxicated with the space. And when the train comes to a halt, you come across a station which is no more than a house made out of huge tree trunks lost in a plain and an old muzhik with a bushy beard who tells the truth in a quiet voice. Suddenly you remember the big cities, the magazines, witty people, men of letters, all the refined hypocrisies of every level, the odious little things that adorn life, the stampede for money – and you have a sudden revelation of another way of looking at life.

This revelation is intense in all Vsevolod Ivanov's good pages, above all because he puts us in contact with a new type of human being, without any doubt one of the greatest and healthiest of our time: the Siberian peasant.

To begin with, above all for the Western reader, the books of Vsevolod Ivanov represent a great documentary interest. The life of the small Siberian village, the Kirghiz encampment, the steppe, the towns lost in the *taiga* (brushwood), the irresistible spontaneity of the uprising of the people of the land of Siberia against the White reaction in 1918, observed on the spot through small details with no apparent historical importance; the psychology of these admirable Siberian peasants, our brothers in the Revolution; and an entire vast panorama, far too vast, I might say, for several books, moving, living, in which crowds of men from Europe and Asia mix together with crowds of events ... This is what you find here. All this is true, adding a great deal of the unexpected to what we already know of the Russian Revolution.

For we know little of what has been its effect in Asia, in the Altai gorges and in the Mongolian plains, where it has nonetheless penetrated like a ploughshare dug deep in the soil. Somewhere the peasants over there, wearied by the agitation of the Whites, take down their guns. A revolt is being prepared in a neighbouring town. They know about it, and a great ambition comes to them. They are going to take *Armoured Train no.14-69*, four or five oblong steel boxes towed by a locomotive containing men and artillery. There are officers and soldiers in the wagons. The soldiers are passive instruments. The officers are old professional soldiers, brought up in the barracks of the old regime, tired, embittered, alcoholics, who only know how to talk about women, the female, in other words, or the service. There is no spirit in them. These men, running along in their train under fire from the peasants, go back and forth between a blown-up bridge and a blocked track, identifying themselves by the chatter of their machine guns. Do you know what the Red partisans do to to stop this armoured train? A man, a comrade, lies down on the rails, tormented by the most frightful anguish ... Then the Chinaman Sin Bin U, in whom pity is stronger than the fear of death, climbs towards this man and tells him 'Go away!' The Chinaman remains there. The Reds have taken the train ...[3]

Revolt appeared elsewhere in the countryside because the militia came to seize a clandestine distillery and a militiaman was killed (*The Partisans*). Yet elsewhere, pushed to the limit by conscription, the muzhiks go to look for three Red soldiers hidden in the woods, and ask them to place themselves in charge of 'the children'. An old man says, referring to these Red fugitives, long hunted for the reward on them:

> We did well not to kill them; they come at the right time (*The Coloured Winds*).

* * * * *

There are passages that bring to mind the history of Merovingian times,[4] such as the ambush carried out by the Kirghiz on a market, where suddenly among the carts filled with animal hides and cattle an angry confrontation begins in the middle of the celebrations. The Russian Whites have brought along their tricolour flag bearing the holy cross on it; it is next to the green flag of the Mongols. Then the German colonists appear on the battlefield, coming in their heavy carts to gather the spoils of the vanquished, counting them methodically with their fingers (*The Coloured Winds*) ... We saw many of these massacres in the Ukraine at the time of the Makhnovschina. It was in an ambush like this that Makhno killed Grigoriev.[5]

Long conversations take place drawing up plans in *yurts* – huge tents of skin where you lie on cushions and cloths – between Kirghiz khans and White Atamans, enemies who are nonetheless allies, accomplices until the time when one or the other will be free of the Reds ... Ataman Trubyshev reminds us of Semyonov and Baron Ungern, the half descendant of the Teutonic Knights who colonised the Baltic provinces,[6] who dreamed of setting up a Russo-Mongol Empire, committed innumerable atrocities, and when finally handed over to the Reds by his own officers, was shot at the end of 1922.

And this confused war of peoples, races and classes, whose eddies pass back and forth over the same poor villages (the same village has three of its chairmen of the soviet murdered in succession) is the revolution; thousands of yellow, swarthy and white poor people, harassed by the necessity of fighting for their bread and livelihood, feel in a confused way, if strongly, what they have to do, and what they cannot avoid doing, so that the Revolution appears to us as the magnificent result of their disparate efforts, in which it hardly matters whether they understand it or not. The feeling of the irresistible spontaneity of the uprising of the Siberian peasants is what matters. The collective enthusiasm is only a by-product of it.

★   ★   ★   ★   ★

Vsevolod Ivanov makes the men live who do these things. In many respects they are primitive people. Look at how these Siberians speak and think:

> They spoke slowly, with effort.
> Their minds, unaccustomed to strange ideas and to everyday work functioned badly; each thought was painfully grasped with flesh sticking to it, like you retrieve a hook from a fish you have caught.

Their moral code is ignorant of the rules laid down in the old countries. It is not very different from that of the Barbarians observed by Tacitus, or the hard and practical Hebrews of the Bible.[7] During a battle someone shouts 'Take care of the cattle!' (*The Coloured Winds*). Kill or be killed in war, what could be more simple? Semen, coming back from hunting, sees a Red soldier sleeping in a wood and fires a shot at him (forty roubles reward), but then falls to thinking that 'we ought to aim at the head of the game whose plumage is so thick ...' The death of an enemy is a mere hunting episode. In *The Coloured Winds* the Reds shoot the captured officers without even thinking about it, incidentally, just like carrying out a necessary duty. A few seconds before himself falling, Anton Slernev, the leader of the partisans, getting ready his last bullet, says 'we shall see!' There is no further comment from the writer.

The logic of these men is something special. The partisans shoot Dmitry Smolin, who has come freely among them to see his father, because his father has killed a Red soldier. But afterwards, after taking him prisoner along with other Whites, they make the one who is really to blame the head of the group 'in compensation' ... The law of the blood feud does not yet seem to be separated from instinct. Sixteen villages in a district conference pronounce in favour of the Soviet system and one against. The majority have the opposing delegates shot ...

This is without doubt a primitive mentality. Again we see that Vsevolod Ivanov, in whom realism is in no way restrained, has revealed the thinking of these primitive people searchingly. In order not to judge them too harshly we should recall what European man, both German and French, came to on the battle fields of the Great War. To understand which of the two is the better we must compare the Red partisan of the social war in Siberia with the man in the trenches ...

Here, for example, is a little example taken from *The Partisans*. It has Jack London written all over it, but it contains, in a savage abridged version, all the great disquiet of the Dostoyevskys and the Tolstoys. Three hungry Bolsheviks lying down in a clearing are found by a sick man. The sick man reassures them:

> 'I won't denounce you. I cannot kill all three of you. And if the muzhiks
> kill you they will not share the money with me. But then, I have had

enough of doing people favours! Let them go to the Devil!'

He cast a crafty and clever glance over them, pulled some fire from the coals, and said:

'I have been searching for the truth for thirty years, my boys. I looked for it among the wanderers in the taiga, and they tied me to a cedar tree and burnt my feet up to the knees ... I don't believe in people, they are scum and wild beasts ...' He drew a slice of bread out of his pocket and threw it to them: 'Stuff yourselves!'

Nikita's sole response was to lift himself up painfully, draw close to the little man, and kick him in the teeth.

The little man wiped his bloody lips, spat, and said slowly:

'That's all right, then'.

This great anxiety about the meaning of life and whether mankind can develop higher – his regeneration or resurrection –which for half a century has dominated the whole of Russian thinking often appears among Vsevolod Ivanov's characters, all the more real because the writer seems to ignore it. The matter was hardly ever talked about in the course of the Revolution; they hardly had the time even to think about it. Being materialists, revolutionaries reject outright all mysticism, even purely moral, and any idealism since it contains a mystical component. However, necessarily they were, and they are, in reality very great idealists.

Kallistrat Efimich, a thoughtful old peasant 'tormented with a need for the truth', has lost his faith. But such a will comes out of him, and there is so pure a conscience in him, that he 'works miracles' in the villages. This is the old man whom the peasants in revolt against Kolchak make into their leader (*The Coloured Winds*).

As head of the partisans, he shares the command with the soldier Nikita, a worker who has come from the distant towns, a real Bolshevik, as hard as iron, completely so, who only any longer believes in the strength of poor people. Sometimes these two leaders, face to face, question each other in short dialogues, in which each word falls as heavy as a stone into a a chasm. The old peasant believes in love for humanity. The worker only believes in knowledge and strength.

'Without love', says Kallistrat Efimich, 'war will go on forever. There
must be an end of it!'

'Let men fight! When they have had their fill of it they will make a
better life ... Rub out the bourgeoisie to begin with ...'

'But in the end', asked Kallistrat Efimich, 'when they ask you, when
they come to you, how do you reply?'

'I know what to reply'.

'To everyone? Without love?'

'Without love'.

This isn't true. This man is not without love; he only believes that he is. This
worker from the towns has only come to fight in the Siberian *taiga* by being
moved by the greatest of love for humanity, but he does not admit it, because
his thought has been formed in other schools, and because he is strong. For
these two men understand that they complement each other. The two men like
each other. One represents implacable logic, and the other the living soul of the
ragged rebels grouped beneath a red rag. 'I myself', says Nikita to Kallistrat
Efimich, 'provide the blood; you provide the bread.'

Hardness. Love. All the thinking of the revolutionaries is contained in these
two words.

Let us attempt to sum up in a few poor abstract words the psychology of the
magnificent Red partisans of Siberia. Their thinking is based upon a direct,
concrete and practical view of realities. Their morality is utilitarian. It is necessary to live and to survive, to conquer, in other words. They think but little.
They act. They only speak in the same way they act, in little, short and precise
words. They have, without knowing it, a deep internal life. They are born for
the future: and that is all they know. To an American soldier whom they have
captured, and whom they want to bring over to the Revolution, they only know
how to say, with great fraternal gestures, and then a cry of hatred, five words
they have understood from the Yankee in spite of the language barrier:

> 'Lenin! ... Soviet Republic! ... Proletariat!'
> 'Imperialism! Down with it!' (*Armoured Train 14-69*)[8]

Form in Vsevolod Ivanov is adequate to the content. There are no descriptions, no accounts, no landscapes, no explanations and no psychological developments. Actions and thoughts, thoughts and actions, are identical. Speech is brief, simple and direct. The language has nothing 'literary' about it. Entire books are written in dialogues in which the sentences on average have five or six words. We find a large number of words in dialect or Chinese, or Kirghiz ... To tell the truth, I think that Vsevolod Ivanov is far too prone to reproduce the local Siberian speech; reading it often becomes fatiguing, and the chances of the work lasting a long time are reduced, since there is a limit to how far you can diverge from a great classical language as rich as literary Russian.

However, this action writer is a poet. In several short stories, which in any case I hold to be more successful than his novel, Vsevolod Ivanov yields to his inner poetry, and it has a powerful effect which in no way clashes with the activity of the rough people of the Siberian land, but explains it, accompanying it like a bass chorus.

I can only compare Vsevolod Ivanov's lyricism with Walt Whitman and certain Vedic poetry.[9] Were the Californian lumberjacks, and the pioneers who founded Manhattan and later New York, all that different from the lumberjacks and pioneers of Siberia, of whom we will only know in a century what republic they will have founded? But if I may be allowed to quote a few brief passages from this Russian writer. The song of the land echoes with its ample refrains the drama of the life of the partisans. Listen:

> The wind had gone away. The smell of pungent herbs rose from the earth. The dull blue sky trembled in the mountain rivers like an enormous blue fish.
>
> And the mountain tops were like red ducks in the blue clouds ...
>
> Firmly, and urgently, the land was calling for human flesh. The mountains were calling upon their soul.
>
> The men were eating happily as if they were bread, slimy herbs melting on their lips ...

Here is his description of the priest Isidore:

> He had a shaggy, bearded head, and a heavy, jerky voice impregnated with the greenness of the marshes. He walked in great strides, draped in

his cassock of dark green fabric. His leafy head seemed moulded into a clod of earth. His hands are clods of earth. His sharp and clear eyes were like subterranean water.

The man is moulded in stone. The land is living. Here is another man:

His shoulders are the earth turned over by the plough, and his neck a fresh millstone. His voice is lost in the meadows ...
His voice: spring herbs. It grows in the soul like restlessness.

The land:

The snows were melting, melting. The land was born, pink. Flesh-coloured, chubby like newborn babes, the mountains were running before the clouds ...
The wild boar is digging up the mountain soil. The mountains are digging through the clouds: they have white fangs. And the rivers, closing their eyes, are throwing themselves off the mountains to bite the earth with their foamy teeth.

And now:

Was I not right to think of the animism of the Vedas in connection with these effusions? This man of the revolution in Siberia has a pantheistic intuition, like his Hindu ancestor. Don't you feel that the rivers are alive, alive with rain, living and shaking the land?

... a patch of my land is flowering! And the pupils of my eyes are clods of earth in the grass!
With the light foot of a wild beast I will go all the way round the world ...

Vsevolod Ivanov above all notices nature's colours and scents. The development of a love for colours and a sense of smell has often been noted among childlike people. Obviously, this poetry may appear a bit monotonous to those who frequent literary cafés and are more accustomed to the capricious rhythms of Dadaism and jazz bands. I am reminded of Pierre Hamp's cruel witty remark: 'Pederasty, the Goncourt Prize[10] and royalism are the three great literary illnesses'.

From the remoteness of Siberia I expect Vsevolod Ivanov to reply:

'The green wind is fertile and clear. Be healthy, be gentle!'

★   ★   ★   ★   ★

Along with a wealth of health, experience and observation, Vsevolod Ivanov has the numerous failings of the young Russian writers educated by the Revolution, and not in literary schools. Frankly, he composes badly; in this sense I find him noticeably inferior to Pilnyak, and he has no better mastery of the Russian language. He goes overboard with incidents, details and very trivial facts. His observation is rich, but his psychology is often poor. The great number of his characters ends up giving the impression of the crawling along of a variegated crowd, which is not always the end in view. Vsevolod Ivanov succeeds better with short stories than with full length novels. In spite of the beauties the book contains, *The Skyblue Sands* cannot be read without effort. Moreover, it is more a chronicle about the Civil War in certain parts of Siberia than a novel, and a chronicle far too packed and too detailed; the author has obviously neither synthesised nor organised the events in accordance with general ideas. He seems to be providing us with the raw materials.

I am also a little taken aback by Vesvolod Ivanov's naive partiality. It often bestows a little of the detestably false smell of official literature upon what he writes. Basically, as far as he is concerned, the Reds are always strong, beautiful and healthy, and the Whites wretched, unhealthy, unintelligent and old. Even as such they could appear to us like living people, whose effort to live is always moving. A minimum of artistic impartiality in Vsevolod Ivanov ought not to be incompatible with a sound revolutionary standpoint. But the fact is, as someone may object to me, that the 'human material' of reaction must obviously be inferior to that of the Revolution: hence its defeat. I know this, and it is good to bring it out: but the writer has to distrust conventional class spirit, and go contrary to class feeling pure and simple, in order not to prevent him from seeing the enemy as he really is: a living human being.

From other points of view, Vsevolod Ivanov has the most typical defects of the general run of writers of the transitional period. Like Boris Pilnyak, he owes everything to the Revolution; he loves the Revolution; he writes an epic and true praise of it; but he does not appear to want to make sense of it, and does not seek to understand it other than as a great drama in which we must blindly follow the Great New Force. From the new Russian writers, above all from those who are portraying with so much talent Bolshevism and the Bolsheviks, we have the right to expect a deeper understanding of what the Communist revolution has thought, wanted and tenaciously stood for. In their preoccupation with being apolitical, in other words, with appearing to be revolutionaries in practice without being communists, the best of them appear to keep a convenient way open towards bourgeois letters. It is true that Vsevolod Ivanov's peasant origins fully explain his distance from proletarian ideology.

I once heard it said by an American who was acquainted with Vladivostock, Irkutsk, Lake Baikal, the Yenissei and the *taiga*:

Siberia has as much of a future as the United States had a century ago ...

This half continent, of infinite natural wealth, was for a long time only the great prison camp of a tyranny. The robust Jacques[11] whose fame is sung by Vsevolod Ivanov have just flung wide open the gates to their country's future. To this first writer brought up in their milieu will obviously belong the credit for having made some of the life giving breath of the great Siberian winds sweep over today's literature.

Victor Serge   28 February, 1924.

Notes

1. I am taking up again the series of these reports which more urgent tasks have prevented me from continuing for several months. The readers of *Clarté* who wish to place the present article in the sequence of these reports would do well to refer to the studies that appeared in *Clarté* in 1923. The last three dealt with *The New Writer and the New Literature*, Boris Pilnyak and I. Libedinsky. In the ones to follow I hope to be able to provide overall views and a precise critical documentation on the main features of intellectual life in Red Russia – V. S. (author's note). Translated from *Clarté* no.56, 1 April 1924 (translator's note).

2. Henri Camille Bordeaux (1870–1963) was a French writer; Pierre Benoît (1886–1962) was a French man of letters, the author of *L'Atlantide* (1919), a utopian novel (translator's note).

3. It is very important to be precise about the time in which Vsevolod Ivanov's stories are placed. They are at the end of the Omsk government (1920). The overall governor, Admiral Kolchak, made a minister in a democratic government by the Right Socialist Revolutionaries, after an easy 18th Brumaire prepared by the Allied military mission, had installed an indescribable regime. Kolchakism was only able to last by shooting workers in large numbers, by reprisal expeditions into the countryside, in other words devastating and burning villages, thanks to a police force that added Sino-Mongolian methods to those of the old Okhrana. When they evacuated Perm in 1919 the White command burnt alive in barns some hundreds of Red soldier prisoners. Ataman Ungern had his prisoners fed into a locomotive boiler. The whole country ended up rising up against this regime which had been legally recognised by France and Britain after they had supported it in practice. Handed over to the Reds by the French General Janin, who saved his own skin thereby, Kolchak was shot in Irkutsk – V. S. (author's note). Roman Feodorovich, Count von Ungern-Sternberg (1886–1921) captured Urga (now Ulan Bator) in February 1921, and shot all the local government officials. He fell into the hands of the Red Army in August and was tried and shot. Pierre Thiébaut Charles Maurice Janin (1862–) was a French general active in Russia during the Civil War. The episode of the suicide of Sin Bin U referred to here appears in 'Armoured Train 14-69' translated by Keith Hammond in *Vsevolod Ivanov: Selected Stories*, Raduga Publishers, Moscow, 1983, pp.336–7. Another English translation printed along with Zamyatin's *The Islanders* was published by Trilogy Publishers, Anne Arbor, 1978 (translator's note).
4. The kingdom of the Franks was founded by Clovis (481–511), of the house of Merwing, after whom the dynasty was named (translator's note).
5. The Ataman Nikifor A. Grigoriev (1878–1919) was a Tsarist officer who had gone over to the Bolsheviks, but who staged an uprising in Kherson in May 1919, and was killed by Makhno at a conference three months later (translator's note).
6. The Ataman Grigory Semyonov (?–1946) sought to succeed to Kolchak's power, and established himself in China in alliance with the Japanese. His notorious Asiatic Division was commanded by Baron Ungern. The Teutonic Knights were an order of military monks formed in 1224 to convert the Prussians to Christianity by the use of force (translator's note).
7. In his *De origine et situ Germanorum*, the Roman historian Cornelius Tacitus (c.56–119 A.D.) contrasted the robust simplicity of the German tribes with the over-civilised Roman Empire. The reference to the Bible is presumably to the 'eye for an eye, tooth for a tooth' of the Mosaic code (translator's note).
8. 'Armoured Train 14-69', in *Vsevolod Ivanov: Selected Stories*, Raduga Publishers, Moscow, 1983, pp.274–5 (translator's note).
9. The *Rig Veda* is a book of 1028 Hindu hymns probably composed between 1500 and 900 B.C. for use in the sacrificial rituals of an aristocratic cult. The *Artha Veda* in particular reflects an atmosphere of simple animism and sympathetic magic (translator's note).
10. The Goncourt Prize is a prestigious award established with a legacy of the Parisian novelist and man of letters Edmond de Goncourt (1822–1896). The first award was in 1903 (translator's note).
11. The Jacquerie was a French peasant uprising in May–June 1358, so-called after a typical peasant, 'Jacques Bonhomme' (translator's note).

Gorky and Fedin

A New Book from Maxim Gorky[1]
Maxim Gorky worked hard during the heroic years of the Russian Revolution, but produced little. His unceasing activity at this time was above all that of a 'protector of literature and the sciences', a devoted defender of the intellectuals who had lost their way in the revolutionary storm, and, often being hostile to the proletariat, were often abused by them. The great writer welcomed with great impartiality all those wounded and crippled in the social conflict, providing they were, by whatever label, servants of culture. He intervened for them with the Cheka. He intervened for them with Lenin, who welcomed him smiling and lent him an attentive ear.[2] He stood surety ... he protected. He cleared up things. The majority of the young Russian writers of today – and we have an admirable constellation of them – recognise him as their master; it is from him that they learned their art during the years of famine and typhus.

Was his activity as a man of feeling, a humanist and a citizen (and something of a troublemaker ...) of the Revolution going to deprive us of a writer? We might well fear it. Literary creativity requires other conditions to exist. Then later another worry came to us: would not Maxim Gorky, smitten as he was with culture – and today's culture, however we look at it, is always that of the bourgeoisie – so sensitive to the inevitable cruelties of the Civil War, and so shaken to the depths of his being by the disagreement between the intellectuals and the proletarian revolution, little by little stand aloof from the country and Communist thinking? We heard him harangue the young Red soldiers leaving for the Polish front: we read the pages he devoted to Lenin ...

... For such of his actions, and such of his writings, like the little unjust and cruel book on *The Russian Peasant*,[3] seemed to remind us of the worst times in Gorky's revolutionary career, the articles in the *Untimely Thoughts on 1917–1918*,[4] which, throughout, are nothing but the cry of revolt of an intellectual, linked, in spite of himself, by his internal cultural confinement, to the old order of things, against a proletarian revolution he profoundly misunderstood.

Gorky left Russia in 1922, having been infected in the depths of his lungs by tuberculosis from long ago, the result of privations in earlier years. He went to live in Sorrento, with his books, his Russian and European friendships, and his hard work.[5] Not long ago Mussolini's loutishness meant that his home was searched by police – 'yet another', he no doubt told himself, with a wry smile through his thick moustache.

We are here far from the conventional novel of bourgeois literature, whose schema you know all too well: her and him, her lover, his mistress, their sofas, their money, their heavy, heavy, incalculable stupidity, and their poverty of which they were unaware through living petty lives of that sort.

This book by Gorky, *The Artamanov Business*[6] is, in its way, a profound attempt to explain modern times. Three generations live in it. In it we see a whole peasant people rise from serfdom to the proletarian revolution, represented by a line of rough workers.

The first of the Artamanov brothers, a sort of clearer of virgin land, a hard pioneer, crafty and practical, made his appearance in a harmless little Russian provincial town just after the emancipation of the serfs (1861).[7] He was originally a serf, but a serf who managed the lands of a prince.[8] He now sets up a spinning mill, so to speak, with his bare hands; he dies on the job, a pioneer builder, through over exertion while transporting a machine.[9] Two of his three sons continue his work and his life, with all their father's roughness. Their industry grows, and their fortune is made. The memory of their origins no longer haunts them. The power of money is all too familiar to them. The grandsons of serfs have become employers, producers and businessmen. 'The future', they say, 'belongs to us businessmen!' The first Russian Revolution (1905) seems to proclaim new times for them, the rule of industry and commerce.[10] But everything changes around them, more quickly than they themselves change. Little by little the employers' patriarchal and despotic authority vanishes; there are more workers, more working class poverty, and more consciousness of poverty; underground struggles break out between the police and the clandestine Socialist parties; a strike breaks out ... And the third generation of the Artamanovs, bourgeois as they are, is disquieted. The emancipated serf's granddaughter, an affected young lady who despises her parents' crude lack of culture, finding that the spinning mill smells bad (... Oh horror!), becomes a proper city lady, completely idle. One of the pioneer's grandsons is, it is true, a born employer, but in comfort, after having made his fortune, continues to administer and collect profits, convinced of his divine right as an exploiter. Soft in manners and a weakened soul, only knowing how to make good investments, the entire energy of the race appears to be concentrated on a grandson who bears the name of his grandfather. Ilya is a lost child, whose obstinacy and terrible strength we merely glimpse in an outbreak of discord. This third Artamanov, the great grandson of rich manufacturers, is a revolutionary student, a Bolshevik, and a Russian pioneer. He is also himself the first of a new race ... Famine, study, imprisonment, exile and the revolution become his life. He hardly appears in the book in which towards the end we everywhere feel his presence. And what, in fact, does his personality matter? It is mixed up with the events.

We feel the coming Revolution covering everything with its shadow and a confused murmur so vast and so different in reality from all that we expected, of which we did not take much account to begin with. Father Artamanov, old, broken and fallen into a cantankerous senility sees bayonets rise up in the midst of his factory. 'You have no money', an old man tells him whom he has exploited for thirty years, 'you have nothing. As for your judges, I don't care a straw for them. I am my own judge ... This is the end of men like Cain!'[11] Soldiers killed Artamanov's son in a train as he fled with his money and his mistress, on account of his well fed appearance.[12] Artamanov the Bolshevik does his bit, here and there, for the destiny of his people.

Can we see how great this book is? Gorky's habitual mastery can be found here in all the characters. Women's destinies, from marriage in accordance with the old rites of the Russian countryside, to old age and death, after a wholly animal and ill-nourished existence among the poor, or as overfed matrons among the rich, are soberly depicted here in all their tragic realism.

A very strong work which reveals in Gorky's thought its fidelity to a concept of life and art very close to that of Marxism. The characters are as distinguishable in the picture as they are in life; but it is the entire generation and masses and classes that are important, and are tested. Is the theme, essentially, not that of history in action, looked at through the destinies of one family? The importance of economic factors, which it would be superfluous to mention, very quickly occurs to the reader. Historical truth is not twisted. One of the aims of emancipating the serfs was, in fact, to provide the manufacturers with hands; serfdom was incompatible with the development of industry. And whoever wishes to understand the origins of present day Russia must, in fact, go back over the course of history down to the year 1861, the date of the abolition of serfdom, in other words to the substitution of the economic constraints of modern capitalism for the juridical constraints of an old order based upon barely concealed force.

Gorky owes this breadth of thinking and this new fertilisation of his talent to the Revolution. But why does he stop depicting things the moment the revolution begins? The book leads us to the threshold of the red October, but not beyond it. Isn't it only a prologue? We do not think so. Gorky admirably understands some of the origins of the Revolution, its rise in the countryside, and its slow germination since serfdom; but connected by his origins to the Russian soil rather than to the factory, and linked by his immense culture of brilliant self-education to the Russian intelligentsia rather than the proletariat, it is no doubt easier for him also to understand the revolution as the unleashing of elemental social forces rather than the deliberate and conscious work of a class called upon to change the world. The internal dualism that has ravaged our great Gorky in the course of these latest years, the perpetual conflict between the intellectual, restricted in spite of himself by the inclinations of his thinking and by the old bourgeois culture, and the instinctive revolutionary and friend of Lenin, the master of historical materialism, thus reveals itself in this book, cut down to a certain extent, by the abrupt silence of the final pages, in which the Revolution takes place.

Victor Serge

Note: A miserable book, cobbled together out of pious legends and certain base slanders referring to a tragic anarchist adventure, and those who were its perpetrators and victims at one and the same time, has allowed the bourgeois press, particularly in the provinces, to defame outrageously our comrade Victor Serge.[13]

It is no use being angry, since these repugnant procedures have become common coin among the irreconcilable enemies of the proletariat. But we should at least make it quite clear that either close up or from afar off, Victor Serge never took an effective part in this old individualistic enterprise.

In the whole affair the only 'bandits' were the dishonourable folklorists who satisfy their hatred of Communism by producing and repeating such stories.

Notes

1. Translated from *L'Humanité*, 5 August, 1924 (translator's note).
2. Cf. V. I. Lenin, *Letter to Maxim Gorky*, 15 September 1919, Collected Works, vol.xliv, Moscow, 1970, pp.283–5; B. D. Wolfe, *The Bridge and the Abyss: The Troubled Friendship of Maxim Gorky and V.I. Lenin*, 1967 (translator's note).
3. Gorky's *O Russkom Krestianstve* (*About the Russian Peasantry*) was published in 1922 (translator's note).
4. Gorky's *Untimely Thoughts on Revolution, Culture and the Bolsheviks, 1917–1918* consists of articles written for *Novaya Zhizn* between 1917–1918, a paper that was banned by the Bolsheviks on 16 July 1918. They were translated into English by Mark D. Steinburg and published by Yale U.P., New Haven, 1995. Cf. Victor Serge, *Year One of the Russian Revolution*, London, 1972, p.104 (translator's note).
5. Gorky lived in a villa in Sorrento between 1921 and 1928, after which he returned to the USSR., only to serve as an ideological prop to the regime as President of the Writers' Union (translator's note).
6. *Delo Artamanovykh* was published in Berlin in 1925; English translation, *Decadence*, by Veronica Scott-Gatty, London, 1927 (translator's note).
7. English version, op. cit., n.5 above, p.1 (translator's note).
8. English version, p.3 (translator's note).
9. English translation, pp.72–5 (translator's note).
10. English version, p.209 (translator's note).
11. English translation, p.321 (translator's note).
12. English version, p.312 (translator's note).
13. For Serge's involvement in this affair, cf. Richard Parry, *The Bonnot Gang*, London, 1987. In February 1937 *L'Humanité*, no longer defending Serge from this accusation, accused him of being 'the brains behind the Bonnot gang of 1911' (translator's note).

Constantine Fedin[1]

Constantine Fedin is surely one of the most remarkable among the young Russian writers of the aftermath of our Revolution. He is also one of the most typical in his links with the past and present of Russian society, as well as by his leanings. He occupies one of the foremost places among those whom Communist criticism has labelled 'fellow travellers' of the Revolution. For revolutionaries, knowing very well where they are going, often have fellow travellers for an hour or a day who wholly follow or go along with them whilst in reality following their own paths towards other destinations.

Let us run over the very typical autobiography of Fedin. Let us compare it with that of a young French literary man of the average type: a bourgeois childhood, university, cafés, literary circles, small magazines, editorial offices, important magazines, literary awards and salons. The War made a terrible break in the careers of those who entered public life around 1914; but this, so it seems, is only a break for the most part, after which the normal course of bourgeois existence starts up again of itself. The dead serve to advertise the living.

Look on the other hand at the life of this Russian, and you will be able to see what the works of such people can give to the western countries. He has a provincial childhood, followed by the blasts of the 1905 revolution. Then come studies in Moscow during the years of reaction.[2] The hangman Stolypin is laying down the law, and policemen are keeping watch over university lecture halls. Then study and poverty in Germany. 'Hermann and Dorothea' are dancing in the little Bavarian villages.[3] A skinny Russian student with awkward movements scrapes at the violin. It is Fedin (he has to live as well). Then come the War, internment in Lower Saxony and periods of withdrawal into himself, fruitful observations and socialist friendships. Then there is a period of employment in the first Soviet embassy in Berlin, unfurling its red flag in the very heart of the imperial capital in the midst of the War. Then return to Russia among the repatriated Russian prisoners, crippled, wretched and radiant.

Then the Revolution, crackling with shootings, celebrations, restless activity, victories, famine, typhus ... 'I was a journalist, a lecturer, a teacher, a typesetter, secretary of the town executive, an agitator, a recruiter on behalf of the Red Cavalry, a party member, a volunteer and soldier myself, and a fighter at the front.' Then Petrograd in year two of the Revolution, starving, depopulated, betrayed, blockaded, besieged and magnificent Petrograd, where two hundred thousand emaciated workers in mud huts want to hold out and do hold out in spite of 'the coalition of fourteen states allied against Bolshevism' (Lord Winston Churchill said this himself).

And there in Petrograd is the Bashkirian Division of Mongol cavalry come from Central Asia to defend the first Socialist commune in Europe against the British fleet and Yudenich ... with Fedin among them.[4] Then years of peace, which are years of work. Fedin, a convincing writer, only publishes works composed and completed with care, reworked on several occasions. 'I think', he says, 'that the Revolution is over for me. I have left the Party, I have heavy shelves full of books.' We will make no comment on these words. You can have heavy shelves full of books without leaving the party of the proletariat. But for that he would obviously have to put off the old man, overcome the deep influences of bourgeois culture, and, in a word, become *another man, an authentic revolutionary*, a proletarian, in other words. And this interior change is less easy for an intellectual than for any other person: the example of Fedin shows us that, if there was any need to prove it in the first place. For no imprisonment is deeper than that of the mind, and intellectuals are basically the most enslaved of the servants of bourgeois society.

Fedin is the author of a great book which already appeared years ago, which has been translated into German and is going to be translated into French, *Cities and Years*, a novel with a unique structure and a strong content in which the author's personal experience occupies an important place. Some admirable pages in it describe the epic grandeur of the worst days of the Revolution. Several Communist profiles are sketched out with the vigour typical of the simple men of iron and flesh of that time.

But the hero of the novel is more of a Tolstoyan. He is a hesitant and enthusiastic intellectual, sensitive and scrupulous, weak and good living, all-embracing and incapable of understanding obvious truths completely understandable to any proletarian. He goes through the War and the Revolution loving and being loved, a self-contained sleep walker, without doing any harm, without shedding blood, and 'without treading on a single flower', at least, so he believes, in his immensely unrealistic candour.[5] But chance places in the hands of this man, who also believes he is a revolutionary, a real counter-revolutionary with whom he is connected by the particular obligation of personal acquaintance. His duty should be to arrest him and have him shot. The man has Red blood on his hands. The man is an implacable class enemy, irreconcilable and sure of himself. But André Startsov is not, himself, a man of class. The social war, a formidable reality, is less real in his eyes than the truly miniscule drama of his heart and his conscience. He deceives his comrades in order to allow the enemy to flee. He does not want to have the blood of this rifleman on his hands. He still does not understand that the blood of the victims of this rifleman nonetheless comes down on his own head. (I knew a libertarian who carried out a similar act during the Civil War[6]). Little by little towards the end he loses his reason, and is killed. We feel that it is the natural solution that this uncertain, weak and broken person has to disappear in the storm. Before his reason gives out the truth appears to him, in pieces but overwhelming:

> 'I understand,' he says, 'why I always felt oppressed. I do not know what darkness enfolded me ... Do you know what it is? It is the mistake of thinking that I am not responsible for the horror that the world is full of. As if I am not to blame for it! My conscience does not allow me any peace. Conscience is a terrible thing ...
>
> 'I now understand that I must take the whole weight of this horror upon myself and not evade it by saying that the universe is to blame and not me ...'

The book should bear as a subtitle 'The Drama of a Conscience During the Revolution'. But what is the author thinking? At times he seems to touch on the real solution, which is unreserved adherence to the revolution. For there can be no individual innocence in the social conflict: there can be no effective revolt of the spirit without any hands-on action; there can be no question of conscience that remains valid in the face of the crying need (for whoever understands and condemns a system whose inevitable results are exploitation, hunger, social evils and war) to be with the class that can and wants to change the world. And the very fact of being with this class completely absolves us of all responsibility for the crimes of the rich classes.

Fedin's conclusions are not the correct Communist ones. When we have closed his beautiful book we ask ourselves if the disappearance of the best and purest does not seem to him to be a natural law in a world where fratricide holds sway. For the book as a whole rather suggests this conclusion, influenced by fatalism and pessimism. As opposed to the reactionary saying that 'man is a wolf to man', we think that man is what society makes him, and that the need for collective production offers him the greatest and purest perspectives.

Constantine Fedin has just published a short story, *Transvaal*,[7] truly composed in this fatalistic and pessimistic spirit: the story of a crafty and strong peasant who participates in the Revolution in order to enrich himself. The writer only seems to see the largely negative aspects of the Revolution in the countryside. The fact is that you often need the eye of a revolutionary to discern clearly the outlines of a new society under construction in the present transitional period. In some things Fedin remains too far from us, and too alien to proletarian thinking for this to be easy for him. This is a great loss: because his talent, of the highest value, would take on a new force if he were enlightened by revolutionary thinking – to which he sometimes comes close.

Leningrad, February 1927   Victor Serge

Notes

1. Translated from *L'Humanité*, 6 April, 1927 (translator's note).
2. i.e. during the period from 1906 onwards when Stolypin and Pobedonostsev were the chief ministers of the Tsar (translator's note).
3. *Hermann and Dorothea* was a narrative poem by Goethe published in 1797 set during the time of the French revolutionary wars (translator's note).
4. Serge does not appear to have had a high opinion of their fighting abilities. Cf. *Memoirs of a Revolutionary*, Oxford U.P., 1975, p.93 (translator's note).
5. 'If only he had taken one blemish and trampled on one flower', Mark Slonim's translation, in *Soviet Russian literature: Writers and Problems*, Oxford U.P., 1964, p.133 (translator's note).
6. Cf. Victor Serge, 'The Endangered City', in *The Revolution in Danger*, London, 1997, pp.68–9; *Memoirs of a Revolutionary*, Oxford U.P., 1975, p.94 (translator's note).
7. *Transvaal* came out in Leningrad in 1927. An English translation is included in Eugene Jolas and Robert Sarge (eds.), *Transition Stories*, New York, 1929 (translator's note).

Recollections of Maxim Gorky: Fedin and Gorky[1]

July 10, 1945. A certain period of my youth comes to life in me again as I read Constantine Fedin's *Gorky in Our Midst*, published in Moscow in '43.[2] It is remarkably well done; Gorky is living, natural; Blok, also, and even Zamyatin – portrayed in a few lines. I knew Gorky well during this period. That endangered Petrograd, polar and with such a tragic internal richness, had been mine. I can follow the recollections of Fedin (1919–21) step by step. Fedin himself I got to know only years later when I reviewed his books *Cities and Years*, *The Brothers*; I saw in him a young Russian Romain Rolland preoccupied by human problems in an inhuman epoch; full of a barely voiced but very profound protest against all that was stifling mankind, incapable of understanding the revolutionists who knew and felt all of that but, out of necessity, adopted surgical measures ...

Fedin related the remark of Gorky to me: 'The party commissar is at one and the same time policeman, censor and archbishop: he grabs hold of you, blue pencils your writings, and then wants to sink his claws in your soul.' Fedin had a handsome thin face, a broad forehead, thin lips, penetrating grey eyes, an air of self-effacing discretion – and great confidence in himself. (Married, two children.)

He must have suffered unbelievably, and if a free Russian literature some day becomes possible no one will be able to explain better than he the nature of that suppression under the terror. He has survived, and even in becoming a master craftsman of that flexible and docile special literature which accumulates such enormous silences, has manifested a minimum of the indispensable conformity necessary to exist and still is occasionally producing worthwhile works, for example, this *Gorky*. The young and uninformed reader, foreign or Russian, will finish reading this book enriched and even enthusiastic. He will see a great man close up, he will be initiated into a powerful form, and into an art which basically manifests itself as a form of love for mankind.

However, if a book is judged with an objective severity, what indignation! The lying in it – through omission and silence – is infinitely greater than the truth. Everything is truncated. To all that I have just noted there is not a single allusion. To the grumbling and sometimes vehement bitterness of Gorky, to his constant struggle against the terror and the abuse of authority, a struggle which made him ill, there is not an allusion. That Gorky spent more time intervening with the Cheka in order to save intellectuals and other victims than with writers cannot be denied. That he had confidence in Lenin because his intercessions were customarily crowned with success cannot be learned. (One day I brought a message from Zinoviev to Gorky in his appartment on Kronversky Prospekt – Zinoviev had censored an article by Gorky. He received me with fury. 'These Bolsheviks – you don't know them! How many crimes and stupidities! Tell Zinoviev that I have had enough of them!', etc. I had to tone down the violence of the message and Gorky, moreover, yielded and his article went through censored).

The lie by omission sometimes produces something outrageous. There is a beautiful and true to life portrait of Alexander Blok, but 'he (Alexander Blok) never says that he was reduced to silence'. Alexander Blok is depicted as a rallier to the regime. He was a revolutionist, a stubborn though discreet protestor. He never said that he was suffocating. Allied with the destroyed and persecuted Left Socialist Revolutionary Party, he maintained a friendship with Ivanov-Razumnik and André Biely; he was put in prison and a moving essay on Alexander Blok in a cell of the Cheka was published. He died in good part from sadness and privation, with the beginnings of scurvy. Constantine Fedin describes the funeral of Blok. I was there. He is silent about its being a double demonstration of mourning and of silent protest: in the first row of his friends, not far from Liubova Dmitrievna Blok, walked Olga Gumileva, with her big brown eyes in a child's emaciated face, the widow of the great poet Nicholas Stepanovich Gumilev, who had just been shot ... Constantine Fedin is silent on Gumilev, silent on that persecution which rocked Petrograd, silent on Ivanov-Razumnik, one of the stimulating forces in Russian thought, because Ivanov-Razumnik disappeared in 1933.[3] What abominable silences!

There are a few lines on the defence of Petrograd – but not one allusion to Trotsky who saved the doomed city. There is a scene from the Second Congress of the Communist International in the Tauride Palace,[4] at which Lenin spoke, but not a word on the friends who surrounded Lenin in an affectionate circle and who did not leave him during the entire day – Zinoviev, Bakayev, Evdokimov,[5] all three of them shot. There is an absolute prohibition against mentioning those who were shot! I am uneasy over not finding the name of Vsevolod Mikhail Eichenbaum – and reassured to find that of Nicholas Nikitin, who has disappeared from the literary scene. Can this be an act of courage? (Nicholas Nikitin is mentioned only incidentally). The remarks of Gorky upon Lenin are faithfully reported, but not the remarks of Gorky upon Trotsky, whom he admired without liking, and whom he often criticised. In general I recognise Gorky's style and the themes upon which he often spoke to me: 'No phosphorous for the mind', the mysterious, contradictory, elementary strength of the muzhik – the drama of the city devoured by the country – the mission of the intellectuals – Russian incompetence, Russian anarchy – the beginning of new times. One word is missing, the word 'planetary transformation' – and an essential motif, the *bezozrazia* (god-awful mess[6]), the abominations which Gorky collected and denounced with a tireless bitterness.

Constantine Fedin visited Gorky while the cannons were thundering on Kronstadt. That provides a guarded page where the anxiety of Gorky can be glimpsed. I saw him several times during that period and I once met him at the Cheka, Godokhovaya 2; he was taking steps on behalf of the prisoners; he was grey and taciturn. I spoke to him about the case of R. Abramovich and Theodore Dan, both of them arrested, and whom the president of the Cheka, Semyonov, a narrow-minded redhead, wished to shoot. Zinoviev perhaps might have let it be done. Gorky promised me to intervene with Lenin, and the protection of the threatened men was doubtless due to this.[7] There is not an allusion in Constantine Fedin to the terror, and moreover Petrograd was living under the terror even more than it was under conditions of famine or of literary experiences. Is it now forbidden to speak of the 'Red terror'?

I again ran across the remarks of Gorky on the tortures which the Siberian peasants inflicted upon their prisoners, Communists for the most part. (Gorky had been informed about them by Vsevolod Ivanov). One day I asked Gorky where this tradition of refined torture, which it is difficult to invent, came from. 'From *The Golden Legend*',[8] he replied.

Still another enormous omission – in order to cover up a state crime – Boris Pilnyak is not mentioned.

And Fedin writes: 'Art consists in expressing sensations as well as possible; and the most lucid sentiment – that is to say, the truth – is the one which can be expressed with the most perfection.'

He shows Gorky's attitude towards the mission of the writer very well, an attitude which Gorky passionately inculcated in the young. Literature was a calling, a method of serving humanity which engaged the personality totally and permanently, and demanded honesty and conscientious craftsmanship. Gorky liked to call himself *masterovoy* (master craftsman[9]). Such has been the guiding idea of several great schools of Russian writers. Literature contributes to the elevation of mankind from obscurity to consciousness; it has the mission of telling men the truth about mankind.

I once asked Yuri Tynyanov (whom Constantine Fedin said so greatly resembled Pushkin, and who also resembled a rabbi born old) why, with such a profound spirit of opposition, writers proved so unwilling to struggle. 'Because,' he said to me, 'each one thinks he has something important to do, and therefore is afraid to take risks, and prefers to humiliate himself and gain time.' I admire Fedin for having swallowed so many humiliations, known so many hideous things without losing faith in himself – the feeling of his dignity – the will to create, and of knowing how, with cynicism and sadness, to be able to adapt himself so as to be able to write a little book which is, in spite of everything, living, moving, human, precious in several senses, like a gem from the Urals mounted in mud.

An edition of 25,000 copies – consequently, paying very well.

Victor Serge

Notes

1.   Reprinted from 'Recollections of Maxim Gorki' translated by James M. Fenwick, in *The New International*, vol.xvi (whole no.143), July–August 1950, pp.249–251 (editor's note).
2.   Fedin's *Gorky Amidst Us* came under attack for allegedly misrepresenting Gorky's views. Cf. John Manson, 'The Carnets' (from which this is an extract), in Susan Weissman (ed.), *The Ideas of Victor Serge*, *Critique*, nos.28–29, Glasgow, 1997,p.238 (editor's note).
3.   Ivanov-Razumnik was several times arrested between 1921 and 1941, but was captured when in exile by the Germans during the 2nd World War and taken back to Germany, where he died. Cf. *Memoirs of Ivanov-Razumnik*, London, 1965; Serge, *Memoirs of a Revolutionary*, pp.151, 271 (editor's note).
4.   The Second Congress of the Third International took place in July and August 1920 (editor's note).
5.   Ivan Petrovich Bakayev (1887–1936), the head of the Leningrad G.P.U. under Zinoviev, and Grigory Yeremeyevich Evdokimov (1884–1936), the former Central Committee Secretary who had read out Lenin's *Testament*, were among the first to be arrested after the assassination of Kirov. As supporters of Zinoviev, they were defendants along with him at the first Moscow trial, the trial of the 16 (editor's note).
6.   The word *Bezozrazia* in Russian means something disgraceful, an outrage, a scandal (editor's note).
7.   Raphael Abramovich Rhein, (1880–1963) and Fyodor Ilyich Gurvich, known as Dan (1871–1947) were important Menshevik leaders who had been arrested and exiled. Abramovich had been allowed to go to

Germany in August 1920, but Dan, who was in prison at the time, was accused by Lenin of helping to organise the Kronstadt mutiny. He was released and allowed to go abroad after a hunger strike in January 1922. Cf. R. Abramovich, *The Soviet Revolution, 1917–1939*, London, 1962, pp.165, 199 (editor's note).

8. The Golden Legend is the name popularly applied to the *Historia Longobardica seu Legenda Sanctorum* written by Jacobus de Voragine between 1270 and 1280, a collection of the lives of the saints, often with very lurid descriptions of their martyrdoms (editor's note).

9. *Masterovoy* is an archaic term in Russian, simply meaning a workman, or a factory hand (editor's note)

Mayakovsky[1]

Almost all the great Russian poets at the end of the old order understood, in their own way, the meaning of the Revolution.[2] A place in the first rank among them goes to Vladimir Mayakovsky, whose open pride crammed with beautiful talent is claiming, in the name of Futurism, to open up new ways for proletarian art.

Like Italian Futurism, Russian Futurism wanted to break with the past, destroy classical values, exalt the individual, and sing the praises of machines, trains, bridges, towns and the realities of modern life. Twenty years soon passed from Marinetti's first manifestos, without Western Futurism, already outmoded, keeping the least of its grandiloquent promises by producing any masterpiece. With the tameness that is peculiar to intellectuals and artists, its apostles have followed the dominant direction of society. The Italian Futurists became imperialists and fascists. During the war in Tripolitania Marinetti sang of 'the beauty of entrails smoking in the sun'. Today he is admiring the *Duce* Mussolini.[3] But the Russian Futurists allowed themselves to be carried off by the current towards the Revolution. Mayakovsky spoke of the horror of the war cemeteries (*War and the World*) and then the Glory to Us! of *Revolution*.[4] Here and there – we are going to look closer – Futurism seems to us to be tragically linked to the past, in its naive pretence of avoiding it.

The Scythian Laforgue[5]

Mayakovsky began to write, with genuine originality, about 1909 (at the age of sixteen). The influence of David Burliuk,[6] disgust with conventional literature, and a vigorous temperament were to decide the direction of his thought. All his poems up until the Revolution are basically heart-rending. In contrast with Italian Futurism, whose exuberant, often joyful and stunning, indeed amazing vitality no one would dream of denying, Russian Futurism was gloomy, contorted, cynical and neurasthenic. That is how far the Italy of 1905–10, with imperialism being born, was from economically backward Russia, where a democratic revolution had just been defeated (1905).[7] This is because the wealthy Marinetti belonged to a bourgeoisie at the height of its power, whereas the hungry

Mayakovsky was from an intellectual youth without a future. Only the form of his first verses is innovatory. He has his own brutal and swaying rhythm with violent images, which almost always indicate an unhealthy imagination. The basis of this poetry is the hopeless suffering of old:

> The street's caved in like a nose after syphilis
> The rivers all all leching, drooling, obscene.
> (*And Yet*, 1910)[8]

> And beyond the street-suns, the sorriest of sights, sank
> the flabby moon, unwanted old junk ...
> (*Great Big Hell of a City*, 1910)[9]

> The hours drag on like a vulgar insult ...
> (*Petersburg Again*, 1911)[10]

> We, prisoners of the city lazar-house ...
> (*A Cloud in Trousers*, 1914)[11]

The only other style of this boisterous futurist, who shows off in the noisy artistic taverns of St. Petersburg in a gold-buttoned shirt, is when he collapses into the eccentric taste of snobs:

> I will make myself black trousers
> Of the velvet of my voice
> Yellow tunic of three yards of sunset sky.
> (*1911*)[12]

His break with sentiment is so superficial that misused sensibility often expresses itself in this cynicism with singular freshness. He says of the stars:

> Does someone therefore call these little spits diamonds?
> ....

Is it therefore necessary that at least one star shines
every night on the roofs?
(*Listen*, 1911)[13]

Your eyes are sunk in your face
Like two tombs shafts ...
And I am alone like the last eye left
Of a man on his way to join the blind![14]

Have you not encountered before this desolate view of the universe, the anguish
of being alone? Do you not remember having read in Laforgue any verses like
this?

But in his breakdown Mayakovsky also finds images that straightaway take
us back to the atmosphere of Stolypin's Russia.

Where cities are hanged
And in cloud-nooses congeal
....
I alone go to shriek
That on crossroads policemen are crucified
(*Myself*, 1912)[15]

I mentioned Laforgue. Laforgue was also a Bohemian, went hungry, suppressed
his suicidal feelings, and felt defeated by the evil city. The sharp irony of an old
aristocratic culture was his main impulse.

Mayakovsky is of an oriental race, in a country bursting with energy. He has
the dumb anger of a sickened plebeian. An angry rebellion broods within him.

And if I today, the brutal Hun,
won't clown for you – what will you do
If I laugh and spit with joy,
Spit in your face I will.
(*How D'Ye Like This*, 1912)[16]

Mayakovsky the 'Bolshevik' could express himself in this way, but not the Anarchist Laforgue, the Reader to the Queen of Prussia.

About woman, the one of them said:

> O woman, mammal with braided hair! (*Laforgue*).

And the other:

> You stare like an oyster from the shells of things.[17]

The similarity in the inspiration of these two very different decadent poets seems striking to me. When he first set out Mayakovsky was a Scythian Laforgue.

In his beginnings as a 'Futurist' he expressed only decadence in every fibre of his being, the breakdown of Russian bourgeois culture.

From 1906 to 1914 Russia went through terrible years. The defeat of the 1905 Revolution was felt for a long time in the minds of the intellectuals. It was a time of individualistic (Artybashev, *Sanin*), mystical (Merezhkovsky, Biely) and sexual-mystic (Rozanov[18]) meanderings. How well we understand Mayakovsky when he says to himself:

> I see in you, on a cross of laughter,
> A cry that you are being tortured, crucified.
> (*Vladimir Mayakovsky*, 1913[19]).

In a poignant poem he describes monstrous funerary obsequies of laughter:

> Behind the hearse, life, sobbing the old mother, is going
> grey with a laughter that is dead ...

Later:

> If someone laughs, it seems as if you have split his lips
> open for him.

If Mayakovsky, the defeated Bohemian of the great capitalist town, had kept to this beautiful talent, today, after October 1917, in spite of his audacious images, he would only have belonged to the past. But in the Revolution he was able to renew himself.

The Poet's Resurrection
His origins predisposed him to it.

At the time of the 1905 Revolution the poet was eleven years old. His family lived in the Caucasus. The child soon felt hatred for the Cossack hangmen. The first verses he read accompanied an illegal proclamation. 'The verses and the Revolution mingled in my head.' At twelve years old the child frequented a clandestine Marxist circle and thought of himself as a Social Democrat. Then came the death of his father, his arrival in Moscow, hunger, and difficult studies, broken off and resumed on several occasions. Mayakovsky joined the Bolshevik Party at the age of thirteen (1907). At fourteen, a tall, awkward youth, he took part (as 'Comrade Constantine') in a conference of the Moscow sections, and belonged to a committee along with Lomov, Smidovich and others.[20] His first arrest was in an illegal printshop. He swallowed a list of notes containing addresses together with the binding. Then he was freed, and there was a new frenzy of activity. Some comrades tunnelled under a Moscow street in order to free some convicts. The thing worked. Then he was arrested again. This time Mayakovsky spent eleven months in the Butyrky prison. It was there that he made contact with literature, and there where he wrote his first detestably Symbolist verses. When he was freed he left the Party to enter Bohemia. One evening the Futurist David Burliuk said to him 'You have genius, my friend!' Mayakovsky was convinced of it. He wore a blouse decorated with glints of sunlight. He and his Futurist friends distributed a joint manifesto entitled *A Slap in the Face of Public Taste*.[21] The individualistic litterateur, a bit of a snob, had put the revolutionary adolescent behind him.

In literature, as in the bourgeois world, the day comes when you have to make your mark by doing something different from those who have gone before, and even to start out by affronting public taste. Russian poetry was no longer evolving in these years. Blok, Balmont, Biely and Briusov belong to the already classical great poets around whom conventional schools become mummified. Between their poetry polished for the use of depressed intellectuals and real life the gap grew wider from day to day. The merit of the Futurists was to sense this. Mayakovsky's merit lay in being a rebel:

> We must today smash the world's skull
> With blows to the head!
> (*A Cloud in Trousers*, 1914).

His satirical pieces are bitterly pessimistic. Internal revolt ends up in rancour, and rancour in jeering (*An Ode to Judges, Port*[22]). The intellectuals disgusted him. A learned man 'isn't a man, he is a two-legged impotence':

> He isn't disgusted
> That man grows tame and submissive,
> Since in a split second
> He can work out a square root.

In 1914, to begin with the war only inspired in him extravagant and atrocious images ('the bushes in the streets are bleeding like a heart torn by the fingers of bullets'). Nonetheless, life goes on behind the lines, the 'good life' of the killing times. You get used to it. And so does the poet. His first masterpiece, *A Cloud in Trousers*,[23] a long, violent, and highly lyrical love poem, dates exactly to 1914. He also wrote some worthless little pieces for magazines. How this poet tails behind the vast mass! As long as those behind the lines forgot about the war, he forgot about it. But when the Revolution began to stir amid defeats and accumulated suffering, he wrote his great apocalyptic piece *War and the World*, to the rhythm of the prayer for the dead (1916). As a soldier whiling away his time by sketching portraits of his commanders, he dreamed up another great composition, *Man: The Life, the Birth, the Passions, etc.*, of Mayakovsky (1916).[24] It is going right over the top – *Me! Me! Me!* with overwhelming force, exaltation, passion, and fall: then utter despair. 'The world declaims the prayer of the dead.' This is the last line. Do you see how this Futurist, this mad individualist, this vehement and passionate man belongs completely in his despair to the past: to a society that is done for?

It is fortunate that the following lines of his *Collected Works,* entitled *Revolution*, date from 26th February 1917:

> Today topples your thousand-year old Before.
> Today the foundations of worlds are revised ...
> ......
> It is the first day of the workers' deluge!
> ......
> We've gained victory!
> Glory, Glory to Us!
> .....
> Today ascends unbelievably red
> All-time Socialists' glorious heresy.[25]

'We' haven't won, poet. You haven't even conquered your neurasthenia. But the Putilov workers did overthrow the autocracy. And that is why, Futurist, in spite of the past weighing down on you, you are going to be reborn, if only because you know how to follow the present!

The Poet of Proletarian Citizenship

Mayakovsky has kept up with the times. The October Revolution was not a crisis of conscience for him. His obstinate will to break with all traditions – one of the dominant traits in his Futurism – and his instinctive hatred for bourgeois society served him well. Soon he became the poet of proletarian citizenship (*Mystery-Bouffe*, 1918, *Orders to the Army of the Arts, Left March*,[26] *The Poet to the Worker*, 1919, *Satirical Poems*, 1920–22).

I cannot help seeing here a first completion of his destiny. His point of departure had been in a revolt against the finished, cultivated, scented, aristocratic and false verses of the poet laureates of the bourgeoisie. During the war he had aimed reproaches at them of this type:

> Haven't you had enough, poetic gentlemen,
> Of pages, palaces, love, and lilac bushes?
> If you are the creators of it

> I don't give a fuck for art!
> (*Brother Writers*)

That road was now seething, in a furnace. The street was full of shouts, flags, ideas in millions of heads, and actions flourished by millions of hands. Literature is a wretched thing. The old boredom, the snobbery of artistic cafés and the odious futility of sophisticated versifying can all go to the devil:

> Enough of pennyworth truths
> .....
> Streets for paintbrushes we'll use
> Our palettes, squares with their wide-open spaces.
> .....
> Into the streets, the crowds among,
> Futurists,
> Drummers,
> masters of rhyme!
> (*Order to the Army of the Arts*[27])

> Forget it!
> Spit on
> rhymes
> and arias,
> And the rose bush,
> And other such mawkishness
> from the arsenal of the arts!
> .....
> Comrades!
> Give us a new form of art
> That will pull the Republic out of the mud!
> (*2nd Order to the Army of the Arts*[28])

Mayakovsky did exactly what he said, helping the Republic out of the mud, and working as a living poet on the street. They were heroic years, of blockade, famine, Denikin, Yudenich and Kolchak. The republic was bleeding from a thousand wounds. The poet was a propaganda worker. Commissioned by *Rosta* (the Russian Telegraph Agency) he designed agitational posters which caught the attention of the masses throughout Russia every day. 'Have done about three thousand posters and about six thousand captions' (*Autobiography*[29]). And in the meantime he produced a great work: *One Hundred and Fifty Million*.

This role suited him admirably. He had an athletic physique, with the head and fists of a boxer and endowed with a voice ideal for resounding in the squares, and every now and then Mayakovsky emerged among the crowds on the days of the big demonstrations and declaimed in the street where he was replied to in chorus.[30] When Lord Curzon's ultimatum[31] brought angry crowds rolling out along the arteries of Moscow, Mayakovsky 'opening his mouth wide' taught them the slogan of the hour:

> Lion of Britain, whine![32]

These are untranslatable words. *Whine* is here pronounced like the command *'To the left!'*

Some of these satirical poems are little masterpieces. For example, there is that devoted to the *Trash*.

> Glory, glory to the heroes!
> .....
> And now lets thrash out about trash.

The trash are the petty bourgeois who have worked their way into the Red Republic. Mayakovsky sketches out an indescribably picture of them. Madame is preoccupied with the Revolutionary War Council's ball; she wishes to appear there in a dress decorated with soviet motifs. The master is calculating salary rises. A cat is purring on the *Izvestia*. And 'on the wall is Marx, in a little red frame'. A canary is whistling in its cage ...

> Marx from the wall looked on appalled
> Then suddenly

Opened his mouth:

.....

'Hurry
Wring that damned canary's neck
So that Communism
By canaries won't be wrecked'.[33]

Thanks to this contact with the reality of the revolution Mayakovsky the satirist, along with Demyan Biedny, remains one of the most typical Russian poets of these years.

'One Hundred and Fifty Million'

Of his great 'communist' compositions, that about the '150,000,000' is the most remarkable. For its originality, breadth and power of expression this poem is a unique work. It is, after all, a splendid piece. We should note along with Trotsky that it has enormous defects.[34] What we might call 'the internal tragedy of Mayakovsky the Futurist' reveals itself in every line of it. To begin with the work appeared without the author's name, for:

150,000,000 is the creator of this poem
Its rhythms – bullets
Its rhymes – fires from building to building
The printing press of footsteps
Has printed this edition
On the stony paper of the squares.[35]

It begins with a call of revenge and of hunger 'for all those who can go on no longer'. Men and things, everything is shaken in masses. In clumsily laboured lines we feel the vibration of a universe on the march. Everything shakes, 'cars, motor bikes, lowly things', the routes 'tired of leading toward wells' which want 'asphalt and the din of the express train'.

The provinces,
The fish, the insects

> One hundred and fifty million men,
> A hundred provinces,

all of which crowds together, crawls along, mounts up, and goes 'like a lava flow' – 'across the white guard of the snow' – across the ocean, towards America. And this universe of hungry rebels on the march is the colossal Russian Ivan, who is going to take the fat colossus Wilson by the throat in Chicago.

It rains hyperboles. Chicago has 14,000 streets; 700 alleys run into each ... etc. There are also abundant discoveries:

> Wilson's clothes
> Are woven by the finest care of the poets
> His underpants are not underpants
> They are sonnets!

The Whitmans, Lincolns and Edisons[36] form Wilson's court. 'While smoking, Whitman swings a censer, with a new rhythm'. 'Chaliapin is there, completely made up, ever ready to sing.'[37]

The confrontation of Ivan and Wilson is described with a wealth of stunning images. It is a social war of people and things, of all that is red against all that is white. 'The Rockefellers[38] are strangled with their own detachable collars ...' Wilson launches himself in vain at Ivan, and after using armies and pestilences, as a last resort

> The poisoned army of ideas:
> Democracy, humanism, isms and isms!

In vain.

> In the clash of an international Tsu-shima[39]
> the fleet of the past sails.

And now:

> 'Call us Abel or Cain[40]
> It doesn't matter to us!

> This is the future!'
> In place of faith inside souls
> Steam and electricity[41]
> Everything will be joy
> In the eyes of us great children.

Communist criticism rightly criticises this poem for its abuse of hyperbole,[42] coarse symbolism, the vulgarity of some of its expressions, the purely conventional character of its myths, and a deep basic resemblance – under a greatly contrasting form – with the old Russian *bylina* (legends). Ivan the giant reminds us too closely of the knight Ilya of Murom (L. Trotsky, G. Lelevich[43]).

In my opinion these criticisms can be levelled at all the present work of the Communist poet.

Futurism or Pastism?

At every turn, in titles, subtitles and lyrical invocations, Mayakovsky identifies himself. On perhaps a hundred occasions he makes the word 'me' a first line. In itself this mad individualism has nothing communist about it. It is exacerbating a psychological illness of capitalist society. Obviously there is revolutionary individualism. We all know that human individuality will flourish in the free communist society of the future; but we know that this will not be in the isolation of childish pride, but on the contrary, in the unanimity of collective life. And the revolutionary artist of today should learn from the proletariat – the class, above all, of collective endeavour – at least to have an inkling of the future. A Walt Whitman, who is so highly individual and yet so deeply imbued with feeling for collective life ('as a whole') in this respect seems to me to be far closer to proletarian art than Mayakovsky, entangled as he is in literary individualism.

Nor is hyperbole, his unending way of going on, any more a feature of proletarian thinking. Far from it, revolutionary realism is distinguished by concrete precision in estimating things, a feel for what is possible, and a contempt for extravagance. The development of technology and working with machines develops the thinking of the worker towards exactitude and precision. Exaggerations are more the work of minds trained outside the disciplines of production. Habitual hyperbole marks an idealism detached from reality, speculating about it in a free and easy manner. So on this point as well Mayakovsky's Futurism is really 'pastism'.[44]

Although an iconoclast, every time Mayakovsky is taken over by deep emotion he returns to his idolatrous past. The prayer for the dead provides the theme for *The War and the World*. The end of the poem smacks of biblical prophecy. In the *Mystery-Bouffe* (written in 1918, and staged by Meyerhold) the entire plot, which is otherwise exploited with very original vigour, is Christian. There is Noah's ark, the flood, Paradise, Hell, and the promised land.

Mayakovsky ends his last great love poem (*About Turn ...*) with a beautiful lyrical invocation of Faith, Hope and Charity.[45] Such is the strong vitality of the old man within him. Verhaeren (and Whitman even more so!) have freed themselves from the past to a far greater degree. Expressing the joy of life – by way of example – is often with them completely separated from old myths.

However, this great poet, moved by the desire to be a revolutionary, has made a great effort to renew himself. His influence stretches to all schools. He is the leader of the Communist-Futurist movement, whose most talked-about organ is the magazine *Lef*. To appreciate his work in all fairness it is necessary to place it in contemporary literature alongside that of the utterly outmoded Marinetti, or the poets of Western Europe. Then you can see at first glance how far this poet of the Revolution has gone from the cafés and salons where 'what remains' of 'literature' in the western countries is vegetating ...

We will talk again about his work and his magazine in a short while. But is Mayakovsky *the* poet of the Revolution? Does Russian Futurism really express the first attempts at proletarian art? To these two questions the resounding voice of the poet replies in the affirmative: Yes, or even more so: *A thousand million times yes!* This is not at all our opinion. Futurism appears to us to be woven out of the past. The *enormous* step towards the future: outmoded. The proletariat must understand that unceasing development is made out of the past, the present, and the future. The hatred of traditions: outmoded. We need *revolutionary traditions*. The overwheening individualism: bourgeois thinking. The abuse of hyperbole: a disorganisation of the imagination peculiar to some decadent forms of bourgeois art. The fascination with the grotesque, the brutal, the loud and the shocking: excesses very alien to revolutionary thinking that is aspiring to a new culture, in other words, a new *equilibrium* of thought. Reminiscences of Christianity:[46] outmoded, outmoded.

Futurism was an aspect of the decadence of bourgeois art. At a time when the separation between culture and the structure of society was growing wider, its merit was occasionally to foreshadow a new beauty destined to remain unexpressed for as long as artistic creation was to remain the privilege of the rich and productive work the task of wage labourers. Has it succeeded, in Russia, in renewing itself sufficiently to become an element in a *possible* revolutionary art? Maybe – its successes in this direction are already noteworthy. But what we see most clearly in Mayakovsky is the drama of a poet who cannot, in spite of his keen desire to do so, escape from the past. The intellectuals of our time are all, to the depth of their very souls, prisoners of bourgeois decadence. And their attempts to escape it, however brave they may be, are hopeless. We will only escape from these hellish circles of decadence by the revolutionary efforts of that class that is called upon to 'begin the world again'.

Victor Serge

Notes

1. Cf. the study of Vsevolod Ivanov in our no.56, and in our collection for 1923, Boris Pilnyak, Y. Libedinsky, etc (author's note). Translated from *Clarté*, no.lxix, December 1924, pp.504–8 (translator's note).
2. The contrast in Russian literature is striking between the attitude of the poets and that of the novelists towards the Revolution. The Poets Alexander Blok, André Biely, Nicolas Kluyev, Serge Yesenin, C. Balmont, Valery Briusov, Vyacheslav Ivanov, Serge Gorodetsky and Vladimir Mayakovsky praised it. The novelists Andreyev, Merezhkovsky, Kuprin, Bunin, Zaitsev, Amfiteatrov and Chirikov – to quote only the great names – hated it. This is too general a feature for it not to relate to causes that merit analysis. It seems to me that among writers, the poets, being more emotional, expressing the moment rather than the period, are more inclined to grasp the deep lyricism of a revolution. On top of this, poetic creativity does not necessarily require the long inner crystallisation of types and mentalities that moulds the novelist's personality and makes a conservative out of him, in the psychological sense of the word (author's note). Ivan Alexeyevich Bunin (1870–1938) was a playwright, novelist and critic; Boris Constantinovich Zaitsev (1881–1972), a writer and critic, was chairman of the Moscow Union of Writers in 1921–2, but then emigrated to Paris; Alexander Valentinovich Amfiteatrov (1862–1938) was also a playwright, novelist and critic (translator's note).
3. Filippo Tommaso (Emilio) Marinetti (1876–1944) was an Italian prose writer, novelist and poet, and one of the founders of Futurism. Excerpts from his *Futurist Manifestos* can be found in Viktor Woroszylski's *The Life of Mayakovsky*, London, 1971, pp.39–41. On his evolution rightwards, cf. Antonio Gramsci, 'A Letter to Leon Trotsky on Futurism', 8th September 1922, in 'Culture and Revolution in the Thought of Leon Trotsky', *Revolutionary History*, vol.vii, no.2, 1999, pp.118–20 (translator's note).
4. Mayakovsky's *War and the World* and *Revolution (A Poet's Chronicle)* were published in 1917 (*Vladimir Mayakovsky: Selected Works in Three Volumes*, translated by Dorian Rottenberg, Raduga, 1985, vol.i., pp.27–54 and 71 (translator's note).

5. The Scythians were a nomadic people who inhabited the Ukraine in the 6th century B.C. Jules Laforgue (1860–1887), a French poet and one of the originators of Modernism, was appointed Reader at the Court of the Empress Augusta of Germany in 1880. Mayakovsky had read Laforgue in translation (E. J. Brown, *Mayakovsky: A Poet in the Revolution*, Princeton University Press, 1973, p.76) (translator's note).

6. David Davidovich Burliuk (1882–1967), a poet and painter and the originator of cubo-futurism, was the first to uncover Mayakovsky's talent (translator's note).

7. The 1905 Revolution in Russia, after forcing the Tsar to grant a constitution which satisfied the liberals, was suppressed with some brutality, and its leaders, including Trotsky, were put on trial and exiled (translator's note).

8. As translated by Dorian Rottenberg, *Vladimir Mayakovsky: Selected Works in Three Volumes*, Raduga, 1985, vol.i, p.53. *And Yet* was written in 1913 and published in March 1914 (translator's note).

9. Mayakovsky's *Great Big Hell of a City*, in the English translation by Dorian Rottenburg, in *Vladimir Mayakovsky's Poems*, Moscow, 1972, p.72 and *Vladimir Mayakovsky: Selected Works in Three Volumes*, Raduga, 1985, vol.i, p.51. The date given there for the poem is 1913 (translator's note).

10. Mayakovsky's *Petersburg Again* was written in 1913 and published in 1914 (translator's note).

11. Mayakovsky's *A Cloud in Trousers*, in the English translation by Herbert Marshall, in *Mayakovsky*, New York, 1965, p.108. The date given there for the poem is 1915. Dorian Rottenberg renders the title as *Cloud in Pants* and translates this piece as:
    We, chain-gangmen of the leper-house city (*Vladimir Mayakovsky: Selected Poems in Three Volumes*, vol.ii, Raduga, 1986, p.18 (translator's note).

12. Mayakovsky's *The Fop's Tunic*, writtten in 1913 and published in 1914, as translated in Viktor Woroszylski's *The Life of Mayakovsky*, London, 1972, p.68 (translator's note).

13. Mayakovsky's *Listen!* was written in 1913 and published in March 1914. A different version of this piece appears in Vladimir Mayakovsky, *Poems*, translated by Dorian Rottenberg, Moscow, 1972, p.28:
    Now Listen,
    it must be for somebody stars are
    set gleaming
    Somebody who longs
    that over the rooftops
    one star at least should come alight? (translator's note).

14. Mayakovsky's *A Few Words About Myself* (May 1913), as rendered by E. J. Brown, *Mayakovsky: A Poet in the Revolution*, Princeton University Press, 1973, p.88. Another translation appears in Vladimir Mayakovsky, *The Bedbug and Selected Poetry*, translated by M. Hayward and G. Reavey, London, 1961, p.59 (translator's note).

15. Mayakovsky's *On the Trampled Pavements*, in the English translation by Herbert Marshall, in *Mayakovsky*, New York, 1965, p.95. The date given there for the poem is 1913. Other translations of this piece appear in Vladimir Mayakovsky, *The Bedbug and Selected Poetry*, translated by M. Hayward and G. Reavey, London, 1961, p.53 and by Dorian Rottenberg in *Vladimir Mayakovsky: Selected Works in Three Volumes*, vol.i, Raduga, 1985, p.49 (translator's note).

16. Mayakovsky's *How D'Ye Like This!*, 1913, as translated in Viktor Woroszylski, *The Life of Mayakovsky*, London, 1972, p.63. Dorian Rottenberg (*Vladimir Mayakovsky: Selected Works in Three Volumes*, vol.i, Raduga, 1985, p.52) renders this piece as:
    And yet if I, rude Hun out of Asia's spaces,
    won't want to grimace before your herds,
    I'll burst out laughing, and spit,
    yes, spit in your faces. (translator's note).

17. Mayakovsky's *Take It!*, as translated by Maria Enzensberger in *Listen! Vladimir Mayakovsky's Early Poems*, 1913–1918, London, 1987, p.44 (translator's note).

18. Vasily V. Rozanov (1856–1919) was a writer and critic who shocked the society of his day with his discussions of sexuality and the family (translator's note).

19. Mayakovsky's *A Few Words About Myself*, part of a book entitled *Me*, was written in May 1913 (translator's note).

20. A. Lomov (Georgi I. Oppokov, 1888–1938), a supporter of the Bolsheviks since 1903 and Lenin's firmest ally on the Central Committee pressing for the seizure of power in 1917, was arrested and shot during the purges; S. N. Smidovich (1872–1934) joined the R.S.D.L.P. at its foundation, and was active in the Bolshevik Moscow Regional Bureau in the years before the Revolution (translator's note).

21. *A Slap in the Face of Public Taste (Poshchochina obshchestvennomu vkusu)* was signed by Burliuk, Kruchenyk, Mayakovsky and Khlebnikov, and came out in 1912 (translator's note).

22. Mayakovsky's *An Ode to Judges* came out in 1915, and *Port* was first published in *An Ode to Judges no.2* (translator's note).

23. 'Do you want me to be irreproachably tender?
    Not a man, but a cloud in trousers!' (author's note).

24. Cf. note 20, above (translator's note).

25. Mayakovsky's *Revolution*, 17th April, 1917, as translated by Dorian Rottenberg, *Vladimir Mayakovsky: Selected Works in Three Volumes*, vol.i, Raduga, 1985, pp.69, 71 and 72 (translator's note).

26. Mayakovsky's *Mystery Bouffe* was translated into English by George Rapall Noyes and published in *Masterpieces of the Russian Drama*, New York, 1933, pp.801–881. *The 1st Order to the Army of the Arts* was published in December 1918, the *2nd Order to the Army of the Arts* in 1921, and *Left March!* in 1918 (translator's note).

27. *Order of the Day to the Army of the Arts* (1918) as translated by Dorian Rottenberg, *Vladimir Mayakovsky: Selected Works in Three Volumes*, vol.i, Raduga, 1985, pp.76–7 (translator's note).

28. *2nd Order to the Army of the Arts*, 1921, in Mayakovsky, *The Bedbug and Selected Poetry*, English translation by M. Hayward and G. Reavey, London, 1961, pp.148–9. Another translation by Dorian Rottenberg appears in *Vladimir Mayakovsky: Selected Works in Three Volumes*, vol.i, Raduga, 1985, pp.84–5 (translator's note).

29. Mayakovsky's *I Myself* (1920) as translated by Dorian Rottenberg, *Vladimir Mayakovsky: Selected Works in Three Volumes*, vol.i, Raduga, 1985, p.41 (translator's note).

30. Mayakovsky was over six feet tall, and had a stentorian voice (translator's note).

31. George Nathaniel, Viscount Curzon (1859–1925) was British Foreign Secretary from 1919 to 1923. As the Red Army approached the frontier of ethnic Poland in the war between the two states in July 1920 he reminded the Soviet government that Poland's eastern frontier had been fixed there by the Allied Supreme Council in December 1919 (translator's note).

32. *Left March! For the Marines* (1918) as translated by Herbert Marshall, *Mayakovsky*, New York, 1965, p.129. Dorian Rottenberg, in *Vladimir Mayakovsky: Selected Works in Three Volumes*, vol.i, Raduga, 1985, p.77 translates it as:
    Let the British Lion brandish his crown,
    And roar until he's dumb and deaf (translator's note).

33. *The Trash* (1920–1921) as translated by Herbert Marshall, *Mayakovsky*, New York, 1965, pp.138–40. Dorian Rottenberg renders the title as *Rot* (Vladimir *Mayakovsky: Selected Works in Three Volumes*, vol.i, Raduga, 1985, pp.82–3) (translator's note).

34. Trotsky's criticism of this poem can be found in 'Class and Art', 9th May 1924, in *Leon Trotsky on Literature and Art*, New York, 1977, p.78 and *Literature and Revolution*, Michigan U.P., 1960, pp.152–6 (translator's note).

35. Mayakovsky's *One Hundred and Fifty Million*, as rendered by E. J. Brown, *Mayakovsky: A Poet in the Revolution*, Princeton University Press, 1973, p.204 (translator's note).

36. Abraham Lincoln (1809–1865) was the President of the USA during the American Civil War; Thomas Alva Edison (1847–1931) made a fortune from his inventions, which included the gramophone, the light bulb and the motion picture (translator's note).

37. Fyodor Ivanovich Chaliapin (1873–1938) was a popular operatic bass vocalist, who abandoned his democratic ideals after the failure of the 1905 Revolution (translator's note).
38. John Davison Rockefeller Jnr. (1874–1960) was a rich industrialist, the head of Standard Oil. He is notorious for ordering the Ludlow massacre at a sit-in strike at the Colorado Fuel and Iron Company, where 40 were killed (translator's note).
39. In May 1905, during the war with Japan, the Russian Baltic fleet, having sailed all round the world, was annihilated by the Japanese fleet off the islands of Tsu-shima (translator's note).
40. Cain is described as murdering his brother Abel in Genesis iv, vv.1–16. The contrast intended here is between the murderer and his innocent brother (translator's note).
41. I very much doubt whether this would be enough (author's note).
42. 'Vladimir Ilyich definitely did not like Mayakovsky's *One Hundred and Fifty Million*. He thought the book was affected and contrived' (Anatoli Lunacharsky, 'Lenin and the Arts', 1924, in *Lenin Through the Eyes of Lunacharsky*, Moscow 1981, p.152). This was something of an understatement. 'Aren't you ashamed to vote for printing 5,000 copies of Mayakovsky's *One Hundred and Fifty Million*? It is nonsense, stupidity, double-dyed stupidity and affectation', Lenin wrote: 'as for Lunacharsky, he should be flogged for his Futurism' (V. I. Lenin, 'Letter to A. V. Lunacharsky', 6 May, 1921, *Collected Works*, vol.xlv, Moscow, 1976, pp.138–9) (translator's note).
43. Ilya of Murom was a hero of Russian folk epic (*bylina*) (translator's note).
44. Mayakovsky was most irate about Serge's comment here. Cf. *Memoirs of a Revolutionary*, Oxford U.P., 1975, p.268 (translator's note).
45. Mayakovsky's *About This* was written in 1923. Faith, hope and charity are the virtues praised in I Corinthians xiii (translator's note).
46. These shock me in Mayakovsky the Futurist. I find them more natural in Alexander Blok or André Biely (author's note).

Tikhonov and Serafimovich

The Epic Literature of the Revolution (N. Tikhonov and Serafimovich)[1]
It is a fact worthy of note that the war of 1914–1918 has not given birth to an epic literature. There was never any parallel in the past for so much and so sustained human energy being devoured by history. Never had so many, and such civilised peoples been so completely absorbed in the sole task of murder and destruction. Never before had the individual been subjected to such infernal trials as those which ground him down in the ant hills and furnaces of modern battles. Never had the mass slaughters been of such an extent. The whole of the unforgettable people of ancient Greece at the height of its splendour could be contained in one mortuary at Verdun ...[2] Many of the people of our time have a full acquaintance with the terrifying immensity of these things at the highest level. Were they not one of the most important causes of the Russian Revolution and of the revolutionary storms that swept over western Europe? The inability of the literature created during the War to measure up to present day requirements by expressing what had gone on – and what was really required after such an experience – with a creative power proportionate to the greatness of the men and events is all the more striking.

However little we think about it, the reason for this is obvious. *An epic literature that takes the imperialist war for its theme is impossible*. Obviously, I would not for a moment dream of denying that writers could, given insight, talent, luck, book sales and academic awards, cultivate the epic genre – which is a genre like any other. But it requires more than this to create an epic literature which is not just entertainment for budding academicians; there must be a deep rapport between the writer and his time, his characters and his readers, an identification that runs so deep that all of them come to life, brought together by a sort of Unanimism.[3] The writer's script has to express the feelings of the thousands and millions of men aroused during the action.

On account of an unavoidable double contradiction, great works that distill the experience undergone by the masses cannot be created from the memory of the imperialist war of 1914–1918. *Those who fought the war*, the human cattle who slaughtered and were slaughtered, caught between the execution posts of their 'fatherland' and the enemy barbed wire, those who carried on the war, understood neither what caused it, nor why it was fought. If they had known, they would not have marched. As far as the war itself is concerned, they have only commented on what is horrible and disgusting about it. The toilers of town and country, launched into this great adventure by their ruling classes, either were, whether or not consciously, in absolute disagreement with the events or with themselves. It was first necessary to make them drunk with lies to get them to be killed. The rich literature that resulted from their sufferings condemns the War. And those *on whose behalf* the war was fought, considered as a class, only know about the gains, the over-dramatised and picturesque events, the secret goings-on and the unspoken under-the-table deals. Even though their class wields a monopoly over culture as a whole, their writers, used to entertaining the well-fed, did not find in this experience, very different from that of the trenches, the material for creating epics. In any case, there was no common language possible between patriotic literary men and the soldiers who survived the great slaughter, the disagreement being only one aspect of the class antagonism between them.

N. Tikhonov: Twelve Songs

These thoughts occurred to me while reading two Russian books, for there is in Red Russia a literature that is both epic and sincere. It is even the pre-eminent form of literature. There is the story told by the old writer Serafimovich, the son of a Cossack, who went through exile in Siberia, and the *Twelve Songs* by the young poet N. Tikhonov, a soldier in the red cavalry not so long ago, risking his life with sabre slashes so that the land should remain the property of the peasants, and the rule of law in the hands of the Soviets.

N. Tikhonov is now one of the masters of Russian poetry. His verses are forged with the sonorous strength of metal. The revolutionary war provides him with subjects. His audacious rhythm is continually adding to the tradition of Russian poetry innovations, foreshortenings, ellipses and contrasts between modern ways of thinking and the wealth of popular speech. And his outlook on life? ... *The Ballad of the Nails* describes in eighteen lines the sacrifice of a torpedo boat under orders. The men did not flinch, and not one returned:

> Could nails from such people be fashioned, you'd see
> No tougher nails in the world would there be.[4]

The Ballad of the Blue Envelope strikes three chords: will, inevitability and piti-less veiled irony. No western European writer would have been able to write it without adding a fourth: despair. The revolutionary soldier Tikhonov knows nothing of despair. His strength comes from accepting fatal losses with clenched teeth and an expression impassive to the point of irony ('could nails from such people be fashioned ...'). Messengers are taking dispatches from the battlefield to the Kremlin. There is the gallop of horse across the steppe, the rush of the locomotive along the rails, the soaring of the aircraft in the sky and night, and then crash. Trapped under his machine

> He said, his mouth with black earth stuffed full:
> 'The envelope first – then my leg – don't pull!'[5]

In the Kremlin another man receives the blue envelope now spattered red, reads the dispatch, and wipes his hand on his tunic: 'I already know all it has to say. It's been brought just half an hour too late!'[6] And even more implacable is *The Ballad of the Deserter*. His wife is told: 'Your husband is a coward, your cows will be taken from you, and your sheep will be slaughtered.' Then, when he returned: 'Give me back the cattle, I know all about it, I am ready'. He received:

> Two slices of bread,
> a cube of sugar –
> and in addition that night
> six ounces of lead.

The poet makes no comment. There is no indignation. Necessity is higher than human law, and all the revolutionary writers are dominated by the feeling of unavoidable necessity. *The Song of the Soldier on Leave*:

> 'Shall I let you off – to take your leave
> Of your wife? Is she dying, indeed?

> There's one gun less if you go away
> No, I can't, just can't let you go!
> Tonight the decisive battle begins
> Left about march, lad! No.[7]

What cannot be translated in these poems is their virile music. The proud controlled eloquence, the intimate interaction between the human and the inhuman realised by perfectly uniting will and necessity shows here one of the most definitive traits of revolutionary proletarian thought, which referring to Lenin I called 'the strength of unity'.[8] Wrangel was defeated when the Red Army led by Frunze took the fortifications of the Perekop isthmus by storm. This was one of the most audacious exploits of the Civil War, and was perhaps the only thing that could have finished it off. Tikhonov expresses this in two verses all the more perfect for being concise:

> There are children, blind and lame, in our rear,
> Children of long slaughter –
> There are towns in our rear on shattered roads
> Without bread, without hearth, without water.
>
> And beyond the mountain is rest and joy.
> A mirage? – it matters not.
> With a sound like a storm goes up the cry
> 'We'll win!' from a thousand throats.

And after the victory in the Crimea:

> And we lay down under the trees
> Under the rocks in the grass,
> And waited – the first time in four long years
> For sleep to come at last.
>
> We dreamt – if we lived for a hundred years
> We'd not see the like again,

No songs can be made up about it, no words
Are there to describe it all.[9]

The last song in this booklet (*Cavalry*) reminds us of Alexander Blok's *The Scythians*. There is very much the same proud feeling of defiance directed at the old civilisations, but with a thinking more narrowly focused, as if reduced purely to the will to win. One morning, when they get up, after the cavalry has come through there from the East, the western towns see:

What has been cut, sculpted, and printed with red iron,
On stones, on the roads, on walls
– scratches of five pointed stars –
traces of broken veins.

(It is well known that the five pointed star is the badge of the Red Army). Tikhonov's poetry has awakened deep echoes among Russian youth. Tikhonov has founded a school.

A. Serafimovich *The Iron Flood*

A. Serafimovich has entitled his novel *The Iron Flood*. The Russians, being revolutionaries, have a predilection for iron. There is 'the iron cohort' of the party (Bukharin). Iron discipline is 'Communist discipline'.[10] It requires much pure metal for particular difficult tasks.

This Iron Flood would be better called 'the flood of flesh'. Trapped in the gorges of the Caucasus by the White Cossacks, a hundred thousand Red peasants – men, women, old people, children – taking with them all they have, leading their flocks, a real migration of a hunted people – open up a road to Kuban, where there is corn, where you can live, where a Soviet army is coming to meet them. The crucial points of the story are those of a strategic problem. There are a hundred thousand mouths to be fed and no food. There are so many days' journey to be allowed for crossing mountain and forest, under burning sun or hot rain. The enemy holds the passes; he must be brought out of hiding. The enemy is well supplied, well armed, and war is his profession. The crowd of tattered labourers must fight him, or die. Any tactician who calmly weighs up the situation can only conclude, so it seems, that the Whites are on the winning side. But he would be greatly deceived: flesh is sometimes made out of steel. Will power can work miracles, and so can revolutionary feeling. Nothing is exaggerated, either in the story or in my reasoning. On how many occasions, from a human point of view, has the Russian Revolution been lost! But every time a 'miracle' (nothing mysterious about it) of revolutionary will has saved it.

What transforms this flood of flesh into a flood of iron – in the first instance – is the will of one man. All the gestures of the leader, who rises from the mass, and embodies it, lifted to the level of consciousness, only express the will to live of a hundred thousand people. The personality of this leader, through too much power, comes down to anonymity. Where does the individual end, and the flood begin? We do not know. The individual is providential. Perhaps without him the flood would pour over into chasms. The shot that pierced his forehead would pierce the foreheads of a hundred thousand. It is the towering role of the individual in history, the giant stature of Lenin! (The leader here is a peasant soldier called Kujukh: 'short, stocky man, with a square, hard-set jaw. His small, grey, gimlet eyes glittered under his heavy brows'[11]). When he speaks, it is only to say what they all feel, and what is dictated by necessity. Mass consciousness and historic necessity shine in his brain: the insignificance of the individual, the mighty role of the classes, and the laws of history! Do you understand why his will is mixed up with the events in such a way that you do not know if it determines them, whether it is born out of him, or whether the opposite is true?

Led by this man, who has been chosen by an assembly similar to a riot, after they have nearly killed him – the cries of 'betrayal' overcoming his calm voice – the iron flood breaks through every obstacle, not without leaving behind it a trail of bones. When the last of the horses die they have to abandon the wounded, the sick, the lame, and many of the children. When one person collapses exhausted at the side of the road those next to him turn their heads away, hastening their steps. The leader knows that every moment of the journey gained means a chance of being saved. He does not tolerate a minute more of stopping than is strictly necessary. He does not pardon any weakness. He has made all his subordinates sign a death sentence in advance: 'if an order is disobeyed, even slightly, the penalty is death'.[12]

German cruisers perched like toys of grey steel on the dazzling blue sheet of the sea bombard from afar this crowd, a long gray serpent gliding along the dust of the roads.[13] The Cossack artillery showers its shrapnel over them. Children at the breast are suddenly transfixed by a death coming as if from another universe. Frantic battles are unleashed. Serafimovich has collected together in this book an astonishing amount of factual observations. He has depicted the *peasant war* as a whole, and in detail. I cannnot quote from his documentation where everything would be new for the western reader. I will only pick out two particularly powerful pages. Cossacks and Red peasants from the same villages split between Whites and Reds are fighting bitterly. This is why, suddenly remembering their nature as cultivators and neighbours used to settling their differences with fist fighting, they put down their guns in order to lash out at each other with fists in front, to come to grips with each other to throttle and to injure each other, fighting man to man. This indecisive battle seems more humane and natural to them than anonymous bullets mowing down often unknown lives ... On another occasion when the human flood was full of fatigue and anger, some people set up a gramophone on a peasant *telega*.[14] The black vulcanite disc turns and a loud warm laugh, the professional laugh of a fat actor, with a well stretched mouth and a gourmet's lips breaks out among the revolutionary fighters who have neither drunk, nor eaten, nor slept, not spoken in a human manner for many days, for whom life's terrible excitements ceaselessly keep going on. Laughter infects them; this laughter, without check and restraint, incomprehensively mounts up into a torrent, putting the grinning stamp of madness on the swarthy faces of the crowd. But the leader wakes up: an order given in a hard voice kills off the laughter of madness.[15]

The truth of this account very likely surpasses that of a good naturalistic work. I have the impression that Serafimovich has become the narrator of an episode in the Communist revolution in the Caucasus such as we have all known about.[16] The book ends – just as the Civil War ends – with the peasants' victory. Then from the throng of survivors an incredible cheering breaks out for the leader, who had so often to control them. The last lines of the book, so full of bloody tumult, could well be a transcription in poetic prose of one of the final verses of Tikhonov's *Perekop* ('... free of blood for the first time ...').

As the veil of smoke vanished towards the star-bestrewn sky so their jubilation waned into intangible weariness around the fires, and the great sea of people fell gently to sleep, smiling.

The fires went out. It was quiet. The night was blue.[17]

The war was fought with so much fury by these men only so that they could truly put an end to it.

The Iron Flood, which appeared last year in Moscow has had the success it deserved. In spite of various imperfections that this is not the place to elaborate on, it is surely one of the most forceful of the works of the new proletarian literature.

★　★　★　★　★

Have I succeeded in showing how far these works are removed from the war literature of the West? We find nothing of the officially laid down patriotism, of the conventional and artificial, 'well intentioned' literature, so called perhaps because it is deprived of feeling. Nor is there anything of the pacifist literature of those who were stupefied by the War. Serafimovich and Tikhonov do not prettify war. Terrible pages abound in them. Nor do they attempt to 'discredit' it, a vain preoccupation for as long as there are great factory owners making guns and ammunition. The revolutionary people whose spokesmen they are is waging it *out of necessity on their own behalf*. The have suffered immensely from it. They wanted to win outright, in order not to die. With victory they come to understand their strength. To accomplish a new task in history, the expropriation of the old ruling classes – one might say, to move towards the conquest of life – they had to attain, what the Civil War accomplished at great risk, the unanimity of the toiling masses, to make leaders arise who embodied these classes, and to make themselves the conscious instrument of historical necessity.

In the sphere of literary creativity the profound agreement between the individual – whether fighter or writer – and his class and the unavoidable task of his class – whatever sacrifice it imposes upon him – makes it possible for an epic literature to appear today in Red Russia that is impossible anywhere else.

Victor Serge　　　　**(Leningrad, December 1925)**

Notes

1. Translated from *Clarté*, no.79, December 1925 – January 1926, pp.389–91 (translator's note).
2. The Battle of Verdun (1916) was one of the great slaughters of the First World War. The German Field Marshal Falkenhayn tried to bleed the French army to death by bombarding its forts in a salient on the Western Front (translator's note).
3. Unanimism was a literary movement pioneered by Jules Romains and Dos Passos at the beginning of the twentieth century. It sought to express the personality of the individual in terms of the collective psychology of a group (translator's note).
4. N. Tikhonov, 'The Ballad of the Nails', 1919–1922, translated by Peter Tempest, in V. Shoshin (ed.), *Nikolai Tikhonov: Poems*, Raduga, Moscow, 1988, p.141. Serge translated some of Tikhonov's poetry into French (translator's note).
5. N. Tikhonov, 'The Ballad of the Blue Envelope', 1922, translated by Dorian Rottenberg, in V. Shoshin, *Nikolai Tikhonov: Poems*, Raduga, Moscow, 1988, p.143 (translator's note).
6. Op. cit., n.5 above, p.143 (translator's note).
7. N. Tikhonov, 'The Song of the Soldier on Leave', 1922, translated by Dorian Rottenberg, in V. Shoshin (ed.), *Nikolai Tikhonov: Poems*, Raduga, Moscow, 1988, p.144 (translator's note).
8. Below, p.297.
9. N. Tikhonov, 'The Perekop', 1922–1924, translated by Avril Pyman, in V. Shoshin (ed.), *Nikolai Tikhonov, Poems*, Raduga, Moscow, 1988, p.139 (translator's note).
10. Serafimovich's *The Iron Flood* (Moscow, 1924: English translation, Martin Lawrence, 1935) is a novel based upon the retreat of the Red army from the Taman Peninsula along the eastern seaboard of the Black Sea from Novorossisk to Tuapse, and then inland through the Caucasus to Kuban for thirty-three days in the summer of 1918. He did not witness it first hand, but relied upon eye witness reports. The commander, Epifan Iovich Kovtiukh (1890–1938), a former Cossack officer, later described it in *From the Volga to the Kuban and Back* (Moscow, 1926). Cf. Victor Serge, *Year One of the Russian Revolution*, London, 1972, p.301. As Deputy Commander of the Byelorussian Military District Kovtiukh was later accused of participating in the so-called 'Generals' Plot' of 1937 and shot in the following year. The phrase 'iron discipline' occurs in the English translation of Serafimovich's book on p.105. 'Iron cohort' was first used in one of Bukharin's articles written in 1922. Cf. Alfred Rosmer, *Trotsky and the Origins of Trotskyism*, London, 2002, p.17, n.2 and 39 (translator's note).
11. A. Serafimovich, *The Iron Flood*, English translation, p.10 (translator's note).
12. English translation, p.104 (translator's note).
13. English translation, p.69 (translator's note).
14. A *telega* is a Russian word for a peasant cart. The English translation renders this as 'on the back of a pack-horse' (p.172) (translator's note).
15. English translation, pp.172–3 (translator's note).
16. Since its characters were recognisable people, it laid the author open to the accusation that he had exaggerated the role of some and underplayed that of others, arousing a storm of controversy. Kovtiukh objected that it made him out to be some sort of a saint, and Serafimovich was later criticised for 'failing to show as fully as he should the extent of Party leadership in the event' (translator's note).
17. English translation, p.246 (translator's note).

The Iron Flood by A. Serafimovich[1]

A hundred thousand men on the road. A hundred thousand peasants dragging the remnants of their possessions, their children, their old people, their sick and their wounded in wretched handcarts. A hundred thousand hungry, desperate peasants, harassed by the enemy, threatened with death ... And in the minds of these people, as in the times of the great primeval migrations, the implacably clear necessities of the matter are:–

On the one side there is the sunless sea, clothed in blue splendour – the deadly sea – no hope of salvation there. On the other, there is the mountain and the enemy. The enemy is everywhere, cavalry, artillery and infantry commanded by old experienced officers. The pass is their only chance of salvation. This arid route between sea and rocks, raked by machine guns, where every corner is an ambush, a road of pitiless famine, with not a field of wheat for a hundred leagues around, leads along the coast of the Caucasus towards Kuban, a land of heavy ears of corn belonging to the Reds, the land of the Soviets!

This doomed people, determined to live *despite everything*, is a red peasant people. By red we mean poor, and by poor we mean revolutionary. The regular troops of the Socialist Republic of Georgia (which sort?[2]) close off the South to them. The Cossacks of the White generals harass them: this immense crowd of human beings is to be killed in the name of the fatherland of the rich. The cruisers of His Majesty the German Emperor, perched like toys of grey steel on the azure sea, fire from a distance upon the unending ribbon of a wretched and tattered grey crowd in flight ...

They are a people with only one chance of survival: to endure it all to make the journey. They know only one law: necessity, and only one rule: to be strong, in other words, united, inflexible, disciplined, enduring, courageous and implacable. There is one spirit and one head: the leader.

With no food, they must march, march and march, with hunger in their bellies. So much the worse for the weak if they fall by the way. To pick them up means risking everybody's future. So much the worse for the wounded, so much the worse for the poor little children, who can't go any further, and so much the worse for their mothers ... They must march or die, and this people wants to live. Either the bones of these hundred thousand men, women and children will whiten in the sun on the clear ribbon of the road or, cut down by a third, they will win through to the North, the land of wheat, the land of the reds, before the last of their strength is exhausted ...

★   ★   ★   ★   ★

Such a book, one of the most poignant and sweeping that I know, a magnificent and true book – the history of the Russian Revolution includes several episodes like this – is *The Iron Flood* by A. Serafimovich.

A Serafimovich is an old proletarian writer, a Don Cossack in origin, exiled during his youth and then for a long time neglected, poor all his life, poor up to now, and a longtime revolutionary.

And he has to be a revolutionary to the depths of his soul to paint this fresco of thousands of men on the move, a 'chronicle of the Civil War', roughly and densely true like those of some of the good chroniclers of yesteryear. War is by no means prettified in it – as if you can prettify war! There are some terrible pages. The Communist writer is also the only one to be able to talk about war without lying about it: his class, even if it knows how to wage war – and win – bears no responsibility for it, and will end up forging its guns into ploughshares. The Communist writer is also the only one capable of describing the worker and peasant mass without either flattering or denigrating it, just as it is. The Red peasants whom Serafimovich depicts for us have all the faults and all the weaknesses of a present encumbered by the weight of their past. They are about to kill their leader, but a change of heart come about and they chose him. On twenty occasions he appears to be their enemy, precisely because his authority embodies their strength to the ultimate degree. His life is more often threatened by the knives of the partisans than the bullets of the enemy. Serafimovich knows the Russian peasant all too well.

Serafimovich's book is one of the best works of proletarian literature in the Russian language. Nine years after the October Revolution, from now on we have the right to be proud of the contrast between European culture and a literature that produces such works.

Victor Serge

Notes

1. Translated from *L'Humanité*, 11 December, 1926 (translator's note).
2. The Mensheviks were strong in Georgia, and proclaimed an independent republic there on 26 May 1919, with Noah Zhordania as its president. It allowed passage to armies operating against the Bolsheviks during the Civil War, and was reconquered by the Red Army in 1921. Cf. L. D. Trotsky, *Social Democracy and the Wars of Intervention in Russia*, London 1975 (translator's note)

Alexei Tolstoy[1]

February 24, 1945. Deaths follow one after the other, so many deaths! It is a time of death. This morning was the announcement of the death of Alexei Nikolayevich Tolstoy, a minute paragraph in microscopic type in *El Popular*.[2] Orders will come and there will be fine articles.

It was in 1923, in Berlin's Tauentzienstrasse, an airy business quarter with pretty, green turf growing between the rails of the streetcar track, that I saw our handsome Serge Zorin of the dark days in Petrograd coming along the sidewalk, tall, fair haired, with the air of a Viking. With him was a stocky gentleman with a massive head and heavy chin, not a soldier, but a reflective bourgeois, with, I believe, little brown crossed eyes, behind a pince-nez which was askew: Alexei Tolstoy. He was negotiating with Zorin the question of his rallying to the support of the Revolution and his return to Moscow.

'How interested he is!' exclaimed Zorin. '*Gosisdat*[3] must put out a complete edition of his works – and the author's rights must be guaranteed to the last kopeck!'

All three of us were in a little café when Zorin began to evoke the Chudin affair, concerning which he retained a profound sadness: 'In him we shot a very fine fellow, a man of 1905, and he was not guilty, but there was nothing else to do'. (It was this conversation which crystallised in my mind the idea for one of the dramas in *Conquered City*[4]).

After 1926, in Leningrad, I got to know Alexei Tolstoy better, at first at the sumptuous dinners of the historian Pavel Eliseyevich Shchegolev,[5] to which came Anna Akhmatova, thin, delicate, white as a porcelain statuette, firmly unyielding and very affected (the pose with her long fingers on her shoulders) and her beautiful, sad, grey-green eyes, Karl Radek and Larissa Reissner, amazon and intellectual, an extraordinary human achievement ...

They are all dead now, even little Pavel Pavlovich with his childish head like that of a young official out of a comedy by Gogol. Tolstoy and Shchegolev made millions of roubles with melodramas on Rasputin and the empress.[6] They enjoyed life and believed in a moderate counter-revolution, liberal and agrarian. They called themselves 'sympathisers' of the C.P., uneasy sympathisers, cynical and inoffensive.

'My office boy at *Byloe* (*The Post*) got drunk,' related Shchegolev, 'and confessed that he was a stool pigeon for the Cheka. I said to him: "I'll not fire you, my friend; I like it this way, now I know where I stand".'

Shchegolev detested Trotsky. I remember that he went into a sort of hysteria in front of me in speaking of that 'little journalist, that correspondent for reactionary sheets in Kiev'[7] – and that there was an incident, smoothed over by Pilnyak. (Leon Trotsky had already fallen from power, of course). Alexei Tolstoy, on the contrary, never spoke of Trotsky but with respect and admiration.

Alexei Tolstoy felt himself insecure, and he sometimes wrote magnificent pages, a short story on a Civil War fighter disorientated by the N.E.P., for example. He spoke a magnificent Russian. He was rather proud and reserved in manner, but easily became warm, sensitive and moving. With Liuba and Vlady[8] we went several times to his home at Dietskoye Selo. His wife was a Russian beauty like those Kustodiev used to paint,[9] plump with clear eyes.

Their traditional household, small white house, garden, birches, Paul I furniture, collections, miniatures, old books, landscapes and great comfort, was simple and luxurious. Alexei Tolstoy invited us to hear the first chapters of his Peter I.[10] He was greatly influenced at that time by the seventeenth century peasant Possoshkov, who died in the Peter-Paul fortress.[11] He thought of his novel as an oppositional work which would trumpet the suffering and the power of the peasants. He said: 'What we are living through is a return to the revolutionary and autocratic barbarism of Peter the Great'. (This was during the farm collectivisation period, and it seemed probable that Stalin would fall because of the famine, and that the 'Right', Rykov, Tomsky and Bukharin,[12] to which Alexei Tolstoy was friendly, would win on a programme of appeasing the peasantry).

Alexei Tolstoy read in a serious and velvety voice, full of emotion. His first identification of Stalin with Peter I was that of a discreet pamphleteer, for the historical novel was an evasion for him. (All the top flight writers used this evasion: Tynyanov with Griboyedov and Pushkin, Kaverin with *Lieutenant Kizhe*, and others with Pugachev or Catherine the Great and even Toussaint L'Ouverture ...)[13]

When I became too compromised our relations naturally became less frequent. Tolstoy skirted disgrace, but Boris Andreyevich Pilnyak, who was incontestably first among the young writers, the leader (along with Vsevolod Ivanov) of Soviet literature, was plunged into disgrace and persecution, rescued by Stalin, then semi-boycotted once again, and censured by Yezhov (the future successor of Yagoda in the G.P.U., the future executioner's victim.[14]

Gorky returned from Italy, but I did not see him again; his secretary Kriuchkov (of the G.P.U.) closed his door in my face (Kriuchkov was shot with Yagoda[15]). Furthermore, Gorky was unrecognisable, ascetic, and like a skeleton. I happened to meet him on the street, and was startled to see the dead man behind the living one.

He wrote official articles, really abominable, justifying the secret trials in the name of culture, proclaiming that 'the enemy who does not surrender has to be exterminated',[16] and privately he gave vent to bitter outbursts. He internally resisted this scornful and violent bitterness, he sometimes burst out and entered into conflict with Stalin. All his old friends, such as Julia and Ekaterina Peshkova,[17] broke with him because he let his former collaborators on *Novaya Zhizn* be imprisoned, Ginzburg and Sukhanov,[18] whose honesty he was aware of, because he refused to offer the slightest objection to the execution of technicians,[19] and became the contrary of himself.

It was in this atmosphere that, at a meeting of forty writers at Gorky's home, which Stalin attended, Pasternak and Alexei Tolstoy had the courage to complain of the censorship. Stalin rebuked the Secretary General of the Proletarian Writers, Leopold Averbach, who had immediately attacked their proposals as counter-revolutionary – and left, taking Tolstoy in his car. (Averbach, the nephew of Yagoda, was shot in 1937 or 1938).

The personal friendship of Alexei Tolstoy and Stalin was thus born in an excess of frankness and courage, probably stimulated by vodka. Stalin was liberal and warm-hearted, as he sometimes sought to be. He granted a passport abroad to the son of Alexei Nikolayevich. Alexei Tolstoy was seduced. The comparison with Peter I flattered Stalin – the reforming Tsar had only to be humanised, and this was an order.

In the same epoch began the disparagement of Pokrovsky's great (Marxist) *History of Russia*, considered up to then as a fundamental work, but which contained a terrible portrait of Tsar Peter. (Pokrovsky was to die in isolation, under the disapprobation of the schools, just in time to escape a worse fate). Alexei Tolstoy recast his *Peter I*, not without internal struggles, and made a play out of it, which Stalin came to see, beaming with contentment.

During the height of the famine Alexei Tolstoy one winter night gave a royal party at Dietskoye Selo, with a buffet which set all Leningrad talking, violin orchestra, and troikas for driving the guests through the snow. We said: *Pir vremya chumy*, 'the feast during the plague'.[20]

Alexei Tolstoy was a writer by birth, loving and understanding the human problem, a good psychologist and a student of manners, a worshipper of his profession and a possessor of a fine feeling for language: everything necessary to make a great writer, if only the despotism and the cowardice which despotism imposes had been absent. He needed a great deal of money and official favour. He feared disgrace, censure and repression, to which his émigré bourgeois and aristocratic past made him more vulnerable than others. He had the zeal of an apostate, but he probably suffered a great deal, for he was intelligent, liberal, and rather good. He probably found an internal justification for his conduct in his love of Russia, a love which embraced the inevitable suffering of the chosen and martyred people, and in his expectation of a new Russian greatness, which he could really envisage only in terms of an empire.

The ralliers group of 1923, *Smenovekhovtsi* (the 'New Orientation'),[21] of which he had been a member, had been decimated – and more than decimated – by the terror from 1929–30 on.

A member of the Union of Soviet Writers, Alexei Tolstoy had seen his friend Boris Pilnyak, and Tarassov-Rodionov, and Galina Serebriakova,[22] and the stage director Meyerhold, and Babel, and so many others disappear. He saw the Old Bolsheviks shot,[23] who had admitted him to their company when they were in power, and whom he had admired. He had a profound knowledge of the totalitarian tragedy.

He never made the slightest protest, he explicitly endorsed – as was requested – all the crimes. It is true that he had described at length the execution of the *Streltsy* under the walls of the Kremlin, at which Tsar Peter forced his boyars and his favourites to kill them with their own hands,[24] as he himself did, thereby establishing an obvious and common bond of complicity.

He died at 62, a millionaire in a country of the greatest misery, weighed down with honours, having obstinately suppresed a nameless sorrow.

(I once ran through a historical novel on the Civil War, written on request by Alexei Tolstoy at the time, in 1935, when the recent past was being violently falsified: in it Lenin was inspired by Stalin, they won the revolutionary war, and Trotsky was not mentioned[25]).

Notes

1. Reprinted from 'In a Time of Duplicity' translated by James M. Fenwick, in *The New International*, vol.xvi. no.2 (whole no.141), March/April 1950, pp.117–120 (editor's note).

2. A Stalinist-controlled paper published in Mexico and edited throughout the preceding period by Lombardo Toledano (translator's note). Serge was living in Mexico at the time, and Vicente Lombardo Toledano (1893–1969) was a leading Stalinist who slandered Trotsky and other exiles there during and after the Second World War (editor's note).

3. The state publishing trust (translator's note).

4. Chudin was a young revolutionary who had interceded with the authorities and obtained the release of some speculators. He was arrested and shot along with them by Dzerzhinsky. Cf. Serge, *Memoirs of a Revolutionary*, Oxford U.P., 1967, p.81; the figure of Arkadi Ismailov in *Conquered City* is based on him (English translation by Richard Greeman, London, 1978, pp.142–3, 148–51, 177) (editor's note).

5. Pavel Eliseyevich Shchegolev (1877–1931) was a literary historian who edited the journal *Byloe* along with Burtsev dealing with revolutionary history before the First World War. It resumed publication in 1917–26. He collaborated with Alexei Tolstoy in writing the play *The Conspiracy of the Empress* in the 1920s (editor's note).

6. Grigory Yefimovich Novykh (1872–1916), nicknamed 'Rasputin' (the debauchee) was an ininerant holy man who gained influence over the Empress Alexandra and direct access to court, which he abused to appoint his favourites to high office. Many were the stories about his sexual behaviour, which brought the regime into such disrepute that he was murdered by one of the aristocracy (editor's note).

7. Trotsky spent the period 1907–1914 based in Vienna, from where he reported on the Balkan Wars and wrote wrote articles on culture for the *Kievskaia Mysl* (*Kievan Thought*). Cf. Fritz Keller, 'Trotsky in Vienna', *Revolutionary History*, vol.vii, no.2, 1999, pp.49–52 (editor's note).

8. Serge married Liuba Russakova in 1919. Driven insane by political persecution, she died in a mental institution in France in 1985. Vlady Kibalchich (1921–), their son, is still alive and lives in Mexico (editor's note).

9. Boris Mikhailovich Kustodiev (1878–1927) was a Russian set designer, graphic artist and painter who developed a portrait genre in which the sitter was tied in with the interior or the landscape (editor's note).

10. Tolstoy's *Peter the First*, which was still incomplete at the time of his death, was serialised in Novy Mir between 1929 and 1945, and Tolstoy was awarded the Stalin Prize for it (English translation by Tatiana Shebunina, London, 1956). The screenplay appeared in 1935 (editor's note).

11. Ivan Tikhonovich Possoshkov (1652–1726) was a Russian economist, the author of *On Poverty and Wealth* (1724). He was imprisoned in the Peter-Paul Fortress after the death of Peter the Great (editor's note).

12. The Right Opposition was a group formed in the Communist Party in 1928 which supported the continuation of the N.E.P. and opposed the turn to forced collectivisation. Bukharin and Rykov were both defendents in the Trial of the 21, but Mikhail Pavlovich Efimov, known as Tomsky (1880–1936), the supposed head of the Soviet trade unions, committed suicide before he could be brought to trial along with them (editor's note).

13. The poet and diplomat Griboyedov is the hero of Tynyanov's *Death of Vazir Mukhtar*. *Lieutenant Kizhe* (1928)

was also written by him, and not Kaverin (English translation by Mirra Ginsberg in *Lieutenant Kizhe and Young Vitushishnikov*, 1990). Yemelyan Ivanovich Pugachev (1742–1775) was the leader of a major Cossack and peasant rebellion against Catherine the Great in 1773–75. François Dominique Toussaint L'Ouverture (1743–1803) led a great slave revolt in Haiti during the French Revolution (editor's note).

14. Nikolay Ivanovich Yezhov (1895–1940) was head of the N.K.V.D. at the height of the purges, often named the Yezhovschina after him. As such he prepared the trial of Hendrik Yagoda (1891–1938), his predecessor in office in 1988. Yezhov was himself hanged not much later (editor's note).

15. Pyotr P. Kriuchkov (1889–1938), Gorky's secretary, a member of the G.P.U., was accused of causing the death of Gorky and his son, and shot in 1938 (editor's note).

16. Maxim Gorky, 'If the Enemy Does Not Surrender – One Exterminates Him', *Izvestia*, 15 November 1930

17. Gorky's first wife, from whom he early separated (translator's note). Julia Kolberg-Gogua was Serge's cousin, and a friend of Stalin's wife. Ekaterina Pavlovna Peshkova had formerly been an S.R., and both worked with the Red Cross in Moscow helping political prisoners, among them Serge himself. Cf. *Memoirs of a Revolutionary*, Oxford U.P., 1975, pp.321–2; Susan Weissman, *Victor Serge: The Course is Set on Hope*, London, 2001, pp.165–8 (editor's note).

18. Abram Moysevich Ginzburg (1878–1931) had been a member of the Supreme Council of the Economy since 1922. Nikolay Nikolayovich Himmer, known as Sukhanov (1882–1940), was a major historian of the Russian Revolution, who edited *Novaya Zhizn* in 1917–18. Both were ex-Mensheviks arraigned in the so-called 'Menshevik Union Bureau' trial of 1931. Gorky wrote a letter to Yagoda from Sorrento approving of Sukhanov's arrest. The article referred to (n.16 above) concerns this trial (Israel Getzler, *Nikolai Sukhanov: Chronicler of the Russian Revolution*, Basingstoke, 2002, pp.161–2) (editor's note).

19. In May–July 1928 53 innocent engineers who had supported Smena Vekh were accused of sabotage in Shakhty and the Donbas coalfields, and 5 of them were shot (editor's note).

20. Pushkin's play *The Feast During the Plague* was one of his Little Tragedies written in 1830 (English translation by Antony Wood in *Mozart and Salieri: The Little Tragedies*, London, 1983) (editor's note).

21. The *Smenovekhovtsi* were those who agreed with the views of the magazine *Smena Vekh*, which argued that the Russia of the N.E.P. was on its way back to capitalism (editor's note).

22. Galina Yosifovna Serebriakova (1905–1980), who had been married to both Sokolnikov and Serebriakov, was sent to Siberia for twenty years, where she became a camp informer (editor's note).

23. Stalin closed down the Society of Old Bolsheviks in 1935, preparatory to murdering most of them in the purges (editor's note).

24. The boyars were the Russian nobility. In 1698 the old-style Russian soldiers called *Streltsy*, who were opposed to Peter's 'westernising' reforms, had rebelled against him, but were defeated, and Peter had over a thousand of them executed (editor's note).

25. The novel referred to is Alexei Tolstoy's *Khleb*, published in Moscow in 1937 (English translation *Bread* by S. Garry, London, 1938) (editor's note).

André Biely (Boris Nikolayevich Bugayev)[1]

The true greatness of the artist – very different from success and fame, which can be manufactured – consists above all of passion, expansiveness and radiance. Radiance means setting alight, a living inner flame that ascends ceaselessly, which ceaselessly pursues nourishment, discoveries, conquests, initiation, creation. This is necessarily revolutionary in the twilight of a pitiless and reactionary society.

These signs, which are so powerful that they sometimes overflow from the moral to the physical, and help to shape it, enable us to recognise the man of worth who cannot be forgotten, who leaves his mark on the world and bequeaths to us a work. The scale of this work will depend on the detailed circumstances of society and may be quite minimal if, for example, the creator has to struggle, as is normal, against the forces of social conservatism and is more or less suffocated by them. Biely's work is substantial, although he could never realise his full abilities and display his merits unreservedly. It was enough to meet him once, to encounter the amazing gaze of his blue eyes, never to forget him. I had the good fortune of knowing him in Petrograd, in Berlin, and at Dietskoye Selo at various turning points in the evolution of his thought. He was a poet above all, and a very great stylist, one of those foremost in the front rank – who completed the formation of the literary language on the eve of the Revolution, something which involves the coming to consciousness of a sensibility and a conception of the world. (Outdated today, certainly. There has been a breaking point in history. Ten days, and then ten years and more, have shaken the world. But are we not all toiling in order to become outdated? I mean so that humanity should make its way by leaving us behind, and even by going over our bodies and our minds?)

A poet above all, pursuing research into semantics, a musician, seeking to give words a sound which was pure, rich and precise. Even more, he was eager to understand in order to transform and to make fertile. Attaching by a myriad of links known to him alone every line of writing to the whole universe. When I saw him – strong features, gently moulded, wearing the black skullcap which he was never seen without – it made me think of a Renaissance humanist, but one liberated from the brutality of his time, and, as a result, rather out of place in our own ...; he possessed all the knowledge of the day without it having become a dead letter for him – it was still sensual and alive. He was a poet because for him the stars would never become mere numbers in a catalogue, even though he was fond of catalogues of stars. He was the son of mathematician, I believe, and a good mathematician himself, a product of the Moscow academic bourgeoisie which, raised at the end of the old regime lacking all faith in the future, was to form a whole constellation of exceptional men who were ripened in the pregnant atmosphere of the end of an old world and amid the germination of a new world still being born.

He followed winding paths, from the mysticism of Soloviev, whose disciple he was when he was very young, to Steiner's anthroposophy; from symbolism to the Revolution, already in 1905 and again in 1917, 1918, 1919 and until his death. He was one of those like Blok, Yesenin and Kluyev, who hailed a rebirth in the proletarian revolution. 'Russia, there is your bride. – Greet the portent of Spring.' – 'I know: a vast – and radiant – atmosphere – Come down on us all. – The burning torment of the century. – Go and put a halo around the forehead of all men.' He must have suffered greatly from the contradictions of the Revolution, from throwing himself headlong into it, feeling pain from its live embers, but without ever failing to recognise its essential meaning. After that, it was of little importance that he himself was not properly recognised. – He came to us from afar, from the depths of the old Russian culture, which belonged to east and west at the same time, which is not yet known and deciphered, which cannot be deciphered unless we make an appeal to it; by it he was drawn as by a magnet towards the total renewal of society.

Devoured at the age of fifty-three.

In a Moscow museum can be seen a powerful painting by Vrubel. The painter had given the god Pan human eyes full of concentrated light. Boris Nikolayevich had eyes like that. And what ardour there was in his voice, and what faith! It was entirely ours except for the form of words. (Forms of words have their importance; his were often very different from ours; this needs to be discussed; but not just now.) The imprint he leaves behind is deep, vast, pervasive, difficult to pin down, complex as he was himself.

He did not believe in death. We must admit that we are terribly defenceless in face of it. Men have always made great efforts to deny it by lying to themselves, a way of overcoming it which is not entirely illusory. We do not yet know how to respond to it, we are naked in its eyes, silent in face of the pain delivered by its scythe. Doubtless this is because we ourselves are incomplete: we are the mere rough sketches of consciousness, the defective instruments of a work that is scarcely started. When they have conferred, by the reorganisation of everything, a new value on life and on living beings, men will feel quite different and much less powerless in the face of death. But even at this boundary, there is no other hope. Biely knew it better than most of us.

(Born in 1880. Works, *Four Symphonies*, *Epic*; novels: *Petersburg*, *The Silver Dove*, *Moscow*; memoirs: *On the Border between Two Centuries*. 40 volumes.)

1.   Translated from *Europe*, 15 May, 1934, pp 114-16. (translator's note)

Part Three

Historians of the Revolution

L.D. Trotsky

L. Trotsky: Materials for a Biography of Lenin[1]

Lenin: Notes for a Biographer collected together by L. Trotsky in a remarkable little book which has recently appeared in Moscow includes in particular: (1) A portrait (practically complete in our opinion, but in any case of great value) going back to 1903 (in London, editing *Iskra* [*The Spark*] of Russian Social Democracy); (2) A series of studies, unequal in length and fragmentary, on the October Revolution, the Brest-Litovsk Peace, the dissolution of the Constituent Assembly[2] and the formation of the first proletarian government; (3) A study of Lenin as an orator, unique so it seems to me, in being penetrating and expressive; (4) a few pages from a pamphlet on Lenin and Wells which will be of great significance for readers who do not confine themselves to enjoying the humour in it: the contrast between the two men is really that between two cultures, one that is ending and the other that is being born.

It is essential to think of this book as the author himself introduces it: not as a completed work, or even as definitively sketched out, but as a collection of materials designed to be used for a biography of Lenin. It therefore emerges that once the gaps in it and their fragmentation are explained, there are really precious materials there. One gap draws our attention: the period which goes from 1903–4 to 1917, during which Lenin and Trotsky moved towards and away from each other on several occasions, is not explained in this book. That does not prevent us from hoping that Trotsky will devote some chapters to it in a later edition. The documentation supplied on the preparations for the October Revolution and about the background to the Brest-Litovsk negotiations is of prime importance, but does not lend itself either to an analysis or to a brief discussion. It evidently gave rise to lively polemics among the Russian militants.

Trotsky is one of the great writers in the Russian language today. His style, however, is neither that of a literary man nor of a 'brilliant' journalist – how misleading these adjectives are – it is essentially the elastic, taut, exact, muscular style of a revolutionary dialectician in possession of all the resources of his language. He needs this style and no other for a portrait of a man of whom it can be said that it was 'Marxism in human form, Marxism in action', the science, consciousness and energy of an exploited class rising to take over everything, in other words. This means that you cannot find in these materials for a biography either unimportant details, nor purely visual details; you see there the clearly marked out, proudly upright and living outline of a revolutionary leader; and little by little you come to understand how he came to be what he was.

The prime, absolute importance of the personality of Lenin, with whom thinking, day to day work, 'private life', relationships and activity became one, always going towards one sole aim, were such that even 'in discussions with others or in learning foreign languages ... he had only one goal before his eyes.'[3] This 'tenseness of striving towards his goal',[4] this monolithic unity can only be found in a Marxist revolutionary, since Marxism is at one and the same time organically inseparable theory and practice, thought and action, knowledge, will and doing.

What did the genius of Lenin consist of at the time of October 1917? *In a very accurate theoretical understanding of a social situation from the point of view of the proletariat, the forces in play, their antecedents and their possibilities; in understanding what alone is possible; in a concrete understanding of the means to do it (organisation); in an infallible will which comes from a lifetime's habit of not separating ideas from facts, nor the word from the thing itself.*

It was necessary to undertake the working class revolution in October 1917 because it was both possible and necessary at the time; it might no longer be so fifteen days later. Lenin's genius consisted of seeing this and, at the same time, of doing everything that had to be done. He had waited for that precise moment for nearly twenty five years.

For, as Trotsky reminds us on several occasions, we cannot separate the work done in October 1917 from that of the long years before then, or separate the revolution from the formation of the party designed by Lenin from 1903 onwards, the only one in the international Socialist movement, as *the means for the revolution* – he 'went abroad' – not as a leader in the general sense of the word, but as 'leader of the revolution, which he sensed and perceived was welling up ...'; he gave himself 'the practical aim of speeding the outbreak of the revolution and of securing its victory';[5] he said later (in 1910) 'The split of 1903' – which split the Menshevik and Bolshevik Social Democrats over the organisation of an illegal party – 'was in a way an anticipation' ...'[6]

It was indeed an anticipation of the taking of the Winter Palace and the Kremlin. To seize power it was first necessary to make 'the iron cohort', and separate the 'soft' from the 'hard'. Trotsky *shows* that between 1900 and 1903 Lenin formed himself as the man who would conquer and then die, his task done: 'the leap from illegality to the seizure of power on October 25, 1917 was enormous; but this was, so to say, outward, the shooting upward of a man who had already weighed and measured all it was possible to weigh and measure ...'[7]

Future revolutionaries will be formed more and more after this still unique pattern. Neither Cromwell nor Robespierre equal it. Too great a historic distance separates us from the former. The other was defeated. Both of them belonged to a class that is in no way ours. The proletariat does not have to imitate the bourgeoisie, even when it was really great; ; its role is to make changes in order to change society. The complete unity of Lenin's life and work reveals certain decisive advantages in the strength of the working class and of the greatest men of this class. They are new men; the party they forge is a powerful new reality.

But these essential truths can only be assimilated by militants through study and a whole patient labour of reeducation; they are often so much more difficult to grasp because the action of bourgeois democracy and culture incessantly leans towards dividing contemplative thought from productive labour and activity; and the political education of democracy tends to discredit the very name of the coalitions of base interests that make up the old parties. And the main importance for the Communist movement of books devoted to Lenin is that at the moment they are the only ones to provide us with more than a theoretical training, a living example.

Notes

1. Translated from *Bulletin Communiste*, 10 October 1924 (translator's note).
2. The Constituent Assembly convened to draw up a constitution for Russia met after the Bolshevik seizure of power on 18 January 1918. It was dissolved the day after (translator's note).
3. English translation by Tamara Deutscher, *Lenin: Notes for a Biographer*, New York, 1971, p.47 (translator's note).
4. Op. cit., n.3 above, p. 169 (translator's note).
5. Op. cit., pp.68–9 (translator's note).
6. V. I. Lenin, as quoted by Trotsky, op. cit., p.30 (translator's note).
7. Op. cit., p.31 (translator's note).

A portrait of Lenin by Trotsky[1]

This article, which belongs among the *Chronicles of Intellectual Life in Russia*, was written at the end of last summer. Since then, following the appearance of an important preface to the volume of his *Collected Works* relating to the year 1917,[2] the political work and activity of L.D. Trotsky have been subjected by the Central Committee of the Russian Communist Party and the leading organisations of the Communist International to the most severe criticism.[3] The reader who wishes to form a firmly based opinion about this important polemic will find abundant documentation in the *Cahiers du Bolchevisme* and *International Press Correspondence*.[4] We can only mention here the writings of Stalin, Zinoviev, Kamenev, Molotov, Bukharin, Rykov and Kolarov.[5]

What no one has denied, as far as we know, is the general accuracy and vigour of the portrait of Lenin that Trotsky traces. And that is what, above all in our eyes, makes up the value of this book: all considerations of history and doctrine apart – and history is never over and done with and the Bolshevik Party and the International have pronounced on doctrine as is their historic role, it remains that here is one of the most living, fascinating and truest of the portraits of Lenin that we may have. – **V. S.**

★　★　★　★　★

The reasons for which revolutionary Russia founded a Lenin Institute are, even if only studied superficially, very much opposed to the personality cult peculiar to the individualistic mentality of the bourgeoisie. And the numerous studies devoted to Lenin in recent Russian literature by Krupskaya, Stalin, Zinoviev, Yaroslavsky,[6] Trotsky and Maxim Gorky provide an extraordinarily valuable contribution to the international workers' movement as much as to our intellectual life, since the life of Lenin offers a unique historical and outstanding example of the *strength of unity* (individual life, collective life, thought, word and action, *not as an assembly, but as a whole*), by which the proletariat will triumph. Bourgeois society thrives on the divorce between thought and action; its thinkers almost exclusively have as their mission providing an 'educated' public with intellectual stimulation without any real relationship with work and life, and hence inoffensive. The genius of the great gravediggers of this society has resolved this contradiction. Marx's thinking was action, since it desired 'no longer to understand the world, but to change it'. Lenin's thinking was changing the world, from the day when the London émigré gave birth to the *new reality*, the Bolshevik Party, a collective entity in which theory and practice make up one and the same thing, to 25 October 1917, to Brest-Litovsk and until the N.E.P., the alliance with the countryside. In this sense Lenin was truly a new man, just as the party he created was profoundly new, very different from the old parties in which it was a necessary tradition to substitute talk for action.

Lenin was at times as solid as a rock, and at others as flexible as steel, as we can see with great clarity in *Lenin: Notes for a Biographer* put out by Trotsky.[7] The great definitive book on *The Life of Lenin* remains to be written. Trotsky only claims in these 168 pages to be providing fragmentary materials, which need to be taken up again and completed on a thousand points. Several chapters, it seems to me, are well-nigh completed (Lenin editing the old *Iskra*, London, 1903).[8] Others do no more than point to problems and mark out subjects for future studies, and, obviously, heated arguments as well. The long period that stretches from 1903–1904 to 1917, during which strong disagreements developed between the founder of the Bolshevik Party and the one destined to become one of the greatest fighters in the decisive days of the Revolution is for the time being passed over in silence.

I will not attempt to subject these *Notes for a Biographer* to criticism. To do that you would need the competence of an old Russian veteran. Nor do I intend to summarise the book. Trotsky is an exceptionally wise observer, who expresses himself elegantly in dialectical language. No one can show better than he, in words that are hardly the norm in lyrical language, the great poetry of the Revolution to which he has devoted a remarkable page in his essays on literature.[9] In this book he succeeds in showing us Lenin as living, simple and natural, but raised to the height of his stature after 1903. The leader of 1917–18 and the hero of today were already contained in the London émigré. Insofar as the internal mechanism of such a destiny can be understood, we understand it here.

One autumn morning in 1902 Trotsky, who had escaped from Verkholensk (Siberia) and arrived in London, knocked on the door of Vladimir Ilyich Lenin, who was already one of the leaders of the youthful Russian Social Democracy. Lenin was then collaborating in editing *The Spark* (*Iskra*) along with Plekhanov, who was to die a patriot in Finland (1918)[10] and Martov, who was to be one of the stalwarts of Menshevism until his death (1923). The extent to which Lenin was already 'himself', i.e. the embodiment of the proletariat's consciousness and will, can be seen from this significant detail taken from old conversations:

> The same morning, or perhaps the next day, I went for a long walk with Vladimir Ilyich. He showed me Westminster (from outside) and some other architectural landmarks. I do not remember how he actually said it, but the inflection in his voice meant: That's their famous Westminster. 'Their' meant, of course, not the one belonging to the English, but belonging to the enemy. This inflexion in Lenin's voice, seemingly accidental, was organically his own; it was this tone of voice that always made its appearance when Lenin spoke about some cultural treasures or new achievements, about the arrangements of the British Museum, about the wealth of information contained in *The Times*, and also, many years later, about German artillery or French air force. *They know, they have got, they made it, they achieved* – yes, but what foes they are! In his eyes the shadow of the exploiting classes lay over the whole human culture, and this shadow was always as visible to him as daylight.[11]

We should compare this Lenin with a Jaurès, to whom there was nothing *alien* in the culture of France and Europe, bourgeois France and Europe, whose language and ideas, like the proud stones of luxury hotels, bore the mark of the civilisation of property owners. Did not Jaurès' supreme eloquence take in the entirety of the oratorical culture of bourgeois France? And were not the leaders of the 'powerful' Social Democracy in Germany in 1914 used to identifying themselves with the glory of the Empire, *without even thinking about it*? Did they not talk about 'our Germany' in the same way as Sembat[12] was to talk of 'our Latin culture' during the War? The leading spirits of Socialism in those days (the whole range of whom – Millerand,[13] Ebert, Mussolini, MacDonald and Léon Blum – the bourgeoisie was grateful to have at its disposal after the War) were oblivious of the feeling of living as enemies, *in the camp of the enemy*. Their inner life was not that of proletarians weighed down by the whole heavy machine of the bosses and the state. The contradiction between their deepest thinking, identical with that of the bourgeoisie's politicians, and their talk as spokesmen for the working class contained the germs of all their betrayals. Lenin, exiled in London, for whom 'the shadow of the expoiting classes lay over the whole human culture', already had the spirit of the founder of the dictatorship of the proletariat. The remark that Trotsky recalls Plekhanov making about Lenin at the time of the Second Congress of the Russian Social Democracy (1903), that 'from such stuff Robespierres are made' is all too true, 'and even something much greater', exclaims Trotsky.[14] For it is objectively far greater to ensure the life of a social revolution than to die stoically and desperately one morning in Thermidor.

Perhaps this is an opportunity for refuting a basically reactionary legend: that of Lenin's asceticism. Zinoviev and Krupskaya have already applied themselves to denying it.[15] It is dangerous because because it attempts to model the type of new proletarian revolutionary on the basis of the social reformers of the past. Ilyich resembled neither Calvin,[16] nor the straightlaced puritan Robespierre, wholly obsessed with reason and abstract virtue. The real revolutionary is a far more complete human being than his predecessors. In a fresh chapter 'The True and the False', which he added to his book from *Pravda* at the beginning of October, Trotsky subjects this point of view sketched out in Maxim Gorky's portrait of Lenin to a severe criticism.[17] And he describes Lenin's delight in life, and his readiness for laughter – as noticed by everyone, even if they only saw him in meetings – his attentive love for children, and his appetite for relaxation. Gorky had written '... the wonderful man who felt the need to sacrifice himself, to offer himself as the victim of hostility and hatred in order to bring about the labor of love and beauty'. Trotsky takes up these words: '*To offer himself as a victim ... No, this is false, untrue, unbearably false! It jars on one's ears like a screw scraping on a glass. Lenin did not sacrifice himself. On the contrary, he lived a full life, a wonderfully abundant life, developing, expanding his whole personality, serving a cause which he himself freely chose ...*'[18]

Lenin's *predestination* is what comes out most clearly in the portrait dated by Trotsky in 1903. You must excuse me if I make use of an old Calvinist word. All the words we use bear the stamp of the development of capitalist culture, and when we seek to make them express the thinking of a new class that has not yet won its right to culture by struggle, a secret force reveals itself in them, which tends to corrupt their very meaning.

'There is an entire mythology in language,' said Nietzsche, who was himself one of its greatest victims. Lenin's predestination springs from the fact that he was the only one at the time, in the Russian revolutionary movement and the Socialist International, to understand correctly, from a class point of view, how the period was developing, and to subordinate himself completely, at all times in his life, to the double realism of commitment to the proletariat. Trotsky explains the unity of Lenin's personality by the *'tenseness of striving towards his goal'.*[19]

> Lenin went abroad neither as a Marxist 'generally speaking', nor in order to devote himself to some 'general' literary-revolutionary work ... he came as a potential leader, as the leader of the revolution which he sensed and preceived was welling up. He came in order to build, in the shortest possible time, an ideological base and organizational framework for that revolution. When I spoke about Lenin's tense concentration on his goal – concentration which was both passionate and disciplined – I did not see it as an effort to achieve a 'final triumph' – no, that would have been too vague and meaningless – but I saw it as a concrete, direct, immediate work toward the practical aim of the outbreak of the revolution and of securing its victory.[20]

> '... he would make use of any circumstance and disregard all formalities in straining toward his goal – this was indeed Lenin the leader' (p.19[21]).

> '... this most powerful 'engineer of revolution', had only one goal before his eyes, and toward this final goal he was pressing, whether in politics or in his theoretical or philosophical studies, in discussions with others or in learning foreign languages. His was perhaps the most determined utilitarianism ever produced in the laboratory of history'.[22]

In his London reminiscences Trotsky places the delicate silhouette of Martov at the side of Lenin. *'The elaborate subtlety of Martov's ideas made Lenin anxiously shake his head ... Lenin was hard, Martov soft. And they both knew it. Lenin would glance at Martov, whom he highly esteemed, with a critical and somewhat suspicious look; and Martov, feeling this glance, grew uneasy, and his thin shoulders would twitch nervously'.*[23] I remember the striking contrast between these two men, the one delicate, graceful, slender and fragile, with a high and straight forehead, a weak chin, poor teeth, and a twisted, nervous, gentle, searching and intelligent expression, but tinged with despair – the sad end of a broken nonentity. Ever since I knew Martov I understood that this gentle and flabby intellectual, so ingenious, scrupulous, honest and indecisive, was to be the inevitable loser in his duel with Lenin. Lenin first appeared to me crossing the Kremlin courtyard with giant strides with thick-set shoulders, a vigorous heavy head, and when speaking on a platform a sharply astute, ironic and decisive expression, or rather a curt gesture, ready with both hands to manipulate material arguments concretely and freely ... He, with his *permanent tenseness towards his goal*, was fashioned from head to toe to carry off success.

The superficial observer over whom modern bourgeois ideas hold sway might gather from this Lenin's *subjective power*, an immense will allied with genius ... No doubt, but without denying the importance of that mysterious x-factor which is the basis of individual superiority, there is little difficulty in disposing of that part of the mystery. The flame of revolutionary subjectivity was not the property of Lenin alone in the Russian Revolution. A number of men, of whom there were many, who were very capable of combining knowledge with strong intellect, obviously had it to the same extent as he did. All who lived in Russia during the great years of 1917–1921 encountered, notably among the Revolution's dissidents, the Left Socialist Revolutionaries and the Anarchists, great subjective revolutionaries.[24] So how did it come about that out of so many ardently revolutionary temperaments it was Lenin's alone – and that of the Bolshevik Party – that showed itself capable of winning, enduring, and living? Because it happened to be there? – no: because it formed an indissoluble unity with a true insight into what was realistic and possible. It was insight allied with determination. But the word 'allied' must here be understood as expressing the idea of a metallic alloy fusing two metals completely together to make them a thousand times more resistant. Marxist practice is only the external, visible expression of theory; and theory is only the precise articulation of existing social reality and what it is possible to get from it. Lenin's energy and that of his party was able to be applied by an extremely accurate understanding of the facts.

In the chapter dealing with the preparations for October 1917 Trotsky shows how Lenin, perceiving *perhaps the unique moment* in which the revolution was possible, fearing that it might escape, applied himself passionately to goading on his party. 'The hour has come!' Never has the unity between understanding the world and changing it appeared more clearly than in this signal of a hand raised:

> Had we not seized power in October, we would not have seized it at all. Before October our strength lay precisely in the fact that the masses were pouring into our party because they believed that it would do what others had failed to do. If the working classes had detected in us the slightest sign of vacillation, of hesitation, or of a divergence between our words and our deeds, within two or three months the tide would have ebbed away, just as it ebbed away from the S.R.'s and the Mensheviks. The bourgeoisie would have obtained a respite ... the proletarian upheaval would have been postponed indefinitely. Lenin understood, sensed, and felt this: hence his anxiety and fear, his distrust, and his frantic pressure saved the revolution (p.66[25]).

Two historical experiences seem to have very much confirmed this reasoning: the factory occupations in Italy (1919) and the offensive called off by the German Communist Party (1923). In both cases, insofar as we can judge after defeats, there was a possibility of seizing power – or of a serious attempt at seizing power – by the workers. The opportunity missed will no doubt come up again; but it is nonetheless true that the Revolution has been put back for an indefinite period.

★　　★　　★　　★　　★

Once the Soviet republic had been set up, it was necessary repeatedly, at dangerous turning points, to avoid an almost inevitable overthrow. The Red October was not the most difficult step. The fate of the proletarian state, still very shaky, held on by only a thread when the Brest-Litovsk negotiations were going on. It was similarly the case later in 1919 when Denikin advanced on Tula and Yudenich on Petrograd, and finally at the time of the Kronstadt revolt, of which the N.E.P. was to a certain extent a direct consequence. Lenin saw clearly and correctly on all these occasions; he knew how to say exactly how to make a sudden turn, and in which direction. (Not because he was by nature free from making mistakes; but even his mistakes remained those of a realist following the direction of history, so it came about that events corrected them, all the more so because he knew how to admit them boldly, as opposed to making the party and the proletariat suffer the dire consequences, which is the habit with even the more farsighted of the statesmen of the bourgeoisie. The example of M. Cuno who, by the hostilities in the Ruhr, led capitalist Germany to the brink of revolution can serve as a witness to this.[26]

Trotsky's book contains some very striking pages about the time of Brest-Litovsk. One of the most remarkable appears to me to be that where he describes the episode about the 'Uralo-Kuznetsk Republic'.

> And if the Germans maintain their offensive? And if they march on Moscow?
>
> Then we shall withdraw further East, to the Urals (replied Lenin) ... The Kuznetsk basin is rich in coal. We shall set up a Uralo-Kuznetsk Republic based on the regional industry and the Kuznetsk coal, and supported by the proletariat of the Urals and by as many workers as we can move with us from Moscow and Petrograd. We shall hold out. If need be, we shall retreat even deeper, beyond the Urals. We may reach Kamchatka, but we shall hold out. The international situation will be changing a dozen times; from the redoubt of our Uralo-Kuznetsk republic, we shall spread out again, and we shall return to Moscow and Petersburg. But if now we senselessly involve ourselves in a revolutionary war, if we let the elite of our working class and our party perish, then, of course, we shall return nowhere ...'
>
> Lenin was by no means joking; true to himself, he was analysing the situation through to its very end, to its worst possibilities. To him the concept of the Uralo-Kuznetsk republic was absolutely necessary in order to strengthen his own – and other peoples' – conviction that all was not lost and that there was no room, that there could be no room, for the strategy of despair'.[27]

Never to despair, but basically to hold on to the last resources in order to keep going, and an utter contempt for phrases and gestures for their own sake.

The man who was prepared to hold on 'as far as Kamchatka' had no intention of going on about a 'revolutionary war' whose pointless heroism had seduced the Revolution's romantics. He signed the infamous peace (*pokhabny mir*) of Brest-Litovsk because *'at the moment there is nothing more important in the world than our revolution'*.[28] And as far as he was concerned, this rested on a realistic feel for the international situation. Lenin was waiting in Smolny for the break up of the structure of the victorious Central Powers, and looking forward to the splintering of the great Allied states; the German Revolution of 1918 and the demobilisation crisis among the Allies in 1919 showed that he saw correctly.[29]

★   ★   ★   ★   ★

... Of all the peoples in Europe it is the English who pride themselves on being the most realistic and practical. We will in no wise contradict them. The Englishman is a manufacturer, a sailor, a conqueror, a trader, and a coloniser. The English bourgeoisie is the oldest of all. English democracy is the most experienced and the most counter-revolutionary (from William Pitt to Churchill-Curzon-MacDonald-Chamberlain[30]). Her realistic policy was crowned by the defeat of her German competitor; but she must have a secret weakness, since after her striking military and financial victory the British Empire appears to be so shaken today (internal political crisis, economic detachment of the dominions); and it has since had to write off the debts of a few adventures that were hardly expected to increase its prestige: the intervention in Russia, the Irish Civil War, the Greek campaign in Asia Minor, and the pathetic misadventures in Arabia.[31] The solution to this enigma is that the realism of the bourgeoisie, however far-sighted it may be, is that of a class in decline. It is not dialectical. Not being able to understand the contradictions inherent in the capitalist system, whose expression it is, it continues to judge the events of an imperialist epoch ravaged by the crises resulting from the War with the common sense and reasoning dating from a time when capitalism was at its height. It is the well known example of the honest tradesman who in a time of economic chaos and inflation is inclined to hold on to his business habits from before the War. In the end it means bankruptcy. Trotsky supplies an ironical formula for the contrast between proletarian (dialectical) realism and the 'positive', mummified, Pharisaical bourgeois (or petty bourgeois, if you like) realism, hampered by a fatal blindness in some pages he devotes to Wells and Lenin. This most imaginative (!) of great British writers, and a Socialist to boot, came in 1920 during a winter of civil war and famine to visit 'the Dreamer in the Kremlin' (*sic*; this 'Dreamer' was in fact about to cross off Thermidor from the calendar of the Russian Revolution) and tell him: 'I believe that through a vast sustained educational campaign the existing capitalist system could be civilised into a Collectivised world system.'

Trotsky adds: 'Wells does not make it clear, however, who is going to introduce this 'vast sustained educational campaign' and who will be subjected to it: Are we to suppose that English "milords" with "domed" heads will exercise it over the English proletariat, or, on the contrary, that the English proletariat will subject 'milords" heads to this education?[32] '*What a petit bourgeois! What a Philistine!' he kept repeating* (after his conversation with Wells), *raising both his arms, laughing and sighing in a way characteristic of him when he felt ashamed for another man.'*[33] We can easily understand the regret and contempt, mingled with a certain shame for the human spirit, that the greatest of the founders of the new realism had to suffer at seeing the whole of bourgeois culture flourishing among the best intentioned people in their blissfully satisfying stupidity ...

Victor Serge

Notes

1. Translated from *Clarté* no.75, 1925, pp.255–8 (translator's note).
2. In the autumn of 1924 the state publishers were preparing to issue volume iii, part i of Trotsky's *Sochinenya* (*Collected Works*) covering 'From February to October' (1917) in a print run of 5,000 copies. Since they had taken the initiative in promoting the Lenin cult against him, Trotsky took the opportunity of writing a preface emphasising the equivocal role played by Zinoviev and Kamenev during the Russian Revolution, drawing parallels with the Comintern's mishandling of the events in Germany in 1923. This preface, generally known as *The Lessons of October*, had the effect of renewing the struggle for power in Russia after the death of Lenin. The text itself can be consulted in *The Essential Trotsky*, London, 1963, pp.113–77, or *The Challenge of the Left Opposition, 1923–25*, New York, 1975, pp.199–258 (translator's note).
3. A plenary meeting of the Central Committee of the Russian Communist Party held in Moscow (January 17–20, 1925) condemned Trotsky's preface for reopening the party conflict ('Resolution on Comrade Trotsky's Actions', *Against Trotskyism*, Moscow, 1972, pp.246–55). This was ratified at the 5th Plenum of the Executive Committee of the Comintern on 21 March–6 April 1925 (translator's note).
4. *Cahiers du Bolchevisme* was the theoretical magazine of the French Communist Party, and *International Press Correspondence* (often known as *Inprecorr*) was the weekly publication of the Comintern (translator's note).

5. These replies were collected together and published in a large volume with a preface by Rykov entitled *Za leninizm* (Moscow, January 1925). The articles by Stalin, Zinoviev and Kamenev and the resolution of the C.P.S.U. condemning Trotsky were republished in English by the C.P.G.B. in a book entitled *The Errors of Trotskyism* (London, May 1925, pp.148–316, 378–92). Vyacheslav Scriabin, known as Molotov (1890–1986), a relative of the famous composer, was one of Stalin's oldest and closest associates. Vassil Kolarov (1877–1950) was one of the Comintern's most important leaders, until he was forced to make a self-criticism for the failure of the 1923 coup in Bulgaria (translator's note).

6. Nadezhda Krupskaya (1869–1939) was Lenin's widow. She later produced more extensive reminiscences (*Memories of Lenin*, English edition, London, 1930). Emelyan Yaroslavsky (1878–1943) was one of Trotsky's most prominent opponents at this time (translator's note).

7. The French translation has just appeared in the *Librairie du Travail* series (author's note). The subtitle of Trotsky's work, *Materialy dlya biografa* would be better translated as 'Materials for a Biographer', but we have quoted it throughout in the standard English edition, *Lenin: Notes for a Biographer*, translated by Tamara Deutscher and introduced by Bertram D. Wolfe, New York, 1971 (translator's note).

8. Chapter i, 'Lenin and the Old Iskra', op cit., n.7 above, pp.29–71 (translator's note).

9. i.e. L. D. Trotsky, *Literature and Revolution*, Ann Arbor, Michigan, 1960, or Redwords, 1991 (translator's note).

10. George Valentinovich Plekhanov (1856–1918) was the pioneer of Russian Marxism, and founder of its first working class organisation, the League for the Emancipation of Labour, but he opposed the Russian Revolution in 1917 (translator's note).

11. Op. cit, n.7 above, p.34 (translator's note).

12. Marcel Sembat (1869–1922) was a leader of the French Socialist Party who joined the government during the First World War (translator's note).

13. Alexandre Millerand (1859–1943) was notorious for being the first French Socialist to sit in a bourgeois cabinet. Friedrich Ebert (1871–1925) was joint chairman of the German Social Democracy during the First World War, which he supported enthusiastically, and later first President of the Weimar Republic. Benito Mussolini (1883–1945) had been a left-talking Socialist before the war, but seized power as the first Fascist dictator four years after it. James Ramsay MacDonald (1866–1937) was an early leader of the ILP and the Labour Party. He was Prime Minister in the first Labour government of 1924. Léon Blum (1872–1950) became leader of the French Socialist Party after the War and supported the left bloc that placed Herriot in power in 1924 (translator's note).

14. Op. cit, n.7 above, p.69. Maximilien Robespierre (1750–1794) was the Jacobin leader of the French Revolution at the height of the Terror (translator's note).

15. Zinoviev's *Leninizm. Vvedenie v izuchenie leninizma* was published in Leningrad in 1925 (translator's note).

16. Jean Calvin (1509–1564), who taught the theory of predestination, was an austere religious reformer who ran the city of Geneva along the lines of a police state (translator's note).

17. *Pravda*, 7 October 1924: op cit., n.7 above, pp.165–84 (translator's note).

18. Op. cit., n.7 above, p.174 (translator's note).

19. Op. cit., n.7 above, p.169 (translator's note).

20. Op. cit., n.7 above, pp.68–9 (translator's note).

21. Op. cit., n.7 above, p.46 (translator's note).

22. Op, cit., n.7 above, p.47 (translator's note).

23. Op. cit., n.7 above, p.48 (translator's note).

24. With an atrocious irony, which very much shows the importance of a *correct teaching*, circumstances often made them in practice into objective counter-revolutionaries, who had to be fought, and even imprisoned ... (author's note).[25] Op. cit., n.7 above, p.88 (translator's note).

26. The mistakes of a good realistic policy – in other words one inspired by an exact understanding of the social process and which goes along with history – can be corrected. Those of a policy that is inspired by a false

concept or which go against the flow of history cannot be repaired, such as when Émile Ollivier 'light-heartedly' declared war on Germany in 1870. Alternatively a better example could be quoted to me: Napoleon's blindness when in his campaigns in Russia and Spain he did not take account of the forces similar to those which, organised in his own armies, had given him his victories, those of the national uprisings of the peoples. The Napoleonic armies had the advantage over all the armies of the states of the semi-feudal ancien regime of encompassing a nation in arms (author's note). By encouraging the general strike against the French occupation of the Ruhr in 1923, Cuno brought about hyper-inflation in Germany and exposed the government to uprisings from both the right and the left. Émile Ollivier (1825–1913) was a republican politician who became a Bonapartist, and was head of the government of Napoleon III that declared war on Prussia in 1870, which France lost disastrously. Napoleon's invasion of Russia in 1812 met with stiff resistance, and he was forced to withdraw in weather conditions that inflicted substantial casualties upon his army. His invasion of Spain in 1808 met with scant resistance from the government, but during the Peninsular War that dragged on until 1814 Spanish guerrillas were a constant drain upon his resources and manpower (translator's note).

27. Op. cit., n.7 above, pp.108–9 (translator's note).
28. Op. cit., n.7 above, p.100. *Pokhabny mir* is a colloquial term meaning 'obscene peace'. By signing the treaty of Brest-Litovsk with Germany in March 1918 Russia was obliged to give up Latvia, Lithuania, Estonia, Poland, the Ukraine and Georgia, losing much of its industry and the best of its agricultural land. The Left SR.s, who wished to carry on a revolutionary war against the Germans, split from the government and began to make terrorist attacks upon it. There was also a deep division within the Bolshevik Party, whose Left also wished to continue the war. Cf. Ronald I. Kowalski, *The Bolshevik Party in Conflict*, Pittsburg U.P., 1991 (translator's note).
29. The mutinies in the bases of the High Seas Fleet at Kiel and Wilhelmshaven in the autumn of 1918 brought an end to Germany's participation in the First World War. For the mutinies caused by the delay in demobilising the Allied armies at the end of the War, cf. *Revolutionary History*, vol.viii, no.2, 2002, pp.115–52 (translator's note).
30. William Pitt, the Younger (1759–1806)) was the Tory Prime Minister in 1783–1801 and 1804–6 who financed and organised the states fighting against the French Revolution and Napoleon. Winston Spencer Churchill (1876–1965) was responsible for orchestrating the similar attacks of the foreign interventionists against the Bolsheviks during the Russian Civil War (1918–22).
31. The troops landed by the British government at Murmansk and Archangel in 1918 were obliged to withdraw, and further support provided to the White armies during the Russian Civil War also came to nothing. Britain was forced to concede independence to most of Ireland in 1921. British support for the attack on Anatolia did not prevent Kemal Ataturk from defeating the Greeks at the Battle of the Sakarya River and advancing on the British forces blocking the Dardanelles at Chanak. This so discredited Lloyd George's government that he fell from power in 1922. In an attempt to protect the emir of Jordan British troops entered the Hejaz, but the Wahhabis marched in in 1924 and added it to the kingdom of Ibn Saud (translator's note).
32. Op. cit., n.7 above, p.161 (translator's note).
33. Op. cit., n.7 above, p.156 (translator's note).

The Memoir Writers of the Revolution[1]

It would be possible to make some fine books of revolutionary history and education simply by selecting among the notes, memories and memoirs of the Russian militants. The obvious usefulness of this literature which one day historians will study line by line has been well understood in the USSR. For some years several periodicals have been collecting these documents together. *The Historical Commission of the Communist Party (Ispart)* has published a great number of them in its magazine *The Proletarian Revolution*. It is a precious documentation. Psychology, politics and sociology will here find fruitful material for study. The artist and novelist will here find the wherewithal to recreate in strong works one of the decisive turns accomplished by humanity. The revolutionary worker will here become acquainted with the first of his brothers to have succeeded. These men were truly great, lifted above themselves by their understanding of what they intended to do, and by the events themselves; and great also in the suffering they underwent, the energy they showed, their courage, their enthusiasm, their joy in living, their joy in winning, and their joy in changing the world ...

It is a literature where inexactitudes no doubt abound, in the context of ascertained truth. Fighters engaged in mass activity are surely not able to think about how they will then be reconstructing the phases of it with scientific precision (which obviously does not exist in the history of social change). The value of their reminiscences lies above all in the sincerity with which they are expressed, and how exact an impression they convey, as well as in revealing significant details erased by time. Without details, there is no longer any *living* history.

The writers of these memoirs are not as a rule acquainted with the art of writing ... which hardly matters to us! They have experienced, acted and thought so well! It so happens that pages signed by unknown names nonetheless have an astonishing sharpness that comes to them, not from art, but from life. The memoirs about the October Revolution that are the most well known, best written and best documented are those of Shliapnikov, Trotsky, Antonov-Ovseyenko, Larissa Reissner (*The Front*), Dybenko (*The Mutineers*) and

Mstislavsky (*Five Days*).[2] The only work of this type as far as I know that has been translated into French is John Reed's *Ten Days that Shook the World*,[3] a beautiful book, moreover. But there additionally exist in the Russian language hundreds of autobiographical accounts which we owe to valuable revolutionaries, known and unknown. The picture they provide of the Revolution is magnificent.

I have in front of me a volume of these memoirs devoted to the uprising of October 1917. How we perceive from it the heavings of the anonymous mass which was the flesh, the blood and the strength of the Revolution! I cannot resist the temptation to reproduce a few extracts from it here.

From V. Bonch-Bruyevich (*Memoirs*)[4] comes this episode, of no historical importance, but very revealing about the strong moral discipline of the Red Guards trained in the factories:

> We are only allowing in Communist and Left SR workers. They are chosen by the factory, the district gives its approval, and then the St Petersburg Committee. A few rejections took place, one man being judged too young; I remember one comrade who was rejected for falling asleep. On one occasion I found my comrades very dejected: 'now what terrible thing has happened', I thought to myself. They pointed to a young lad, a very devoted boy, and told me that it was necessary to shoot him. He had scrounged a bottle of liquor in a cellar while at work. He explained, genuinely sorry, that his father had induced him to do it. Their sense of discipline was such that his comrades wanted to shoot him ... They finally agreed, when I asked them, to confine him to my strict surveillance, which saved his life.

I. Flerovsky (*Kronstadt During the October Revolution*)[5] describes a number of details which deserve to be known about how the sailors took part in the events; it is a story which, at times, the sense of collective action rises to the most sound and human level of pathos. On the eve of the uprising a meeting of the crews took place. There were final speeches to rouse the men to arms!

Flerovsky writes: 'when I was in the presence of thousands of attentive faces, when I saw the mass of eyes fixed on me, something irresistible and very frightening arose within me. My throat closed up to begin with, then a shiver went all the way through my body. I felt as never before the links that bound me to that mass of faces and eyes. I wanted, not to speak, but to throw myself into it, to feel the multiple force of the proletarian revolution, a great dream on the point of becoming a reality. I could only with great difficulty pronounce a few words':

> 'Comrades, exceptional events are coming to fruition in the history of the world and of our country. We are going to make the social revolution. We are going to defeat, gun in hand, the power of capital. The immense happiness, never to be forgotten, of making the dream of the oppressed become a reality, happened to us ...
>
> Five years have passed, and the picture of the first minutes of the meeting that preceeded the uprising is still alive before my eyes. I doubt if any of those who took part have forgotten it. There were neither applause, nor shouts, nor exclamations, but warm embraces, demonstrative handshakes, tears on weather beaten energetic faces, and shining eyes ...'

These are such pages as to make us love the revolutionary struggle, by transmitting across space and time that great liberatory enthusiasm without which men will run along in the old ruts indefinitely ...

Podvoisky (*Memoirs*[6]), who led the assault on the Winter Palace on 25 October, gives us a lively account of it. There is Lenin, jumping with impatience in Smolny, with his ears open, straining for the sound of the guns. There are the sailors, on a gray square around a brazier, blaming the delay and the 'diplomacy' of the leaders. This palace, with its blacked-out windows, behind which a dozen disconsolate pale gentlemen were discussing, was the final obstacle to be removed for power to belong to the Soviets! When the signal was finally given the assault was a rush. Enthusiasm grew with the force of a tempest.

A few grenades went off. Once in the corridors of the Palace all hesitation ceased ... In spite of machine gun bursts, sailors, Red Guards and soldiers flung themselves over the barricades, overturned the Palace defenders, and rushed in there. The court was occupied ... then the stairways ... corps after corps engaged on the steps ... Terror seized hold of the cadets ... The government's defenders were overthrown ... The flood reached the third floor. The cadets threw down their weapons. The flood of sailors, Red Guards and soldiers swept past them.

Where are the guilty men? Closed doors are forced open. Here is the flood in front of a door guarded by cadets petrified with fear:

'Is the government here?'
    'The sentries' bayonets are lowered. 'Down with your weapons!' The mass flows into the room. Antonov is with them. What was once called the Provisional Government is there, almost physically dead, wrapped as in a shroud with mortal fear of the mass ...'

... Until 1917 the proletarians had always – and everywhere – been defeated. Those in Russia today have a literature and an entire history of the winners, in which the feeling of working class power is unfolded, an inspiring literature that ought to be spread worldwide.

Victor Serge   Leningrad, 19 November 1926

Notes

1. Translated from *L'Humanité*, 19 December, 1926 (translator's note).
2. Alexander Gavrilovich Shliapnikov (1887–1937) had been a Bolshevik since 1903, and imprisoned for two years after the revolution of 1905. He acted as liaison between the Bolsheviks inside the country and those abroad, returning in 1917 as a member of the St. Petersburg Party Committee. As the founder of the Workers' Opposition, and then a supporter of the Left, he was killed in the purges. The 2 volumes of his *On the Eve of 1917* came out in Moscow in 1923 (English translation by Richard Chappell, London, 1982). The reference to Trotsky is probably to *The History of the Russian Revolution to Brest-Litovsk*, Moscow 1918, of which an English translation can be consulted in *The Essential Trotsky* (London, 1963, pp,.21–111). Vladimir Alexandrovich Antonov-Ovseyenko (1884–1938) was a supporter of Trotsky who led the assault on the Winter Palace in 1917, later served as Consul-General in Catalonia during the Spanish Civil War, and was recalled and purged by Stalin. His *The Building of the Red Army in the Revolution* was published in Moscow in 1923. Pavel Yefimovich Dybenko (1889–1938) was a sailor who played an important part in the agitation in the Baltic fleet, and was killed by Stalin after the secret trial of the generals. *The Mutineers* was published in Moscow in 1919 (translator's note).
3. John Reed (1887–1920) was an American journalist and founder member of the American Communist Party, who died of typhus in Moscow on his return from Baku. His book appeared with a recommendation from Lenin that it be translated into all languages (original English edition 1926, reprinted on several occasions, e.g. Harmondsworth, 1974) (translator's note).
4. Vladimir Dmitriyevich Bonch-Bruyevich (1873–1955) was a Bolshevik almost from the beginning, who organised the circulation of the party's literature. His *Ot iyulya do oktyabr (From July to October)* was published in *Proletarsk. Rev.*, 1922, 10. His fuller reminiscences (*At the Battle Stations of the February and October Revolutions*) later appeared in full book form in 1931 (translator's note).
5. Ivan Petrovich Flerovsky (1888–1959) was a Russian revolutionary and journalist, member of the Military Revolutionary Committee during the Revolution, and then head of the Baltic Fleet in 1918. He became a newspaper editor and later head of a department in Tass, the Soviet news agency. His *Kronstadt v oktyabr. revolyutsii (Kronstadt in the October Revolution)* was published in *Proletarsk. Rev.*, 1922,1 (translator's note).

6. Nikolay Ilyich Podvoisky (1880–1948) joined the R.S.D.L.P. in 1901, and as a member of the Military Revolutionary Committee in Petrograd in 1917 led the actual detachment that stormed the Winter Palace. His memoirs, *God 1917* (*The Year 1917*) were republished in Moscow in 1958 (translator's note).

Twice Met (Parijanine)[1]

Parijanine's life and mine crossed only twice: both times were unforgettable. In the Year Three of the Russian Revolution's calendar (1920), I was living in the hotel Astoria, which was the principal 'House of the Soviets' in Petrograd. Zinoviev lived two floors above me, and Evdokimov and Bakayev were my neighbours ... Parijanine, my peaceable companion, see how it is: no sooner do I recall you than I am back again, among the ghosts of the great ones, all shot now ... Our meetings together had no importance other than the simply human; but they were of such a kind, and our age is such an age, and we ourselves are such in ourselves, that in thinking of you I see and test the intimacy that binds the dead with the living, and now history sweeps us on, whoever we may be, more or less along the same track, history which works its way through the bodies of us all, inexorably.

We lived under close guard and discreet surveillance. The gate officer rang me with the news that a Frenchman, duly armed with a letter from Guilbeaux,[2] was asking to see me. A few moments later I opened the door to one misshapen and with gentle eyes, eyes of a timid, sly sort of man. He appeared to have some difficulty with his walking, but that was just an impression he gave. I can see him now, swaying over the dark red carpet, holding out a letter to me, and explaining how he had just been on his way back to France, only without a cent to his name, and how Guilbeaux had offered him some hope of doing a little work with me in the French Section of the Third International's Executive ... Work I certainly had. For Lenin, for Zinoviev, for Trotsky, for the International itself, whose agitation was the sole weapon at our disposal on a world-wide scale, there were texts to translate, revise, edit, correct, print, disguise in a hundred ways, and then transmit via Finland, Estonia (enemy territories), or via Murmansk, the Arctic Ocean and the little northernmost ports of Norway ... I employed the most variegated persons on my staff, demanding of them only a knowledge of languages and a strict minimum of punctuality. Madame de Pfehl, who had lately been received at court ('... and I can assure you, Comrade, the Emperor was a really good sort, so far as I knew him, a splendid man he was, and loved the people ...'); Madame de Pfehl was the usual translator employed in my departments for the Proclamations of the President of the Communist International to the Proletariat of the World. Her style, which at times recalled that of the Comtesse de Ségur (née Rostopchin), was brushed up by Monsieur Konstantin P---, who not so long ago had been an editor on the official *St Petersburg Gazette*. Monsieur Bak,[3] a former businessman and journalist for a steel cartel in the days of the Empire, a small, smooth-faced gentleman, appallingly refined and reserved, was agreeable to translating articles on theory, but not revolutionary appeals. 'Pardon me, citizen', he would remark, 'My conscience ...' Naturally I respected his conscience.

I had scarcely any time to see faces properly; no time to chat, to dream, to get to know a man, except in a hurry. There was little sympathy between Parije and myself. 'Communist?' I had at once asked him. 'No, not exactly: a sympathiser...' This was a sympathiser, quitting the land of the Revolution in the middle of civil war – blockade – famine – terror? That did not please me, but it was his business. In any event, he spoke perfect French (quite the scholar), and he knew Russian inside out. All this would be happening in June: we were making arrangements for the Second World Congress of the Communist International, and I had just received a bulky manuscript of Trotsky's. I passed half of it on to Parije. I thought I saw him wince slightly as he pondered on the title of the work: *Terrorism and Communism*. It was subtitled: *Anti-Kautsky*.[4]

'Does that upset you?' I asked him, a little ironically. 'Oh, no', he replied mildly, 'No more than the terror does ...' I have kept a memory of that sentence, or of one very like it, illuminated by a distinct, though reticent, glance from those eyes ...

We had to do the job quickly, very quickly. Trotsky had just finished dictating the book to his secretaries in the course of his endless travels on the train-cum-mobile-headquarters that for two years now had been transporting him from one front to the next, through devastated territories lying prey to epidemics, warring bands and peasant counter-rebellions, whole tracts disputed by flags of red, white, blue-and-gold (Ukrainian), black or green. The 'white nights' lit up the city with a huge and everlasting twilight, whose spell was unending, soul-stirring, and rather fatiguing. We spent more than one of them crouched over the pages of *Anti-Kautsky*. I can see Parije now, sitting in the wan light inside his room at the Hotel International, working through this book of victorious civil war, with all his scruples of a grammarian, a poet, a romancer, polishing up those powerful, caustic pages. (The Hotel International, if I remember, later got back its old name of Hotel Anglia). It is entirely possible that Parije occupied the same room there in which, six years later, a quite different poet, whom he admired so much, Sergei Yesenin, would write his last lines with a rusty nib dipped in a few drops of his blood, before proceeding to hang himself. In these same rooms I knew others again who vanished: Raymond Lefebvre, Lepetit, Vergeat, Sasha Tubin. Dead, and then more dead.[5]

My memories of Parijanine are today hard to separate from that particular book and that particular epoch. More recently the work has been re-issued under a misleading title: *In Defence of Terrorism*. In it Trotsky does not defend what is usually meant by terrorism, but does demonstrate the unconditional necessity for the working class to prove its strength and its ability to use all the severities of war, in those revolutionary periods when its only choice is to win or die ... There too he refutes Austro-Marxism, the doctrine of the great Socialists of Vienna, Karl Renner, Friedrich Adler, Max Adler, Otto Bauer.[6] Kautsky in this period was in some sense the ideologue of the Weimar Republic, the most liberal democracy that ever was, sealed, it is true, in the blood of Liebknecht, Rosa Luxemburg and the Spartacist workers. The Austrian Marxists thought that they could put off the future by avoiding the seizure of power, with its accompanying cost of a difficult, dangerous struggle. Wisely, prudently, acutely, they legislated on behalf of the working class. In Vienna they were going to build the finest working class housing in the world, the very best municipal baths, the most brilliantly lit public halls ... Dead, and then more dead. Karl Kautsky has just passed away in exile at Amsterdam, Otto Bauer has just died in exile in Paris, ravaged by his sense of defeat; the Third International has a thousand bullet-holes in the back of its neck ... This much has to be said: looming through all these deaths and defeats, the thinking embodied in that book of 1920 is still masterfully and prophetically alive. (And many of the objections it provoked from the Menshevik defenders of working-class democracy in the Revolution, have acquired a fresh potency; that debate is certainly not finished)

Once the book was out of the way, Parije took the train for Finland. I took the Moscow train, travelling with Angel Pestaña of the CNT (he died last year);[7] in the restaurant car we met Frossard and Marcel Cachin.[8] In Moscow, the Second

Congress of the International laid down the Twenty-One Conditions for its affiliates. It addressed am appeal to the Anarchists, and discussed Lenin's theses on the colonial question,[9] which were fiercely contested by Serrati (dead, and then more dead ...).[10] Lenin, smiling and good-natured, passed among us in his old jacket dating from exile days, brushed clean for the occasion. In the President's chair, beneath the gold ceiling of one of the throne-rooms in the Kremlin, Zinoviev would be tossing his long, soft locks. The throne had been put away in a nearby ante-room where typists were busy setting up their machines. A few paces from the throne and the Remingtons, a map, spread out over the hangings on the wall, attracted various groups to discuss around it. Lenin, Radek and Zinoviev were standing there with foreign delegates, their eyes glued to the progress of the little red flags that Tukhachevsky was pushing towards Warsaw[11] – on the way to rip up the Versailles Treaty, to create a Soviet Poland, than tomorrow a Socialist Germany, and soon a United States of Socialist Europe. All of us had in our briefcases Tukhachevsky's theses on the Red Army in the service of the International ... One evening a despatch from Kharkov spread the rumour that Tukhachevsky, Rakovsky and Smilga had entered Warsaw ...[12]

I lost sight of Parijanine; several years later I resumed contact with him by post. We were working as joint translators on *Against the Stream*, the volume by Lenin and Zinoviev dating from the War.[13] I was living for a while in Berlin, then in Vienna. The International was torn asunder by successive crises, in the wake of bungled (or simply crushed) revolutions in Germany and Bulgaria. The succession to Lenin now lay open. Zinoviev and Kamenev were now inventing 'Trotskyism' for the purpose of refuting it,[14] and in the shadows, noiseless as yet but growing larger and larger, was the silhouette of Stalin, who was unknown not only to the masses but even to the old militants of the Party and the International. At the very height of some obscure battle against Trotskyism, Parije and I, he in Paris and I in Vienna, decided to translate the splendid book that Trotsky had just devoted to Lenin, a work that was becoming heretical.[15] We refrained from putting our names to the book, which was published by Hasfeld. Parije was fighting the good fight: the fight, that is, for a clear mind and for good faith kept before history.

Years went by: dark years, going darker and still darker. The revolution changed its face, ridden by deep-seated maladies for which there was no cure. It was all a tale of persecutions, lengthening proscriptions, heresies annihilated. Men stopped thinking, men stopped talking. Poets declaimed hexameters in support of the death penalty, today against engineers, tomorrow against economists, the day after that against old Socialists. The Soviet Union became the vastest prison on earth. For myself, this was to last for ten years. Then, in 1936, Wullens[16] came to see me in Brussels with greetings from Parije. Things were not well with Parije, not well at all ... It had very nearly been curtains for him, nobody had really got to the bottom of this sudden illness of his. Was he maybe beginning to feel he had had enough of it all?

I was to see him again in '37, after an interval of seventeen years, in a small hotel in Ivry, one of those small hotels occupied on a weekly rental by couples, troubled or else troublesome, by émigrés, by people without families, by unemployed men with an allowance for lodging, by abandoned or self-abandoned folk of all kinds; here sleep is sold at the fag-end of night, a dowdy, almost comfortable establishment ... Parije had grown stout; he opened his heavy eyelids to us, rather put out, because he was not used to having visitors. In the room there was wallpaper of the colour that goes with poverty, some books on a tiny table, manuscripts spread over the bed, a bottle of wine at the bed's foot. He gave out the breath of defeat, of weariness with living, of loneliness. What could he do now? What use would it be? If you are not a climber or a faker, or one of those sharp gentlemen who know how to get banknotes, in units of hundreds or of thousands, rolling out of the presses of journals which are subsidised by unspeakable swine: when once and for all you have taken seriously ideas, places, and some faces which deserve to be trusted and to be loved, there comes a day to you, during epochs of reaction, when you ask yourself quite suddenly and simply whether there is any usefulness or point in going on with this drab and even slightly disgusting game, which is life ... Parije, living on unemployment benefit, was still writing short stories and poetry. Duhamel had just carried a few of his poems in the *Mercure de France*; this was, I am pretty sure, the last satisfaction he was to experience as what is generally called a 'man of letters' ... Together with Wullens, we summoned back, in that waiting-room for death, Moscow, the Revolution, the fullest twenty years, charged with hope and suffering, that there have been for centuries, the old comradeships, the defeated friendships, the betrayals, the recantations, the shootings, and our own friendship, formed across time, distance, misunderstanding and even mistrust, but still close and solid, made weightier by sorrow, of which there had been plenty. It was good, and rather miraculous, to meet again like this after so many years, after all the traffic of life and its shipwrecks. We kept telling this to one another in the café, over a snack together, and at certain moments the eyes of Parije became young once more and very mischievous. He delivered himself of a few ironical wisecracks, and of various plans, which, it was plain to see, he did not believe in ... We were supposed to see him again, but we never did. He died on his pauper's bed, in the shadow of the poverty-coloured wallpaper, alone and weary of many things, but faithful, together with a few others, to a few things that are of overriding importance.

Notes

1. This article was translated from *Témoins*, no.23, May 1960, by the late Peter Sedgwick, and published in *International Socialism*, no.20, Spring, 1965, pp.13–15. Parijanine was the pen name of Maurice Donzel (1885–1937), who translated several of Trotsky's works into French, including *My Life* (editor's note).
2. Henri Guilbeaux (1885–1938) was a syndicalist who attended the Kienthal and 1st, 2nd and 5th congresses of the Comintern, but moved to the far right in the 1930s. Cf. Victor Serge, *Memoirs of a Revolutionary*, Oxford U.P., 1975, p.144 (editor's note).
3. Bak, who was a lawyer, was shot for counter-revolutionary activity in 1921. Cf. *Memoirs of a Revolutionary*, p.150 (editor's note).
4. Trotsky's *Terrorism and Communism* was first published in 1920 (and since, London, 1975) (editor's note).
5. Raymond Lefebvre (1891–1920), opposed the 1st World War, and had been wounded at Verdun; Louis Bertho, called Jules Lepetit (1889–1920) was an anarcho-syndicalist jailed for his opposition to the war; Marcel Vergeat (1891–1920) was a lathe operator and syndicalist who supported the Zimmerwald manifesto. Sasha Tubin, their Russian interpreter, had been a comrade of Serge's in the underground in France. All four perished at sea near Murmansk on their way back to France. Cf. Frederick Strom, 'How Lefebvre, Lepetit and Vergeat were Drowned', *Communist Review*, no.1, May, 1921, pp.19–20; *Memoirs of a Revolutionary*, p.112 (editor's note).
6. Karl Renner (1870–1950) was an Austrian Social Democrat and Chancellor for a brief period; Friedrich Adler (1879–1960) had opposed the First World War, and was later Secretary of the 2nd International; Max Adler (1873–1937) was a famous sociologist and a member of Austrian Social Democracy; Otto Bauer (1881–1938) was its most prominent theorist (editor's note).
7. Angel Pestaña Nuñez (1886–1938) attended the 2nd Congress of the Comintern on behalf of the CNT, the mass Spanish anarcho-syndicalist trade union federation. Cf. Gerald H. Meaker, *The Revolutionary Left in Spain, 1914–1923*, Stanford U.P., 1974, pp.288–99 (editor's note).
8. Louis-Oliver Frossard (1889–1946) was General Secretary of the French Socialist Party in October 1918 and for a while joined the Communist Party, but went back to the S.F.I.O.; Marcel Cachin (1869–1958) had been a member of Guesde's party, and then as a right-wing Socialist had supported the First World War, when he had been sent with money to contact Mussolini and help bring Italy into the war. He remained a cynical Stalinist to his death (editor's note).

9. The 'Theses on the Conditions of Admission to the Communist International' (the Twenty-One Conditions), proposed by Trotsky and written by Lenin, were adopted on 6 August, 1920;. Lenin's 'Theses on the National and Colonial Questions' were accepted on 28 July, 1920. Cf. Alan Adler (ed.), *Theses, Resolutions and Manifestos of the First Four Congresses of the Third International, London*, 1980, pp.92–7, 76–81 (editor's note).

10. Giacinto Serrati (1874–1926) was the leader of the Maximalist wing of the Italian Socialist Party, who to begin with opposed membership of the Comintern on the basis of the Twenty-One Conditions (editor's note).

11. Taking advantage of the Russian Civil War, the Poles advanced into the Ukraine in the Spring of 1920, but their supply lines were over-extended, and the Russian army counter-attacked and invaded Poland. Before their defeat at the Battle of the Vistula in August 1920 it looked as if the Russians would take Warsaw.

12. Christian Georgievich Rakovsky (1873–1941), one of the pioneers of the Balkan Socialist movement, and Ivar Tenissovich Smilga (1892–1938), who had helped Lenin prepare the October insurrection, were sent to support Tukhachevsky as military commissars. Rakovsky was later a defendant at the Trial of the 21, and Smilga was shot without a trial of any sort (editor's note).

13. This was the volume of Lenin's works dealing with the period of the First World War, roughly corresponding to volume xxi of the 1977 English edition (editor's note).

14. On the invention of 'Trotskyism' by Zinoviev and Kamenev, cf. Alfred Rosmer, *Trotsky and the Origins of Trotskyism*, Francis Boutle, London, 2002 (editor's note).

15. Cf. above, pp.297.

16. Maurice Wullens (1894–1945) was a Flemish anarcho-syndicalist schoolteacher, the co-founder and editor of the magazine *Les Humbles*, for which Serge published several articles in the late 1930s, along with Magdeleine Paz, Poulaille and André Breton (editor's note).

Part Five

Writers Under the Terror

Boris Pilnyak[1]

There are reports from Moscow of the arrest, or to be more precise, the disappearance of the most renowned of the Soviet writers, Boris Pilnyak. What is certain is that foreign journalists accredited in the USSR do not know what has happened to him, and that *Literaturnaya Gazeta* (*Literary Gazette*) has named him as among the 'enemies of the people'. That makes things clear, despite the uncertainty. According to some rumours he is being blamed for having helped Radek and his wife during the period of disgrace preceding their arrest. Boris Andreevich Pilnyak is certainly quite capable of a 'crime' of this sort. For years he has held on with great difficulty, constantly under suspicion, pretty well boycotted, excluded from the place in Russian letters which was his by right. All this because of his bad attitude, or, to put it better, his independence of mind, backed up by a deep human feeling ... I know him well, I know his weaknesses, I've seen all the little acts of cowardice he has been guilty of over the least ten years in order to make up for his talent and his spirit, and thus avoid banishment, prison and deportation. I am thus all the better placed to do him justice. From outside it is impossible to imagine the terrible pressures to which a man of ideas is subjected by totalitarian regimes: if you know this, then you no longer have the heart to condemn the small retreats, the little acts of pusillanimity, and even the low tricks which the regime succeeds in forcing on those who strive to maintain, even silently, hidden and disguised, a conscience that is at least slightly free ...

Of German origin, Pilnyak is nonetheless a writer who is specifically and – if I may be permitted a big word which is absolutely the right one – magnificently Russian. Recently turned forty, he has behind him some twenty volumes in which there is an abundance of very powerful pages. His personality was formed during the Revolution, the whole period of which he spent in obscurity in provincial towns. He emerged in the foreground of the new post-revolutionary literature, which was born, amazing in its freshness and greatness, straight after the end of the civil war, in 1922–25. He was without doubt the greatest of them. Two or three of his books have been translated all over the world: in French I know of translations of *The Naked Year* and *The Volga Falls to the*

Caspian Sea, published, unless I am mistaken, by Gallimard. Few writers have been able, like Pilnyak, to condense into a novel or a novella the reality, the illusion, the lyricism both human and inhuman, and the humble details of everyday life belonging to the Revolution. Hence precisely the dangerous conflict with official literature, which, from the time of the first victories of the bureaucracy over the proletariat, has put the novelist of the Soviet world into an ever more untenable position.

By 1927–28 the bureaucratic regime was demanding from writers a propaganda literature strictly inspired by current slogans. The standard of living of the masses, which had been visibly improving since 1921–22, began to get rapidly worse as the result of the consolidation of the dictatorship of a clique which made ever more mistakes: the enforced collectivisation of agriculture, a sort of war on the peasantry, was soon to produce the harsh famine of the years 1932–35. Human feeling (which is, however, the only moral basis for any socialist conviction) has become under these conditions a 'counter-revolutionary sentiment'. This is written and proclaimed everywhere. Does it not lead to pity for the starving, the persecuted, the defeated, the executed? Now the hypocritical official doctrine insists, however outrageous this may seem, that amid the convulsions of a vast land there is no-one who is starving or persecuted and that the masses enthusiastically approve the executions necessary for public well-being.

When, in 1929 or 1930, he returned from a small town in the Volga region whose dire distress he had observed at first hand, Pilnyak took from his notebooks the material for a novella, published in its time in a French translation in Europe, 'Mahogany'. In it a sort of moaning arose from the Russian soil. It described former heroes of the civil war, now drunks and tramps, recalling the epic days when they captured cities ... Nobody could read this work in Russian, but, when the signal was given, the whole Russian press denounced it as a counter-revolutionary slander. Pilnyak, literally hunted down, had to make due apology. He protested that he was optimistic and loyal. And this was quite sincere, for he loves Russia and the Revolution too much not to keep for them, even through the bitterest experiences, an absolute trust and fidelity. The Central Committee of the Communist Party demanded that he should adapt the condemned work in a conformist fashion. He agreed. From this thankless labour, under the control of the censors, emerged an acceptable novel (for the pedants of the bureaucracy): *The Volga Falls to the Caspian Sea*, of which one well-informed critic wrote: 'This book shouts out lies and mutters the truth.'

Pilnyak was a close friend of the Bolshevik essayist Valerian Polonsky, who died a few years ago, of typhus, on his way to exile; he was a friend of the Bolshevik novelist and critic Voronsky, one of the most remarkable writers of the USSR, who long ago disappeared into an unknown prison; he was well acquainted with most of the Soviet leaders of the recent past, and he even, in some circumstances, had the advantage of Stalin's personal favours. But today, as we observe the disappearance – hounded and described as enemies of the people – of the men who made the October Revolution and of the first years of Stalinism, a Pilnyak, who belongs to both those generations, must be eliminated. Will he merely be boycotted and deported? Will he be sent, like so many others, into a concentration camp? Will they go so far as to kill him? It will doubtless be a long time before we know. Perhaps the greatest of today's Soviet writers, one of the most original and powerful writers in the world, has just disappeared in Moscow, in the most alarmingly mysterious circumstances: and we know nothing more.

Count Alexei Tolstoy, a right-minded novelist under Tsarism, a White émigré in 1917 who went over to the Soviets in 1923, will be happy to replace him on the platform at congresses ...

1.   Translated from *La Wallonie*, 31 July & 1 August 1937, p. 8. (translator's note)

Bezymensky[1]

Yet again, in the flood of terrifying news which comes to us incessantly from Moscow, along with the disappearance of a President of the Council (Sulimov, President of the Council of People's Commissars of the Union of Soviet Socialist Republics), the disappearance of a member of the Political Bureau (Rudzutak), and the execution of seventy-two railway workers at Irkutsk,[2] I find a familiar name, and one of symbolic importance. I recently noticed here the disappearance of a great Soviet writer, Boris Pilnyak;[3] and now in his turn the most famous of the Russian Communist poets, Bezymensky, has left us.

I remember a miserable little dwelling in Moscow towards which, in 1926–27, I always joyfully made my way. There, in the tiny delapidated rooms of an old monastery, lived a tall young man of singular ugliness, with a very high bald forehead, an equine profile and a square jaw – who was one of the most remarkable brains of our younger generation. A group leader at thirty-two or thirty-four years old, he gave the impression of being the most intolerant, the most imperious, the most rigorous in his aspirations, and in some respects the most exasperating theoretican of Communist literature ... He aspired to renew everything for the revolution, to rethink everything from the Party point of view, and to impose a new spirit on poetry, the novel and criticism ... George Lelevich, the son of small Jewish artisans, a former fighter during the Civil War in the Volga region, was the inspiration behind the *On Guard-Na Postu* group – a combat post. He lived very poorly with his companion and his little Varlin. Above the papers strewn across his work table on a postcard there was a portrait of the other Varlin, the great one, who was shot at the time of the Commune. Where is Lelevich today? It was almost three years ago that we learned of his departure to a concentration camp from a press cutting. Going off along with him for the same forced labour went his friend, George Gorbachev, the most corrosive literary critic of the Leningrad Communist press ... [4]

It was at Lelevich's place that I met a slightly round-shouldered young athlete, with a very young face and an enormous forehead beneath which burned charming blue eyes. 'This,' Lelevich told me, 'is our best poet, the true creator of poetry among the young Communists ...' And he added confidentially: 'He is a magnificent type, forever young, with the spirit of a true Bolshevik ...'

Bezymensky went from success to success, and not undeservedly. His fame was based upon a poem entitled *The Party Card*.[5] All the anthologies reprinted it. He employed lively, expressive and familiar language; with a simplicity that occasionally attained great power, he expressed the feelings of the young revolutionary generation, for whom the party card symbolised discipline, total devotion, the feeling of a life devoted to a noble cause and to the march towards Socialism all at the same time. People committed suicide at this time because they could not survive being excluded from the Party. Bezymensky became an actor, naturally in parts written to order, passionate to begin with, and then official. Delegated by the youth – the *Komsomol* – we saw him come to the platform in the workers' clubs and at Party congresses to proclaim the greatness of the epoch in an intelligent, well-pitched voice which declaimed the words energetically and youthfully. Over and over again he repeated praise for the great Party, the daily appeal for heroism, and rhyming praise for the Leader ...

And so the years passed. Almost all his friends suffered persecution, having argued or thought a bit ... Bezymensky adapted, manoeuvered, and remained the official poet, a sort of permanent poet laureate, producing almost as much, though less originally, as Mayakovsky, but much more in line with agitational needs. His reputation grew, the magazines paid him at a high price for each verse, and he was brought out in millions of copies: he was in the two daily state newspapers, *Pravda* and *Izvestia*, at the same time. To tell the truth, poetry no longer accounted for much of his work, in which all spontaneity had evaporated. But among the literary figures in the propaganda service he belonged in the front rank in conviction, zeal and talent.

For years we did not shake hands with each other. I never forgave him, in my conscience, for having abandoned his imprisoned or deported comrades of yesterday. I found him too smart. The verses he published in the magazines on the occasion of the successive trials in order to demand, according to the circumstances, the death penalty for the engineers, the old Socialists or Lenin's companions disgusted me. He provided the most heart-rending of these two months ago on the occasion of the execution of the red Marshal Tukhachevsky[6] – 'this vermin Tukhachevsky', he cried – but at that very moment he was already himself suspected, already threatened, and no doubt obliged to versify this in order

by going over the top to try to avoid the sword suspended over his own head ...
But he was not to escape it.

... It's done. It is said in Russia that exclusion from the Party means 'political death'. We know that for the writer or the poet it brings along with it the impossibility from then on of publishing a line. For the militant it most often also involves internment in a concentration camp ... Bezymensky, expelled from the Party a few days ago, immediately disappeared, and is finished. The most remarkable of Communist poets has just been suppressed by a stroke of the pen. And in the great drama in which have disappeared two generations of revolutionaries, the heroic one of 1917 and the bureaucratic one of 1926–36, it is only an episode among thousands of others ...

Victor Serge

Notes

1. Translated from *La Wallonie*, 21/22 August, 1937 (translator's note).
2. Daniel Egorovich Sulimov (1890–1939) joined the Bolshevik Party in 1905, and was repeatedly elected to the Central Committee after 1921, even having a Caucasian town named after him. He was arrested in 1937 and shot in 1939. Jan Ernestovich Rudzutak (1887–1938) was a veteran Latvian Bolshevik trade union activist who had been Deputy Premier of the USSR and head of the Party Control Commission. He refused to acknowledge the confessions wrung from him by torture and was shot in July 1938. On 19 August 1937 the East Siberian *Pravda* reported that a military court in Irkutsk had tried and sentenced to death alleged members of a 'Trotskyist-Rightist anti-Soviet terrorist organisation' accused of carrying out sabotage on the East Siberian Railway and plotting the assassination of Soviet leaders (translator's note).
3. Pilnyak was denounced for 'counter-revolutionary writing' in May 1937, and disappeared shortly afterwards. He was later accused of being a Japanese agent, and shot (translator's note).
4. Lelevich and Gorbachev were arrested in January 1935. Lelevich was shot two years later, and Gorbachev perished during the Second World War (translator's note).
5. Bezymensky's *Partbilet N.224332* came out in Moscow in 1930. It was reprinted in 1968, along with a collection of poems and memoirs (translator's note).
6. Field Marshal Mikhail Tukhachevsky (1893–1937) was one of the most successful Russian commanders during the Civil War, and a pioneer of modern tank warfare. He was arrested and shot during Stalin's secret Trial of the Generals in June 1937. For Bezymensky's verses on this, cf. Robert Conquest, *The Great Terror*, Harmondsworth, 1971, p.277 (translator's note).

Meyerhold[1]

Meyerhold began his work of reviving the theatre well before the Revolution. Between 1905 and 1917 – between the two revolutions, in other words – Symbolist poets, end of empire novelists, painters and decorative artists such as Bakst,[2] creators of the first Russian ballets like Diaghilev and Nizhinsky[3] and even revolutionaries, whose pent-up passion everywhere made itself felt, created an atmosphere in which the theatre had to submit to a total overhaul in order to survive. The whole of Russian society was going through a sort of metamorphosis. No one was less sure of the future than a grand duke or a governor general. The bourgeoisie even wished for the storm to draw near. 'Let the coming of the tempest be all the more violent!' exclaimed Gorky at the end of a poem, and this line became the motto of the Anarchists.[4] Lenin chose from it for his papers another expression no less significant: 'the spark will kindle a flame'.[5] Lenin, in exile in Paris or Geneva, entrusted Lunacharsky with managing the Bolshevik Party School in Bologna where several of the future leaders of the USSR were trained[6] (and who were shot in 1936–37). On emerging from the courses of the Bologna school, after tiny meetings in the great western cities, in illegal circles in the Russian cities and in the salons of the intelligentsia at Merezhkovsky's, Andreyev's and Gorky's places, the theories, attempts, first failures and first successes of Meyerhold were talked about, because he belonged to the small number of great Russian artists – and hence European – inspired by the dynamism of the time.

After the workers' insurrection had seized power Meyerhold came over to the Soviets very early on and set himself to work for new audiences who had not so far been entertained by the theatre. Suburbs devastated by the Civil War, troops on leave from the trenches, Red cavalry who had come from far-off fronts, peasants, shepherds, hunters from the North or the East, and delegates to governmental congresses who were all this at the same time invaded the theatres, filling them with a naive and lively enthusiasm, demanding feelings and ideas, and requiring that they should communicate with each other and the universe. This was no longer the refined and aesthetic public with its over-critical attitude and weakened vital feelings of the years never to return. And there could be no question of his putting on stories of sexual encounters spiced up with triple meanings or rarified French psychology. The life of the masses required something very different, and even love did not have the taste of perfumed pastry or scent. It was in some way necessary to rediscover the ancient drama on stages poor in material, décor and accessories, using actors who often went hungry. And it was then, in the time of Lenin, Trotsky and Lunacharsky, that what can be fairly called the genius of Meyerhold came to be revealed.

Meyerhold was daring. No scenic convention prevented him from searching for a powerful idiom, one that was understandable, in other words, and which brought feeling to the maximum intensity. So much the worse for the sets, and so much the worse for the frightened old critics who survived the deluge. The stage turned round, broke up, went out of alignment, and was covered with scaffolding or superimposed planes, often broken, barely giving the spectator's thinking a few summary indications: for it was not a question of putting together easy viewing for him, but of freeing his imagination, even by irritating him a little. The stage was covered with real buildings, eating really went on there, and coolies transported real bales of cotton onto it. All the movements on it were stylised with a slight exaggeration which made them move beyond everyday reality in order to enter the sphere of a more intense reality, almost to the point of becoming oppressive. Circus stunts – and Meyerhold was even blamed for it – for there are imbeciles, there really were! – were suddenly combined with impeccable dramatic action, a black typist strangely spinning round, or an actor becoming a jester or a circus clown, and tragedy was violently overturned by the grotesque. As if it isn't the most obvious truth that the jester and the circus clown, unknowingly and oblivious to gravity, are walking among us at any time, even in the heart of revolutions!

Meyerhold followed current events. The propaganda plays he put on – *Roar, China!*, or Mayakovsky's *The Bedbug*,[7] for example – were the only great ones, for he imbued the theme with so frenzied a spirit that the propagandists, among whom the constipated pedants were becoming a majority, as the years wore on, began no longer to recognise it. During the performance Meyerhold noiselessly opened a side door and stood close to a wall at an angle to the stage and the auditorium, looking at both of them, tall, bony, greying, with a terribly misshapen nose and an extremely unwelcoming penetrating expression, a beautiful Gothic mask with a proud forehead. He was at his place in a world being transformed, sure of himself, reaching the summits of his work, beloved of the crowds, and known to a universe in which his work added something to the radiance of Soviet achievements ...

When he joined the Communist Party he found himself enmeshed in conformism. Holding himself apart from political discussions, he was a good specialist 'non-party Communist'. The Stalinist regime to begin with showered him with encouragement. They tried to build him a theatre that would respond to all his daring ... and he fell in two months, removed from the stage, his theatre closed, his cast disbanded, and his life as a creator probably over[8] – alone, old, faced with the ruins of a work unique in the world, passionately built up for the entire length of his life. No one can understand anything of it. Why this absurd vengeance by a Vandal tyrant? We can only reply that there are precedents for it, after all equally inexplicable as well. Tairov, another first rate stage director, has been brutally disgraced in the past year. Akhmetelli, the great man of the Georgian theatre, has just been shot in Tiflis, no doubt because he was linked by friendship to the Old Georgian Bolsheviks who had been shot before him.[9] In his own fall Meyerhold brought down with him a member of the government, Kerzhentsev, the Director of Fine Arts, accused of having encouraged for years his 'low quality insipid juggling and stunts' (speech by Zhdanov[10] a member of the Political Bureau, at a recent meeting in Moscow).

The official explanations for the suppression of the most living and the most famous State Theatre in Moscow are crammed with this type of arguments. The truth is that Meyerhold knew quite closely the men of the Revolution, who have now been suppressed. Their thinking is familiar to him, and he belongs to their family. Could this witness be left with the platform of the theatre? The regime that has been set up pitilessly removes from its path whoever reminds it of its own past, for there is for it no worse reproach nor any worse danger than this simple reminder.

Victor Serge

Notes

1. Translated from *La Wallonie*, 29/30 January, 1938 (translator's note).
2. Lev Samoylevich Rosenberg, called Léon Bakst (1866–1924) was a Russian graphic artist who revolutionised

theatrical design in scenery and costume to bring them into line with each other (translator's note).

3. Sergei Pavlovich Diaghilev (1872–1929) was a world renowned producer of theatre, opera and ballet; Vatslav Formich Nizhinsky (1889–1950) was the foremost Russian ballet dancer and choreographer in Diaghilev's ballet company (translator's note).

4. Gorky's prose poem, *Pesnia o burevestnike* (*The Song of the Storm Petrel*), written in 1901, was a call to revolution (translator's note).

5. This motto appeared on *Iskra* (*Spark*), the newspaper of the R.S.D.L.P., which first came out in Leipzig on 24 December 1900 (translator's note).

6. The Otzovists organised a party school at Bologna in Italy in November 1910 (translator's note).

7. Mayakovsky's play *Kop* (*The Bedbug*), a futuristic satire on the N.E.P., which Stalin had just brought to an end, was first performed in 1929 (translator's note).

8. The Meyerhold Theatre was dissolved in January 1938 as 'alien to Soviet art'. Meyerhold himself was arrested on 20 January 1939, and confessed under torture to have been a Trotskyite since 1923 (his 1923 production of *Earth in Turmoil* had been dedicated to Trotsky). He was shot in Moscow on 2 February 1940. Cf. David King, *The Commissar Vanishes*, Edinburgh, 1997, p.165 (translator's note).

9. Alexander Vasiliyevich Akhmetelli (1886–1937) had been the principal director of the Rustaveli Theatre in Tiflis. Stalin carried on a particular vendetta against the Georgian Bolsheviks led by Mdiviani, who had already opposed Stalin with the support of Lenin in the last years of his life (translator's note).

10. Andrei Alexandrovich Zhdanov (1896–1948), who replaced Kirov as head of the Leningrad Communist Party, was one of the foremost functionaries of Stalin's regime, and dictator of culture during the postwar period, which became known as 'Zhdanovism'. When he died in mysterious circumstances, all his associates were executed (translator's note).

On Literary Creativity[1]

25 March, 1944. I am writing a small essay – slapdash, but full of matter and complete, on 'the writer's message', defining the need to write in this way: 'To start off with grasp, focus on, understand, interpret and recreate life; by externalising them set free the confused forces you have felt fermenting within you by which the individual plunges into the collective unconscious. This will be transmitted by the Testimony and the Message in the work itself ...' Perhaps the deepest source of it lies in the feeling that wonderful life is passing, flying, inexorably slipping away and the desire to catch it in its flight ... It was this feeling of despair that drove me when I was about sixteen to note the precious moment that made me discover that *existence* (human, 'divine') *is memory.* Much later, when your personality has become enriched, you discover its limits, the poverty and shackles of the self, and you discover that you only have one life, and one forever circumscribed personality, but containing many possible futures, and is not unique in the sense that it is intermingled by means of countless roots, relationships and interchanges (most of them inexplicable in rational terms) with other human existences, and the earth, beings and everything. Writing then becomes the search for a multiple personality, a way of living different destinies, of entering the other person and communicating with him. All the characters in a novel and even the forest trees and the skies become part of the life of the writer, since they spring from him. The writer takes hold of the feeling of the world he has brought to life, he is its consciousness and he thus escapes the ordinary limits of self, which is at the same time intoxicating and enriched with lucidity. (There are no doubt other types of writers, individualistic ones, who only seek to assert themselves and can only see the world through themselves).

It should be remembered that a work of art which 'is a work of lucid will and trance' only refers to a work that springs from the depths and is not deliberately constructed, even if in the latter there is also a springing up, but it is subordinated to external necessity, and therefore sickly, since it can be subordinated. There is a sort of suffering and relief in writing. It is amazing that an analytical novel of literary creativity has not yet been done; there are too many psychological blocks and inhibitions opposed to it.

I am writing a novel at the moment set in France the day after the defeat.[2] I am often overwhelmed by it, held up by the darkness. I do not know what my characters are doing, where they are going, a fog surrounds them, I feel myself exhausted, I have no desire to go on – I doubt if it is worth the effort. And then the impetus – helped by the will to work – is born again of itself. I have to continue in such developments as regards N., in accordance with the 'plan' of the book – a vague plan which is not carried out; I feel the need, which I cannot analyse, on the contrary to take up Z., but I do not know, and in any case I know neither visually or exactly what he is doing, although I know the direction he is following and sometimes the end to which he is being led. Occupied at the moment with Félicien Mûrier, I suddenly feel the need to take up Karel Tcherniak. I knew that his destiny was leading him to suicide – without being sure of it. For several days now I have been tormented by the feeling of Karel Tcherniak inside me, usually while falling asleep and probably during my sleep. It prevented me from seeing the other characters. I finally found a key phrase, insignificant and apparently empty: 'Tcherniak opened the window', and I knew that the solution to the problem was ready inside me, and that I had to do no more than write it, – but I did not know what was the solution, it would have been impossible for me to describe it in advance. I set myself to write, and in a few hours this piece was completed, and finished off. 'Karel Tcherniak opens the window with effort, he fears the return of everyday life. He sees Véronique in the court ... Véronique appears at the time the window opens.' I had not consciously thought about her during the previous minute ... 'Karel Tcherniak was not thinking about suicide today, but he is going to throw himself in the sea without thinking about it, obeying an unconscious decision that has come to a head, which the Véronique-event has brought about.' I ask myself what associations of ideas have linked together these themes within me, these moments of life with the action of opening a window? I only found a beautiful line of Pasternak: 'To open a window means to open the veins ...', but I also feel that opening a window is a great joy, in many cases. (Karel Tcherniak's internal life follows its own course, Karel Tcherniak is not me, even if he has something of me inside him, i.e. that I understand him and see him from the inside, by identification.)

When I spoke about this with H. L.[3] he says: 'We have only begun to decode the mind ... the brain is infinitely mysterious ...' And I: 'And it is barely more than a half century that it was even discovered! As a nerve centre, an organ, and a seat of nervous life and thought, the brain had been discovered before, in the eighteenth century; but it required time to pass from the study of this organ, which thus far tells us little about the psyche – to the study of the psyche in depth; this has been the real discovery of the soul, a soul infinitely richer, more mysterious and more baffling than the soul of mystical intuition – a real soul.'

The Difficulty of Writing : The Russian Writers

10 September, 1944. H. L., seeing me working on a novel, asked me if I felt I was in full possession of my capacities?

– No. I never felt further from this feeling. The novel about the Moscow Trials[4] was painful for me to write, but I very much had the feeling of having given it all I could give, and of a duty carried out faithfully. And how long would it remain unpublishable? – *Les Derniers Temps* will be a sincere and probably satisfying book, but no more than that, apart from a few pages where human understanding will be increased a little. It is fearfully difficult to create in a void, without the slightest support, without the least atmosphere. If I could allow myself to go deeper, to shake off the weight of external and internal constraints (the latter a reflection of the former), the book would be worth a hundred times more and I would feel a hundred times better. But this is psychologically almost impossible. Writing only for the drawer when I am over fifty, in the face of an uncertain future and without excluding the hypothesis that the tyrannies will go on longer than what remains of my life, what would that give you? A fairly rich focus on the background of despair; and I rather prefer a practical compromise with social constraints than deliberately plunging into despair. Yet again: remain rational: things can and must change sufficiently before long for me to breathe more freely. For compromise is all the same an act of confidence – of mutilated and stiff, but living confidence. I am even asking myself if my name alone will not be an obstacle to publishing the novel.

It is strange to observe that I am at present writing, in this free country of the American continent, like the Russians were writing about 1930 when the last spiritual liberty was expiring over there. Pilnyak, Fedin, Tynyanov, Kaverin, and even the facile Lavrenyov – spoke to me in the language to which I now

speak to myself in solitude. Lidia Seifullina got drunk and became neurasthenic; Pasternak awaited imprisonment ... Osip Emelyanovich Mandelstam,
an authentic poet, in secret read us a story inspired after the manner of
Giraudoux; impressions of the Caucasus were mixed up with allusions to freedom of the imagination that no power could destroy (no power apart from censorship and the political police). When he had finished his reading, his thin and
irregular face, with disquieting eyes, was lifted up: 'Do you think that it can be
published?'. Zoschenko lifted up his yellow, reticent and regular face to say
'That doesn't seem too scandalous to me ...' I had the painful impression of the
crafty and twisted revolt of a fearful infant who was looking for some way of saying something without seeming to do it.[5] Some time later Mandelstam stupidly
tried to commit suicide by throwing himself out of too low a window. And he
'had worries'. – One night, at my place, he felt hemmed in and constrained. 'It
is because you are a Marxist', he admitted. And as I was showing him a volume
of photos of *Paris by Night*, the constraint quickly fell away in front of the pictures. 'Thanks to these pictures, confidence has returned to me ...'

Notes

1. Translated from *Carnets*, Julliard, Paris, 1952, pp.96–98, 134–5 (translator's note).
2. *Les Derniers Temps*, translated as *The Long Dusk*, New York, 1946 (translator's note).
3. H. L. is no doubt Herbert Lenhof, a Freudian psychoanalyst who befriended Serge in Mexico (translator's note).
4. *The Case of Comrade Tulayev*, English translations Penguin, Harmondsworth, 1968 and Bookmarks/Journeyman, London, 1993 (translator's note).
5. Osip Emelyanovich Mandelstam (1891–1938) was one of Russia's foremost poets. John Manson places this reading of Mandelstam's *Journey to Armenia* in his flat in Leningrad in 1933 ('The Carnets' in Susan Weissman, *The Ideas of Victor Serge*, *Critique*, nos.28–29, Glasgow, 1997, p.231. On Stalin's treatment of the writers in general, cf. Jean-Jacques Marie, 'Staline et les écrivains', *Cahiers du Mouvement Ouvrier*, no.17, April/May 2002, pp.83–93 (translator's note).

The Tragedy of the Soviet Writers[1]

I want to deal with this problem only in the context of the most important aspects of present day reality. These notes are from a writer who feels as if he has been struggling for twenty years in the midst of more and more surprising events, and where in various ways he incessantly saw men (and works) perish, whose basic aim was to express conscience.

I recently received from afar, and by devious routes, two messages at the same time which complement each other in their tragic significance. The literature of our post-war time without peace, that is to say, without reconciling the victims, without any intention of reconstructing the world, and without renewing our confidence in man, is a reflection of anguish more than anything else. It shows how narrow a margin of creative freedom is left by social reality to the intellectual, even when to give himself an inspiring illusion, and no doubt to raise himself up to the level of nightmare, he is pleased to lay claim, like certain French authors, to 'a dizzy freedom'. If there were however fairly sincere exchanges today, and if we were not living cut off by immense prison barriers, we would have noticed the rare appearance in Russo-Soviet literature of a welcome clarity. Among a host of war books, sometimes written with undeniable talent, but whose general arguments, supplied by the relevant authorities, are known in advance, a few poems have appeared which only bear the official stamp in the same way as a soldier wears his uniform. It so happens that suddenly we see the man under the uniform, and that this man has an intense face, and a personal identity. The Regime of Directed Thought has sensibly decided that at a time of the worst suffering it might as well allow some comfort to the human spirit; on the one hand it has authorised a suitably supervised religious revival, and on the other a lyrical poetry strictly limited to the great theme of love. Love is indeed more dangerous to tyrannies than you might think at first sight, and they know it. In their enjoyment of togetherness the man and woman must not find absorbing diversions likely to lessen their zeal for work, their obedience to the supreme orders of the state, or their devotion to the Leader ... I remember a young worker, 'fed up with ideology', who wrote to the old Maxim Gorky: 'I would like the peasant, instead of embracing his tractor, to embrace the peasant woman, I would like fields where grass would grow and not nails, I want "'to enjoy myself!" And the great writer, who had now become official, replied in an indignant tone: "Enjoying yourself – that is the parasites' oldest motto: Let others work, while we enjoy ourselves".' (*Pravda*, 20 December, 1931). For precisely that reason Russia's most remarkable lyric poet, Serge Yesenin, lived under a harassing disapproval that finally drove him to commit suicide in 1925. A few years later the same internal conflict drove to suicide Vladimir Mayakovsky, the poet of hope in the dictatorship ... But perils less psychological than lyricism threaten the absolute state during wartime. Since all youth is frustrated of the right to go on living, it therefore seems wise to allow the song of love which, since it helps life to go on, can also help fighting and dying go on. And the fact is that, alongside a patriotic prose that is over-whelming in its monotony, Soviet Russian literature has just produced some poems of love of noble vigour and with a freshness of sentiment and thought which are enough to show that Russian man continues to live intensely, even under the heaviest constraints. I have to hand the ninth number of the review *Znamia* (*The Standard*) for 1945, which contains a poem by Margarita Aliger, *Your Victory*, in 6,700 lines.[2] Until quite recently the author was only a young unknown. The work is simple, written in the classical language of the Russian poets of the nineteenth century, and at times it reaches the heights of a lyricism packed with life's experience, lucid passion and emotional intelligence appropriate to the greatest emotional radiance.

> Let he who falls in the reddened dust,
> His helmet pierced by a shell splinter,
> Let he who falls pardon the two who live
> Their sacred right to earthly caresses.

As a whole, in spite of inevitable and probably sincere concessions to the ideological phraseology of the time, this work seems of the first order to me; and I see nothing to compare with it in the four European languages in which I try to follow literary output.

The Poet's Resistance

At the same time as I received the official literary review containing this poem, I learnt after a delay of some years, for secrecy is the rule, of the death (we should say murder) of one of the most significant Russian poets of the last thirty years: Osip Emilievich Mandelstam. He would have been a bit more than fifty if he had lived. About 1913, along with Nikolai Stepanovich Gumilev, he had founded the school of Acmeism, which had the aim of expressing the 'immediate truth' in perfectly complete forms. (N. S. Gumilev, one of the four or five Russian poets of the first magnitude at the outbreak of the Revolution, openly professed counter-revolutionary opinions, and was shot in 1921). I remember a gathering at Mandelstam's home in Leningrad in 1932. The poet had collected together a number of writer friends to read to us a prose work he had brought back from a journey to Armenia. I will not name here any of those present, my comrades and friends, in order not to compromise the survivors. A Jew, rather small, with a face of concentrated sadness and restless and meditative brown eyes, Mandelstam, highly regarded by literary people, lived poorly and with difficulty. He was hardly ever published and he produced little, not daring to struggle against the condemnation of the censors and the diatribes of the orators of the Associations of Proletarian Writers. The sharply outlined text he read us put me in mind of Giraudoux at his best, but here it was not a question of Suzanne's spacious dream in front of the Pacific; instead, it was a question of the poet's secret resistance to the strangler's noose. The visions of the lake of Erevan and the snows of Ararat raised in the murmur of a breeze a demand for liberty, a subversive praise of the imagination, support for uncontrollable thought ... Having finished reading, Mandelstam questioned us: 'Do you think that this will be publishable?' Admiring landscapes was not forbidden. But would the censors fathom the language of protest in these landscapes? I do not know if these pages ever saw the light of day, for not long after that I was shut away in the Internal (and secret) Prison of Moscow (for expressing unauthorised opinions). I learn that Mandelstam later tried to commit suicide: that he wrote during the terror an epigrammatic quatrain in which an allusion to the Leader could be seen, and was imprudent enough to let it be known to several people; that he was arrested; that from 1942 onwards his few friends considered him as deceased in captivity, in unknown circumstances ...[3] It is allowed to publish a great poem of love. But it is mortally forbidden to ask of the state what has happened to disappeared poets and prose writers. Even love must hold its tongue on the threshold of the dungeons.

Under Threat of Death

The history of the massacre of the Soviet writers in 1936–9 has not been written. No account of it has been published. What publisher, what magazine, would have welcomed such an account? Since everything had passed into obscurity, it could only be fragmentary. But, published or not, this drama is one of the basic cultural facts of the present age. A friend, one of the most remarkable writers of the revolutionary generation, said to me in Moscow: 'Our consciousness as Soviet writers is very different from that of Western men of letters. Not one of us escapes the fear of possible execution. There is not a single one of us who does not exclaim bitterly in his solitude: "Ah, if only I could create freely!" ' The anguish of this extraordinary creator has been fully justified: nobody knows what became of him. His fifteen powerfully valuable novels have been withdrawn from the libraries. His colleagues no longer dare to pronounce his name. Such has been the fate of several master-writers of the first order, in whom should be recognised the true founders of Soviet literature. Boris Pilnyak, the author of *Ivan and Maria*, of *The Naked Year*, of *Wood of the Isles*, of *The Volga Falls to the Caspian Sea*; Babel, author of *Red Cavalry* (*Konarmia*) and *Tales of Odessa*; Voronsky, a former revolutionary convict, who was the leader of Soviet literature from 1918 onwards (*Art and Life*, *Beyond the Dead and Living Waters*, *The Eyes of the Hurricane*), was certainly shot for belonging to the Left Opposition; the old Ivanov-Razumnik, philosopher and historian, one of the intellectual guides of the generation of 1917 ... (Ivanov-Razumnik had just published a biography of Shchedrin when he disappeared. I had news of him in prison, through a young poet, my cell companion for a night, who did not know for sure why he himself was shut away; I thought I could discern that the master and his pupils had been blamed for harbouring a hidden attachment for the idealist philosophy of Mikhailovsky and Peter Lavrov[4]) ... So also for the theatrical producer Meyerhold, whose innovative genius renewed the Russian theatre between 1902 and 1936. So also for Riazanov, the historian of Marxism, who died in exile at the beginning of the war ...[5] Naturally I do not know enough to draw up a list of lesser-known writers, of the young, of authors of revolutionary memoirs, who disappeared in their hundreds. No one knows that list, except perhaps the directors of the Secret Services of the Political Police. And the *perhaps* which I put here is ambiguous, for the police chiefs who carried out the purges have themselves disappeared. The rule is that once the man is suppressed, his works are eliminated, and his name is no longer uttered, erased from the past, and even from history. I have just read the very beautiful memoirs of Constantine Fedin on Maxim Gorky. They refer to a time when I knew Maxim Gorky quite well, while he was still maintaining a brave moral independence, did not hesitate to criticise revolutionary power, and ended up receiving from Lenin a friendly invitation to go into exile abroad ... It is possible for me to vouch for the astonishing accuracy of Constantine Fedin's notes, and the honesty which he has put into gathering the habitual discourses of Gorky, whose gesture and voice I seem to encounter again. On each page, however, I notice the omission of ideas expressed on several occasions, of historical facts, and of names ... I nervously admire the skill, tenacity and paralysed honesty of a writer who successfully traces a truthful and powerfully living portrait whilst unfailingly conforming (but not without distress, I imagine) to the rule of obedience.

None of these vanished writers whom I have just named, with the exception of Riazanov, was the victim of an openly stated accusation. (And Riazanov was accused in the press of having conspired with the Socialist International to prepare war against the USSR, which amounts to madness; he was condemned in secret, by an administrative measure. In reality, he had shown several oubursts of indignation and some gestures of generosity towards persecuted Marxists.) None was the result of a legal verdict, in the least bit public. Several, like Pilnyak, Babel, Meyerhold and Riazanov, were personally known in both hemispheres. They had works translated into English, French, German, Spanish, Catalan, Czech, Yiddish and Chinese ... No Pen Club, even those who had held dinners on their behalf, asked the slightest question about their cases. No literary journal, to my knowledge, commented on their mysterious end. Books on Soviet literature were published abroad that passed over them in silence, or only mentioned them incidentally and evasively ... A universal complicity surrounds their sufferings.

Universal Western Caution

On the attitude of the journals, i.e., of the intellectuals who create the journals, in the presence of these mysteries and these crimes, I will allow myself to cite one example which I can very much vouch for from my own experience. When the old German Marxist Otte Rühle, the biographer of Karl Marx and author of many works of recognised importance, a militant of the German revolution of 1918, died in Mexico in 1943, I offered to supply an essay on him to an important South American journal, where there were numbers of his friends. My proposal was first welcomed with interest, although my heretical reputation aroused a certain disquiet. But as soon as I expressed the intention of mentioning, among the struggles carried out by Otto Rühle, his participation in the John Dewey Commission which proclaimed Trotsky's innocence after the Moscow Trials, I received the categorical reply: 'No. Impossible.'[6] From a rational point of view, I have never completely understood why it was not possible, unless it was that an unjustifiable fear warped the conscience of the review's editors. The same evil is today diffused at both ends of the map of the world. A new Parisian journal, popular and sympathetic, called *Maintenant*, published last January a study of the poet Marcel Martinet, who died in the occupation (author of *Les Temps Maudits*, 1918, *La Nuit*, 1920, *Une feuille de Hêtre*, 1935). The author of these warm-hearted pages passes over in complete silence the struggles which the poet kept up for twenty years for the integrity of revolutionary thought. This is an omission close to impiety: Marcel Martinet, whose moral courage never wavered, would have rejected it as a betrayal. I understand that it is still practically impossible to publish today in Paris a hundred clear lines on the problems which I am dealing with here. And I believe that friends of the poet, being obliged to chose between total silence on his death and his work and this mutilated in-memoriam, have all the same preferred a provisional monument to be erected for him from which his true greatness is missing ...

Can a civilised person who sees a crime committed under his window, in broad daylight, without himself or anyone else allowing themselves to intervene, or even to make an audible shout, retain afterwards his own complete self-esteem, his clarity of judgement, his critical spirit, and his capacity to create, if he is an artist? The writer who is informed of what happens in the world – and I maintain that it is the duty of the writer to be so informed – is often in the uncomfortable position of this civilised person. Once his conscience is wounded, he can only escape the oppressive contamination of directed thought, all the more directed by terror and psychological perversion, if he confronts the whole inhumanity of the problem with a firm decision not to cooperate. Here are posed, it is true, complex questions of faith, inseparable from the social environment and from personal interest. Yet we should still demand of religious or political faith that it does not obliterate conscience. The faith of modern man should be compatible with clear knowledge, loyalty, a simple mental hygiene, and a sense of the dignity of himself and others: otherwise it becomes a regression to mentalities previous to our culture considered in its superior forms. It all too frequently happens under our eyes that the writer (in more general terms, the intellectual) gives proof of a blindness which at times borders on imbecility, and at others on knavery. We are therefore witnessing the disintegration of universal values by the insincerity imposed by playing a double game with ourselves and others. That such insincerity can be repressed into the unconscious and that the writer believes himself, in surrendering to it, to be perfectly sincere or devoted to a supreme *reason of state*, is no less disquieting.

The Song of the False Witness

I would not dream of underestimating the importance of the literary work of the French Resistance, to which so many of my friends have given so many deaths, and so much suffering. That work obviously attests a precious vitality. And that is why I feel in reading certain of its texts an asphyxiating unease. That poetry should arise to scourge the executioners, to exalt the heroism of the tortured, to guard the proud memory of the shot, is undoubtedly one of its most human missions in the present time. But that such poetry should often be signed by poets who elsewhere praise the hangman, praise the torturer, insult the shot and speak untruths over the tombs of another Resistance *inspired* by the same motives – the defence of man against tyranny – that leads us, by a terrible alchemy, to the negation of all accepted values. Pure gold becomes no more than stirred-up mud. The conscience of the writer shows itself to be full of dark undercurrents. The impassioned voice of song is nothing more than that of the false witness. The poetic quality of the work of Aragon has sometimes appeared to me to be moving, and even excellent; but how many men from whom he sought instruction, whom he has loved, or pretended to love, in Russia and in the Third International, have suffered torture and death by shooting without his having been moved by it? Without his having posed in their cases the elementary question of innocence or guilt? Without his having questioned himself on the sinister gravity of repressions paradoxically justified by 'revolutionary humanism'? On another occasion, in 1937, in *Commune*, I believe, Aragon wrote some incredible pages about the accused in the Moscow Trials.[7] Whether they had or had not plotted, these old Socialists at least deserved the human respect accorded by the victors to the Nazi leaders at Nuremberg. (It has become difficult to doubt that respect for the truth would have saved these men, now that the archives of Nazism are in the hands of the Allies. Verifying some of the insane accusations made against them has now become easy. I venture to write that it has been done[8]). The Poet of the Communist Resistance was among others the friend of Bruno Jaszienski,[9] the Polish Communist writer whose novels were published by *L'Humanité* (*Je brûle Paris*, a successful title ...), whom I knew in Moscow timidly faithful to the 'general party line', and who was to die in a concentration camp in the Far East ... Aragon was the friend of the Secretary General of the Association of Proletarian Writers, Leopold Averbach, the most official of the directors of Soviet literature, shot where, when, how? But shot he certainly was, because he was the nephew of the People's Commissar of the Interior and chief of the Political Police, Yagoda, who was himself shot.[10]

The allegiance of the writer to the party of a great power accustomed to shooting many people is in this precise case sufficient explanation. But in that case, how can one understand these lines on the 'traitors' written by another poet of the same party (Paul Éluard[11]):

> They have praised our executioner to us
> They have itemised the evil for us
> They have said nothing innocently –

Yes, how do we understand them? Let us note the psychological disintegration. Let us note that the poem, perfect as it may well be in its flow, gives a false note. The reader is expecting to hear the voice of a defender of freedom, of an enemy of the murderers of the innocent, and the reader is deceived, and we feel uneasy about it. But what, then, is happening in the minds of these poets? The poet is suddenly stripped of his clarity. 'What is truth?' asked Pontius Pilate of the condemned man.[12] Thousands of men formed by the intellectual disciplines of scientific thought – it seems – reply in fact: 'It is the command of the Leader of my party.' This is the death of intelligence, the death of ethics.

Committed or Directed Thought

In lesser degrees, numbers of other writers of the Resistance, less clearly classified, suffering from the disinformation around them, incur the same criticism. They seem to have discovered the annihilation of man by totalitarian machineries only by having suffered it for several years. Have they not seen it before, elsewhere? Do they not know that this drama is not national, that Europe and our whole civilisation is riddled with it? It is very much a question, under these worthy pens, of 'committed thought', of 'participation in action', of 'making up one's mind', of 'responsible literature', and even of consenting to perish for the just causes of our time ... But what exactly do these formulas mean? Do we only want to apply them in the narrow confines of the patriotism of an already obsolete movement? Do they intend to confer on these words an esoteric sense to the detriment of their universal sense? 'Committed Thought' – is it allowed here, but over there effaced humbly before directed thought? 'Participation in action' – is it legitimate against one oppression but to be condemned against another? That would be only a return to the tribal mentality of past ages: 'Thou shalt not kill' the man of the same tribe, but it is praiseworthy to kill the man of the neighbouring tribe ... 'Responsible literature', rightly extolled by Jean-Paul Sartre[13] – does it limit its own responsibility to certain determined historical cases in order to renounce it in the face of certain others? This should be made clearer. The conscience of the writer cannot evade these questions without betraying itself. And these questions today interest the conscience of everone, I mean, of all men for whom the old magic of words, and of living works created with words, remains a means of clarifying and ennobling life.

Notes

1.   This article was first published in no.1 of the 'Les Égaux' series of René Lefeuvre in 1947, and again in *16 Fusillés à Moscou*, by Éditions Spartacus in 1984 (pp.167–76).Our translation is an improvement upon that entitled 'The Writer's Conscience' published in *Now*, no.7, February–March, 1947, pp.52–8. It was also

reprinted in David Craig (ed.), *Marxists on Literature*, Harmondsworth, 1973. We have restored the subtitles of the French edition, and certain passages that were inadvertently omitted (translator's note).

2. Margarita Iosifovna Aliger (1915–) wrote her narrative poem *Zoia* in 1942 (translator's note).

3. Mandelstam was first arrested in 1934, and then again in May 1938 and sent to the Far East. Driven half mad by his sufferings, he died in a psychiatric ward. Cf. Robert Conquest, *The Great Terror*, Harmondsworth, 1971, p.445 (translator's note).

4. The young poet Serge met in prison was called Petrovsky. For a fuller account of this incident, cf. *Memoirs*, pp.286–7 (translator's note).

5. David Goldendakh, called Riazanov (1870–1938) was Russia's foremost scholar of Marxism. He perished in the purges. Cf. *Memoirs*, pp.250–1; Boris Souvarine, *What Became of the Revolution*, London, 2001, pp.130–137; Brian Pearce, 'D. B. Riazanov', in D. B. Riazanov, *Marx and Anglo-Russian Relations and Other Writings*, London, 2003, pp.18–31 (translator's note).

6. Otto Rühle (1874–1943) was a former Reichstag deputy and a founder member of the German Communist Party, famous for his biography of *Karl Marx* (English translation, 1929). He cooperated with the Dewey Commission in 1937, and later assisted Trotsky in compiling *The Living Thoughts of Karl Marx* (London, 1940) (translator's note).

7. Louis Aragon (1897–1982) was a poet who joined the French Communist Party in 1927 and defended the enormities of the Stalinist regime throughout the 1930s, only breaking with it during the suppression of the Prague Spring in 1968. He played a particularly shameful role during the campaign for the release of Victor Serge from the USSR. Cf. Richard Greeman, 'The Victor Serge Affair and the French Literary Left', *Revolutionary History*, vol.v, no.3, Autumn 1994, p.156; Jean Damien (Georges Henein), *Qui est Monsieur Aragon?*, Cairo, 1944. (translator's note).

8. Attempts by Natalia Trotsky, backed by several prominent figures such as H. G. Wells, George Orwell and Professor C.E.M. Joad, and aided by the American and British Trotskyists, to question those on trial at the Nuremberg War Crimes Tribunal about the supposed contacts of Trotsky with the Germans were avoided by the tribunal ('Nuremberg Prosecution Asked: 1. To Give Representation to Natalia Trotsky. 2. To Produce Evidence of Moscow trials', *Socialist Appeal*, March, 1946 (translator's note).

9. The Polish poet Bruno Jaszienski (1901–1941) was arrested as a 'Trotskyite' on 31 July 1937 and sentenced to 15 years. He died of typhus in a Vladivostok transit camp. He was rehabilitated after 1956. Cf. Robert Conquest, *The Great Terror*, Harmondsworth, 1971, pp.446 and 585. Shortly afterwards Stalin closed down the Polish Communist Party completely, and practically annihilated all of its members who were in exile in the USSR. Cf. Isaac Deutscher, 'The Tragedy of the Polish Communist Party', in *Marxism, Wars and Revolutions*, London, 1984, pp.91–128; Ludwik Hass, 'Trotskyism in Poland up to 1945', *Revolutionary History*, vol.vi, no.1, Winter 1995–6, pp.38–9; 'La Dissolution du parti communiste polonais et ses échos', *Cahiers du Mouvement Ouvrier*, no.17, April/May 2002, pp.69–82 (translator's note).

10. Yagoda was the head of the N.K.V.D. who organised the first Moscow Trial, of the 16; he was himself a defendant in the third trial, of the 21. Jaszienski had relied upon Yagoda's protection (translator's note).

11. Eugène Grindel, known as Paul Éluard (1895–1952) was a surrealist poet and a staunch defender of the Moscow Trials, even though he did not join the French Communist Party until 1942 (translator's note).

12. John, xviii, v.38 (translator's note).

13. Jean-Paul Sartre (1905–1980) was a novelist, playwright, and a leading proponent of existentialism. He was was taken as a prisoner of war in 1940, but released a year later. He advocated responsible and committed writing in 1945 in the first issue of his journal *Les Temps modernes*, one of the few mainstream French journals to publish Serge's work in the 1940s. (translator's note).

Index